KOREA
THE WAR BEFORE VIETNAM

KOREA:
The War Before Vietnam

Callum A. MacDonald
Lecturer in Comparative American Studies
University of Warwick

THE FREE PRESS
A Division of Macmillan, Inc.
New York

The Free Press
A Division of Macmillan, Inc.
866 Third Avenue, New York, N.Y. 10022

First American Edition 1987

Printed in Great Britain

printing number

1 2 3 4 5 6 7 8 9 10

Library of Congress Cataloging-in-Publication Data
MacDonald, C. A.
Korea, the war before Vietnam.
Bibliography: p.
Includes index.
1. Korean War, 1950–1953. I. Title.
DS918.M263 1987   951.9′042   86–22943
ISBN 0–02–919621–3

To Ala, Kathy and Clare

Contents

List of Maps

List of Plates

Foreword

Korea, although a limited war, had repercussions far beyond the battlefield. As I prepared the material for this book, it seemed to me that the topic fell naturally into two broad sections and I have arranged the narrative that way at the expense of some repetition. 'War and politics', Section 1, deals with the impact of the conflict on the US and its allies. It is concerned with high politics and strategy rather than with the details of military operations. 'The problems of limited war', Section 2, deals with the military experience of Korea, a conflict which frustrated American commanders and contradicted their cherished beliefs on how war should be waged. It is more concerned with the fighting and the details of bureaucratic rivalry at the Pentagon.

The research for this book was only made possible by a fellowship from the American Council of Learned Societies which allowed me to visit archives in the United States in 1981–82. I would like to thank the American Council and its representative, Richard Downar, for their encouragement and financial support. I owe numerous debts to archivists and librarians and would like to thank the following individuals and institutions for their assistance with various collections: Edward J. Boone Jnr, MacArthur Memorial Library, Norfolk Va.; Staff Sergeant Hardman, Air Force Historical Section, Bolling AFB; Kathy Nicastro, Diplomatic Records, US National Archives; Wilbur Mahoney, Modern Military Records, US National Archives; the Harry S. Truman Library, Independence, Missouri; the Public Records Office, London; the US Army Military History Institute, Carlisle, Pa.; the Citadel, Charleston, South Carolina; the Library of Congress; the Warden and Fellows of University College, Oxford; the British Library of Political and Economic Science; the National Archives of Canada.

My research was also facilitated by conversations with British veterans of the war, especially Ashley Cunningham-Boothe, Henry O'Kane and Eric Stowe. Colleagues at the University of Warwick, particularly Dr Robin Clifton, read early drafts of various chapters which benefited from their comments. I was also able to test some of my ideas out on the participants in the conference on the Korean War, held by the British Association for Korean Studies at the University of Newcastle in September 1985. Lastly I would like to thank my family for their tolerance and support and my agent Gill Coleridge for her efforts on my behalf.

University of Warwick CALLUM A. MacDONALD

Key to Sources

CNA   Canadian National Archives
DS   Department of State Decimal File
FIR   Far Eastern Air Forces Intelligence Roundup
FR   *Foreign Relations of the United States*
FRC   Federal Records Center
HSTL   Harry S. Truman Library
HVP   Hoyt Vandenberg Papers
MMR   Modern Military Records
MACL   MacArthur Library
MCKP   McKinlay Cantor Papers
MCP   Mark Clark Papers
MRP   Matthew Ridgway Papers
NTP   Nathan Twining Papers
PRO   Public Record Office
SRRKW   Selected Records Relating to the Korean War

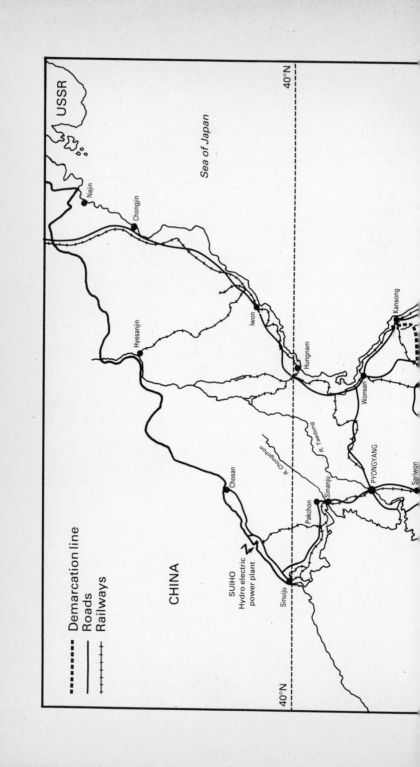

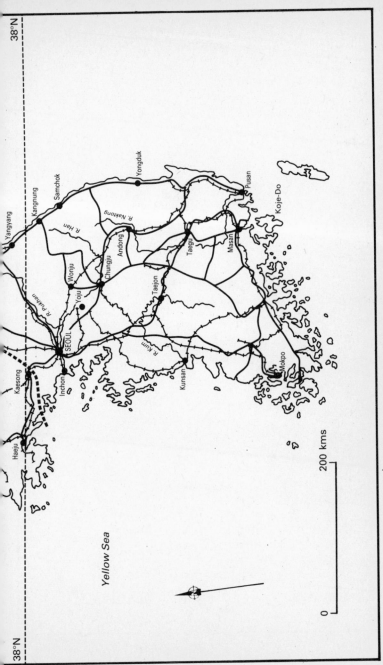

Yellow Sea

38°N

38°N

Yangyang

Kangnung

Samchok

Yongduk

Pusan

R. Han

R. Naktong

Andong

Taegu

Masan

Koje-Do

Chungju

Wonju

Yoju

R. Pukhan

SEOUL

Inchon

Kaesong

Haeju

Taejon

R. Kum

Kunsan

Mokpo

200 kms

0

1. KOREA

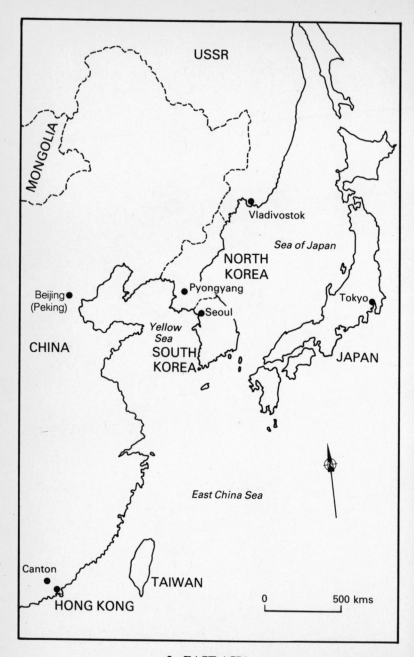

2. EAST ASIA

PART I
War and Politics

1 The Cold War and Counter-Revolution

On 25 June 1950 North Korean troops crossed the 38th parallel in an attempt to unify the peninsula under the communist regime of Kim Il Sung. The South Korean state, based on right wing groups headed by Syngman Rhee, was to be eradicated in a quick military campaign. On one level, the attack was the latest act in a civil war which had been taking shape since the liberation of Korea from Japan in 1945. Korean developments, however, did not occur in isolation. The United States and the Soviet Union, the victors of 1945, divided Korea at the 38th parallel to accept the Japanese surrender. As in Europe, this temporary line rapidly became permanent, delineating the boundary between US and Soviet spheres of influence. Within their respective zones, Russians and Americans attempted to define the parameters of change. While Moscow supported the left, Washington entered a political alliance with the right, placing conservatives in control of the security apparatus bequeathed by the defeated Japanese in an attempt to contain communism. Thus the North Korean attack was not merely an episode in the struggle amongst Koreans. On another level, it represented a clash between the Soviet and American power systems. The war amongst Koreans was soon overshadowed by the war between the blocs. When the fighting ended in 1953, a solution was imposed on both Koreas by the great powers. Unification, their common war aim, remained unrealised.

In the nineteenth century, Korea was a closed peasant society which paid tribute to the Chinese emperor in Beijing. The hermit kingdom was part of an inward-looking pre-capitalist Chinese world rather than the international capitalist system of the leading industrial powers.[1] Korea, however, was wrenched out of isolation by the decline of China and the impact of Russian and Japanese imperialism. By the end of the century it had become the prize in a three-way contest between a decaying China and the rising empires of Russia and Japan. By the beginning of the new century, Japan had emerged victorious from this struggle, defeating China in 1894 and Russia in 1905 to become the dominant power in Korea and the neighbouring Chinese province of Manchuria. The last vestiges of independence were suppressed in 1910 when Korea became a Japanese colony.[2] Japan's contiguous empire in

North-East Asia became the springboard for further expansion. During the Bolshevik revolution, Tokyo took advantage of Russian weakness to intervene in Siberia, temporarily occupying Vladivostock. As World War Two approached, Japan's continuing ambitions in the area produced a series of military clashes along the Soviet–Manchurian border. China was also exposed to Japanese power. In 1932 the last vestiges of Chinese sovereignty in Manchuria were eliminated. In 1937 China itself was invaded, setting off a conflict which did not end until 1945.[3] Thus both the Soviet Union and China had historic ties with Korea, common borders and a legitimate security interest in the political future of the peninsula.

In Korea itself, the Japanese pursued a programme of modernisation. Some groups benefited and collaborated with the colonial regime.[4] Japanese rule, however, was generally unpopular. In 1919 there were nationwide independence demonstrations which were only put down by force.[5] Order was maintained by a colonial bureaucracy backed by a powerful police force. This was recruited from Koreans displaced by social and economic change and became the enduring symbol of Japanese rule. By 1941 there was one policeman to every forty Koreans as Japan mobilised its empire for participation in World War Two.[6] By this stage, opposition to colonial rule was dispersed and divided. The collapse of the independence movement in 1919 was followed by the establishment of a Korean Provisional Goverment (KPG) in Shanghai in 1921. This was a self-constituted group, divided against itself and increasingly cut off from Korea.[7] Amongst its founders was Syngman Rhee, a fierce nationalist and anti-communist who had been imprisoned and tortured for his opposition to the Japanese. In 1904 he had left Korea for the United States where he publicised the cause of liberation. Despite quarrelling with the KPG in 1942, he spent the war years campaigning in Washington for its recognition as a legitimate government, an effort which proved unsuccessful.[8]

The KPG was tolerated by the Chinese government as a possible counterweight to the Korean left and the Soviet Union.[9] The Korean communist movement, like the nationalists, was plagued by factional struggles. In the 1930s however, it emerged as the main source of resistance to Japanese rule. Attempts were made to organise the peasants and a guerrilla movement emerged in the remote border regions which collaborated with the Chinese communists. The Japanese responded with repression. Many communists were jailed or forced into exile. In 1941 the remaining guerrillas retreated across the

Soviet frontier to await the results of the war. Prominent amongst them was Kim Il Sung who was to play a leading role in the North after liberation. The communist record in the resistance was to prove an important source of legitimacy in the political struggles which followed the Japanese surrender.[10] By 1945, therefore, China and the Soviet Union had established links with Korean political groups, a process which had led to destabilisation and war at the end of the nineteenth century. This was an outcome which the United States was anxious to avoid. Washington hoped to avert a power struggle on the peninsula and to secure its future through international cooperation.[11]

Despite the conclusion of a friendship treaty in 1882, the US took little interest in Korea before Pearl Harbor. It acquiesced in Japanese annexation and refused to raise the independence issue after World War One.[12] This was neither forgiven nor forgotten by Syngman Rhee.[13] Washington was more interested in China than in the fate of nations on the Asian periphery and lacked the power to challenge Japan in the area. US involvement after 1945 reflected the vast expansion of American military and economic strength which had taken place since 1910. It was dictated, however, less by an intrinsic interest in Korea itself than by concern about more vital contiguous areas, China and Japan. It was also influenced by US relations with the Soviet Union, Japan's historic rival in North-East Asia. In Washington, the Korean problem was viewed as part of a larger whole.[14]

The United States wished to construct a stable capitalist order in the Far East as part of a global system which reflected US economic and strategic interests. The American vision embraced self-determination for colonial peoples and an open door for trade and investment. The area was to be developed as part of a liberal world economy dominated by the United States. The situation in North-East Asia was merely part of a larger problem. The impending collapse of Japan created a power vacuum which the Russians might attempt to fill. It was no part of US policy to defeat Japan only to replace it with the Soviet Union as a threat to American interests in the Far East. A related issue was the rise of radical nationalism. The war fatally weakened the European empires in Asia and stimulated the rise of liberation movements which were hostile to the restoration of colonial rule. Washington sought a postwar system which met demands for self-determination and accorded the Russians a role in the Far East without compromising US interests.[15] The Russians were neutral in the Pacific war until August 1945. US policymakers worked to commit the Soviet Union against

Japan, reducing American casualties and speeding the Japanese defeat, without allowing Moscow to impose its own solutions. President Roosevelt sought agreement on a postwar system which would contain both the USSR and radical nationalism. Both were to be coopted into an international order dominated by the United States.[16]

China occupied a key role in Roosevelt's plans. Although technically one of the Big Four during the war, China was weak and divided. Since the nineteenth century it had been dominated by foreign powers and plagued by domestic unrest. In 1927 civil war broke out between the Guomindong regime of Generalissimo Jiang Jieshi (Chiang Kai-Shek) and the communists under Mao. Superimposed on this internal struggle was the Japanese invasion of 1937. Although supposedly cooperating in a united front against Japan, the Guomindong and the communists maintained at most an uneasy truce.[17] Roosevelt hoped to transform China under American tutelage. It was to provide both a balance against the Soviet Union and a model for former colonial peoples seeking self-government. In pursuit of this goal, Roosevelt attempted to avert renewed civil war between Jiang and the communists. The communists were to be coopted into a coalition government and their long-term appeal undermined by political and economic reforms. The result would be the emergence of a Chinese third force, neither reactionary nor communist, linked to the US by bonds of ideology and self-interest.[18]

This was a daunting task which had not been achieved by 1945. China remained weak and divided, hovering on the edge of civil war. At the Yalta conference in February 1945, the Russians were mobilised behind American policy at the price of rail and port concessions in Manchuria. The immediate aim of this bargain was to secure a Soviet pledge to enter the war against Japan but it was also part of a wider political strategy. Roosevelt hoped to avert a civil war in China and the danger that Moscow and Washington would be drawn in on opposite sides. At the price of limited gains in Manchuria, Stalin would be coopted behind American goals in China. Deprived of possible Soviet support, the communists would have little option but to enter a coalition with the Guomindong. Roosevelt was legitimising limited Russian gains to secure support for a political solution in China conceived in American interests.[19] The President was 'using the Soviets'.[20]

Roosevelt also sought Russian support in Korea, important because of its strategic position between China and Japan. There was concern in Washington that Stalin might promote revolution to dominate the peninsula and use the Korean model as an example to other colonial peoples.[21] Roosevelt wished to transform Korea into an area of great power cooperation, rather than an area of competition which might draw China, the US and the USSR into postwar confrontation. He also wished to use Korea to demonstrate his own ideas about the treatment of former colonial peoples.[22] In order to accommodate great power interests and nationalist aspirations, Roosevelt developed the concept of international trusteeship. The great powers would collaborate to guide Korea towards independence, a process which the President believed might take up to forty years. At the Cairo conference in 1943, the US, Britain and China promised Korea independence 'in due course'. A four power trusteeship was discussed with Stalin at Yalta. There was no formal agreement, however, since Russia was still at peace with Japan. As in Manchuria, Roosevelt was prepared to recognise a legitimate Soviet interest in areas bordering Russia. Moscow was to be drawn away from unilateral action and into an arrangement controlled by the United States. There was also a role for China which was to become a regional power in an international structure which included yet contained the Soviet Union.[23]

In the postwar period, however, the Yalta system rapidly broke down. It depended on US–Soviet cooperation and on the ability of each power to control events in China and Korea. Both assumptions proved to be unfounded. After the Potsdam conference of July 1945, US policy was defined by distrust of the Russians, a development which reflected the emerging quarrel over the division of Europe. The death of Roosevelt in April 1945 was also a factor. He had never institutionalised his policy which was made in the White House rather than the State Department. His successor, Harry S. Truman, was advised by officials who favoured a tougher line with Stalin. The new administration began to doubt the possibility of cooperation with Moscow and regarded Soviet actions in Eastern Europe as preludes to global communist expansion.[24] The postwar international system would have to be constructed to exclude the Russians. This view dictated the American attitude towards revolutionary change in China and Korea. The leading role of communists in both areas promoted the belief that revolutionary nationalism was the tool of the Soviet State. Washington's goal became 'the prevention of revolutionary change linked to global Soviet expansion'.[25]

The main area of concern in the Far East was China, which had been central to Roosevelt's concept of a new order in Asia. Relations between the Guomindong and the communists collapsed in the wake of the Japanese defeat. Each side raced to occupy as much territory as possible, the nationalists openly assisted by the United States, the communists enjoying the tacit support of Soviet forces which liberated Manchuria following a Russian declaration of war against Japan on 8 August 1945. Despite an attempt at mediation by Truman's Special Envoy, General Marshall, in 1946, civil war broke out the following year. By the end of 1949 the Guomindong had been driven from the mainland and preserved a precarious existence on the island of Taiwan (Formosa), one hundred miles off the South China coast. In October 1949, Mao proclaimed the People's Republic of China in Beijing.[26] The Marshall mission was the last attempt to stabilise China by negotiation. Thereafter, Washington abandoned any pretence of disinterest and reluctantly backed Jiang as the only means of containing communist expansion.

In March 1947 the President enunciated the Truman Doctrine, pledging US support for free peoples resisting communism. What occurred, however, was less the assumption of new burdens than the reordering of existing commitments. This process was to have implications for US policy in the Far East. The Truman administration committed itself to containment, conscious of its limited economic resources. The President faced a Congress determined to keep taxes low and to balance the budget. Truman himself was pledged to fiscal responsibility and recognised limits on what he could ask of the American people. In this situation, Washington discriminated between areas and interests. Europe emerged as the first priority. China was considered neither strategically nor economically important enough to warrant an unlimited commitment of American power.[27] Moreover Washington, although backing Jiang as the only non-communist alternative in China, was well aware of the failings of the Guomindong as a vehicle of containment. During and after the war, the nationalist regime proved itself inept and corrupt. As Truman bitterly recalled, the Guomindong leaders were 'all thieves, every last one of them. . . . And they stole seven hundred and fifty million dollars out of the thirty-five billion that we sent to Chiang.'[28] In China, US resources and prestige would be engaged in a losing cause. Thus, while the United States promoted economic reconstruction in Europe through the Marshall plan and guaranteed the security of the area by joining NATO, China was supplied on a strictly limited basis. Nor was there any question of military intervention. As the Guomindong moved towards defeat in 1949, Washington attempted to distance itself from the wreck. The China White Paper of July 1949 condemned the communists as tools of the Kremlin but attributed the nationalist collapse to the failures of the Guomindong rather than to any lack of American support.[29]

The collapse of China into war and revolution destroyed the Yalta system and forced Washington to seek an alternative means of protecting its interests in the Far East. A new system could only be based on the rehabilitation of Japan, which Washington had intended to weaken and demilitarise in 1945. A revived Japan would be the lynchpin of American influence in Asia. It would be the centre of an offshore defence perimeter in the Pacific, stretching from the Aleutians in the North to the Philippines in the South. This would provide the US with a line of cheaply defended strongpoints as a base for the projection of American influence on the Asian mainland.[30] By the end of 1949 Washington was considering a peace treaty which would exclude the Russians and reflect US strategic interests. While progress was delayed by a debate between the State Department and the Pentagon, the direction of US policy was clear. On 18 May 1950, Truman publicly announced his belief that a settlement was not far off.[31] The revival of Japan, the former imperial power in Korea and Manchuria, was to have an important influence on the origins of the Korean War.

The decisions of 1947 raised a question mark over the US position in Korea. The war ended without firm agreement between Washington and Moscow on trusteeship. State Department planners had been concerned since 1943 about the dangers of unilateral Soviet action on the peninsula. The military, however, accorded primary strategic importance to Japan and had no resources to spare for the Asian mainland which remained a Russian zone of operations.[32] In this situation, the planners wished to conclude firm agreements on the Korean occupation in advance of military action. This might prevent Stalin from imposing a unilateral solution where his forces were dominant, as in Poland.[33] At the Potsdam conference, however, Truman avoided detailed discussions on Korea and the Far East. The successful test of the first atomic bomb in the middle of the conference made Russian participation less essential to defeat Japan. Truman hoped to deal with the Soviet Union from a position of strength and to make no concessions in advance. Either Japan would be defeated before Russia could enter the war or possession of the 'winning weapon' would put Washington in a better position to bargain with Stalin.[34]

Japan surrendered on 14 August 1945, following American atomic bomb attacks and a Soviet declaration of war. As Japan collapsed, Washington moved to limit the advance of Russian power. Truman issued General Order Number One by which Japanese forces in China were to surrender to the Guomindong and not to Mao's communists. The United States was to assume responsibility for Japan itself, excluding the Russians. Korea was to be divided at the 38th parallel, US forces accepting the surrender South of this line and the Russians to the North of it.[35] The parallel was chosen as the furthest limit of American occupation likely to be acceptable to the Soviet Union. The division allowed the US to occupy Seoul, the Korean capital, and the important port of Inchon which lay slightly South of the demarcation line. The military was doubtful that the Russians would accept the proposal, which exceeded immediate American capabilities. While Soviet troops were entering Korea, the nearest US forces were on distant Okinawa, with no prospect of arriving before September. Stalin, however, avoided a confrontation and acquiesced to the American suggestion.[36]

The decision to divide Korea at the 38th parallel has been described as the first act of containment.[37] American power had been projected into a key area of North-East Asia whose future had important implications for China, Japan and the Soviet Union. Unlike Russian interest, which was long-standing, American involvement was new. In acting to contain the Soviet Union, the US was already stepping into the role of its defeated enemy, Japan, in the region. The surrender agreement brought Washington two-thirds of the Korean population and the main agricultural area. The Russians occupied the industrial North. Although intended as a temporary measure, the results were far-reaching. The US and the Soviet Union now faced each other on the peninsula, lacking any firm agreement on the future beyond some vague discussions of trusteeship. The wartime alliance was already under strain. In these circumstances the prospects for unification were not bright. Ironically for Koreans, liberation brought not self-determination and peace, but a vicious civil war, enmeshed in great power rivalry, which was to bring the country death and destruction on a scale it had never known during World War Two.[38]

American and Soviet forces entered a country in the throes of revolution. The collapse of Japan was followed by a mass movement for land reform and the eradication of all traces of colonial rule. A Korean People's Republic (KPR) was founded in Seoul, exercising power through a series of provincial committees which emerged in August 1945.[39] Although exiled nationalists such as Rhee were given a formal role, the KPR was dominated by the left, popular because of its record in the resistance.[40] The attitudes of the occupying powers to this development differed radically. The Russians remained in the background and allowed the revolution to take its course. Soviet interests were guaranteed by promoting communists such as Kim Il Sung into positions of power.[41] Kim was apparently chosen because of his guerrilla record and his four-year exile in the USSR. The Russians distrusted Koreans who had served with Mao in China and had a low opinion of the organisational abilities of communists who had remained in Korea.[42] Despite his debt to Moscow, Kim was never merely a Soviet puppet. He was both a communist and a nationalist, committed to social revolution and unification.[43]

The Americans reacted differently. It is ironic that while the US occupation imposed reforms on Japan, in Korea it preserved the structure of the Japanese imperial state which was employed to crush the left. Washington refused to deal with the KPR and instituted a military government. The American commander, General John Hodge, cooperated initially with the hated Japanese and subsequently with the Korean right which he placed in control of the colonial police and bureaucracy. The right welcomed this approach. Tainted by a record of collaboration, it looked to the Americans to save the South from revolution. The military government brought Rhee and the leaders of the KPG back from exile to provide a facade of legitimacy. Unlike the domestic right, these men were uncontaminated by collaboration. By 1945 an embryo Southern state had emerged. The left was pushed out of politics.[44] The result was civil war. Between 1946 and 1949 the South was shaken by violent social conflict as the right, with the assistance of US occupation foces, launched a counter-revolution, employing the mechanisms of the Japanese imperial state. This offensive was led by the police, assisted by para-military right-wing youth groups. By 1947 there were 22 000 political prisoners in the South, twice as many as under the Japanese. As an American officer informed the journalist Mark Gayn in October 1946: 'the security system was the same we found when we got here. For our purposes it's an ideal setup. All you have to do is push the button and somewhere some cop begins skull cracking. They've been learning the business under the Japs for 35 years.'[45] Other observers agreed. An Australian diplomat reported in November 1947 that real power was 'in the hands of a ruthless police force which works at the direction of . . . the American GHQ and Syngman Rhee. . . . Korean prisons are now fuller . . . than under Japanese rule. The torture and murder of the political enemies of the extreme right is apparently an accepted and commonplace thing.' The Americans were 'too concerned with the suppression of the left' to enquire closely 'into the methods employed by their Korean agents'.[46] Hodge identified the Korean revolution with Russia and saw the extreme right as a bulwark against communism.[47]

Despite the alliance between the military government and the right, the official goal until 1947 remained trusteeship. In pursuit of this aim, an agreement was concluded at Moscow in December 1945, calling for the establishment of a provisional government and a five-year trusteeship leading to independence.[48] The scheme, however, was widely unpopular in the South. While the left supported the agreement, perhaps at Soviet prompting, the right condemned trusteeship as another form of colonialism, winning a new legitimacy by its outspoken opposition.[49] If the left hoped to gain from endorsing the Moscow agreement, it was to be disappointed. Trusteeship was acceptable to Washington only if it contained the Russians and the Korean revolution. As one State Department official remarked in March 1946, the US goal was 'an independent, democratic, stable Korean Government capable of resisting Russian domination over a protracted period of time . . . freedom from Russian domination is more important than complete independence.'[50]

This approach created a fundamental ambiguity in US policy towards the South. In 1946 Washington attempted to form a moderate coalition as the basis for a Korean provisional government. This third force would steer a middle course between the extremes of right and left, ensuring a transition to independence favourable to the United States. Despite attempts to draw away from the right, however, the Americans could not wholly repudiate Rhee. The police and para-military youth groups were regarded as guarantors of order and enjoyed the tacit support of members of the US military government. As one official informed Mark Gayn, little had changed: 'last Spring Washington finally came through with a policy of moderation. But you must've found out that we honor it here only in the breach. To this day our allies are boys like Rhee to whom moderation is anathema.'[51] In the autumn of 1946 the police were employed, with American military assistance, to crush a wave of strikes and peasant uprisings, the last stage in the suppression of the provincial committees which had emerged in 1945.[52] Rhee, however, did not limit himself to the campaign against subversion. His position of control over the police and bureaucracy was employed to secure a powerful voice for the right in the consultative institutions established by Washington after 1945, which were used as platforms to denounce coalition and trusteeship.[53] This foreshadowed the position during the Korean War when Rhee and his police were regarded as embarrassing but necessary in the cause of containment.

The Moscow agreement, therefore, failed to promote stability in the south where the US remained saddled with an expensive and unpopular military government. Nor could the Russians be persuaded to accept American conceptions of a united Korea. Two sets of joint commission talks in Seoul failed to produce agreement.[54] This was perhaps hardly surprising given the American conception of Korean independence and the deteriorating relationship between the powers in other areas of the world. By 1947 Korea was more firmly divided than it had been in 1945. Roosevelt's conception of trusteeship was clearly unsuited to the realities of the Korean revolution and the emerging climate of cold war.

The deadlock over trusteeship coincided with the Truman Doctrine of March 1947 which symbolised the formal opening of the cold war. In the survey of American commitments which followed, the place of Korea was reevaluated. The initial impulse was to accord the peninsula a high priority. It was the only place outside Europe where the US and the Soviet Union were in direct confrontation. In this respect, it differed from China where neither was directly involved in the civil war. The US had drawn a line in Korea and engaged its credibility. It must not appear to weaken in the face of Soviet power. A second set of factors, however, argued against a continued US presence. The occupation was costly at a time of increasing European commitments and fiscal restraint. Low military budgets and a shortage of resources made the Pentagon anxious to withdraw and redeploy its troops to more vital areas. As the JCS reported in September 1947, Korea was strategically unimportant. In the event of war, the peninsula could be neutralised by air power based in Japan.[55] The low military value of Korea conflicted with its symbolic political importance. The US could not simply cut and run, leaving a vacuum which would be filled by the Russians and the Korean left. The conflict between the low strategic value of Korea and its symbolic importance in the cold war was to remain an important factor in US policy.

In September 1947 it was decided that the US should seek to withdraw from Korea 'with the minimum of bad effects'. This involved creating a separate Southern state and endorsing Syngman Rhee as an instrument of containment. While Rhee proved an uncomfortable ally, he remained the only reliable barrier against communism.[56] Partition was to be achieved through the United Nations. It was hoped that sponsorship by the world organisation would both legitimise the new state and restrain the Russians from action following the withdrawal of US forces.[57] By resorting to this device, Washington was attempting to maintain containment on the cheap. At this stage, the UN was not what it later became. Decolonisation had yet to occur and the US and its allies could count on a majority in the General Assembly where the Soviet veto did not apply. Moreover, the UN Secretary General, the Norwegian Trygve-Lie, leaned towards the West in the cold war.[58] It was thus natural to regard the UN as a useful tool.

In October 1947 the US proposed in the UN General Assembly that elections take place before the end of March 1948 to create a Korean national assembly. This would establish a government and security forces, allowing US and Soviet troops to withdraw. Korea would be united and free. The elections would be supervised by a UN Temporary Committee on Korea (UNTCOK) which would guarantee the legitimacy of any government which emerged. This proposal was endorsed over the opposition of the Soviet bloc. Australia, Canada, Guomindong China, India, the Philippines, El Salvador and Syria were nominated to serve on UNTCOK.[59] Of these, El Salvador, China and the Philippines were likely to support the US automatically. Only India and Syria could be regarded as non-aligned. The Americans, however, had unexpected problems with the committee. When the Russians refused to admit it into North Korea, Australia and Canada hesitated to endorse a separate election in the South. It was felt that this would increase tension on the peninsula. There were also well-founded doubts about political freedom in the South which was dominated by Rhee's police and para-militaries.[60] According to the Australian delegate, the US military government was 'supporting the rightists and treats anyone who is not a rightist as at least a near communist. . . . Several spokesmen for the parties have said that a free election is impossible because the rightists with the aid of the police have the whole situation under control. This is probably very near the mark.[61] As far as the Australians and Canadians could ascertain, nobody outside the extreme right wished a separate election and partition. In these circumstances, the Korean hot potato was referred back to the General Assembly where Washington lobbied intensively for a poll in the South. Its efforts were ultimately successful and UNTCOK observed an election in May 1948, despite the continuing reservations of some of its members.[62]

The election took place against a background of violence. The left attempted to boycott and disrupt the poll while police and right-wing youth groups patrolled the villages, terrorising and beating anyone who did not register to vote.[63] The final result merely demonstrated Rhee's control of the bureaucracy and security forces. Although it had observed only 2 per cent of the polling places, UNTCOK endorsed the vote as a legitimate expression of Korean opinion South of the parallel. In December 1948, the UN placed its seal of approval on the new Republic of Korea (ROK) organised by Rhee in Seoul.[64] Rhee's regime claimed to speak for all Koreans and reserved 100 seats in the National Assembly for Northern members. The Russians replied by establishing a Democratic People's Republic of Korea (DPRK) in Pyongyang under Kim Il Sung and withdrawing its troops by the end of 1948.[65] The DPRK, like its Southern rival, claimed to be a national state. According to Kim Il Sung, the ROK was a reactionary puppet regime. Its leaders were traitors and collaborators who would be punished according to the laws of the DPRK.[66] The ultimate result of great power rivalry, therefore, was to institutionalise the civil war in two contending states, both committed to the cause of unification. Armed confrontation across the 38th parallel was added to unrest in the South. This had been foreseen by Australia and Canada which had grave doubts about American policy at the UN. In the end, however, they backed down. Korea was considered too minor an issue to risk American friendship.[67] As the logic of the cold war took hold, to oppose Washington seemed to be to endorse the Soviet Union. Thus doubts about US policy were pushed into the background, a phenomenon which was to be repeated after June 1950.

The US relationship with the new Korean state was discussed in NSC-8 of April 1948, a document which revealed the ambiguities of American policy on the peninsula. NSC-8 represented a compromise between the imperative of a US troop withdrawal and a reluctance to concede Korea to the Russians. The Americans would neither guarantee the new state nor abandon it. The occupation was to be liquidated by the end of the year and a programme of limited military and economic assistance granted to Rhee's government. As far as practicable, defence forces were to be established to deter invasion from the North. Washington would provide equipment and training for these troops. At the same time, the Pentagon displayed a marked reluctance to risk involvement in a civil war and confrontation with the Russians: 'The US should not become so irrevocably involved in the Korean situation that any action taken by any faction in Korea could be considered a casus belli by the US.'[68] This passage reflected distrust of Syngman Rhee and his plans to conquer the North. The ROK was denied equipment such as tanks, heavy artillery and bombers which would allow Rhee to launch a march to the Yalu.[69] Certain sections of NSC-8 displayed pessimism about the long-term survival of the ROK and implied that Washington was seeking a decent interval in which to distance itself from the inevitable collapse of the regime. Simultaneously, however, the document recognised the continuing symbolic importance of the ROK. It was unique in Asia because it was the creation of the US. Washington could not allow its elimination without losing credibility. Such an outcome would also undermine the value of the UN as a cold war instrument. As NSC-8 remarked: 'The overthrow . . . of a regime established . . . under the aegis of the UN would . . . constitute a severe blow to the prestige and influence of the UN; in this respect the interests of the US are parallel to, if not identical with, those of the UN.'[70]

Despite the creation of the ROK in 1948, the last American troops were not withdrawn until the following year. The new republic was shaken by provincial rebellion and mutiny in the army. The sense of crisis was further deepened by armed clashes along the parallel. In these circumstances, the continued presence of US combat troops gave the regime a breathing space and deterred the DPRK.[71] A new round of budget cuts, however, made a long-term reversal of policy impossible, and the last American contingent departed in July 1949.[72] The Pentagon was reluctant to envisage any future commitment to the peninsula. As US troops pulled out, it produced a document on the implications of an attack by the DPRK on the South. This noted that in such a contingency, the US should evacuate its nationals and appeal to the UN. It might even be possible to launch a 'police action' if Moscow did not exercise its veto in the Security Council. A commitment of US forces, however, would be ill-advised in the light of existing strategic commitments and inadequate military strength.[73]

US policy before the war remained based on deliberate ambiguity. The aim was to obtain containment at minimum cost. Rhee would hesitate to attack the North because he was unsure of American backing. Kim Il Sung would refrain from action against the South lest the US intervene. In pursuit of this approach, Washington denied the ROK a guarantee or a military security pact. These would encourage Rhee's ambitions by offering an open American commitment to the South. The Seoul regime was supported by a programme of military and economic aid while a US military mission, KMAG, remained behind to train Korean troops.[74] The DPRK was deterred by the deliberate involvement of the UN. In December 1948 a permanent commission on the unification of Korea (UNCOK) was established. Its ostensible duties were to observe the process of military withdrawal and assist in solving the problem of unification. Its real value to Washington was as a deterrent against action by Pyongyang.[75] In March 1950 a UN military observer group was appointed to monitor the situation along the 38th parallel as a further inhibition on armed attack.[76] In a speech at the National Press Club in January 1950, the Secretary of State, Dean Acheson, sketched out a US defence perimeter in Asia which excluded the mainland. According to Acheson, states in this area would have to look to their own efforts and the United Nations as their first line of defence. Although sometimes regarded as an expression of uninterest, which gave the green light for a North Korean attack, Acheson's speech was in fact an exercise in ambiguity, designed to restrain both sides. In this respect, it was a faithful reflection of American policy. Washington did not express uninterest but refused to spell out in advance its attitude towards an armed assault against its Korean creation.[77] In the meantime, Washington hoped that the worst would never happen.

US policy in China and Korea diverged after 1945. In China, Washington was prepared to cut its losses and eventually let events take their course. The Chinese revolution was beyond control. American credibility and prestige were not directly involved in the fate of the Guomindong. Deeper involvement in the civil war, as desired by Jiang, was likely to commit Washington to a losing cause. The first fatal steps towards direct involvement were never taken.[78] In Korea, however, disengagement was not as simple, despite the demands of 'Europe first' after 1946. The traditional relationship between China and Korea in US policy was reversed and America remained a major influence South of the 38th parallel. This was the outcome of the cold war and direct US/Soviet engagement.[79] From August 1945 Washington confronted the Korean revolution and the USSR on the peninsula. It could not withdraw without appearing to back down in the face of Soviet power. It was committed by the decisions of 1945. While liquidating the occupation in 1948, the US deepened rather than lightened its commitment to the anti-communist bastion it had created in the South. It established the ROK and involved the UN in the process. As NSC-8 recognised, whatever their reservations, neither the Americans nor the world organisation could escape responsibility for its fate.

2 The Korean Decisions

The Asian decisions of 1947/8 represented an attempt to balance commitments with resources. In a period of budgetary restraint, first priority was given to containing communism in Europe. In 1949, however, US policy began to assume new directions which dictated the response to the attack on South Korea in June 1950. Two sets of factors lay behind the changes. The first was international. In September 1949 the Soviet Union tested an atomic bomb, shattering the US atomic monopoly which had existed since 1945. In October Mao proclaimed a People's Republic in Beijing, leading the largest nation in the world into the communist camp. In this situation, it was feared that Washington was losing the initiative in the cold war. A further expansion of communist power would endanger American credibility. Western Europe and Japan would lose faith in US guarantees, seeking refuge in neutrality or an accommodation with the Russians. Washington would have lost the cold war. The second was domestic. The new international climate had political repercussions at home, denting public confidence in containment. The Republicans, denied power in the Presidential elections of 1948, attempted to capitalize on this mood, charging Truman and the Democrats with softness on communism and the loss of China. These developments pushed Washington into a new approach, designed to contain both the Soviet Union and domestic critics. This emphasized military strength and the drawing of firm lines against further communist expansion. Korea became a test case for the new policy in June 1950.

The fall of China forced Washington to seek a new international structure in the Far East to replace the discredited Yalta system. US policy was based on the 'fundamental decision' that 'the United States does not intend to permit further extension of Communist domination on the continent of Asia or in the southeast Asia area.'[1] The reconstruction of Japan as the centre of an offshore defence perimeter in the Far East was integrated with a wider policy for the Asian mainland in the wake of the Chinese revolution. Communist expansion around the periphery of China was to be contained by encouraging stable nationalist regimes supported by American economic and military assistance. These states were to look to their own efforts and to the United Nations as the first line of defence against external aggression, whilst US training and financial aid

18

contained internal subversion.[2] In this respect, Korea was used as a model for American policy elsewhere on the Asian mainland. China itself was regarded as both a danger and an opportunity. It might attempt to spread the revolution to neighbouring countries such as Indochina where the French were engaged in a bitter guerrilla war against communist insurgents under Ho Chi Minh.[3] There was also, however, the possibility of a Sino-Soviet split and the emergence of Chinese Titoism. Washington was anxious to encourage such a trend, turning Chinese xenophobia against Moscow rather than the West. It was hoped that the break might come over Stalin's Yalta gains in Manchuria and his supposed desire to detach the province from Beijing. Such a policy demanded American non-intervention in the closing stages of the civil war. There would be no attempt to protect the last vestiges of Guomindong rule on the island of Taiwan.[4]

US policy on the Asian mainland was related to the process of reconstruction in Japan. A stable and prosperous Japan required an economic hinterland as a source of trade and raw materials. This could be found, as in the imperial past, in Korea and South-East Asia. An independent China might also be integrated into such a structure. The incorporation of the Asian mainland into a flourishing capitalist economy centred on Tokyo would prove the bankruptcy of the Soviet model and undermine states such as the DPRK.[5] The ultimate aim of US policy, as expressed in NSC-48/2 of December 1949, was thus to contain and ultimately to reverse the spread of Russian power in the Far East; a concept which became known as rollback.

The decision to concede Taiwan and encourage a Sino-Soviet split was controversial. At the Cairo conference of 1943, the United States had agreed to return the island, then the Japanese colony of Formosa, to China after the war.[7] This presupposed a friendly government in Beijing, tied to Washington by bonds of ideology and self-interest, an assumption undermined as the cold war deepened and the communists gained the upper hand in China. The Pentagon and General Douglas MacArthur of the Far East Command became concerned at the prospect of the island in Mao's hands. It was feared that he would grant the Russians air and naval bases there, threatening communications between Japan and the Philippines. The Pentagon, however, consistently argued that it lacked the resources to defend the island, a fact which left Washington with little room for manouevre.[8] In early 1949 the State Department considered a scheme for autonomy under the UN, only to dismiss the idea as impracticable. Instead Taiwan was to be defended by economic and diplomatic means, leaving military

security to the Guomindong regime.[9] Since Jiang was as incapable of
saving Taiwan as any other part of China, this was tantamount to
conceding the island to the communists. In the discussions of Asian
policy in December 1949, Louis Johnson, the Secretary of Defense,
attempted to modify this approach, endorsing a JCS proposal to supply
arms to the Guomindong and despatch a military training mission.
This was successfully resisted by the Secretary of State, Dean
Acheson, who argued that Washington must avoid the dying embrace
of Jiang's regime.[10] On 5 January 1950 Truman publicly confirmed this
approach, announcing that US forces would not be used to defend
Taiwan 'at this time'. The ambiguous reservation was included at the
insistence of General Omar Bradley, Chairman of the JCS, who
wished to deny the Russians bases on the island in the event of global
war.[11]

Despite Acheson's belief in a sophisticated approach to China,
Washington refused to recognise the communist regime or to oust the
discredited Guomindong from the UN. China was a bitter political
issue which plagued the Truman administration. Despite the attacks of
Asia firsters who accused the President of appeasement in the Far East
in pursuit of his European strategy, foreign policy remained bipartisan
until 1948. Truman's unexpected victory in the Presidential elections,
however, transformed the situation. Denied power and embittered by
defeat, the Republicans seized on China to discredit the Democrats
and revive the political fortunes of their party. The Republican
leadership passed from the liberal Eastern wing, which accepted the
New Deal at home and containment abroad, to mid-Western
conservatives such as Robert Taft of Ohio. This group argued that
consensus had denied the party power since 1936. It was necessary to
roll back the New Deal at home and abroad. The right wing distrusted
entangling alliances such as NATO and rejected Europe first, calling
for a unilateral display of American power in Asia. Jiang was
portrayed as a martyr, betrayed to the communists by Washington.[12]
China became a symbol of all that was wrong with official policy.
Acheson became the focus of the Republican attack. He was an
upper-class liberal who made no secret of his contempt for men he
considered political primitives. In Republican mythology, Acheson
was at best an appeaser and at worst a traitor.[13]

The Republican revolt fuelled opposition to Acheson's Taiwan
policy at the Defense Department. Louis Johnson was an abrasive
politician who hoped to form a conservative coalition to further his
presidential prospects in 1952. He was prepared to intrigue with

right-wing Republicans and with the Guomindong, less to save Jiang than to discredit Acheson and further his own ambitions.[14] General Douglas MacArthur also sympathised with the Republican right. His connections with the party went back to his service in Washington as Army Chief of Staff under President Hoover, when he gained notoriety for his role in dispersing a march on the capital by unemployed veterans.[15] An austere, aloof figure, MacArthur became a popular hero in the war against Japan. As occupation commander in Tokyo, he cultivated an imperial style. His headquarters was like a royal court where his word was law.[16] One journalist called him the Caesar of the Pacific, a description endorsed by his staff who considered him a military genius.[17] MacArthur believed that the West had a mission in Asia where the future of civilisation was at stake. He resented the Europe first psychology at the Pentagon and accused a narrow clique of making policy. His anger had its roots in World War Two, when he believed that he was starved of support in favour of Eisenhower's campaign in Europe. MacArthur was thus the natural ally of the Republican right and aspired to the Presidency.[18] He angled for the nomination in 1948 when his staff allocated themselves roles in a MacArthur administration.[19] Despite his disappointment on that occasion, MacArthur did not abandon his Presidential hopes, a factor which influenced his attitude on Taiwan. Strategically the island might be, as he argued, a natural aircraft carrier within the US defence perimeter. Politically, it was a weapon in domestic politics. In January 1950, his headquarters attempted to embarrass the administration by leaking a State Department briefing paper predicting the imminent fall of Taiwan, an incident which offered ammunition to Republican Congressmen.[20] This sniping prefigured more dramatic events during the Korean War.

As early as September 1949, Acheson registered concern over the erosion of bipartisanship.[21] The situation made it inadvisable to take any steps towards recognising communist China until Taiwan had fallen and the Guomindong regime had ceased to exist.[22] There was more than domestic politics, however, behind the decision to let relations with China drift. Whatever his distaste for the Guomindong, Truman's dislike of the communists was equally great.[23] His ambiguity was shared by Acheson who regarded the Chinese revolution with deep foreboding. Acheson had no intention of appearing weak by running after Mao.[24] This would merely strengthen those in Beijing who wished to lean towards Moscow in the cold war. According to Acheson, China must learn from bitter experience the costs of

association with the Kremlin.[25] In December 1949 he attempted to
secure a united front with Britain on non-recognition, only to be
disappointed.[26] This was the beginning of an Anglo–American
divergence over China which was to plague relations during the
Korean War. In the end, China was to cause the Truman
administration more trouble at home and abroad than any other issue.

In a speech at the National Press Club on 12 January 1950, Acheson
attempted to answer criticism of American policy in Asia and restore
political consensus. According to Acheson, the American position was
based on an offshore strategic perimeter running through Japan and
the Philippines. He expressed interest in the continued independence
of the mainland states but emphasized that they must look to the UN as
their first line of defence. He defended his stand on Taiwan, arguing
that Chinese nationalism must be turned against the Russians in
Manchuria. The peoples of Asia would see that the Soviet Union and
not the United States was the enemy of freedom and independence.
Although Acheson placed the Asian mainland, including the ROK,
outside the US strategic permimeter, he did not write the area off.
Instead he attempted to deter aggression by deliberate ambiguity,
invoking the UN.[27] The continuing gap between resources and
commitments forced him to resort to this expedient in drawing the line
in Asia. A new assessment, however, was soon under way which
eliminated ambiguity in favour of a global system of containment
backed by military force.

This review was stimulated by the shock caused by the Soviet atomic
bomb test in September 1949, followed closely by the fall of China.
These events produced public anxiety and the impression that the
balance in the cold war was tipping towards the Soviet Union. In
March 1950, the British ambassador, Oliver Franks, found Acheson
obsessed by the need to recapture the initiative and counter the
impression that communism was the wave of the future.[28] In January
1950, Truman authorised research on the super or hydrogen bomb, in
an attempt to restore US technological advantage. Simultaneously, he
initiated the broad review of foreign and defence policies known as
NSC-68.[29] This report, completed in April 1950, treated the Russian
threat as primarily military. This was a new departure. In the opening
years of the cold war, it had been thought unlikely that Moscow would
deliberately resort to armed aggression. Communism was regarded as
a political threat, to be contained by economic aid to key areas on the
Soviet periphery which would restore prosperity and eliminate the
conditions in which communism flourished. In this system large

conventional forces were unnecessary. US membership of NATO was intended as much to reassure Europe as to deter the USSR. It was a psychological rather than a military device, extending the US atomic umbrella over Europe and guaranteeing a climate of confidence conducive to economic recovery.[30]

This situation was transformed by the Russian bomb. NSC-68 predicted that Stalin would have the capacity to launch an atomic Pearl Harbor against the United States by 1954. Alternatively, the Kremlin might employ an emerging atomic stalemate to utilise its conventional forces or those of its satellites around the Soviet periphery. Russian atomic weapons put 'a premium on piecemeal aggression . . . counting on our unwillingness to engage in atomic war unless we are directly threatened.'[31] Thus US credibility was endangered. Western Europe and Japan would lose faith in American guarantees. Doubting that Washington would risk atomic destruction in their defence, they would seek refuge in neutrality. The US would be isolated and the Russians would have picked up the stakes in the cold war. The Soviet Union did not even have to use its new capacities. It merely had to be seen to possess them. This alone would undermine confidence in default of countervailing American action. In this context, communist gains anywhere, however insignificant in real terms, were important because they contributed to an apparent reality. Mao's victory in China might not increase Soviet capabilities but it appeared to do so while raising questions about the American will to resist. On this basis, other peripheral areas such as Taiwan and Korea became important, since their loss would contribute to an apparent shift in the balance of power. If erosion at the periphery continued, the centre would be threatened by a psychological domino effect. The concept of national communism, divorced from the Kremlin, was abandoned. Communist advances anywhere, whether or not promoted by Russia, endangered American credibility. The initiative must be seized from the Kremlin. A line had to be drawn on a global scale and defended, reaffirming the American will to resist. There could be no grey areas in the cold war.[32]

If a line was to be drawn on this scale, military resources would have to be found to support it. At the centre of NSC-68 was an unspoken equation between Soviet Russia and Nazi Germany and a determination to avoid the errors of the 1930s. The only way to deal with Stalin was from a position of military strength. NSC-68 advocated rearmament, both atomic and conventional, which would allow the US to match the USSR on a symmetrical basis. Washington must possess the capacity for a flexible response, avoiding the choice between humiliation and risking atomic war. It should be able to counter the Russians at all levels of warfare, atomic, conventional and limited. This meant creating forces able to fight in local conflicts as well as global war. NSC-68 recognised for the first time the possibility of piecemeal aggression. The allies were also to rearm with US assistance, forestalling neutralism and binding them to the American bloc.[33] NSC-68 was a call to arms which looked forward to the transformation of NATO into a functioning military alliance and foreshadowed the rearmament of West Germany and Japan. It played down diplomacy as a means of dealing with Moscow. Diplomacy was regarded as a dangerous detraction from building positions of strength around the Soviet periphery. Negotiations would only prove productive when Western unity and determination had forced changes in the Soviet system.[34] This was the ultimate goal of NSC-68. Communism was to be rolled back, not only in the Soviet bloc but also in Russia itself. A united Western alliance committed to a policy of strength, would eliminate the Iron Curtain and win the cold war. The first step down this ambitious road was taken with the invasion of North Korea in October 1950.[35]

NSC-68 was based on the economics of military Keynsianism. It rejected the tight budget restrictions of the early cold war in favour of a vast increase in spending. This was regarded as a means of encouraging growth and of consolidating American leadership of the free world. It was argued that the US could afford both guns and butter and must maintain, even in time of peace, a permanent state of semi-mobilisation.[36] Ironically, these recommendations were the product, not of the Pentagon, but of Acheson and his advisers who approached the cold war in military terms. In their view, peace was a technical term. In real terms, the US was already at war with Soviet communism.[37] Louis Johnson's cooperation with the survey was minimal and there was some surprise when he signed the final document. He was a dedicated budget-cutter, determined to curry favour with the Congress by fiscal austerity at the Defense Department.[38] His career was not to outlast the Korean War and the launching of NSC-68. The continued presence of such figures in the spring, however, accounted for the hysterical tone of the document and the absence of precise figures on spending. It was intended to scare other officials, in particular the President, into dramatic action.[39] Although completed in April, NSC-68 was not formally approved by Truman, who referred the survey for further study. The President was clearly unwilling to enter the political minefield of spending in advance of the November Congressional elections. Meanwhile, Acheson began a speaking campaign to create public consensus around the new strategy.[40]

In the spring of 1950 there were signs of a firmer US policy in the Far East as NSC-68 was completed and the political debate over Taiwan continued. Acheson's Press Club speech failed to convince his critics who demanded action to save Jiang. In February 1950, Senator Joseph McCarthy made his first charges of subversion at the State Department, a theme which became a major element in the Republican campaign.[41] The administration attempted to preserve bipartisanship by splitting the opposition. In March 1950, Dean Rusk was appointed Assistant Secretary of State for Far Eastern Affairs, a move dictated by his links with moderate Republicans. In April, John Foster Dulles was made a consultant on the Far East. Dulles was a lifelong Republican and an expert on foreign policy. He was taken on board to divide the Eastern wing of the party, to which he belonged, from the primitives. Dulles was given responsibility for the Japanese peace treaty to preserve a key element in Asian policy from partisan attack.[42]

Although neither had participated in drawing up NSC-68, both reflected its approach to the cold war. In May 1950, Rusk argued that if more countries fell to communism, American credibility would be shattered. The containment system would collapse: 'We can expect an accelerated deterioration of our position in the Mediterranean, Near East, Asia and the Pacific. The situation in Japan may become untenable and possibly that in the Philippines. Indonesia with its vast natural resources may be lost and the oil of the Middle East will be put in jeopardy.' This echoed the psychological domino theory at the centre of NSC-68. According to Rusk, such an outcome could be avoided by a 'dramatic and strong stand that shows our confidence and resolution'. It was better to seek a showdown with the Russians now than in two years time when their atomic stockpile would have grown. Rusk wanted a confrontation over Taiwan. The American fleet should be used to neutralise the island while the UN assumed responsibility for its future.[43] Rusk was supported by Dulles who felt a strong emotional commitment to Taiwan.[44] A muscular Christian, who often spoke as if he had a direct line to God, Dulles regarded his co-religionist Jiang as the defender of Western civilisation in Asia. The communists were dismissed as the anti-Christ.[45] While Acheson did not reverse policy on Taiwan, he did agree to limited arms sales to the Guomindong on 28 May. This reflected his concern with the situation in Indochina and a desire to distract Beijing from any adventure in the area. The Sino-Soviet Pact of February 1950 convinced Acheson that there was little chance of an early split with Moscow and cleared the way to this move.[46] In the early summer of 1950, therefore, pressure was building for a new policy on Taiwan. In the event, however, the showdown demanded by Rusk occurred not over Taiwan but over Korea. Jiang was saved as the by-product of the North Korean attack.

Korea remained a problem in early 1950. In January, Republican Congressmen torpedoed an aid bill as a protest against China policy and Acheson had to lobby to restore the cuts.[47] Rhee embarrassed Washington by his failure to control inflation and his intolerance of dissent. The Korean leader attempted to postpone National Assembly elections to prevent opposition parties increasing their representation. It was feared that he was another Jiang and that his regime would share the fate of the Guomindong. In April, Acheson threatened to cut off American aid unless inflation was controlled and elections held.[48] Despite these events, however, there were signs by early summer that Washington might increase its commitment to Seoul. This trend was more apparent in the State Department than at the Pentagon which continued to accord the ROK a low priority. In an interview with the Korean ambassador on 3 April, Rusk hinted that the ROK might not always lie outside the US defence perimeter.[49] This reflected his desire to draw firm lines against the advance of communism in the cause of American credibility. In June 1950, Dulles visited the ROK during a tour of the Far East. He inspected defences along the 38th parallel and addressed the National Assembly on 19 June, defining Korea as 'an equal partner . . . in the free world' which did not stand alone in the struggle against communism.[50] This was intended to reassure Rhee, following earlier threats to reappraise US aid. MacArthur regarded Dulles' words and actions in Korea as 'a reversal of previous State Department policy'.[51] The likely reaction of the Pentagon to any such development was revealed when the US ambassador, John J. Muccio, lobbied for increased military assistance in May 1950. Muccio was concerned by the changing balance of forces on the peninsula. While the DPRK had been reinforced by Korean units repatriated from China after the civil war, US aid had been delayed by supply shortages and the conflicting demands of other areas.[52] Muccio demanded a supplemental assistance programme and the provision of aircraft to the ROK. The request was not greeted enthusiastically by the Pentagon, which argued that Korea was 'not regarded as of any particular value to the overall American strategic position in the Far East'. The provision of further military hardware could only be justified on political grounds.[53] Rusk authorised a review of the position which was incomplete when war broke out in June 1950.[54] The crisis resolved the tension between the political importance of the ROK and its low strategic value. The doubts of the Pentagon were brushed aside and Washington became militarily engaged on the peninsula.

The American response to the North Korean attack reflected the assumptions of NSC-68. The war was regarded as the first sign of Soviet adventurism, encouraged by Stalin's recent acquisition of the atomic bomb. The DPRK was merely an obedient puppet, obeying orders dictated by Moscow.[55] Few, however, now accept this view. Recent research regards the war as the extension of a civil struggle begun in 1945 and institutionalised in two opposing regimes.[56] Despite North Korean claims that the attack was a justified response to ROK aggression, immediate responsibility for the war seems to lie with Pyongyang.[57] According to Krushchev, Kim Il Sung visited Moscow at the end of 1949 to suggest the unification of Korea at the point of a bayonet.[58] An open military assault represented a dramatic change in policy. Since 1948, Pyongyang had employed guerrilla action and political warfare in an attempt to undermine the Seoul regime. This campaign, however, had made little headway against the police apparatus perfected by Rhee and the guerrilla bands were isolated and crushed.[59] It has been suggested that Kim was under increasing pressure from factions in the politbureau to solve the problem of the South.[60] If such domestic pressure existed, it was reinforced by international considerations. By 1950, it was clear that Washington was rebuilding Japan as the key to the Western position in Asia. The ROK, regarded in the North as a collaborationist regime, might become the tool of a revived Japanese imperialism in Asia, menacing the security of the DPRK. Rhee, backed by Tokyo and Washington, might launch a march to the Yalu. He was known to be increasing his army and lobbying Washington for increased supplies of arms. A revival of the Japanese Empire in North-East Asia might be forestalled by sudden action to crush the ROK. The conditions were favourable for such a coup in 1950. The North Korea People's Army (NKPA) had been strengthened by the repatriation of Korean divisions from China and the supply of Soviet equipment. This situation, however, might not last, putting a premium upon an early employment of force.[61]

A mystery remains, however, about the timing of the attack. It was later revealed that the NKPA was ordered to combat readiness on 10

June. The operational directive for the attack was issued in great secrecy on 23 June, at a time when mobilisation was incomplete and the final shipments of Soviet arms, arranged during the spring, had yet to arrive.[62] It is possible that operations scheduled for August were hurriedly launched in June as a consequence of the visit by John Foster Dulles to the 38th parallel. Kim, like MacArthur, may have seen this as the first evidence of a firmer US commitment, which forced him to strike before time ran out.[63] The decision to jump the gun cost Pyongyang dearly. Moscow was boycotting the Security Council over its refusal to seat the Beijing regime as the representative of China, a fact which allowed Washington to organise a speedy response through the UN and characterise intervention as a legitimate attempt to uphold the rule of law.[64]

It is generally agreed that Beijing played no part in planning the North Korean attack, although Mao may have been consulted in advance.[65] The role of Moscow is more controversial. It is clear that Stalin knew about Kim's plan without necessarily approving the timing. According to Krushchev, the North Korean action appealed because it could be characterised as 'an internal matter which the Koreans would be settling amongst themselves'. There was a good chance that unification would be achieved before the United States could respond.[66] The Russians had something to gain from cautious backing of the DPRK. The revival of Japan was a threat to the Soviet Union as well as to North Korea, raising the spectre of the old imperial unit on the Siberian border. Russian sensitivity on this score was revealed in the Sino-Soviet Pact, which was aimed against the revival of Japanese imperialism. China too had every reason to fear the reappearance of Japan in North-East Asia.[67] Whatever Stalin's role, he left his ally to take the risks. While Moscow supplied the NKPA with obsolete equipment, the Russian role was minimised by reducing the number of Soviet advisers with the North Korean forces.[68] Stalin may even have been taken by surprise at the timing of the offensive. Not only were the Russians boycotting the UN, but they were notably slow to adopt a line on the Korean War for public consumption.[69]

The North Korean military build-up was detected by MacArthur's intelligence organisation in the spring of 1950. The concentration of the NKPA along the 38th parallel and the evacuation of civilians from the border areas were reported to Far East Command (FEC) headquarters and to Washington. Alarm bells failed to ring, however, in either quarter. The information was interpreted within the context of the traditional tension between North and South Korea. As FEC intelligence remarked on 1 March:

> Evacuation of civilians from critical border areas normally could be viewed as an indication that warfare is anticipated, and possibly imminent. In the case of the immediate 38th Parallel areas, this criterion does not necessarily hold. Considering the frequency of clashes between North and South Korean armed force personnel during the past two years, it is likely that voluntary evacuation has been occurring for some time.[70]

Louis Johnson later recalled that invasion scares had become so common since 1948 that they were treated as routine.[71] The American embassy in Seoul, like FEC intelligence, did not believe that an attack was imminent. It was assumed that military action would be avoided until other methods had been exhausted.[72] When Rhee publicised North Korean troop movements in May 1950 and claimed that the ROK was already at war, it was assumed that he was merely attempting to scare Washington into improving arms supplies.[73]

The impact of information on North Korean military movements was further muted because the recipients held their own assumptions about Soviet global stragegy and did not regard the ROK as the area at greatest risk. In an evaluation of the situation on 24 March, FEC intelligence noted:

> That the North Korean Peoples Army will be prepared to invade South Korea by fall, and possibly by spring, of this year is indicated in current reports of armed force expansion and major troop movements to critical 38th Parallel areas. Even if future reports bear out the present implications, it is believed that civil war will not necessarily be precipitated. Soviet intentions in Korea are believed to be closely related to the Communist program in Southeast Asia. It seems likely . . . that military action by North Korea will be held in abeyance . . . until further observation is made by the Soviets of the results of their program in such places as Indo-china, Burma and Thailand.[74]

The belief that the Russians were concentrating on other targets was shared by higher authority. In Washington, Acheson regarded Indochina and not Korea as the critical area.[75] MacArthur in Tokyo remained obsessed by Taiwan. When Louis Johnson and General Bradley visited FEC headquarters on the eve of the North Korean attack, an intelligence briefing failed to raise the possibility of action against the ROK. MacArthur, however, gave his visitors a long memorandum on the strategic importance of Taiwan.[76]

When the NKPA crossed the parallel on 25 June, Washington and Tokyo were caught unprepared. As late as 20 June, Dean Rusk had informed a Congressional committee that there were no signs of an imminent attack.[77] Many of the most important officials had left Washington for the weekend. Truman was visiting his home in Independence, Missouri. Acheson was at his Maryland farm. The Army Chief of Staff, General Joseph Collins, was at a cottage on the Chesapeake.[78] MacArthur was equally surprised. When the first reports reached his headquarters, the fighting was dismissed as yet another border incident along the notoriously disputed 38th parallel.[79] Even Seoul was caught napping, despite the alarm raised by Rhee in May. One third of the army was on weekend leave when the assault began.[80] For all concerned, the North Korean offensive was a Saturday night surprise.

The US response, however, was swift. From the beginning of the crisis the North Korean attack was viewed as a Soviet move with global implications. Failure to respond would be regarded as a sign of weakness, undermining American credibility and endangering the whole edifice of containment. As the US embassy in Moscow argued in a telegram of 25 June, North Korean aggression represented a clear-cut Soviet challenge which the US must answer 'firmly and swiftly as it constitutes direct threat to our leadership of the free world against Soviet Communist imperialism. ROK is a creation of US policy and of US-led UN action. Its destruction would have calculably grave unfavorable repercussion for US in Japan, SEA and in other areas as well.' Stalin's Korean adventure offered Washington the chance to seize the initiative and draw the line against communist expansion.[81] This view was echoed minutes later by Dulles from Tokyo: 'To sit by while Korea is overrun by unprovoked armed attack would start a disastrous chain of events leading most probably to world war.'[82] Truman and Acheson agreed with this analysis. There was no question of inaction. The President approved Acheson's decision to appeal to the UN and returned to Washington determined to hit the communists hard.[83] On the way to the White House he remarked, 'By God, I'm going to let them have it.'[84] Truman cited the lessons of history in favour of intervention. The failure of the Western powers to stand up to Hitler had encouraged Nazi aggression and led to world war. He would not repeat the error in dealing with the Soviet Union.[85]

The exposure of US policy in Korea as empty bluff, threatened the credibility of the adminsitration at home as well as abroad. With the Republican right making political capital over the loss of China, Truman could not afford to let another Asian country fall to communism, particularly one within the reach of American military power in Japan. Democratic Congressmen made the President aware of their anxiety on this score.[86] It was perhaps a desire to forestall domestic criticism which made the administration anxious that news of US action at the UN should appear in the morning newspapers simultaneously with reports of the North Korean attack.[87] A firm stand would deprive the opposition of an issue and compel it to meet the costs of resistance in the Far East. NSC-68 could be launched on the basis of bipartisanship. This strategy worked in the opening stages of the war. The Republicans supported the decision to intervene and accepted an expanded military budget. Truman, however, failed to formalise this consensus in a Congressional resolution. He was unwilling to erode what he regarded as Presidential prerogatives by seeking approval on Capitol Hill. This proved to be a costly error. When the war began to go badly, the Republicans dissociated themselves from decisions which they had supported in June 1950.[88]

The legal basis for intervention was provided by two UN Security Council resolutions sponsored by Washington. As General Bradley remarked on 25 June, American military support could be provided under 'the guise of aid to the UN'.[89] The first resolution, passed that day, called for a North Korean withdrawal. The second, on 27 June, requested UN members to assist the ROK repel aggression and restore 'peace and security' in the area.[90] In the absence of the Soviet delegate, the Security Council was quick to respond to American pressure. There was no attempt to query a finding of North Korean aggression, despite the previous history of tension on the peninsula. Trygve Lie, the Secretary General, lobbied strongly on behalf of the US resolutions amongst non-aligned members such as India and Egypt.[91] The UN was ill-equipped to view the situation impartially, having already backed Washington in establishing the ROK. It was predisposed to view the situation in terms of the cold war. The dominant Western members of the organisation shared the American perspective and regarded the attack as a Soviet probe. Few could credit the DPRK with a capacity for independent action.[92] If the US dominated events at the UN, it also dominated the Unified Command established under the UN flag on 7 July. Although Korea was formally a UN war the world organisation did not attempt to control military

operations, turning over the running of the conflict to Truman, the JCS
and MacArthur in Tokyo.[93]

Thus a new stage in the cold war was ushered in by an appeal to
collective security which drew on memories of the 1930s. The UN
helped legitimise American involvement and mobilise public opinion
behind US policy at home and abroad. As MacArthur was informed on
12 July, for 'worldwide political reasons' it was important to emphasise
the UN role.[94] While the involvement of the world organisation was
useful, it was not essential. Washington was prepared to act in default
of UN backing if the Russians cast a veto, arguing that unilateral action
was in support of the UN charter.[95] Behind the slogan of collective
security, the US was upholding its own selective security and that of
the Western bloc.[96] The appeal to the UN charter concealed the reality
of NSC-68. As the Joint Strategic Plans Committee of the JCS noted
on 14 July, 'The prompt reaction of the United States to Communist
aggression . . . indicates the initiation of a new and stiffened US
policy vis-à-vis Communist expansion which is in consonance with
NSC-68.'[97]

NSC-68 called for a system of global containment. In the wake of the
Korean crisis, Washington drew the line against communism
throughout the Far East. Announcing air and naval support for the
ROK on 27 June, Truman also stated that the US was increasing aid to
Indochina and the Philippines and neutralising Taiwan.[98] The latter
moves were made unilaterally, outside the framework of the UN. The
most controversial was the decision to interpose the 7th Fleet between
Taiwan and the mainland. This threatened to involve the US in the
closing stages of the Chinese civil war and provoke a wider struggle in
the Far East. It was from the beginning a source of anxiety to the UN
allies, who were prepared to support action against the DPRK but
hesitated to risk a conflict with China.[99] The neutralisation of Taiwan
was proposed by Acheson on 25 June and approved without debate.
An announcement was merely delayed until fleet units were in
position.[100] It reflected the growing belief in Washington that
whatever the long-term prospects, the Chinese communists were for
the time being tools of the Kremlin.

At a time of increasing tension with the USSR, it made strategic
sense to guard the flanks of the Korean operation. The JCS had long
been apprehensive about the prospect of Soviet bases on the island and
there was a contingency plan to deny the Russians the use of Taiwan in
the event of global war.[101] Neutralisation, however, also represented
the expression of American determination demanded by Rusk in May

1950. As Acheson emphasised on 30 June, if the Chinese were allowed to seize the island, Asia would fall apart. There would be panic from Japan to the Philippines.[102] This was an echo of the domino theory in NSC-68. It also gave the game away. While neutralisation claimed to be even-handed, favouring neither side in the Chinese civil war, practically the policy favoured Jiang whose regime stood on the verge of extinction. Nor was such a move without domestic political implications.[103] Acheson, however, had no intention of fighting the communists on behalf of the Guomindong. When Jiang offered to send 33 000 troops to Korea on 29 June, Acheson persuaded Truman to decline on the grounds that it might provoke Chinese intervention in the fighting. The JCS agreed, emphasising the unpreparedness of Jiang's men. Guomindong troops would be better employed defending Taiwan.[104] This military estimate reflected the dismal experience of the civil war when many of Jiang's soldiers had deserted or fled.

Although Truman was determined to stop the communists in Korea, the extent of American involvement depended on the capabilities of the ROK and the Soviet response to US intervention. On 25 June there was some hope that the situation could be saved by increased supplies of military equipment and the moral backing of the UN. It was clear, however, that if these moves failed, further action would follow: 'The United States could not meet the situation with half measures. It either had to take a stand and stick to it or take no stand at all.'[105] By 26 June it was evident that more than equipment was needed. At a meeting that day, Truman approved air and naval action in support of the ROK, but restricted operations to the South of the 38th parallel.[106] Despite the fall of Seoul on 28 June, direct attacks on the DPRK were not authorised until the following day. Unknown to Truman, however, he had been forestalled. MacArthur had already authorised bombing raids on his own initiative, a foretaste for Truman of the problems to come with his Korean commander.[107] The reason for official caution was uncertainty about Soviet intentions. While Truman believed that the Russians would back down in the face of firm action, it was unwise to base policy on such an assumption.[108] Korea had long been regarded as an unfavourable spot for a confrontation with Moscow. The Russians held all the strategic cards on the peninsula, where US forces would be operating at the muzzle of a Soviet gun. In the event of Russian intervention, air superiority could only be maintained by an atomic attack on air bases in Siberia. On 25 June, the USAF commander, General Vandenberg, was authorised to make contingency plans for such atomic strikes.[108] In addition, Washington had to consider if the Korean crisis was merely a feint, designed to divert attention from some more vital region. On 26 June US embassies were warned that the attack might be part of a larger Soviet plan. American diplomats were to investigate and report any evidence of a further Russian coup.[109]

Meanwhile, Moscow was given every opportunity to disown its client. The Russians were not accused of direct complicity and the Soviet sphere of influence North of the parallel remained inviolate. On 26 June, to draw the Kremlin out, the US ambassador was instructed to request that the USSR disavow the North Korean action and use its influence to restore peace on the peninsula.[110] Only after the Russians had failed to exercise a veto at the UN and Gromyko had informed the US ambassador on 29 June that the USSR stood by non-intervention did Truman feel free to act.[111] As he remarked that evening, 'This means that the Soviets are going to let the Chinese and the North Koreans do the fighting for them.'[112] The President nevertheless remained careful to avoid pushing Stalin into a corner. In authorising air and naval action against the DPRK he emphasised, 'We must be damned careful. . . . We want to take any steps we have to push the North Koreans behind the line, but I don't want to get us overcommitted to a whole lot of other things that could mean war.'[113] Ironically, Washington began to implement NSC-68 while denying that it was actually confronting the USSR. As the FEC stressed in an order of 30 June, the enemy was the DPRK: 'Statements that any other nation or group of nations is being combated are unauthorised.'[114]

The failure of air and naval support to contain the NKPA led to the commitment of US ground combat forces. This reversed the previous thrust of American military policy which opposed ground wars on the Asian mainland. On 25 June, General Bradley, while endorsing the employment of air power, had questioned 'the advisability of putting in ground units particularly if large numbers are involved'.[115] As the director of the Joint Strategic Survey Committee noted, the Pentagon did not want to commit troops.[116] This reluctance echoed the position of the JCS in July 1949, as the last American units withdrew from the peninsula. Truman and Acheson, however, were conscious of the consequences of failure in Korea. The future of both containment and the administration were at stake in the fighting. As the President remarked on 28 June, 'We will either get results or we will have to go all-out to maintain our position.'[117]

In the early hours of 30 June, Truman decided to risk escalation rather than accept defeat when MacArthur reported that Rhee's forces were incapable of holding without the introduction of American ground combat units. He requested the immediate despatch of a regimental combat team and the early commitment of two divisions for a counter-offensive against the victorious NKPA. Within twenty-four hours the first GIs were on their way from Japan.[118] As the Secretary of the Army, Frank Pace, later recalled, this was a 'fundamental decision . . . although it was largely overlooked at the time'. The earlier despatch of air and naval forces had committed American prestige and left the administration with nowhere to go but forward.[119]

MacArthur's recommendations followed a personal visit to the front on 29 June. In his memoirs, he left a dramatic description of the scene and his own determination to save the situation:

> Across the Han, Seoul burned and smoked in its agony of destruction. There was the constant crump of Red mortar fire. . . . Below me . . . were the retreating, panting columns of disorganized troops, the drab color of their weaving lines interspersed here and there with the bright red crosses of ambulances filled with broken, groaning men . . . everywhere were the stench and utter desolation of a stricken battlefield. . . . In that brief interval on the blood-soaked hill, I formulated my plans. They were desperate plans indeed, but I could see no other way except to accept a defeat which would include not only Korea, but all of continental Asia.[120]

His plans were interesting because they reversed his previous neglect of Korea and his firm conviction that US troops should not be used on the Asian mainland. The reasons are not far to seek. MacArthur blamed unrealistic politicians for creating the situation which he as a soldier had to save.[121] MacArthur himself, however, could not escape responsibility for the fate of the ROK. He had recommended the withdrawal of American troops in 1948 and blocked additional military aid in 1950. His first reaction to the crisis had been dismissive. Indeed his conduct led John Foster Dulles to recommend his replacement.[122] He could, therefore, hardly escape implication if Congress picked over the wreckage of US policy. This would be a poor end to a distinguished career and doom his political ambitions. US ground troops, however, might save the day. MacArthur would be the hero of the hour, a role with political implications in 1952. Moreover, Korea was a useful means of reversing the strategic priority of Europe first, which MacArthur had always resented. These ambitions ultimately provoked a breach with the administration. For the time being,

however, Truman and his Asian pro-consul could agree on the need
for forceful action to save the ROK.

Truman took a calculated risk in despatching troops. The Soviet and
Chinese forces across the frontier far outnumbered anything the US
could field. It had already been concluded, however, that Stalin would
not intervene, clearing the way to firm action against the DPRK. The
administration shared with MacArthur a belief that in these
circumstances, US ground action would be cheap, decisive and swift.
An arrogant display of force would save the situation. On 29 June,
Truman agreed with a reporter's description of Korea as a police
action, a phrase he was later to find embarrassing.[123] Both Washington
and Tokyo underestimated the North Koreans. As General Bradley
ruefully recalled, 'I don't think any of us knew . . . what would be
involved. No one believed that the North Koreans would be as strong
as they turned out to be.'[124] Neither for the first nor for the last time,
Americans underestimated the staying power of an Asian society
against the application of modern military technology. Within weeks
of the decision to invervene, US forces were on the verge of expulsion
from Korea.

The Korean crisis created a new structure of containment in Asia. A
firm line was to be drawn in the Far East as in Europe. In willing this
end, the administration also willed the means. By demonstrating the
military nature of the Soviet threat, Korea cleared the way for NSC-68.
The new era was characterised by 'a military policy of armaments, to
the exclusion of everything else'.[125] It was hoped that decisive action in
Korea would restore bipartisanship at home and confidence abroad,
creating consensus around the programmes of NSC-68. The decisions
of June 1950, however, proved to be the prelude not to a brisk show of
force but to a long and exhausting struggle on the Asian periphery. In
the course of the conflict, the administration was to bankrupt its
political capital at home and strain relations with the Western allies.
The moral crusade under the banner of the UN became a sour little
war.

3 Across the Parallel

The Korean adventure brought immediate dividends for the Truman administration. The Republican attack temporarily lost momentum and the President's ratings soared in the polls. The war was popular. There was little opposition when Truman began to implement the rearmament provisions of NSC-68 in July 1950.[1] If Korea provided the 'springboard for a US global build-up', however, it also posed problems of priorities.[2] The war was important as a symbol of US determination to draw the line against communism and as a means of mobilising the public behind rearmament. It was never intended, however, to place the main emphasis on containment in Asia. Korea was to serve the goals of global strategy, not to dictate its shape. Washington saw the war as an opportunity, 'Not so much to build-up military strength in Asia . . . but to bolster the obviously inadequate defenses of Western Europe.'[3] In September 1950, however, to maintain the initiative in the cold war and the domestic consensus for increased commitments to NATO, Truman authorised the invasion of North Korea. This brought China into the war, threatened a wider conflict in the Far East, and revived partisan debate about foreign policy. It was the most disastrous decision of the Truman presidency. While a general conflict in Asia was avoided, the administration never recovered from the domestic consequences of Chinese intervention.[4]

The Korean crisis seemed to confirm the predictions of NSC-68 about Soviet adventurism and it was within this context that the US response was organised. Washington was determined to create 'positions of strength' from which to deter further Russian action. There was a vast increase in defence spending, new commitments to NATO, and calls for the rearmament of Germany and Japan.[5] Many of these moves had been under consideration before June 1950, but Korea lent impetus to the process and created a receptive climate for the militarisation of the cold war. The moving force behind these changes, as with NSC-68 itself, was not the Pentagon, but Dean Acheson. On 14 July Acheson argued that to meet the demands of Korea and to impress the USSR, economic resources must be mobilised behind rearmament. The President must 'ask for money and if it is a question of asking for too little or too much, he should ask for too much.'[6] Acting on the advice, Truman asked the Congress for increases in the defence budget of $10 billion on 19 July.[7] On 30 September the National Security Council adopted NSC-68 as 'a statement of policy' for the next 'four or five years'.[8] In the following months appropriations 'tumbled over' each other,[9] not only to expand the conventional forces but also to improve atomic striking power. Atomic weapons construction was accelerated and the Strategic Air Command received a substantial share of the new expenditure.[10] These developments were welcomed by the Western allies as a further stage in the decline of isolationism and the assumption of global responsibilities by the US. As the Canadian ambassador to Washington, Hume Wrong, remarked on 1 August, 'Perhaps the best result of the Korean affair . . . is that it has made it possible for the people of the United States to accept the load involved in making their military power equal to their world responsibilities.'[11]

The drain on existing resources caused by the fighting made the early implementation of NSC-68 all the more important. The abilities of the North Koreans had been underestimated and increasing amounts of manpower had to be committed simply to avoid defeat. MacArthur's estimates of force requirements went up from day to day.[12] The administration had to take risks elsewhere. As early as 9 July, the JCS warned about the 'crippling effects' of the fighting on the ability of the armed forces to fulfil current war plans or to meet further limited emergencies.[13] In order to prevent Korea from becoming a strategic trap, endlessly consuming men and materials, Washington tried to avoid broadening the Soviet or Chinese roles. It was also anxious to avoid triggering a war with the Soviet Union for which the US was unprepared. Strict orders were given against the violation of the Russian and Chinese borders by US aircraft and the city of Najin (Rashin) was removed from the target list because of its proximity to the sensitive Soviet frontier. Truman carefully refrained from charging Moscow with responsibility for the war and sacked Francis Matthews, the Secretary of the Navy, when he advocated a preventive attack on the USSR.[14] In the last analysis, however, the administration relied upon the existing US atomic superiority to deter further Soviet moves. While the Russians were not openly threatened with the bomb, the message was communicated by subtle signals such as the despatch of SAC bombers to British bases in July 1950. Although this was officially described as a 'training mission' the aircraft were at their war station.[15] The US strategic plan, OFFTACKLE, called for an air atomic offensive from these bases in the opening weeks of a global conflict.[16] Even this move, however, contained an element of bluff. SAC lacked sufficient aircraft and bombs to perform its alloted role in OFFTACKLE.[17]

As NSC-68 was launched, US forces were retreating down the Korean peninsula. By August 1950, MacArthur's command had been forced into a narrow perimeter around Pusan. The situation was so serious that in mid-July MacArthur and the Army Chief of Staff, General Joseph Collins, discussed the use of the atomic bomb against the DPRK. MacArthur's idea was to use the bomb to strike a 'blocking blow' which would cut North Korean supply lines from Manchuria. The subject was not pursued, although emergency use of the 'winning weapon' was not ruled out if it became necessary to save US forces in Korea from 'disaster'.[18] The long retreat raised political problems. It was feared in Washington that if the US was left to face the burden of the war alone and was humiliated, the American people would question the value of alliances. They would revert to isolationism, endangering the whole system of containment. This concern led to pressure on the UN allies to deploy forces to Korea. Although Britain, Canada and Australia had contributed naval contingents and Australia also had an air squadron serving with MacArthur, this was considered insufficient by the Americans. The US was still bearing the burden of the ground fighting. When the Canadians argued that their three warships were more than a token, one US official sourly remarked 'OK, three tokens'. This attitude was resented but it could not be ignored.[19]

The problem for the major allies was that low defence budgets in the pre-Korea period left them stretched to cover all the risks. Britain, Canada and others implemented their own budget increases under the impact of the war and American pressure. They shared with the US a perception of the North Korean attack as a Soviet probe, signalling a new and dangerous development in Russian policy. The shift from economic to military containment was accepted with little internal debate.[20] Until their own rearmament gathered pace, however, the allies were reluctant to strip existing capacity for Korea. Nobody had foreseen the possibility of a UN 'police action' and the resources for such a commitment could not be created overnight. The allied governments faced a delicate balance of risks. If they were drawn into Korea they would undermine their ability to fight a global war or to resist limited aggression in more vital areas. Britain, for example, was concerned about the Soviet threat in Europe and the Middle East.[21] While Korea could not be written off like Czechoslovakia at Munich, neither, as Prime Minister Attlee argued on 6 July, should the situation

blind the West to the dangers nearer home.[22] It was hoped in London
that the affair could be settled by US forces in Japan.[23] Canada
occupied a similar position. Ottawa recognised a moral commitment to
'collective security', but was reluctant to fulfil it at the expense of risks
in NATO.[24] Washington, however, had a powerful lever to secure
allied compliance. It was made clear that American assistance for
defence and rearmament was dependent on physical support for the
US in Korea. Containment was indivisible. Congress would not
support collective action outside Korea if the allies proved reluctant to
help the US there and left the Americans to pay the butcher's bill.[25]

US pressure for the commitment of ground forces was exercised
both directly and through the UN. On 14 July the UN Secretary
General, Trygve Lie, asked for offers of ground contingents because of
the 'urgent need for additional effective assistance' at the front. At
staff talks in Washington on 20 July, General Bradley raised the matter
directly with the British, requesting a brigade for an eventual
counter-offensive.[26] The British agreed on 24 July, a decision based on
political rather than military considerations. If Britain failed the US in
a 'tough spot', Anglo-American relations would suffer. The despatch
of a brigade, however, would reassure US opinion, consolidate the
British image as a major ally and strengthen the government's hand
with the Truman administration.[27] London strained its military
resources to outfit a brigade, but the US request proved merely a first
instalment. On 16 August Bradley outlined the desperate position at
Pusan and warned that if the US was driven from Korea, the American
people would demand scapegoats. Attention might initially focus on
the Pentagon, but Britain ultimately might have to share the blame.
Infantry were needed immediately and not in October when 29
Brigade were scheduled to arrive.[28] The Foreign Secretary, Ernest
Bevin, emphasised that Britain was already taking 'tremendous risks'
in key areas and 'begged' Washington not to further weaken British
defences. On 17 August, however, London reluctantly agreed to send
a second brigade immediately, drawn from the garrison in Hong Kong
which was already understrength.[29] Once again the motive was
political. Britain, dependent on the US for military assistance in
NATO and financial aid for rearmament, could not afford to alienate
Washington.[30] The other major allies, Canada and Australia, made
their decisions for similar reasons.[31] In retrospect they all over-
estimated the leverage a troop commitment would guarantee over
US policy in the Far East.[32]

Both the US and its allies found Rhee an uncomfortable partner.

The ROK fought under the UN flag and was the creation of the world organisation. It remained what it had always been, however, a police state dominated by Syngman Rhee. As the Australian ambassador to Japan reported after a visit to Korea in September 1950, 'Every observer with long experience of Korean affairs holds the opinion that we have at present in South Korea a reactionary government closely associated with unscrupulous landlords and bolstered by a vicious police force.'[33] Rhee's activities were embarrassing and threatened public support for what was initially a popular war. In the early days of the conflict, the DPRK was condemned in the West for atrocities against POWs and civilians.[34] Such events were inescapable in a civil war and undoubtedly occurred. As the journalist James Cameron recalled, the NKPA often killed POWs, providing the American press 'with precisely the propaganda they so badly needed'.[35] Such reports confirmed the illegitimacy of the DPRK. Behind the front, however, the North Koreans appear to have made a genuine effort to win over the population, introducing land reform and appealing to nationalist sentiment. The arrested revolution of 1945 was completed. There was no systematic policy of terror. Large-scale massacres occurred only at a later stage when the revolutionary regime in the South was collapsing after Inchon.[36] In the summer of 1950, it was the ROK which pursued a policy of terror. This was the result of the perennial insecurity of Syngman Rhee. As Muccio later complained, he treated most of the population as subversive.[37]

Before the fall of Seoul, Rhee ordered the execution of political prisoners. It was estimated that 50 000 died in the ensuing massacres.[38] Mass graves were discovered at Taejon by the advancing NKPA and their existence reported in the West by Alan Winnington of the *Daily Worker*.[39] While such incidents were exploited by the communists for their propaganda value, they had not been invented. A French priest witnessed the Taejon incident and tried unsuccessfully to intervene.[40] American personnel attached to the ROK Air Force, under the command of Colonel Dean Hess, found bodies floating in the sea off Chinhae in August 1950:

> Several were in an advanced state of decomposition and all had been tied together. . . . Our enquiries disclosed that these had been Communist spies . . . captured by the South Korean forces. Ammunition was scarce . . . the spies had been taken out onto the water and, with hands bound behind their backs, shoved overboard. Our men lost their taste for swimming in the bay.[41]

Hess, an admirer of Rhee, accepted assurances that this had been an isolated incident. In fact it was all too common in the summer of 1950. James Cameron recalled that behind the lines, the ROK police intensified their campaign against subversion, a term broadly interpreted during the war. The methods employed to secure confessions were the gossip of rear area headquarters.[42] Cameron himself encountered a group of prisoners on their way to execution and was sickened by the sight. Their condition was:

> quite sensationally appalling. They were skeletons . . . and they cringed like dogs. They were manacled with chains . . . compelled to crouch in the classical Oriental attitude of subjection. . . . Sometimes they moved enough to scoop a handful of water from the black puddles around them. Any deviation from their attitude brought a gun butt to their heads.[43]

This medieval spectacle was taking place only yards from US Army HQ and within five minutes of the UN commission building in Pusan. It had been 'going on for months. Nobody had said a word.'[44]

As Cameron pointed out, the US and its allies chose to remain silent. In the words of one UN official, it was important not to damage the morale and efficiency of the ROK police.[45] There was self-censorship by the press and where this was insufficient, pressure from governments. On 25 July, the British Foreign Office noted with concern that the newspapers were 'showing great interest in reports of the shooting by Korean Government Police of a number of Communist prisoners'.[46] The News Department intervened with editors to divert this unwelcome line of enquiry. It was pointed out that such incidents were more frequent and violent in the North where there was no free press to report them.[47] In the US, the administration also brought discreet influence to bear. Acheson attempted to give the ROK a positive image by arranging background briefings emphasising the achievements of the Seoul regime. This was intended to prevent correspondents 'falling unconsciously for commie line that ROK is reactionary govt not representative of people'.[48] Despite Acheson's fears, most American journalists were prepared to overlook Rhee's failings in the larger cause of anti-communism. While admitting that the ROK was not a perfect democracy, it was argued that the regime had a better record than a communist police state such as Poland. Rhee might be something of a dictator but he was 'our' dictator.[49]

While there was broad agreement between the US and its allies on intervention in Korea and a shared readiness to overlook the failings of

Syngman Rhee, no such consensus emerged over the unilateral American decision to 'neutralise' Taiwan. In the spring of 1950 Acheson abandoned hopes of an early Sino–Soviet split, assuming that China would act as a Russian satellite in the immediate future.[50] Thus the Taiwan decision, like the Korean intervention, was intended to draw the line against Soviet expansion. As Acheson argued on 28 July: 'We do not believe Formosa [Taiwan] can be limited to a facet of the Chi[na] problem; it involves our attitude toward present Commie determination to seize Asia, a determination which US feels we must oppose in the interest of our own nat[ional] as well as world security.' In Russian hands, the island would pose a grave threat to the US position in the Western Pacific.[51] Thus China was part of the Russian problem. Major allies such as Britain and Canada, however, continued to distinguish between Chinese and Soviet communism. They did not see China, like the DPRK, as a slavish satellite and regarded Korea and Taiwan as separate issues.[52]

Britain recognised the Chinese communist regime in January 1950. While the Americans emphasised the role of 'selfish' economic interest in this decision, trade was intended to serve a political as well as an economic purpose. Bevin was anxious to avoid driving Beijing and Moscow together and wished to leave Mao an opening to the West.[53] This approach was justified on broad political and strategic grounds. Britain faced a Soviet threat in Europe and the Middle East and was unwilling to add China to its problems. Hong Kong was a permanent hostage to China and the situation in Malaya, where a communist insurgency had broken out in 1948, could only be worsened by conflict with Beijing.[54] Moreover China was a commonwealth issue. Despite Indian independence in 1947, Britain had not abandoned hopes of an Indian contribution to Middle East defence in the event of war.[55] Nehru saw the Chinese revolution as an expression of Asian nationalism. He wished to act as a bridge between the new China and the West and opposed any attempt to isolate Mao's regime.[56] While India voted for the UN action in Korea, Nehru was an outspoken critic of US action in the Taiwan straits.[57]

'Neutralisation' faced London with a possible choice between commonwealth unity and American friendship. At best it would drive China into the arms of the Soviet Union. At worst it could provoke a Sino-American conflict which would divert US resources from Europe and even lead to global war with Russia. The Chiefs of Staff had few illusions about the fate of Britain in these circumstances.[58] The government had no wish to run such risks on behalf of the discredited

Guomindong. The situation was made no easier by the belief that US policy was dictated by domestic political considerations.[59] Britain made its concern plain. The issue was raised through diplomatic channels and British fleet units assigned to MacArthur's command were forbidden to police the straits. At the same time, London hesitated to carry dissent too far. In deference to US opinion it tightened trade controls against China and postponed voting in favour of seating the communist regime on subordinate organs of the UN.[60] Although Canada had not recognised Beijing, Ottawa took a similar line.[61] Both countries sought a solution to the Taiwan problem which would keep the Korean war limited and avoid a wider conflict in the Far East.

Acheson was conscious of the dangers and prepared to placate allied opinion, but not at the cost of surrendering Taiwan.[62] He attempted to keep his distance from the Guomindong regime. The interests of the US differed from those of Jiang. The Generalissimo regarded the island as a stepping stone for the reconquest of the mainland. The US was concerned only to keep a strategic position in the Pacific defence perimeter out of hostile hands. Jiang was warned against attacking the mainland from behind the shield of the 7th Fleet. He was informed in blunt terms that Washington would consider such action 'an unfriendly act'.[63] On 19 July Truman attempted to calm allied concern about 'neutralisation' by announcing that the US sought no special rights on Taiwan and would not prejudge the ultimate political status of the island. This could be settled by peaceful means under the UN charter after the Korean war was over.[64] There was a fine distinction between defending Taiwan and aiding Jiang which was difficult to apply in practice. At the end of July the National Security Council agreed a programme of military aid to improve the defences of the island, a step which involved cooperation with the nationalist regime.[65] The administration had little alternative. If it wished to hold Taiwan, it had to use the available military material, Jiang's army. It was explained to the allies that the US intended to supply guns and tanks for purely defensive purposes. It had no intention of promoting an invasion of the mainland.[66] It is doubtful if Beijing viewed matters in this perspective. Washington was arming its political enemies and preventing the final act of the civil war. In August, through the Russians, China accused the Americans of aggression at the UN.[67]

A programme of limited military support did not satisfy the Pentagon. On 24 July it recommended that Jiang be allowed to launch pre-emptive air strikes against troop and shipping concentrations on the mainland. The JCS feared an invasion and doubted the ability of an overstretched 7th Fleet to prevent a landing.[68] Jiang had been pressing for authority to bomb the mainland since the beginning of the month.[69] Acheson, however, viewed the proposal as political dynamite. It would put the US in a minority of one at the UN and might provoke Chinese intervention in Korea where the military situation was already desperate. Such a development might easily escalate into global war.[70] He succeeded in quashing the idea, which revealed the degree of sympathy for Jiang which had always existed at the Defense Department.

The most powerful challenge to official policy, however, came not from the military bureaucracy in Washington but from General MacArthur, who had become responsible for the defence of the island as US commander in the Far East. In retrospect it was unwise to vest military responsibility for both Korea and Taiwan in such a figure, given allied sensitivity and MacArthur's sympathy for Jiang.[71] The General rapidly displayed an ability to embarrass the administration and alarm the allies, whose fears of a wider war were soon summed up in one word – MacArthur. At the end of July, MacArthur made an inspection trip to Taiwan. This was his right as responsible commander and the visit had been cleared with the Defense Department. Acheson, however, had not been consulted. He would surely have objected to an expedition which so closely identified the UN commander in Korea with the political hot potato of Taiwan.[72] If MacArthur's mere presence on the island was annoying, his actions there were even more unwelcome. He publicly displayed his solidarity with the Guomindong and privately encouraged Jiang's ambition to bomb the mainland.[73] He further eroded 'neutralisation' by arranging to base three US air squadrons on Taiwan.[74] MacArthur implicitly criticised Acheson by including no diplomats in his entourage and by ignoring the US embassy in Taipei. On his return to Japan he argued that the diplomats had lost the confidence of the Generalissimo.[75] Jiang stepped up his military activity after the visit. It was feared in Washington that he hoped to play off the Defense and State Departments to his own advantage. The visit had given him the impression he could defy 'neutralisation' and get away with it.[76] Truman and Acheson rapidly moved to contain the situation. The air deployment was cancelled and it was emphasised that only the President could authorise raids on the mainland: 'The most vital national interest requires that no action of ours precipitate general war or give excuse to others to do so.'[77]

This message was pushed home when the President's special representative, Averill Harriman, visited Tokyo on 6 August. He was to convince MacArthur of the importance of avoiding war with China. Harriman emphasised the importance of UN unity and the need to avoid trouble over Taiwan which would 'give the Russians a chance to develop an entering wedge'. He found the General a reluctant convert. While he promised to obey orders 'as a soldier', MacArthur emphasised the possibilities of stirring up trouble in China and regretted the bombing ban. Harriman left Tokyo unconvinced that MacArthur was in 'full agreement' with the official line.[78] This suspicion was confirmed on 26 August, when Truman learned about the contents of a letter solicited from MacArthur by the Veterans of Foreign Wars (VFW), an organisation which was hawkish on the China question. In his message to the VFW, MacArthur emphasised the strategic importance of Taiwan and went on to criticise those who argued that by defending the island, the US risked alienating Asia. Such people did not understand 'oriental psychology'.[79] This was a sideways blow at Acheson and his policy towards Jiang in the pre-Korea period. The letter was doubly embarrassing because it appeared on the eve of a UN debate on Taiwan in which the US denied any intention of establishing a special position on the island. MacArthur was emphasising its strategic value to the US defence perimeter, implying the permanent denial of the Cairo declaration of 1943 pledging the island to China.[80]

Truman was furious and ordered the withdrawal of the letter. It was too late to stop publication but at least an appearance of official sanction could be avoided. When Louis Johnson hesitated to deliver the order he was fired. His position was already under threat as a budget-cutter in an administration newly committed to military spending. Nor had his intrigues against Acheson with the Republican right gone unnoticed. His hesitation to discipline MacArthur was the last straw. He was replaced by General George Marshall, the 'architect of victory' in World War Two and a figure greatly respected by Truman.[81] In the long run, the appointment did nothing to ease relations with MacArthur. Marshall was the living symbol of the Europeanist clique which had discriminated in favour of Eisenhower in World War Two and which continued to neglect the Far East in the cold war. Truman also considered removing MacArthur from his commands in Korea and Taiwan and restricting his authority to Japan. He had no doubt that the General was playing a political role, appealing to the Republicans in the hope of reversing global strategic priorities and improving his own chances of the Republican nomination in 1952. As the President's Assistant Press Secretary, Eben Ayers, remarked, 'MacArthur is regarded as a Republican and seemingly playing the Republican line in Far Eastern . . . policy.'[82] In the end, however, the President failed to act. With controversial new commitments to NATO under consideration, he could not afford the Republican storm which would be provoked by the demotion of MacArthur. Nor, on military grounds, did he wish to risk replacing his commander in Korea at a crucial stage in the war.[83]

It would be a mistake, however, to overemphasise the differences between MacArthur and Washington at this point. In condemning appeasement of Chinese communism, MacArthur was attacking a straw man. The administration might not back the return of Jiang to the mainland but it was moving towards the permanent denial of the island to Beijing. MacArthur's greatest crime was to state publicly what was being implied privately in Washington. The reality of the developing US position was revealed in the American response to a British initiative at the end of August. Bevin, concerned by the resumption of US arms sales and MacArthur's actions, suggested that the problem of Taiwan should be put before the UN. The General Assembly could establish a committee which would decide when peace and security had returned to the Pacific and the island could be ceded to China under the terms of the Cairo declaration. This would meet US insistence on 'neutralisation' while reassuring India and China about the long-term future of the island. Beijing would be given an incentive to refrain from military action at the straits or in Korea. While agreeing to study the idea, Acheson refused to confirm the Cairo declaration.[84] There was strong pressure against handing Taiwan over at any future stage. The JCS defined it as strategically important, irrespective of the situation in Korea. Acheson himself had always argued that it was one thing to cede the island to China and another to give it to a regime which was an arm of 'the Moscow conspiracy'. He wanted to encourage a liberal alternative to Jiang and an independent Taiwan, guaranteed by the UN.[85] When the JCS objected that a UN commission might give the island to Beijing, Acheson replied that the question would be settled on terms 'agreeable' to Washington.[86]

The American decision to cross the 38th parallel in October 1950 brought Chinese troops across the Yalu. Chinese intervention in Korea ultimately killed any resort to the UN over Taiwan and confirmed the de facto alliance with Jiang which Truman had earlier hoped to avoid. In contrast to their alarm over Taiwan, the major

allies, led by Britain, were curiously blind to the risks involved in
eradicating the DPRK. The US was committed to the goal of rolling
back Soviet power by both NSC-48/2 and NSC-68. The UN had a
theoretical commitment to Korean unification dating back to its
original involvement in 1947. Neither, however, was prepared to act at
the cost of global war with the Soviet Union. Nevertheless, a strong
feeling developed in Washington after the war began that its outcome
should not be a mere return to the status quo. It was argued that in
default of Soviet action to save its North Korean satellite, the US and
the UN should seize the opportunity to unify the peninsula. This would
have an electrifying effect in Asia and constitute a notable victory in
the cold war. The administration was careful not to rule out unification
and kept its options open. On 10 August, in a speech to the Security
Council, the US ambassador declared that Korea should not be
condemned to exist 'half slave and half free'. On 31 August Truman
declared that Koreans had a right to be free, independent and united.
The US 'under the guidance of the United Nations' would do its part to
help them achieve this end.[87]

While US forces were grimly holding on in the narrow Pusan
perimeter, discussion of the future of Korea was merely theoretical.
By the end of August, however, Washington had approved
MacArthur's plan for a daring landing at Inchon which would envelop
and destroy the NKPA. The JCS had grave reservations about an
operation which MacArthur himself described as a gamble. On the
other hand, they desired a decisive end to the war which would free
military resources for more important areas. As MacArthur argued,
the Inchon plan was the only alternative to 'a frontal attack . . . [and] a
prolonged and expensive campaign'. He would not be party to a
strategy which penned American troops in the Pusan perimeter 'like
beef cattle in a slaughterhouse'.[88] The Inchon landing, OPERATION
CHROMITE, was scheduled for 15 September. The prospect of
victory in the South forced Washington to elaborate its thoughts on the
future of Korea. These were set out in NSC-81, approved by Truman
four days before MacArthur's forces went ashore. This document
envisaged military operations in the North to complete the defeat of
the NKPA. Such operations, however, were contingent on Soviet
non-intervention. MacArthur's command was to cross the parallel
only 'provided that at the time of such operations there has been no
entry into North Korea by major Soviet or Chinese forces, no
announcement of intended entry, nor a threat to counter our
operations militarily in North Korea.' Reluctance to risk a direct

confrontation with the Russians in their own sphere of influence remained. In the event of Soviet or Chinese intervention before MacArthur reached the parallel, Washington would have no option but to negotiate. If an advance proved possible, the Soviet and Chinese frontiers were to be strictly respected. As a 'matter of policy' only the ROKs were to be employed in the sensitive border provinces.[89] This in effect meant the creation of a buffer zone north of the 40th parallel. Washington would accept less than total unification rather than risk a clash beyond the narrow Korean neck.

The dramatic success of Inchon and the failure of either the USSR or China to respond confirmed the decision to enter North Korea. In the absence of deterrent action by the Soviet bloc, the risks of halting seemed to outweigh the risks of going ahead. On 27 September MacArthur was authorised to cross the 38th parallel. His military directive was based on NSC-81. His objective was 'the destruction of the North Korean armed forces'. If major Soviet units were encountered during the advance, he was to halt and consult Washington. 'As a matter of policy' only ROKs were to be used in the border provinces.[90] Washington remained careful not to define Korean unification as a war aim. It would not fight the Soviet Union on behalf of the ROK. At the same time, it was determined to exploit the surprise of Inchon before the Kremlin could coordinate an effective response. Once MacArthur had crossed the parallel, it would be up to Moscow and Beijing to risk a clash to restore the boundary, rather than up to Washington to risk confrontation to extinguish it. It was assumed that once operations had reached this point, Stalin would not take the risk. He would back away from a bold show of force, a lesson supposedly learned during the Berlin blockade of 1948/9.[91]

In justifying the decision to advance, Acheson argued that aggression must not go unpunished. North Korea could not be allowed to take refuge behind a 'surveyor's line'.[92] This approach displayed both a reluctance to accept stalemate and a desire to maintain the initiative in the cold war. If the campaign was abandoned short of victory, Washington would have to negotiate with Moscow. Discussions would take place at the UN, where the US could not be sure of controlling its allies and where a Korean settlement might be linked with other Asian problems such as Taiwan. At best Washington might find itself blamed by Rhee for the continued division of the peninsula and pinned down there while Moscow rebuilt the NKPA. Rather than risk such an outcome, Truman and Acheson were determined to solve the Korean problem on US terms. They were acting in the context of NSC-68, which regarded negotiations as a dangerous distraction from the goal of building positions of strength. There was to be no diversion from the process of economic and psychological mobilisation behind rearmament.

Domestic factors, related to global strategy, influenced official thinking. Acheson was anxious to display firmness in answer to domestic criticism. The opposition was clearly prepared to make political capital out of any attempt to end the war short of total victory.[93] A halt at the parallel would only give the Republicans ammunition in the November elections. The administration announced plans for German rearmament, a unified NATO command and an increased US commitment to Europe on 12 September. It could not afford the furore which would follow an attempt to restrain MacArthur after Inchon. The General made no secret of his own determination to back Rhee's demands for Korean unification.[94] The last thing that Truman could afford was a debate with MacArthur on foreign policy goals. He would be accused of abdicating victory in Asia in pursuit of 'Europe first'. A successful operation against the DPRK, however, would allow him to carry through his European policies on the tide of triumph in Korea.

Acheson sought UN endorsement of action against the North, believing that an expression of unity would further reduce the chances of Soviet or Chinese intervention.[95] He was unwilling, however, to initiate a debate on the 38th parallel, fearing that this might delay operations and create diplomatic openings for the Soviet Union. On 29 September MacArthur was ordered by Marshall to avoid any implication that his forces might halt at the parallel. This could prove embarrassing at the UN which wished to evade a vote on the issue. The message concluded, 'We want you to feel unhampered tactically and strategically to proceed north of the 38th parallel.'[96] The role of the UN was not to debate but to approve a decision already taken in Washington, a position already endorsed by major allies such as Britain.[97] Marshall came to regret the broad language of his message which MacArthur later insisted overrode the political restrictions on his operations contained in his military directive. In his reply, MacArthur significantly broadened his freedom of manoeuvre in a phrase which was overlooked at the time: 'Unless and until the enemy capitulates, I regard all of Korea open for our military operations.'[98]

The US found Britain prepared to take the lead in sponsoring a resolution which would tacitly approve the advance to the North and set out UN plans for the future of Korea if MacArthur's military operations proved successful. The Attlee government, like the Truman administration, wanted to seize the initiative in the cold war and reap the political capital of a clear-cut victory over communism. A tired cabinet with a narrow majority was anxious to improve its electoral appeal.[99] From the beginning, Korea, unlike Taiwan, was regarded as a Soviet question. On 25 September, Bevin justified British action at the UN on the grounds that if MacArthur halted at the parallel and left the DPRK intact, 'Russia will virtually have triumphed and the whole United Nations' effort will have been in vain. Whatever happens in Korea in the end, we must try to make sure now that just as in the case of the Berlin blockade, the Russians are made to realise that they are up against it and accept that fact.' Failure to act would allow the USSR to reoccupy the North and claim credit for rebuilding what the UN had destroyed.[100] It was hoped that if the temporary nature and limited objectives of UN occupation were emphasised, China would be reassured. As Attlee remarked on 22 September, Beijing would not be sorry 'to see Soviet influence eliminated' provided the alternative did not threaten China. Moreover India, important for its influence on Asian opinion, might feel able to support such an initiative.[101]

The UN resolution, based on an American draft, was presented to the Political Committee of the General Assembly on 30 September. It recommended that 'All appropriate steps be taken to ensure conditions of stability throughout Korea.' These included the 'holding of elections' under UN auspices to secure 'the establishment of a unified, independent and democratic Government in the sovereign state of Korea.' UN forces would remain only long enough to achieve these tasks. A UN Commission for the Unification and Rehabilitation of Korea (UNCURK) was to oversee the execution of the resolution. While the UN gave tacit approval to military operations in the North, it did not make unification a UN war aim. Although Korea was formally a UN war, the world organisation did not attempt to control military operations, turning over the running of the conflict to Truman, the JCS and MacArthur in Tokyo. MacArthur's mission remained to defeat aggression. Unification was dependent on his achieving this end. Thus the US and its allies left open an escape route in the event that their military operations were opposed. It was no part of their purpose to fight a major war for Korean unification.[102] They were later to regret the sweeping language of the resolution, however, which MacArthur was to adopt as his overriding goal during his march to the Yalu.

Despite Western hopes of securing Indian endorsement of the

resolution, Nehru proved reluctant to support operations across the parallel.[103] New Delhi was under increasing pressure from Beijing which began to issue warnings that UN action would be followed by Chinese intervention. This was exactly the kind of East–West confrontation which Nehru had been anxious to avoid since the beginning of the Korean conflict. On 25 September the Vice Chief of the Chinese General Staff informed the Indian ambassador, K. M. Pannikkar, that US aircraft had bombed Manchuria. These incidents and US policy towards Taiwan had convinced Beijing that an American attack was imminent. China must 'act accordingly'.[104] These statements were passed on to London and Washington. The British, however, did not take them seriously, believing that India was being subjected to a war of nerves, sponsored by the Russians to sow dissension at the UN.[105] In order to reassure both Nehru and the Chinese, Bevin reiterated the limitations on UN action, emphasising that non-Korean troops would not be used beyond the 40th parallel. At British prompting, Washington weighed in with an offer to compensate Beijing for alleged raids on Manchuria.[106]

In the US, Chinese warnings were dismissed as bluff. It was assumed that if China had seriously intended to intervene, it would have done so at an earlier stage and not after Inchon when the DPRK was on the verge of collapse. There were no signs of Soviet intervention and it was believed that Beijing would not act to pull Soviet chestnuts out of the fire, jeopardising its chances of Taiwan and a UN seat. It would not make war on an international body prepared to consider such questions on their merits once aggression in Korea was defeated.[107] Acheson was curiously ambivalent about China. He apparently felt that over Taiwan, Beijing would act as a tool of the Kremlin, while in Korea it would follow its own national interest, a case of believing what was convenient to justify US policy. In fairness, he perhaps thought that Chinese and Russian interests coincided on Taiwan but not in Korea. On the one issue, the Chinese, by acting for themselves, would also aid the Russians by granting them bases on the island. On the other they would be entering a war promoted by the Soviet Union, at great cost to themselves and for no tangible gain. They would be cannon fodder for the Kremlin.

In assuming that Beijing would accept US assurances at face value, Acheson was guilty of arrogance and wishful thinking. China did not view the Korean operation as an exercise in 'collective security'. The 'neutralisation' of Taiwan and the advance across the parallel were regarded as moves to encircle and threaten the new China. It was not forgotten in Beijing that the process of Japanese expansion had begun in exactly the same way and that China had been the ultimate victim. While Britain attempted to separate the UN from the US, implying that Korea was not part of a counter-revolutionary strategy in Asia, the Chinese fitted it into the context of US actions in Indochina, Taiwan and the Philippines. In those areas, as in Korea, Washington was arming and supporting reaction. In June 1950, the UN had acted, not as a disinterested body, but as a tool of Washington. Nor could China have faith in the good intentions of a UN commander who had visited Taipei and talked openly of solidarity with the Guomindong. Washington sincerely believed in its own good intentions and later accused Beijing of launching a war of aggression at the behest of Moscow. The subleties of US policy, however, were lost on the Chinese who believed that they were being forced into a defensive war against imperialism.[108]

If the subleties of US policy were lost on Beijing, the oblique approach forced on China by international isolation failed to impress the West. The most open Chinese threat came on 2 October, when Pannikkar was summoned from his bed for an interview with the Foreign Minister, Zhou Enlai (Chou En-Lai), and informed that if UN forces other than South Korean crossed the parallel, China would intervene.[109] This bald statement, which fitted one of the contingencies in NSC-81 and MacArthur's military directive, was ignored. Despite the threat of Chinese entry, MacArthur was allowed to go ahead. Partly this was because Pannikkar was distrusted as being sympathetic to China and 'playing the communist game'.[110] It is perhaps unfair to blame US officials for this since the ambassador was distrusted by members of his own Foreign Office, who made their reservations known.[111] On the other hand, his reports earlier in September, which argued that China would not intervene, had not been treated with similar scepticism. Pannikkar's warning was ignored because it was unwelcome. It came *after* decisions had been taken. Washington found it hard to accept because to treat it seriously would mean countermanding MacArthur's orders and going into reverse at the UN. American credibility was at stake. Acheson chose to regard the warning as a 'Chinese Communist bluff' designed to save the DPRK by offering an opening to Soviet diplomacy at the UN, where the Russians were calling for a cease-fire and the withdrawal of foreign troops. In words which must have returned to haunt him in November, Acheson remarked that Beijing 'would have to put more on the table' if it 'wanted to take part in the poker game'.[112]

Zhou's warning brought only one change in MacArthur's military directive. On 9 October, he was informed by the JCS that 'Hereafter in the event of the open or covert employment anywhere in Korea of major Chinese Communist units, without prior announcement, you should continue the action as long as, in your judgement, action by forces now under your control offers a reasonable chance of success.'[113] This left much to MacArthur's discretion and made certain assumptions about the Chinese. It implied that successful operations could continue even in the event of intervention by 'major' Chinese units. This was a repetition of the 'Gook syndrome', the arrogant underestimation of Asians which had almost led to disaster in July. Washington was about to repeat its error by failing to take the Chinese army seriously. As early as 1 July a Pentagon memorandum remarked that while the PLA might be well led, it lacked armour or artillery. It had only fought weak opposition, other Chinese in the civil war, and had never met a well-trained force with high morale, equipped with modern weapons and possessing the will and skill to use these weapons.[114] Thus, even if Zhou did fulfil his threat, the consequences would not be as serious as intervention by the Russians. The US was to pay dearly for this assumption before the year was out.

Britain was more alarmed by Pannikkar's warning. Bevin noted on 4 October that 'armed intervention by China would be a great catastrophe' and suggested that Beijing be given a hearing on the UN resolution lest it become 'explosive'. The Chiefs of Staff, long ambiguous about the march North, suggested a brief halt of about two weeks, while the UN summoned the DPRK to capitulate. Since Pyongyang had already ignored such a demand from MacArthur on 1 October, this was regarded as a means of conveying further reassurances to the Chinese rather than as a way to persuade the North Koreans to lay down their arms.[115] The Canadians, similarly armed, asked for a postponement of the vote in the Political Committee of the General Assembly.[116] Acheson, however, was consumed by the need for speed. The Chinese could not be invited to the UN: 'Forces were in motion and plans were being made. . . . The UN Command, after a period of regrouping, would be advancing into North Korea and it was now too late to stop this process.' The only proper course was to be 'firm and courageous' in the face of a 'Chinese Communist bluff'.[117] Acheson thus echoed once again the sentiments of NSC-68 and the lessons of Berlin. The Attlee government was unwilling to face Washington on the issue. As Bevin remarked, in the light of American determination representations would have to be 'on the highest level and in very strong terms'.[118] If Britain secured a pause in the fighting, it might be blamed for any difficulties encountered by MacArthur. London, therefore, avoided a confrontation when the UN resolution was brought to a vote on 7 October. The Canadians, who also had reservations, similarly surrendered to US pressure and recorded a positive vote. India, which had consistently refused to endorse the resolution, abstained.[119]

Despite misgivings, the allies allowed themselves to be pulled forward by the momentum of military operations after Inchon. In the euphoria of victory, a commitment to the status quo was the first to suffer.[120] It seemed foolish to press for a halt in successful military operations on the strength of a verbal warning conveyed through an unreliable intermediary. As Bevin informed the cabinet on 9 October, the day MacArthur's forces crossed the parallel, there was 'insufficient evidence' for Indian apprehension that China would intervene.[121] Similarly Canada, while sympathising with Nehru, did not regard Pannikkar's despatches as 'hard evidence' of Chinese intentions.[122] Any effort to halt the advance, therefore, would have rested on flimsy evidence. It would have meant asking Washington to stop short of victory in what was still a popular war on the eve of important Congressional elections. With the US considering new commitments to NATO and financial assistance for allied rearmament, it was not the time to endanger relations with the administration and the Congress. Nor were goverments such as the British beyond calculating the domestic political advantages of rollback.[123] Lastly, the Korean issue was still seen mainly in terms of the Soviet Union. As Bevin emphasised on 4 October, *Russia* did not want war but an extension of its power on the cheap. The best thing to do was to call the Soviet bluff and 'get rid' of the 38th parallel. 'That will be one more artificial frontier gone anyway'.[124] If the Russians could be confronted, the Chinese could be reassured. In the end, London was satisifed with the reassurances it received from Washington on this score. No more than Acheson did Bevin understand the worthlessness of US guarantees to Beijing. When this became evident in November 1950, there was an attempt to make MacArthur a scapegoat. As the General later bitterly remarked, at the time the decision to cross the parallel was supported by everyone concerned except the communists.[125]

In retrospect, it is clear that the decision to cross the parallel was never thought through by the US and its allies. The advance was regarded as an alternative to stalemate and a prolonged commitment of US forces to guard against a renewed threat from the DPRK. Yet it was unrealistic to suppose that North Korea, with its industry flattened and its army decimated, would have been in any position to renew the attack. Nor was Moscow likely to have sponsored such a development. Both the USSR and China would have settled for a return to the status quo in October 1950. It required a vast leap of the imagination to argue, like Bevin, that such an outcome would have represented a triumph for the Soviet Union. Washington and its allies broadened UN aims and gambled on a united Korea. [The US hoped to make a graceful exit after this had been achieved, withdrawing American troops and leaving a rearmed but neutralised Korea as a showpiece of democracy on the Asian mainland.][26] It was highly unlikely, however, that Moscow or Beijing would ever have accepted such an outcome. Even without open intervention, the hostility of its larger neighbours would have ensured a future of unrest for a united Korea. The Korean problem was a political tar baby. It proved easy to become involved but difficult to leave. Indeed the only exit proved to be through agreement with Moscow and Beijing, a solution which could have been achieved at a lower price in October 1950.

4 Disaster

In his memoirs, Acheson criticised MacArthur for pursuing the 'mirage' of total victory in the autumn of 1950.[1] It was a mirage, however, which also seduced the administration. If MacArthur stripped the ambiguity from the UN resolution of 7 October and overrode the limitations in his military directive, he met with little opposition from Washington. As the advance continued with no sign of Chinese reaction, officials began to feel 'pretty good' because the war seemed almost over.[2] At all levels, there was a growing conviction that Zhou had indeed been bluffing in his interview with Pannikkar. In the absence of a credible Chinese threat, it made little sense to enforce self-imposed limitations on MacArthur's operations. To stop short of total victory would be to relinquish the initiative to an adversary whose bluff had already been called. Thus MacArthur did not drag a reluctant administration at his heels in the advance to the Yalu. Rather both shared a conviction that total victory was possible at an acceptable price. It was an illusion which was to be shattered in November 1950.

As MacArthur's offensive moved into North Korea, Truman flew across the Pacific to Wake Island for a meeting with the General on 15 October. The President was primarily concerned with domestic politics rather than with discussing the war. On the eve of congressional elections he wished to emphasise the connection between the Democrats and the victor of Inchon. Roosevelt had engaged in a similar political manoeuvre at Hawaii in 1944.[3] The meeting was important because the General told the President what he wished to hear. MacArthur doubted that the Chinese would intervene. If they did enter the war, American air power would destroy their armies with the 'greatest slaughter'. He hoped to finish the campaign by Thanksgiving and to redeploy US troops to Japan by Christmas. By January 1951, he could have a division available for service in Europe.[4] These reassurances on China, confirmed what the President heard from other sources. On 12 October the CIA reported that while China was capable of intervening, such action was unlikely.[5] Truman and his party returned to the US expressing full confidence in the General and confirmed in the belief that the war was almost over. In Tokyo and Washington 'optimism reigned'.[6]

On 20 October Pyonyang was taken by the advancing Eighth Army. On 24 October Truman congratulated MacArthur on his 'remarkable'

military progress, which would have 'a most profound influence for
peace in the world'.[7] The same day, MacArthur ordered all his forces
to make full speed towards the Yalu, overriding the restrictions in his
military directive on the use of non-Korean troops in the border
provinces.[8] The General was clearly persuaded by his belief in
'oriental psychology' that any pause would be regarded in Beijing as a
sign of weakness, perhaps provoking an intervention which would not
otherwise occur. When the JCS queried his action, MacArthur
justified himself on several grounds. He argued that his move was
dictated by military necessity. The South Koreans alone could not
establish order in the far north. He cited General Marshall's message
of 29 September that he should feel 'tactically and strategically
unhampered' to proceed north of the 38th parallel and further argued
that the restriction on non-Korean troops in the border provinces as 'a
matter of policy' amounted to less than an absolute prohibition. He
also maintained that the entire subject had been covered at Wake
Island. In a later press release, MacArthur maintained that his UN
mission was to 'clear Korea', implying that the resolution of 7 October
overrode any restrictions in his military directive.[9]

This elaborate justification indicates the ambiguity of MacArthur's
position. The original intent of his military directive was that the South
Koreans should fall back if they could not impose order, not that other
UN contingents should come to their assistance. Marshall's message
was not intended to change the thrust of existing orders. MacArthur
was to feel 'unhampered' only within the context of his directive. On
the other hand, the General was justified in maintaining that a 'matter
of policy' was less than a ban. An early draft of NSC-81, containing
such an absolute prohibition, had been changed at the Department of
Defense, perhaps to grant MacArthur the degree of flexibility he now
claimed.[10] It was, however, unusual for a subordinate commander to
reinterpret standing orders without consulting Washington. As for the
matter being covered at Wake, only a close reading of the record could
support the claim. MacArthur had talked about withdrawing non-
Korean troops *from* the border once victory had been secured. The
issue was in no sense discussed and it is doubtful if the presidential
party grasped the implications of MacArthur's phrase.[11]

Washington, however, did not overrule the General.[12] MacArthur's
prestige was at its height after Inchon, an operation which had
originally raised grave doubts. In the aftermath of victory, there was
little disposition to challenge MacArthur's military judgement again.[13]

Politically, it was difficult to curb him on the eve of the elections. This would destroy the façade of unity established at Wake and lend support to the image of softness on communism which McCarthy, with the support of the Republican leadership, was attempting to fasten on the administration. The overriding factor, however, was that the administration, like MacArthur, was tempted by the mirage of victory. Acheson later emphasised the distinction between Korean elections and unification, as provided in the resolution of 7 October, and MacArthur's military directive which was merely to defeat aggression. According to Acheson, the General stripped the resolution of its 'husk of ambivalence' and transformed it into a war aim.[14] Clearly, however, this somewhat artificial distinction between military objectives and political aspirations had been set up only as an escape hatch against the contingency of Soviet or Chinese intervention.[15] A similar argument applied to the restrictions in the military directive overriden by MacArthur. By mid-October, events seemed to justify the abandonment of deliberate ambiguity. The distinction between political and military objectives was not emphasised at Wake where the participants were more concerned to discuss a situation in which the UN resolution was on its way to realisation. If Chinese or Soviet intervention could be ruled out, a point on which Tokyo and Washington agreed, safeguards included at an earlier stage were unnecessary. On 28 October MacArthur received a civil affairs directive which stated that his mission was to occupy the DPRK 'in the name of and on behalf of the United Nations'.[16] There was 'no mention of any part of North Korea being excepted from his military administration'.[17] It was not only MacArthur, therefore, who was carried forward by over-optimism. The administration shared his views on Chinese reactions and colluded with him.

At the Pentagon, officials began preparations to wind down the war and transfer US forces to more vital areas. The *New York Times* expressed the prevailing mood when it remarked on 29 October that 'Except for unexpected developments along the frontiers of the peninsula, we can now be easy in our minds as to the military outcome'.[18] There was concern about the consequences of victory for NSC-68. The administration foresaw problems in persuading Congress to fund rearmament once the Korean emergency had passed. Officials uneasily recalled public pressure for demobilisation in 1945. Such an outcome would leave the initiative with the Russians, despite a successful war. In order to head off this possibility, it was to be made clear that Korea was merely an episode in the wider struggle with communism.[19] The American people must accept a permanent state of semi-mobilisation and never lower their guard.

Rhee remained an embarrassment as victory approached. After Inchon, the civil war amongst Koreans reached new levels of ferocity. As the People's government in the South collapsed, the communists exacted a bloody revenge on ROK police, bureaucrats and their families who had fallen into communist hands. Executions continued in the Seoul prison while fighting raged in the streets.[20] These massacres, however, were paralleled by the savagery of the ROK, both in the reoccupied zones and in the 'liberated' North. The UN advance was accompanied by a right-wing counter-revolution, spearheaded by the ROK forces and attached paramilitary groups. The DPRK later claimed that 'hundreds of thousands' were killed during the brief occupation of the North.[21] Although these figures were never verified, there was clearly more than propaganda to the accusation. In October 1950 the US 24th Infantry complained about the brutal conduct of attached ROK troops. These men were involved in numerous cases of rape, 'unwarranted roughness and downright mishandling. . . . Their ideas of treatment of a fallen foe are . . . diametrically opposed to ours'.[22] An Australian member of UNCURK remarked that a combination of pillaging, looting and general violence by the ROK forces, coupled with economic insecurity, was turning the population of the North against the UN 'to such an extent that some of them consider that they were better off under the old regime'.[23] Reports about the situation began to trickle into the Western press. On 2 November, the *New York Times* carried an article on the execution of 'collaborators' in Seoul, including a woman whose baby was taken from her back at the last moment.[24] In October 1950 the London *Times* produced two articles strongly critical of Rhee's regime. According to the *Times* correspondent, Rhee's defence of 'the local brand of democracy' was 'no less vicious than the atrocities committed in the name of Communism'. The only difference was that ROK terror enjoyed the protection of the UN flag. It was 'a strange way to bring about the unification of the country'.[25]

These accounts were unwelcome to Western governments which wished to portray Korea as a war of liberation against communist tyranny. On 8 November Acheson complained about the 'color writing' in the *New York Times* report which evoked sympathy for the victims. He did not object to the executions but rather to the manner in which they were carried out. The US embassy in Seoul was ordered to urge discretion on the ROK since such press reports were highly damaging to the world position of the US and to the UN cause.[26] In Britain the *Times* articles were followed by a 'Fleet Street scandal' when the proprietor of the *Picture Post* stopped an account of ROK atrocities by James Cameron when the magazine was going to press. This action was probably the result of official intervention which had occurred in the past. Cameron resigned and a pirated copy of his piece subsequently appeared in the *Daily Worker*.[27] The affair caused local branches of the UN Association and of the Labour Party to raise questions about the situation in Korea.[28] While the Foreign Office tried to play down the significance of atrocity stories, there was concern that Rhee's activities might undermine public support for the war and alienate other Asians, particularly the Indians who had opposed an advance across the parallel.[29] Bevin briefly raised the issue with Washington on 28 October.[30] There was no official condemnation of Rhee, however, since it was believed that this would merely play into the hands of the communists.

The atrocity issue became linked to the question of authority in the occupied North. Rhee maintained that his regime was the legitimate government of all Korea. It was simply a matter of extending ROK authority beyond the parallel. This position enjoyed the sympathy of MacArthur who regarded Rhee as an important bastion against communism.[31] The UN, however, was unwilling to resolve the situation in this way. On 7 October to pre-empt both Rhee and his admirer MacArthur, the Interim Committee on Korea passed a resolution making the UN command the agency of civil government in the North, pending the arrival of UNCURK.[32] As Bevin urged on 28 October, Rhee must not be allowed to present the world organisation with a *fait accompli*.[33] There was some sentiment at the UN for UNCURK to organise new elections in both North and South to produce a new government for a unified Korea. This, however, was resisted by Washington. As Truman argued at the Wake Meeting, 'we must make it plain that we are supporting the Rhee regime and propaganda can go to hell'.[34] The ROK must not be put on the same level as the DPRK. Such a course would raise doubts about the legitimacy of UN/US involvement since 1947. Washington favoured elections for the National Assembly seats reserved for Northern representatives in 1948.[35] While the Americans defended the Rhee regime, they found their client troublesome. Rhee threatened to defy the UN and to impose his own authority north of the parallel irrespective of the Interim Committee ruling. He was advised not to 'rock the boat' and damage the position of the ROK at a crucial point in the war.[36] While Rhee appeared to defer to this pressure, it was a paper victory for the principle of UN control. ROK police and officials operated in the North as agents of the UN command but continued to owe their loyalty to the regime in Seoul.[37] This allowed Rhee a *de facto* authority which UNCURK would have found it hard to reverse. By the time it reached Korea, however, the question had become merely academic as the war entered a new and more dangerous stage.

Unknown to Washington or Tokyo, MacArthur's forces were advancing towards eighteen Chinese divisions which had infiltrated into the mountains north of Pyongyang. By mid-November these had been joined by twelve more. At a time when both General and President believed that the war was as good as over, 'the United Nations Command forces of some 150,000 men were advancing unwittingly into 300,000 Chinese troops and 80,000 North Korean remnants and guerrillas'.[38] Failure to detect this deployment represented a massive intelligence breakdown, and later there was frantic rivalry between Tokyo and Washington to shift responsibility. In fact blame could be equally shared. There was an almost total lack of political intelligence on China. The CIA and MacArthur's FEC, took steps to improve their coverage of China but lacked well-placed sources.[39] Both agencies were forced to rely on Guomindong networks, whose information was distrusted because Jiang had a vested interest in promoting tension between the US and China. Thus a report from Hong Kong that China had alerted troops to begin entering Korea on 20 October was disregarded by both Tokyo and Washington.[40] One of the few alternative sources of information was India, whose representative in Beijing had already been written off as a Chinese propaganda mouthpiece. Other forms of intelligence also failed. Signals intelligence (SIGINT) had played a vital role during the Second World War. Allied cryptographers were able to crack the secret of the enigma code machine employed by both the Germans and the Japanese, conferring an incalculable advantage on commanders like MacArthur who often knew about enemy moves in advance.[41] In 1950, however, the resources for signals intelligence in the Far East were 'far short of requirements' and the Americans were forced to rely on the British SIGINT unit at Hong Kong.[42] This clearly failed to pick up any indication of the Chinese deployment across the Yalu. Ironically, it was probably handicapped by Chinese technological inferiority. Radios were rare in the Chinese Army which was forced to rely on older forms of communication, less vulnerable to electronic surveillance.[43] Battlefield intelligence also failed. As Korea broadened beyond the narrow waist, UN forces on the east and west coasts, separated by high mountains, lacked the manpower for aggressive patrolling which might have revealed the presence of the PLA. Air reconnaisance suffered from a lack of specialised aircraft and trained photo interpreters. The Chinese in any case moved by night and had an excellent system of camouflage and dispersal.[44] As a result, the US, while aware that Chinese troop concentrations in Manchuria gave Beijing the capacity to intervene, doubted its intention to do so at a time when Chinese troops were entering Korea in force. As late as 29 October, after the first Chinese prisoners were taken, the Eighth Army was not inclined to accept reports of substantial Chinese involvement in the fighting.[45]

The result of MacArthur's 24 October order was to ensure that the Chinese were encountered under the most unfavourable military and political circumstances. Militarily, MacArthur chose to advance to the Yalu with a divided command. The original plan called for Walker's Eighth Army to advance on Pyongyang from Seoul, while Almond's X Corps was landed on the east coast at Wonsan to advance on the communist capital along one of the few lateral valleys on the peninsula. A juncture between the two forces would have been affected around the original stop line envisaged in MacArthur's military directive. Mines at Wonsan, however, delayed the landing of X Corps until the fall of Pyongyang and it was given a new mission to clear the north-east.[46] Liaison between the two armies remained through MacArthur's headquarters in Tokyo. This might have been justifiable in a mopping-up operation, but against a major new enemy it courted disaster. The Chinese were established on the flanks of both forces. Politically, the move made a major Sino–American clash practically inevitable. Instead of meeting only South Korean troops north of the 40th parallel, the Chinese would be engaged from the first with American forces, narrowing Washington's scope for political manoeuvre or compromise.[47]

Not until early November, when a clash at Unsan halted Walker's offensive, did it become clear that an organised Chinese force was in Korea. Beijing had placed its stake on the table and entered the game. In Washington and other UN capitals, the changed situation produced a new interest in negotiation. The solutions canvassed in the West, however, did not envisage a Chinese role in the Korean settlement. Rather, they were concerned with finding some mechanism which would keep China out, while deciding the issue on unilateral Western

terms. The most ambitious plan was produced in London and
envisaged the creation of a demilitarised zone (DMZ) from the 40th
parallel to the Yalu border. In pursuing this proposal, the government
was acting on the advice of its Chiefs of Staff, who had always been
ambiguous about the march north. Faced with evidence of a Chinese
military presence, the British chiefs doubted that MacArthur could
reach the border without bombing Manchuria, an extension of the war
fraught with dangerous possibilities. A Soviet source in Beijing
warned Pannikkar that if Manchuria was bombed, the Russian air
force would come to the assistance of China, opening up the possibility
of global war.[46] The British, having doubted Pannikkar in October,
were not inclined to repeat their error and took this statement
seriously. At the same time, Bevin's proposal stopped short of offering
China a role in the Korean settlement. Its objective was to secure a
Chinese withdrawal. While MacArthur halted, the Chinese would
evacuate. The DMZ would be run by a UN commission which could
consult Beijing on issues of border security.[49] It was thus a temporary
measure to allow Korean unification under the terms of the UN
resolution of 7 October.

In Washington, the administration was also reconsidering the
position. It was no part of the American purpose to become bogged
down in a major war with China at the expense of US commitments
elsewhere. On 9 November, the JCS called for MacArthur's military
directive to be kept under review and for the problem of Chinese
intervention to be solved by political means.[50] At a meeting of the NSC
on 10 November, Acheson speculated on the possibility of a DMZ in
north-east Korea under the control of the UN. Such a zone might
extend ten miles on either side of the border. This would allow the UN
to hold elections and 'get out'.[51] While differing in detail from the
British scheme, Acheson's proposal shared the objective of reassuring
Beijing while allowing Korean unification on Western terms. The
Chinese had been invited to attend a Security Council debate on a
resolution calling on Beijing to cease its intervention and Acheson
hoped to explore the issue with their delegation to Lake Success.[52]
Pending the arrival of the Chinese, assurances on border security were
to be conveyed through public statements and informal approaches
through the Swedes. Beijing was to be convinced that the border
would be held inviolate and that there would be no interference with
electricity supplies to Manchuria from the Yalu power plants on the
Korean side of the frontier.[53] Washington had long recognised a

legitimate Chinese interest in the issue and had given strict instructions against air attacks on Suiho and other power complexes.[54]

An emphasis on 'political' solutions, however, did not preclude further offensive operations. Although the JCS noted on 9 November that the best military option might be to hold the existing line rather than to continue towards the Yalu, they refused to revise MacArthur's directive. He was still empowered to advance as long as he felt there was a reasonable chance of success. His orders were merely to be kept under review. This despite growing concern about the division between the Eighth Army and X Corps.[55] There were several reasons for this inaction. It was traditional to trust the judgement of the field commander and the JCS hesitated to interfere with operations at a distance of 7000 miles. Moreover, MacArthur was a powerful advocate and the spell of Inchon still lingered. On 8 November the General entered a strong polemic against stopping short of the border. Such action would destroy the morale of his command and condemn the US to an indefinite stalemate along difficult defence lines. At an NSC meeting on 10 November, the chairman of the JCS, Bradley, used MacArthur's arguments against a halt.[56]

On this issue, Acheson did not challenge the Pentagon. This may have partly stemmed from an excessive deference to General Marshall, architect of victory in World War Two and Acheson's former boss at the State Department.[57] Domestic politics were also involved. In the November congressional elections, the Republicans increased their representation after a campaign in which Acheson's record on Asia had been an issue. In some areas, McCarthy's intervention was regarded as decisive. In such circumstances, it was difficult to appear 'soft on communism'.[58] An appearance of weakness in Asia might have repercussions on administration plans for Europe in the new congress. Halting represented a political and military gamble which the administration was not prepared to take. If the Chinese used the opportunity to reinforce their armies and launch a massive attack, responsibility would rest with Washington. Everyone was aware that MacArthur's communications were in some sense 'posterity messages', shifting the blame away from Tokyo in the event of disaster. The administration hesitated to take the risk. This was clear as early as 5 November when Washington clashed with MacArthur over his order to Far Eastern Air Forces (FEAF) to destroy the Yalu bridges and all communications and shelter between the border and the battleline. This carried the risk of violating the Chinese and Soviet borders and overrode a ban on bombing within five miles of the frontier.[59] The importance of this restriction had been proved when two US jets attacked a Soviet airfield in Siberia on 5 October.[60] When Washington learned of the order, it was suspended and MacArthur asked to justify his action. He replied with a flood of 'purple prose', claiming that Chinese pouring across the bridges endangered the safety of his command. The thrust of the message was to assign responsibility to Washington for the outcome if air attacks did not go ahead. In the face of this threat, Truman and his advisers retreated. The operation was allowed to go ahead, provided strict precautions were taken to bomb the bridges on the Korean side only.[61] In the following two weeks, nobody in Washington proved any more willing than on this occasion to run the risks of overruling the general.

Escalating clashes with Chinese troops might have forced the hands of Acheson and the Pentagon. In early November, however, the Chinese vanished from the battlefield and the debate was carried on during a lull in operations while MacArthur prepared for a final advance. The Chinese withdrawal both stimulated MacArthur's confidence and made it difficult to resist his plans on military grounds. Chinese strength and intentions remained a mystery. Some form of 'probe' was necessary to take the measure of the enemy. MacArthur's arguments against any appearance of weakness, moreover, struck a strong chord in official Washington, which operated on the assumptions of NSC-68.[62] A halt would encourage aggression. Any political solution was best reached from a position of military strength.[63] In its anxiety to prove its determination, the administration proposed to its allies a policy of 'hot pursuit' across the Yalu of Chinese aircraft which had become increasingly engaged in November and which were hampering air operations near the border.[64] Nobody paused to consider the contrast between such military action and the public assurances being offered to Beijing on the inviolability of the frontier. The proposal received universal condemnation from other UN members. Britain, for example, hesitated to give a commander such as MacArthur such latitude and was convinced that it would soon lead to the bombing of Manchuria.[65] Washington did not pursue the issue. Acheson was anxious to maintain a united front at Lake Success and to leave no openings for Soviet diplomacy.[66]

In retrospect, Acheson blamed himself for not giving Truman good advice in this period. According to Acheson, everyone knew that something was wrong but nobody did anything.[67] This underestimates the extent to which MacArthur's exaggerated optimism was shared in

Washington. The disappearance of the Chinese convinced MacArthur that his air campaign had proved successful and had decisively weakened his new opponent. The war could still end by Christmas.[68] The absence of the Chinese influenced Washington as much as the field commander. Rusk, for example, found it significant that China had made no military response to the attacks on the Yalu bridges.[69] The tempting idea gained hold that it might prove unnecessary to negotiate with Beijing. In Washington as well as Tokyo, MacArthur's advance became not a 'probe' but a final offensive. On 24 November, the day the operation began, Acheson talked about military measures establishing the conditions for attainment of UN aims on a permanent basis.[70] At Lake Success, Gross boasted about 'chasing the Chinese out'.[71] There was no hint here of accepting anything less than unification, a solution which Acheson had contemplated earlier in the month. Indeed, the Secretary and other officials implicitly accepted MacArthur's definition of his mission as to clear Korea.[72]

In this process, the idea of a DMZ was abandoned. On 21 November it was decided merely to suggest to MacArthur that he halt his advance on the ridges overlooking the Yalu.[73] As Rusk informed the British ambassador, the unoccupied strip would be a zone of manoeuvre and not a DMZ. It would be lightly patrolled and if Chinese infiltration was detected it would be entered by the UN command.[74] MacArthur, however, found even this suggestion unacceptable.[75] Simultaneously, Acheson took action to defuse the British proposal for a DMZ north of the 40th parallel. This scheme was never seriously considered in Washington since it required the retreat of UN forces from their existing positions.[76] As in October, Bevin did not press the issue.[77] A determined stand was unlikely to achieve anything beyond stirring up MacArthur and the Republicans, perhaps endangering British prospects of increased US support in Europe. In the last analysis, moreover, Bevin seems to have shared Acheson's illusion that political proposals could always be made if MacArthur's operation stalled. Nobody predicted the extent of the disaster which occurred.

In retrospect, the idea of a DMZ was viewed as a lost opportunity.[78] This, however, is a considerable exaggeration. Acheson's idea of a zone on both sides of the Yalu would never have appealed to the Chinese, since they would have been required to abandon their own frontier. Bevin's alternative was unacceptable to Washington since it surrendered territory and risked giving Beijing something for nothing. In any case, a DMZ could not be created simply by pronouncement. The complex process of military disengagement demanded negotiation but China displayed no interest. After refusing to attend the debate on Korea, the Chinese sent a delegation to the UN for a hearing on Taiwan. It dawdled through Europe, however, and did not arrive until MacArthur's offensive began. Nor did private soundings by the British produce a response. This suggests that Beijing had decided to settle the Korean problem on its own terms.[79] US determination to deny Beijing a role was matched by Chinese intransigence. China intended to play its Rooseveltian role as regional policeman, but under new management.

On 24 November MacArthur launched the offensive which was to end the war by Christmas. Four days later his armies were retreating in the face of massive Chinese attack. MacArthur never admitted that his assumptions had been wrong. In retrospect he claimed that his plans had been betrayed by 'sources in Washington.'[80] Not only did the Chinese possess advance knowledge of his operations but they were also aware that he was forbidden to attack Manchuria. Without this vital piece of intelligence, Beijing would never have dared to intervene.[81] MacArthur was referring to the role of the British diplomats, Guy Burgess, Donald Maclean and Kim Philby, who had been recruited by Soviet intelligence as students in the 1930s. By October 1950 these agents occupied important posts in the British bureaucracy. Burgess and Philby were attached to the embassy in Washington where Burgess dealt with the Far East, while Philby acted as liaison officer between the CIA and British intelligence.[82] Maclean was head of the North American Department at the Foreign Office in London. The scandal which erupted when Burgess and Maclean defected in May 1951 made a stab in the back theory attractive to MacArthur and his sympathisers. It could be argued that the British spies had kept Moscow and thus Beijing supplied with vital intelligence about US policy. The British were not only appeasers but traitors as well.[83]

The role of Soviet moles in the December crisis, however, has been greatly exaggerated. Whatever the Chinese learned from this source about the restrictions on operations across the Yalu, they could not assume that intervention would not be followed by retaliation. In taking military action, Beijing accepted the risk that the atomic bomb would be employed against Chinese cities.[84] As for tactical intelligence about MacArthur's final offensive, it did not require a Soviet spy ring to provide the enemy with information. Until mid-December, MacArthur refused to impose press censorship in Korea. As a result, correspondents were 'able to phone anything they chose to their

Tokyo bureaus. And the American news services sold their product to the Japanese press and radio . . . [the enemy] had but to listen each day to the radio and read our press . . . and he possessed knowledge of our order of battle, intentions, strength, losses, difficulties and, all too often, plans for the future.'[85] By ascribing the disaster of December 1950 to intelligence leaks, MacArthur was attempting to escape responsibility for his own errors of judgement.

On 28 November MacArthur reported that his command faced an entirely new war against the military power of Communist China.[86] In this situation, three courses seemed open to the administration. It could escalate the war, it could hold a line and attempt to negotiate, or it could evacuate the peninsula. These alternatives had to be considered not only in terms of the military situation in Korea, but also in the context of global strategy and their likely effect on the political situation at home. MacArthur's instinct was to escalate the war.[87] His military reputation and political prospects depended on his retrieving the situation caused by Chinese intervention. When the Army Chief of Staff, General Collins, flew to the Far East on 3 December to investigate the situation, MacArthur argued that the choice lay between escalation or humiliation. Without reinforcements, the use of Guomindong troops, air attacks on Manchuria, a naval blockade and the possible use of atomic weapons, he could not hold a tenable position in Korea.[88] Washington, however, was reluctant to contemplate what amounted to full-scale war with China. It was believed that behind Beijing's action lay the Kremlin. The Chinese would not have attacked in Korea without assurances of support in the event of retaliation. Air attacks against Manchuria or the use of Guomindong troops would bring matching escalation by the enemy. The Chinese air force, as yet not seriously employed against the UN command, might be brought into action, threatening the retreat of MacArthur's forces. Covert or open use of Soviet air and naval units could not be ruled out. In such a situation, the use of the atomic bomb might be unavoidable, leading perhaps to global war.[89]

The United States would enter such a struggle in the worst possible circumstances. Rearmament was still in its opening stages and there was no possibility of holding Europe against a Russian attack. Moreover major allies, such as Britain, would blame the United States for provoking the third world war instead of solving the Chinese problem by political means. Even if global war did not occur, a war with China would pin the US down in the Far East and leave Europe exposed to Soviet power. Washington would be fighting the 'second team', while Moscow exploited Western anxiety about US policy in the Far East to undermine NATO. As Acheson emphasised, war with China might be welcomed by Russia. It would be 'a bottomless pit' which would 'bleed us dry'.[90]

The reaction of the administration, therefore, was to avoid the trap of general war with China. It wished to remain in step with its allies in a crisis which signalled a new willingness by the USSR to run grave risks in an attempt to weaken and divide the Western bloc. It was feared in Washington that Soviet preparedness had been underestimated in NSC-68. Under the impact of the Korean crisis, assumptions were revised and Russian readiness for global war brought forward from 1954 to 1952. It was argued that to meet this imminent danger, Western rearmament must be accelerated. If war was to be avoided, time was short. Moreover, measures to strengthen NATO by the appointment of an American commander and the commitment of additional US troops, delayed by French anxieties over German rearmament, would have to be completed. As Harriman argued, in the current crisis Washington should forget about the details and give a lead to its allies.[91] On 15 December Truman declared a state of national emergency. This was followed by a tightening-up of economic controls and a revised military budget. On 16 December, following a NATO meeting at Brussels which formalised a compromise over German rearmament, the President announced the appointment of General Eisenhower as supreme commander in Europe.[92]

It was by no means clear, however, whether MacArthur's strategy could be avoided. If the enemy chose to escalate in Korea, there would be little chance of avoiding a general war with China and perhaps global war with the USSR. Acheson was convinced that the world stood at the brink.[93] Everything depended on the enemy displaying restraint and limiting his military commitment in Korea. Limitation turned on the possible emergence of an unwritten agreement. Washington would not strike at Manchuria if Beijing did not use its growing air power against the UN command. The conflict would be a competition between Chinese manpower and a numerically inferior UN force backed by the USAF. In this situation, there was some hope of a military stalemate which might lead to negotiation. If China committed its air power, however, Washington would have no option but to retaliate against Manchuria.[94] This might bring in the Russians under the Sino–Soviet pact, forcing the United States to use the atomic bomb. Employment of the bomb had been under consideration from the earliest days of the war. Political and military factors, however, dictated against its use. It was decided that such a weapon should only be deployed as a last resort to save the UN command from disaster. This was defined as a 'Dunkirk style' evacuation under heavy military pressure.[95] The issue arose again in early November with the first evidence of Chinese intervention. On 20 November General Collins authorised a study of the use of the bomb against military targets in Korea, Manchuria and China, noting that in the event of full-scale Chinese intervention, atomic weapons might be necessary to allow MacArthur to hold or to drive to the border.[96] On 28 November the JCS ordered a further top secret study, on the employment of the bomb in the event of Soviet intervention, 'to discourage such intervention and/or to assist in the evacuation of UN forces from Korea.' It also requested comments on the use of atomic and conventional bombs against China 'with or without previous ultimatum'.[97] The existence of these studies raises the possibility that when Truman implied the use of the bomb was under 'active consideration' at his famous 30 November press conference, he was not guilty of faulty expression.[98] He may have been warning the Russians about the consequences of further escalation in Korea.

Washington's decision to limit the war unless further provoked and to accelerate its European programme opened up a serious breach with MacArthur which was to end with his dismissal. The potential conflict between Truman's European strategy and MacArthur's belief in Asia first, which had surfaced in the August debate over Taiwan, had vanished as the mirage of total victory in Korea beckoned. At Wake, it had seemed that both General and President could be satisfied. Truman could have his European strategy and MacArthur his victory over Asian communism. The General could even offer to make troops available for NATO by 1951. It now became a stark choice between the Far East and Europe. A deep and widening gap emerged between MacArthur and his superiors, the Europeanist clique which he had always distrusted.

MacArthur fought his battle with the administration, not only through the medium of despatches but also by appeals through the press to the home front. An early example of this technique had been seen during the earlier friction over Taiwan. When China intervened, the General attempted to evade responsibility and to force his own strategy on Washington, by a series of interviews in which he criticised the restrictions on his command, his inability to strike Manchuria, and the influence of UN allies, particularly Britain, on the foreign policy of the United States.[99] This represented a political threat to the administration. Truman was seriously worried by the results of the November election and by signs that the Republicans intended to capitalise on their gains to attack the administration and its European policies. His political enemies, aided by their allies in the right-wing press, were pursuing a 'campaign of lies, vilification and distortion' which undermined 'the confidence of the American people in their Government'.[100] MacArthur was clearly capitalising on and encouraging this campaign and steps were taken to gag him. On 5 December the President issued an order forbidding officials to make statements on military or foreign policy without previous political clearance.[101] Although issued in blanket form, this directive was plainly aimed at the commander in the Far East.

The chances of avoiding war with China depended on holding a defence line at some point in Korea. With the Chinese army engaged, Washington was prepared to retreat from victory and accept instead a return to the status quo. It would be content with repelling aggression. The difference between military objectives and political aspirations, which had disappeared in October, was again emphasised. As Acheson emphasised on 28 November, 'Our great objective must be to hold an area, to terminate the fighting, to turn over some area to the Republic of Korea and to *get out* so that we can get ahead with building up our own strength and building up the strength of Europe.' He later speculated on the possibility of a cease-fire around the 38th parallel.[102] Such a solution was in accord with the wishes of the major allies. All except the South Koreans were prepared to accept a solution based on a return to the status quo.

If grave dangers existed in relation to MacArthur's preferred option of escalation, however, this approach also was not without its problems. MacArthur maintained that it was impossible to hold a line against the Chinese with the forces available and that he could only withdraw his command into beachheads. Even after the X Corps was evacuated from North-East Korea and brought into line with Eighth Army, he continued to argue that any stabilisation was merely temporary.[103] Thus the United States would be negotiating from a position of military weakness, the antithesis of that called for in NSC-68. As Acheson himself admitted, the Chinese had little incentive to negotiate as long as their armies were advancing. Beijing, backed by Moscow, would use its position of military advantage to demand a high price. Discussion of a cease-fire in Korea would be accompanied by demands for a UN seat, the cession of Taiwan and perhaps a voice in the Japanese peace treaty. These terms would amount to almost a complete surrender in the Far East. Acheson foresaw a total collapse of the Western position in Asia if this position was ever reached. Japan would lose faith in US guarantees and the French would abandon Indochina. The Soviet Union, through its Chinese satellite would 'collect the stakes'. It would have won the great game in the Far East.[104]

There was also the political situation at home to consider. With the Republicans shaping up for a new confrontation over foreign policy, the administration could not afford to appear weak in Asia. As Acheson remarked, in a veiled allusion to McCarthyism, the American people would not understand a policy of appeasement in the Far East and resistance in Europe.[105] The situation was complicated by the inability of the administration to publicise its motives. It could not argue for a settlement with China on the grounds that the Soviet Union was the real enemy. This would only provoke demands for preventive war. Thus there was little room for Washington to negotiate on anything but the most narrowly defined terms, which were unlikely to be acceptable to China. Moreover, the worse the situation became, the greater would be the public pressure for retaliation against Beijing, a fact of which both the administration and General MacArthur were well aware.

The military uncertainties and the political problems of negotiation forced the administration to consider a third option, evacuation. There was strong sentiment in favour of such a course in certain quarters at the Pentagon. The military had never favoured Korea as a suitable area for a major confrontation with communist power. As early as 3 December, both Admiral Sherman, the chief of naval operations, and General Vandenberg, head of the USAF, talked of delivering an ultimatum to China, demanding that it either halt its attack or accept the consequences. If Beijing remained intransigent, US forces would be withdrawn and air and naval warfare waged against the mainland. According to Vandenberg, 'The proposed action against China would not affect our capacity in Europe. All we would need would be the naval blockade and the use of one or two air groups.' This course, however, was ultimately as unacceptable as MacArthur's demands for escalation. It would foreclose the possibility of a truce and mean abandoning the South Koreans. Truman and his civilian advisers were determined to hold in Korea as long as possible, in order to preserve American honour and strengthen the chances of a cease-fire, however slim.[106]

A forced evacuation, however, could not be ruled out. US policy in this contingency had to be considered. As General Bradley remarked on 3 December, 'He would not advocate putting men into China but wondered whether we could come home and just forget the matter.'[107] Although reluctant to become involved in retaliation against China, Acheson agreed. As he emphasised on 4 December, 'If we are pushed out. . . . We could make as much trouble for the Chinese Communists as possible and hold Formosa, retaining what strength we can.' Actions considered at this stage included economic and political sanctions and support of covert operations from Taiwan by the Guomindong.[108] As Acheson realised, once retaliation took place, hostilities were liable to escalate. Limited action against China was likely to lead to the adoption of MacArthur's strategy by the back door. Such an outcome would create serious strains between the United States and its allies. It was recognised, however, that political considerations might leave the administration with little choice.[109]

The US position was explained to Attlee when the British Prime Minister made a hasty trip to Washington on 4 December. Attlee's flight symbolised the strains in the Atlantic relationship caused by Chinese intervention. Britain, in common with the other major allies, was alarmed by the deteriorating military situation and by political developments in Washington. Republican gains in the November elections were a particular source of apprehension. It was feared that under pressure from the McCarthyites, the administration would allow MacArthur to retaliate against Manchuria, an action which might bring global war with the USSR.[110] This concern was crystallised by Truman's press conference remarks on the atomic bomb. The prospect of such a weapon in the hands of MacArthur was viewed with horror. At Quebec in 1943 Churchill and Roosevelt had agreed that the atomic bomb was a joint possession which should not be used without mutual consent. Britain lost its veto after 1945, however, and the bomb became one of the few issues on which a special Anglo–American relationship did not exist. The US established an atomic monopoly and even refused on security grounds to brief the British on the global war plan, OFFTACKLE.[111] This was ironic since British airfields occupied a key role in the contemplated SAC bombing offensive against Russia. US aircraft first arrived in Britain during the Berlin crisis in 1948. Bevin had not insisted on preconditions governing use of the bases, regarding the US military presence as a valuable symbol of American commitment to Europe and evidence of the decline of isolationism. A mere verbal agreement existed, recognising Britain's right to terminate US base rights. Thus London lacked both a veto on the use of the bomb and operational control of the bases from which an atomic bombing offensive would be launched.[112] The Korean crisis emphasised for the first time the dangers of this situation and placed Britain in the front line. As Attlee complained in December 1950, if the US became involved in a war with Russia, Europe would be the first to suffer.[113] The USSR was likely to launch a pre-emptive strike against US airfields in East Anglia. This made the Labour government anxious to define the atomic relationship more closely and to gain some form of veto over US employment of the bomb and of the bases. It was no longer a matter of committing the US to British security but of restraining the indiscriminate use of American power.

Attlee wished to assert British influence in Washington, feeling that in the past the Americans had taken their major ally for granted. Public opinion other than American would have to be taken into account in formulating allied strategy. Before leaving London, Attlee met the French prime minister and talked with the Dominion high commissioners. Although in no sense an allied emissary, he could claim to reflect a general concern that the US would act unilaterally against China, dragging its allies with it. The situation was made no more palatable by the knowledge that in such an event, Britain and the other allies might have little option but to support the United States despite the consequences.[114] The Western security system could not exist without Washington. As Lester Pearson later remarked, the problem was no longer whether the United States would commit its power, but how that power would be used.[115] Attlee's trip was an attempt to keep American power in the proper channels, preventing a diversion of US attention to the Far East, which would leave Europe and the Middle East vulnerable to the Soviet Union.

In Washington, Attlee found broad agreement on the advantages of a cease-fire which would allow the West to concentrate on meeting the Soviet danger in Europe. The appointment of a US supreme commander to NATO and the deployment of US troops was to be pushed ahead.[116] The problem, however, was the price to be paid in the Far East for maintaining Europe first. Attlee was prepared to consider a wider deal with China than any contemplated by Truman and Acheson. The British argued, as they had always done, that nationalism in China was potentially more powerful than communism. China could be detached from the Soviet orbit and used against the Russians. It was unwise to assume an identity of interest between Beijing and Moscow which might not exist. This view supposed that Chinese intervention in Korea was more the product of Chinese national interests than of the Soviet conspiracy. Attlee favoured granting Beijing the Chinese seat in the UN and reaching some solution to the problem of Taiwan, perhaps 'derecognising' Jiang and placing the island under a UN commission. The Prime Minister emphasised the importance of acting within a UN framework and of maintaining the support of Asian opinion.[117] This reflected the importance of India to commonwealth unity. Nehru had always favoured seating Beijing at the UN and solving the problem of Taiwan. Retaliation against China would break up the commonwealth and would also be likely be bring down the Labour government since the left wing of the party would not support measures which alienated India.

The Americans, however, were unwilling to link a Korean cease-fire with a general settlement in the Far East. The response to Attlee's arguments was within the established parameters of NSC-68, with its emphasis on the dangers of negotiation with communists, particularly from a position of military weakness. Truman could see no prospect of a Sino-Soviet split. The President was in no mood to 'give into that vicious government' which was 'actually the Russian government'. According to Acheson, 'The Chinese Communists were looking at the matter not as Chinese but as communists who are subservient to Moscow.'[118] A breach with the Kremlin was a long-term prospect and the West could not base its policies on such a contingency. Concessions on the British scale amounted to rewarding aggression and would cause a loss of confidence in American power throughout the Far East. The Soviet bloc would be strengthened and its appetite increased. Moreover, there was the American domestic situation to consider. As Truman emphasised, the issue of China was 'political dynamite' in the United States.[119] Unless Washington took a firm line with China there was no hope of American backing for NATO. The American people would not understand a policy of surrender in Asia and resistance in Europe. Containment was indivisible.[120] While agreeing with Attlee that Asian opinion was important, the Americans were privately impatient with Nehru whom they regarded as a 'mugwump'.[121] In the world of NSC-68, there was no room for dissenting voices on the nature of the communist menace. Thus while Attlee confirmed US determination to hold in Korea if possible and to seek a ceasefire through the UN, he found no support for linking this with a general settlement in the Far East. Nor did he receive any assurance that a 'makeshift' policy of retaliation against China would not be pursued in the event of defeat.[122] This question, however, dropped temporarily into the background following the return of General Collins from an inspection trip to the front on 8 December. According to Collins, evacuation was not an imminent possibility, a fact which gave the UN bargaining time.[123] Nor did Attlee make progress on the issues of the atomic bomb and control of General MacArthur, questions which he also raised in Washington. Britain aspired to return to the wartime Quebec agreement, under which the two powers possessed a mutual veto on the employment of atomic weapons. While Truman was prepared to pledge to consult London before using the bomb, this part of the communique was hastily revised by Acheson. It contravened the atomic energy act and threatened to raise a storm in Congress, where the Republicans were already complaining about secret deals with Britain.[124] Attlee did not raise the related question of the bases and the American global war plan. The Chiefs of Staff continued to find this situation 'intolerable' but the issue was not resolved until the Morrison–Acheson agreement of September 1951. This was confirmed by the incoming Churchill administration and made use of the bases a matter of joint consultation in the light of the circumstances prevailing at the time. A British veto on the use of the bomb, however, remained as distant as ever.[125] As for MacArthur, when the British tentatively raised the idea of a UN military committee to oversee operations, insulating the war from the direct influence of US public opinion, the Americans reacted angrily and transformed the issue into a question of confidence. According to Bradley, the administration had always acted as a loyal agent of the UN; 'If others did not like what was going on, they should say so and they would be given assistance in withdrawing.' Acheson emphasised the dangers if a similar concern developed over Eisenhower's projected role in Europe.[126] Once again containment was indivisible. The price of Eisenhower in Europe was MacArthur in the Far East. The US spokesmen did not reveal their own increasing disillusion with the victor of Inchon.

By December 1950 Korea, which had originally bolstered global strategy by mobilising Western opinion against the Soviet danger, threatened to conflict with the goals of NSC-68. The document assumed consensus both within the United States and between the United States and its allies on the nature of the communist threat. Chinese intervention provoked an acceleration of the measures called for in NSC-68 but in a far different atmosphere from that envisaged by its authors. The allies were being called upon to assume major new risks and burdens at a time when many had begun to doubt the political stability of the United States. From this perspective, NSC-68 seemed less a programme to avert a conflict than a recipe for global war. In the United States, government programmes were being accelerated, 'not in a period of patriotism and willing sacrifice . . . but in that of a hugely unpopular limited war'.[127] The administration faced a 'partisan rupture' over foreign policy fuelled by the frustrations of Korea and the costs of NSC-68, which culminated in Republican demands for a basic reorientation of US strategy. In the following months, Truman had to cope with both a domestic political crisis and a crisis in US relationships with its allies, provoked by a growing lack of confidence abroad in American leadership.

5 A Crisis of Confidence

In the spring of 1951, US policy developed within the outlines which had emerged in December 1950. Rearmament was accelerated and steps taken to consolidate the Western bloc. In his state of the union message, Truman ruled out 'appeasement' of the USSR and warned that military strength was 'the only realistic road to peace'. The United States was preparing for 'full wartime mobilisation, if that should be necessary'.[1] The first priority remained NATO. In January 1951 General Eisenhower called for the creation of forty NATO divisions by 1952, the assumed year of crisis with the Soviet Union. In the Far East, preparations for a Japanese peace treaty speeded up with the despatch of John Foster Dulles to Tokyo in January 1951 as the President's special representative.[2] Financial and military assistance to Indochina and the Philippines increased and links with Taiwan were consolidated by the despatch of a US military mission under General Chase in May.[3] This ambitious programme, however, was developed against the background of continuing crisis in Korea which both fuelled partisan debate at home and caused grave tensions within the Western alliance.

After the Attlee visit, the focus of attention shifted to the UN. Washington disliked placing the issue of a cease-fire in the hands of an international body and was pessimistic about the prospects of a satisfactory outcome. Multilateral negotiations posed problems of control. The administration suspected that its Western allies, under the misguided influence of India, might promote a settlement unacceptable to the United States.[4] While prepared to go some distance to satisfy his UN partners, Truman could not go too far without causing a political storm at home. The cease-fire was a delicate question, since the Korean crisis coincided with the full-scale assault on Truman's foreign policy known as the 'Great Debate'. Not only did the Republicans redouble their opposition to any deal with China, but they also seized the opportunity offered by disillusion with the war to attack the whole basis of NSC-68.[5]

On 3 January 1951 resolutions were introduced in the House and Senate challenging the right of the President to send additional troops to Europe without congressional consent.[6] In the course of the ensuing debate, the opposition developed an alternative strategy of containment. According to Senator Taft, the costs of containing

79

communist power on the European mainland were prohibitive. The American economy could not sustain the enormous costs of confrontation with the USSR in the area. Peace could be best preserved and the American way of life guaranteed, not by an expensive land build-up in association with NATO, but by a more cost-effective approach based on air and naval power. The US should adopt an offshore perimeter strategy in both Europe and Asia, leaving land defence of the mainland to the nations most immediately involved.[7] This argument reflected distrust of entangling alliances and expanded executive power. Both were symbolised by Korea, an undeclared war fought on behalf of the UN which had ended in disaster. Korea also stimulated disillusion with land warfare. As Senator Wherry argued, Korea was an 'object lesson' in the difficulties of fighting on the Eurasian mainland. Korean losses were 'almost negligible compared to what we would suffer if our ground forces received the full weight of the Red Army in Europe'.[8]

On Korea itself, the Republicans occupied an ambiguous position. While sympathising with MacArthur's demands to escalate the war, spokesmen also called for evacuation. Korea was not the place to engage the massive land armies available to the communists. These apparently contradictory approaches came together on the issue of Taiwan. Whatever happened in Korea, the Guomindong regime was the key to the US position in the Far East. Chinese nationalist rather than US ground forces should be used against Beijing either in Korea itself or as part of a wider campaign against the communist mainland.[9] This meshed with the belief that the American strategic role should be in the air and on the sea rather than on land. The Republicans were more inclined to trust Jiang as a loyal ally, than they were to support the Western powers, which they suspected, rightly, of wishing to dump the Generalissimo in favour of a settlement with Beijing.

Republican policy was unilateralist rather than isolationist. US power was to be deployed without the need for frustrating compromises with allies. The party placed more emphasis on the Far East than Europe, regarding Asia as the key to victory over communism. In this respect, it echoed the arguments of MacArthur. At the same time, however, the opposition was highly opportunist. Republican prescriptions in the Far East reflected a domestic strategy in which an imagined 'free China' was more important than the reality of Taiwan. Republicans enjoyed the luxury of criticising the war without assuming responsibility for its conduct. Unlike the administration, they could manoeuvre freely for partisan advantage.

Once in power, even former diehards, such as Richard Nixon, were prepared privately to admit the weaknesses of an Asian policy based on Jiang.[10]

The immediate effect of the 'Great Debate' was to paralyse the administration at the UN. Already profoundly hostile to the Chinese communists, Acheson found his capacity for even tactical compromises to satisfy allies severely constrained. Any hint of softness in Asia was likely to complicate the already controversial deployment of troops to Europe. As Acheson warned the British ambassador on 5 January, failure to condemn China as an aggressor would doom the UN to the fate of the League of Nations and jeopardise NATO. A wave of isolationism would sweep the country, endangering the American commitment to Europe.[11] Despite an element of exaggeration, designed to bring a recalcitrant ally into line, this danger was viewed as real. Truman was anxious about the collapse of consensus and compared the Republicans to the Know-Nothings of the 1840s.[12]

As Acheson's statement revealed, a breach was beginning to open up between the US and some of its allies in January 1951 over the issue of condemning China as an aggressor. The controversy centred on the activities of the three-man cease-fire committee, consisting of Nazrollah of Iran, Pearson of Canada and Rau of India, established by the Political Committee of the General Assembly on 14 December. Washington was pessimistic about the prospects of this initiative, but hesitated to appear as an opponent of peace. If China refused to cooperate, it would be revealed as an aggressor and the way cleared for condemnation of Beijing by the UN.[13] On 16 December the cease-fire group passed on the terms suggested by the UN command to China. These reflected American insistence on a narrow military rather than a wider political arrangement. On 23 December China rejected this approach.[14] It claimed that the UN terms reflected US influence. The Americans wanted a cease-fire only to gain a breathing space and to deprive China of the military initiative. The issue could not be considered in isolation from political questions. Beijing outlined its own terms, which included the concession of a UN seat, withdrawal of all foreign troops from Korea, the settlement of Korean questions by the Koreans themselves and the removal of US forces from Taiwan. This uncompromising statement was followed by a new Chinese offensive, launched on 31 December, which forced UN forces to abandon Seoul. On 3 January the cease-fire group admitted that it had no recommendations which could be 'usefully made'.[15]

In the face of this response, the US suggested an adjournment of the
Political Committee to consider the situation. It was clear that this was
regarded as the prelude to condemnation of China and consideration
of further measures to punish aggression. At the suggestion of Britain,
however, the cease-fire group was asked to draw up a statement of
principles for the next session.[16] With a meeting of commonwealth
prime ministers taking place in London, Britain did not wish to
alienate India which remained hostile to condemnation of China. As
the Australian diplomat, Watt, remarked, the commonwealth
representatives found themselves 'on the horns of two dilemmas'. No
set of terms acceptable to Washington was likely to find favour in
Beijing. Moreover, while everyone wanted to 'keep in line' with the
Americans, nobody agreed with the steps which Washington
contemplated.[17] The deliberations of the commonwealth conference
influenced the activities of the cease-fire committee on which India
and Canada were both represented.[18]

The 'Five Principles' produced by the cease-fire group on 11 January
attempted to escape the two dilemmas by bridging the gap between the
US and China while avoiding a breach with India which could prove
fatal for both the commonwealth and the UN. Under the terms of the
'Five Principles' a Korean cease-fire would be the prelude to a general
discussion of Far Eastern problems, including the issue of Taiwan and
Beijing's claim to a UN seat. These questions would be considered by a
body established by the General Assembly which would include
British, Soviet, US and Chinese representatives. In Korea itself all
foreign troops would be withdrawn by 'appropriate stages' and the
future of the country decided by the Koreans themselves under UN
principles.[19] These terms faced Washington with a 'murderous'
choice. If the administration accepted them, it would provide
ammunition for the Republicans. If it rejected them, it risked
alienating major allies such as Britain, which were clearly unwilling to
condemn China at this stage.[20]

In the end Acheson advised acceptance, but only in the belief that
the terms would be rejected by the Chinese.[21] Washington was not
committed to a deal on the UN seat and Taiwan by the 'Five
Principles', but there were clear dangers in allowing the issues to be
discussed by an international body on which the US might be
outvoted.[22] As Acheson had predicted, China rejected the UN
approach on 18 January. Beijing remained suspicious of any
arrangement which placed a cease-fire ahead of political discussions
and produced a new set of counter-proposals. These centred on a

seven nation conference, to be held in China, which would settle the Korean issue and other Far Eastern problems, including Taiwan. Beijing's right to a UN seat was to be recognised from the beginning.[23]

In Washington this seemed like a demand for unconditional surrender. On 20 January the US representative on the Political Committee tabled a draft resolution condemning China as an aggressor and calling for the establishment of a special body to consider further measures against Beijing. As a sop to allied concern, the draft also contained provision for a Good Offices Committee, reaffirming the UN desire for a cease-fire. The essence of the resolution, however, was clearly condemnation and Washington made it plain that it expected the support of its allies.[24] The administration had gone to the brink with the 'Five Principles', which were attacked by the Republicans as shameful appeasement. The opposition brought further pressure to bear when a resolution was introduced in the House on 19 January, calling for the condemnation of China. This was followed by a similar move in the Senate. The time for manoeuvre was past. The administration could make no further compromises for the sake of its allies without risking unacceptable political damage at home.[25]

It rapidly became clear, however, that India, supported by Britain and Canada, was reluctant to close the door on further negotiations. It refused to accept China's response as an outright rejection of the 'Five Principles' and instead sought further clarification of the Chinese position. This produced some moderation of the Chinese terms on 22 January. A cease-fire for a limited period was to be the first item on the agenda of the proposed seven nation conference. At the same time, the Taiwan question was to be settled in accordance with the Cairo declaration and 'definite affirmation of the legitimate status' of Beijing in the UN was to be 'ensured'. These concessions were insufficient to deflect Washington, which pressed forward with its own proposals.[26] Acheson was furious at these further contacts with China, accusing the Canadians and the Indians of manoeuvring behind Washington's back. The allies now faced a critical decision at the UN. While Australia and Canada expressed their reluctant support for the US resolution in the last resort, they continued to express reservations about American insistence on further measures against China.[27] The most troublesome ally, however, was Britain. Not only did London urge moderation on Washington, but it also lobbied commonwealth representatives in an attempt to modify the American position.

Britain was concerned lest condemnation of China not only

foreclosed further negotiations but also led to 'extreme' measures against Beijing. The US resolution might clear the way to the type of limited warfare, involving Guomindong forces, mentioned at the Truman/Attlee meeting. London was apprehensive about the military situation, fearing that, by continuing to retreat, MacArthur was 'creating facts' and forcing an evacuation of the peninsula which would compel retaliation against China. It had picked up disturbing rumours of pessimism at the Pentagon and growing sentiment there in favour of withdrawal.[28] On 8 January Attlee wrote to Truman seeking confirmation that the US intended to stand and fight. Although the President affirmed US determination to hold a line in Korea and denied any intention of seeking a UN mandate for limited war with China, London remained apprehensive as long as the retreat continued.[29] MacArthur was still an object of suspicion. His reported statement at the end of January that UN forces were fighting for 'a free Asia' reinforced concern that he contemplated an extension of the war using Guomindong troops.[30]

The Attlee government had to consider not only Indian opinion and its implications for commonwealth unity, but also British opinion. As the Cabinet noted on 18 January, 'There would be great difficulty in enlisting the support of public opinion in this country for any extreme action by the United States.'[31] Chinese intervention ended the popularity of the war. Disillusion with the UN cause was further encouraged by fresh evidence of ROK atrocities. On 15 December, just as the war was going sour, there was a mass execution within the British brigade lines at Seoul. The troops were 'outraged' by the method of killing and by the fact that women were amongst the victims. They also claimed that children were involved, although this was later officially denied.[32] This 'criminal' activity received wide publicity and one soldier wrote to Bevin complaining that the UN should be fighting against such things. He was now wondering 'which side was right' in Korea.[33] The British commander banned any further executions by the ROK police, authorising the use of force if necessary. The incident increased public disillusion with the war. The Americans were concerned lest 'emotional' reporting of ROK activities drive a wedge between the US and Britain.[34] Both the US and UNCURK intervened with Rhee, whose initial reaction had been defiance.[35] According to Rhee, 'There was a war on . . . [and] we have to take measures.' Under pressure, he agreed to review death sentences and to end public executions. These had been introduced because the gallows in Seoul prison had been destroyed during the fighting of September 1950.[36] As UNCURK concluded, little weight could be placed on these pledges. The ROK would probably continue the mass execution of 'subversives' behind prison walls.[37] The Foreign Office, however, was less concerned with the killings than with the publicity which surrounded them. It was satisfied with a cosmetic measure which might contain public disillusion with the ROK and a possible threat to the Atlantic alliance.

Dislike of the Rhee regime was accompanied by growing disillusion with the United States, which was regarded as an irrational giant. There was growing public concern that Washington, under the influence of McCarthyism, was dragging Britain towards global conflict. There was widespread fear of an atomic war with Russia. As Dalton remarked on 31 December, 'The danger of a Third World War in our times is . . . hideous and seems to be growing . . .'[38] The British people, exhausted by the continuing effects of the earlier struggle, were sick of war. Attlee was warned that the public questioned the need for further sacrifices in the cause of rearmament, a policy attributed to American pressure. The problem was complicated by the issue of German rearmament, which according to a survey of public opinion many found 'sinister and repugnant' only five years after the defeat of Hitler. If support was to be retained for containment, the public must be convinced that the defence effort was being undertaken for British reasons. A show of independence was required.[39]

Until this point, Britain had been content to influence US policy from the inside, avoiding an open breach in the Far East. As Bevin emphasised, London must loyally support 'the well-intentioned but inexperienced colossus on whose cooperation our safety depends', while attempting to exert 'sufficient control' over US policy. This could only be achieved by influencing the US government and people 'not by opposing or discouraging them'.[40] A contrary sentiment, however, was gaining strength, fuelled by public concern over American intentions. The Minister of War, Strachey, argued that US hostility towards China posed dangers for global peace. It would be better for Britain to accept an open dispute on the issue than to enter a debate with Washington feeling that America must not be lost.[41] Such an attitude conceded the argument before it had even begun. Younger, Minister of State at the Foreign Office, put this view succinctly when he remarked, 'So long as their own extremists are an embarrassment to them and HMG are not, it is unlikely that our view will have much effective weight.'[42]

A show of independence was not long in coming. On 25 January the

Cabinet, in the absence of Bevin, decided to vote against any condemnation of China which was coupled with a demand for sanctions. In contemplating this action, Britain had to balance two sets of risks. An affirmative vote might lead to moderation of US policy and allow Britain to exert a calming influence from the inside. It might also, however, clear the way for military measures, alienate India and cause domestic political problems. A negative vote might have repercussions on American aid to Europe and in particular on financial assistance for British rearmament. It might also increase the political pressure on the administration to adopt a stiff line in the Far East, regardless of the UN. It was decided, however, that Britain could not vote for a China policy with which it disagreed, without losing both its 'independence' and its 'self-respect'.[43]

Despite the cabinet decision, there were strong pressures for a compromise. Gaitskell, the Chancellor of the Exchequer, threatened to resign on the issue, arguing that a break with Washington over China would have grave consequences for British security. It would 'enormously strengthen the anti-European block in the USA . . . [and] might lead to their virtually coming from Europe which would . . . be the end for us.'[44] Acheson was furious, believing that the resolution would lose much of its force without British endorsement. He blamed the influence of Nehru who was 'following an appeaser role'.[45] The US had already made it clear that military sanctions against China were not envisaged. Additional measures against China would be political and economic. London would not be expected to break relations with Beijing, nor to impose stricter economic controls than it already enforced. This was a gesture towards fears for the safety of Hong Kong. It was argued that passage of the resolution would remove public pressure for action against China and allow the question to be discussed in a calmer atmosphere.[46] Britain's continued foot-dragging led to the application of the stick as well as the carrot. London was warned that failure to support the US would have grave consequences in the congress on the eve of Eisenhower's crucial report on NATO defence needs.[47]

These internal and external pressures produced a compromise which was endorsed at the UN on 1 February. The revised resolution no longer charged China with having 'rejected' the 'Five Principles' but only with 'not accepting' them. The additional Measures Committee was to be established immediately, as demanded by Washington, but was to defer its report if the Good Offices Committee reported satisfactory progress.[48] Since Washington wanted the gesture rather than concrete measures, it had conceded little. Britain's gesture of independence was thus short-lived. The whole episode showed how small was the area of manouevre open to the major allies. Few shared the US attitude towards China, but none could finally contemplate a break on the issue. The US was vital to global security against the Soviet Union. In contemplating a gesture of independence, Britain merely came face to face with its dependence on American military and financial aid. The episode also displayed the difficulties of dealing with China. Washington's intransigence in January 1951 was mirrored in Beijing and there was never any real chance of bringing the two powers together. The problem for the cease-fire group and its supporters was that while the UN was trying to mediate the dispute it was also a protagonist, militarily engaged with Chinese forces. It was difficult for Beijing to accept the bona fides of any UN proposal and difficult also for UN members to avoid the logic of condemning China as an aggressor, since China opposed a UN settlement in Korea.

The Chinese communists did not have to be tools of the Kremlin to demand their own solutions in Korea and the Far East. The cease-fire group and its supporters underestimated the strength of Chinese xenophobia. Emerging from a century of foreign domination, China was determined to reassert its traditional influence in the region against the established power of the US. Although both the US and the UN refused to admit the fact, they were resisting neither 'communism' nor 'aggression' but the re-emergence of China. As long as Chinese armies were advancing, compromise was impossible, and those who attempted to bridge the gap, such as India, were distrusted and condemned by both Washington and Beijing.

British concern about the situation in January 1951 was not misplaced. As Truman confirmed on 9 January, the US intended to hold on in Korea. It remained unclear, however, whether this objective could be achieved. While the State Department emphasised the political importance of holding a line and deflating Chinese prestige, the Pentagon was uncertain whether evacuation could be avoided. Under the influence of MacArthur's pessimistic reports, 'Military chieftains . . . rated as distressingly high the chances that the Chinese would expel UN forces from the Korean peninsula.'[49] Escalation and reinforcement were both ruled out by the need to prepare for global war with the USSR. In these circumstances it was by no means clear that MacArthur could wage a war of attrition without endangering his command. A rout in Korea would jeopardise the defence of Japan for which the Eighth Army remained responsible.

This was an important consideration at a time of increasing tension with the Soviet Union. Japan was the key to the strategic position in the Far East.[50]

On 29 December MacArthur received a directive which represented an uneasy compromise between the political imperatives of the State Department and the military pessimism of the JCS. He was ordered to defend successive positions, inflicting maximum casualties on the enemy, without endangering his own command or the defence of Japan. At the same time, the directive recognised that a point might be reached beyond which orderly evacuation would prove impossible. The JCS suggested the Kum river line and noted that if Chinese forces began massing to assault this position, it would be necessary to 'commence withdrawal to Japan'. MacArthur's views were invited on the conditions which should trigger evacuation.[51]

The directive provoked an extended debate with MacArthur which reflected the familiar argument over priorities. The general placed the demands of the war he was fighting above preparation for a hypothetical future conflict with the USSR. The Far East was being neglected while the US mobilised to support Eisenhower in Europe. As MacArthur argued on 30 December, European security was important, but not at the price of accepting defeat everywhere else. Washington was retreating from victory in Asia and placing an unfair burden on his headquarters. He was ordered to resist in Korea without endangering his command or the security of Japan which remained 'paramount'. It was the General's contention that these objectives were incompatible. If he was to fight it out under existing restrictions, Washington must take responsibility for the consequences. The future of his command must be governed by a clear-cut strategic/political decision at the highest level rather than by a vague and contradictory exhortion to 'deflate the military and political prestige of the Chinese Communists . . . if this could be done without incurring serious losses'.[52]

In MacArthur's opinion, the only choices remained escalation or evacuation. On 30 December he replied to his directive recommending blockade and bombing of China coupled with the use of Guomindong forces against the mainland.[53] When Washington reiterated his existing orders on 9 January, the General requested 'clarification'. According to MacArthur, the administration must decide whether it wished to hold for an indefinite or limited period or to minimise casualties by evacuation. It could not have *both* continuing resistance under existing restrictions *and* a force capable of defending Japan. His command could fight on the peninsula 'for any length of time up to its complete destruction if overriding political considerations so dictate.'[54]

It seemed as if military reality might soon produce convergence between MacArthur and Washington. When the General's request for 'clarification' arrived, the administration was at its 'lowest point'. Seoul had fallen and the retreat seemed likely to reach the Kum river, suggested earlier by the JCS as the last line of resistance.[55] On 11 January MacArthur's directive was repeated for the third time. This was followed by a personal letter from Truman emphasising the importance to global strategy of holding a line in Korea.[56] Despite these exhortations, it seemed as if the UN command was on the brink of defeat and evacuation. As the JCS remarked when reiterating MacArthur's orders, on the basis of available military information protracted resistance appeared to be impossible.[57] Plans were under consideration to evacuate the Korean government and army and to continue the struggle from Cheju-do and other islands.[58] According to Truman, if forced from the peninsula, 'we shall not accept the result either politically or militarily until the aggression has been rectified.'[59]

On 12 January Generals Collins and Vandenberg were despatched to the Far East to assess the situation. It was reported that they arrived in Tokyo convinced that evacuation was inevitable.[60] Collins carried with him a JCS options paper which discussed further measures against China. These included the preparation of a naval blockade, to be imposed when the front had stabilised or UN forces had been driven from Korea, and the removal of restrictions on air reconnaisance of the China coast and Manchuria. It also suggested that the US provide logistics support for Guomindong operations against the mainland and for nationalist guerrillas in south China. US air and naval attacks were ruled out unless China retaliated on US forces outside Korea.[61] Such an escalation might have become inevitable, however, once a policy of military sanctions was initiated. It was this possibility which obsessed Britain and other allies at the UN.

At the later MacArthur hearings the General wilfully misinterpreted this document, claiming that the JCS approved his views on expanding the war. In the light of his military directive and the message from Truman which arrived in Tokyo around the same time, it is difficult to understand how he could have made a genuine error. As Marshall argued in rebuttal, the document was a contingency paper, never approved at high level. It was intended to relate to a situation where evacuation came 'close to reality'.[62] It has been argued, however, that when Collins and Vandenberg flew to Tokyo, such a possibility was being taken seriously. The proposals were a good deal less tentative than they were made to appear at the later hearings. It had been clear since December that, in the event of expulsion, Washington could not simply walk away and accept defeat at the hands of China. National pride and domestic and international credibility would demand retaliation. Thus, in January 1951 the administration may have been 'on the verge of ordering a dramatic expansion of hostilities in East Asia'.[63]

The crisis, however, was quickly defused by the stabilisation of the military situation which rendered the JCS paper 'inoperative'. It was never submitted to the National Security Council. By the time Collins and Vandenberg returned to the US, it had become clear that the Chinese could not drive the UN command from the peninsula.[64] MacArthur's reporting had been unnecessarily pessimistic, reflecting a desire to bolster his argument that there was no choice but escalation or evacuation. While underestimating the impact of air power on lengthening Chinese supply lines, the General had exaggerated the erosion in the morale and efficiency of his command.[65] Under its new leader, General Ridgway, the Eighth Army was preparing to counter-attack, an operation which began on 24 January. A paratroop officer during the Second World War, Ridgway had been groomed for high office at the Pentagon as Deputy Chief of Staff for Operations. He had taken command of the Eighth Army following the death of General Walker in a jeep accident on 22 December.[66] A representative of the dominant Europe first group, Ridgway could be relied upon to understand the importance of avoiding a wider war with China. From the beginning, he was determined to fight it out under existing restrictions. On 17 January, after witnessing what Ridgway had already achieved, Collins reported: 'Eighth Army in good shape and improving daily. . . . Morale very satisfactory considering conditions.'[67] As Acheson later sourly remarked, while MacArthur was fighting Washington, Ridgway was fighting the war.[68] The episode destroyed MacArthur's credibility, already under strain since the events of December. He would never again enjoy a decisive voice with the JCS.[69]

Although no longer regarded as infallible by Washington, the victor of Inchon remained a powerful political factor. As long as the 'Great Debate' continued, an open breach with the General might have unacceptable repercussions in Congress. Moreover, MacArthur represented an element of stability in Japan during the crucial negotiations for a peace treaty. His delicate handling by Washington during the January crisis reflected an awareness of the damage he could do by resignation. It proved impossible, however, to contain MacArthur within the parameters of established policy. A lull in February 1951 proved merely the prelude to an open confrontation with the General which was to provoke his recall and a political storm in the US.

The improving military situation in February/March 1951 raised anew the problem of the 38th parallel. There was a clear consensus amongst the major allies against any new offensive into North Korea which might again expose UN forces to disaster or make it impossible for Beijing to negotiate without loss of face. This view was shared in Washington. It had been clear since December 1950 that the administration would accept a stalemate and a return to the status quo as the price of avoiding a wider war. On 16 February Rusk informed the UN allies that no major operations in North Korea were planned. He did not rule out crossing the parallel for tactical reasons but promised to consult before any action was taken.[70] It proved difficult, however, to produce a formal change in MacArthur's orders which, despite later additions, remained based on the military directive of 27 September.[71]

In February 1951 a 'peculiar minuet' occurred between the State and Defense Departments on the subject of Korea. Neither wished to assume formal responsibility for accepting a stalemate. While the Pentagon insisted on political guidance, State demanded an estimate of military capabilities on which to form a judgement. Neither 'would make definitive recommendations in its own field without the conclusions of the other'.[72] The JCS had sound military reasons for wishing to avoid a halt at the parallel. As the Pentagon insisted, any decision would be 'premature' until MacArthur had developed the main line of enemy resistance. Nor should the Chinese be allowed a safe haven from the attrition imposed by Ridgway's combined operations.[73] At the same time, there was clear evidence of evasion of responsibility. With the 'Great Debate' still in progress, the Pentagon did not wish to assume responsibility for shackling MacArthur with further restrictions, disrupting the uneasy calm between Washington and Tokyo. As Rusk noted on 20 February, while the JCS opposed a major crossing of the parallel, they were unsure of how to handle the situation with MacArthur.[74]

As UN forces approached the parallel in early March, however, State and Defense achieved a broad consensus. While the objective in

Korea was to regain control of territory south of the parallel, it was not to constitute a barrier to military operations. The UN command would wage an aggressive defense, penetrating up to twenty miles inside North Korea. As UN forces approached the parallel, a new appeal would be issued for a cease-fire. If this were rejected, maximum attrition would be imposed on the enemy without 'a general advance . . . [or] military actions directly against mainland China'.[75] This agreement provided the basis for a National Security Council decision in May and a new military directive.[76] By that stage, however, MacArthur was no longer in command.

On 19 March, a draft announcement was prepared for Truman to issue as UN forces approached the parallel. This was intended as much to reassure allies such as Britain as to appeal to the Chinese. It was suspected in Washington that Chinese withdrawal behind the parallel was the prelude to a new offensive. In these circumstances, a declaration was 'useful and necessary' since it would prove that Beijing and not Washington was responsible for continuing the war.[77] The planned appeal kept within the parameters of the Five Principles which the US had accepted in January. It noted that with UN forces approaching the 38th parallel, the UN command was prepared to enter into arrangements which would 'conclude the fighting and ensure against its resumption'. A cease-fire would pave the way to a Korean settlement and consideration of 'other problems' in the Far East.[78] This represented an attempt to fulfil the demands of both international and domestic politics. China was given a hint that issues such as Taiwan would be considered without committing Washington to any concrete concessions.

The proposed initiative brought an open breach with MacArthur which had been avoided in January. It symbolised Washington's readiness to accept stalemate, a concept which he had already condemned on 13 February as 'wholly unrealistic and illusory'. In a press interview on 15 March which breached the presidential directive of 6 December on unauthorised statements, he gave a broad interpretation of war aims, arguing that his command should not be ordered to halt short of 'accomplishment of our mission . . . the unification of Korea'.[79] These transgressions had been ignored by his superiors. Informed of the President's planned statement on 20 March, however, MacArthur took a step which could not be overlooked. He sabotaged the cease-fire initiative, precipitating a crisis in his relations with Washington, alarm amongst the UN allies and a new political furore in the United States.

On 24 March, MacArthur issued his own statement on Korea which cut across the presidential plan. He claimed that recent tactical successes had proved that Chinese manpower could not prevail against the technical resources available to the UN command. China was incapable of waging modern war. The enemy must be 'painfully aware' that if prevailing restrictions were lifted, 'an expansion of our military operations to his coastal areas, and interior bases, would doom Red China to the risk of imminent military collapse.' The Korean problem could therefore be settled on its own merits, without being burdened by 'extraneous matters' such as Taiwan or Beijing's claim to a UN seat. MacArthur was ready to confer with the enemy commander in the field to find a means by which UN objectives in Korea could be realised. This statement amounted to a demand that Beijing admit defeat.[80] No attempt was made to save Chinese face by compromise. Instead China was invited to renounce aggression or accept destruction. The effect was to torpedo Washington's planned initiative. Beijing could not respond without appearing to defer to the threat of American power.[81]

MacArthur's action has been a source of controversy ever since. At the MacArthur hearings, the General denied any political intent. His statement had been 'merely a notice' that 'every field commander at any time can put out'.[82] In October 1951, however, he informed the VFW that he had uncovered one of the most 'disgraceful plots' in American history. The administration planned a sell-out in the Far East.[83] This account seems nearer the truth. The General was deliberately torpedoing a move which would stop short of victory and leave the communists in control of North Korea. From the beginning he had believed that the war was about rollback and not about repelling aggression. Moreover, he suspected that any deal would involve Taiwan, endangering the survival of Jiang's regime which he saw as the key to liberation of Asia. The statement not only made Chinese rejection of a cease-fire inevitable but also opened up once more the prospect of a wider war. It was an appeal to the public to support Republican demands for attacks on the Chinese mainland. This strategy was linked to his own military and political prospects. The General wanted both victory and the Republican nomination in 1952. He could not bear to 'end his career in checkmate'.[84]

The MacArthur initiative alarmed the allies and raised questions about the control of US foreign policy. London was already concerned about MacArthur's earlier statements and the delay in changing his military directive.[85] Moreover, ministers were conscious of the lack of progress on the Good Offices Committee and US pressure for additional measures. A combination of MacArthur and domestic political pressures might yet lead to a dangerous escalation in Korea. Canadian officials were similarly preoccupied.[86] The planned presidential statement was therefore welcome. As the new British Foreign Secretary, Morrison, informed the Cabinet on 22 March, unless some fresh step were taken, there was a risk that MacArthur would 'again advance North of the 38th parallel and seek to justify that course on military grounds'.[87] Britain was working on its own plan for a statement by the sixteen nations contributing troops to the UN force. This would parallel Truman's initiative and provide the basis for a new approach to Moscow and Beijing.[88]

MacArthur's action undermined the confidence in US policy which the administration had been trying to build since December, a confidence necessary for the future of NSC-68. On 31 March the Canadian Foreign Minister, Pearson, publicly warned of the dangers to 'free world unity' which arose when those charged by the UN with military responsibility went 'far beyond that responsibility' making 'controversial statements' which created 'confusion, disquiet and even discord'.[89] In response to protests by the British ambassador, an embarrassed Rusk could only admit that the whole incident was unauthorised. Steps would be taken to ensure that it did not happen again. At the same time, he held out no promise that MacArthur would be curbed. As he remarked, the administration was:

> faced with a bitter dilemma. On the one hand, MacArthur had made a statement entirely at variance with their policy. On the other hand, the political situation . . . was such that were they explicitly to disown him, the whole of their foreign policy might be jeopardised, including troops for Europe . . . the state of Congress had never been more deplorable and difficult. They had accordingly decided to 'roll with the situation' and hope that the Easter holidays and other preoccupations would help them to control it.

He drew the moral that everyone should 'speed the conclusion' of the Japanese peace treaty, implying that this would ease the way towards MacArthur's graceful retirement.[90]

This apparent paralysis of will was hardly reassuring, particularly when new military moves were under consideration. At the beginning of April, Washington, worried by the continuing build-up of Chinese aircraft in Manchuria and Shantung, proposed granting the UN commander authority to retaliate in the event of a mass air attack on his forces. It was explained that the directive would be 'kept on ice' and issued by the President only in an emergency.[91] Britain, however, expressed 'serious anxiety' about such a directive. While sympathising with the desire of the JCS to plan for all eventualities, officials distrusted MacArthur. If he learned about the existence of the order, he might use it to justify widening the war. Washington would find it difficult to resist a claim that an emergency existed. As Field Marshal Slim, Chief of the Imperial General Staff, remarked, the JCS could not be trusted: 'They were scared of General MacArthur: his definition of the scope of an air attack would be what they would work on and this definition might be coloured to suit his own wishes.' An attack on Manchuria might involve Britain in global war. The government remained conscious of the Soviet warning that air strikes across the Yalu would engage the Russian air force in defence of China.[92]

A second source of concern was a US naval demonstration off the Chinese coast scheduled to begin on 7 April. It was feared in London that this was part of an attempt by MacArthur to build up a case for extending the war. He was exaggerating Chinese air strength for his own purposes, while seeking an incident which would present Washington with a fait accompli. A clash off Foochow would be followed by claims of Chinese air attacks in Korea, justifying retaliation on the grounds that Beijing had widened the war. The domestic political situation would make it difficult for Washington to resist.[93] It was reported, wrongly, that the cruiser HMS *Belfast* had been ordered to join the naval demonstration, breaching the agreement that MacArthur controlled British units only in support of the UN mission in Korea.[94] Britain protested about the naval moves, arguing that it was not the time to provoke Beijing. On 5 April Franks informed Rusk that London was suffering from a severe bout of 'MacArthuritis'. The fleet operation looked like 'dragging coat tails', inviting the enemy to come out and fight. The government took 'the gravest view' of this move and insisted that Washington assume 'sole responsibility' for any consequences. Rusk's reply that the naval demonstration was a 'reconnaisance', related to the defence of Taiwan, was not reassuring in view of the British belief that MacArthur wanted 'war with China' while 'we do not'.[95]

Although Truman later maintained that from the first he was determined to relieve MacArthur,[96] the initial reaction in Washington was to avoid a break. As Rusk's statement reveals, officials were acutely conscious of the political implications of an open breach with the General. The instinct of the State Department to 'roll with the situation' was shared by Defense. On 24 March Lovett, the Assistant

Secretary, informed Acheson that he had spent an hour discussing MacArthur with the JCS. It was agreed that the General had breached the directive on unauthorised public statements and undermined the planned presidential initiative. He should therefore be relieved at once. The JCS recognised, however, that the consequences would be 'startling', mentioning the Japanese peace treaty and 'other compelling considerations'.[97] The Pentagon had to consider not only the impact on the closing stages of the Great Debate, but also the future of their military appropriations. Concern that the Republicans would retaliate against the financial programmes demanded by NSC-68 remained a powerful consideration throughout the crisis. The JCS therefore recommended a reprimand rather than relief. As Lovett remarked, echoing Rusk, MacArthur's initiative seemed just about the 'most popular public statement anyone ever made'. It offered victory, peace and a quick exit from Korea. If the President challenged it, he would be 'on the side of sin'. MacArthur had 'gotten us . . . in a tight box from which there seems to be no escape'. While Acheson emphasised the importance of preventing further incidents, he could offer no alternative to a reprimand.[98]

On 24 March a message was despatched to MacArthur, calling his attention to the presidential directive of 6 December 1950. He was ordered to coordinate all future statements with Washington.[99] The despatch was clearly intended to be a final warning, building a record which could be used in the future without precipitating a final break. This, however, was not long in coming. On 5 April the Republican minority leader in the house, Joseph Martin, released a letter from MacArthur, critical of administration policy. A strong advocate of unleashing Jiang, Martin had solicited MacArthur's views. On 20 March the General replied expressing agreement and attacking those who placed Europe ahead of the Far East. According to MacArthur, 'If we lose the war to Communism in Asia, the fall of Europe is inevitable. . . . We must win. There is no substitute for victory.'[100]

For the administration, 'the time had come to draw the line'.[101] As Truman noted on 5 April, 'The şituation with regard to the Far Eastern General has become a political one.'[102] Like General McClellan in the civil war, MacArthur had chosen to fight out his differences with the President in the political arena, raising the issue of civilian control of the military.[103] The country could not have two competing foreign policies, one made in Tokyo and the other in Washington. As Acheson remarked, the question was no longer whether MacArthur should go but how it was to be achieved.[104] Truman refused to act precipitately and sought the advice of his leading officials before revealing his own decision on 9 April. It was vital to establish a consensus. As Acheson emphasised, a grave political crisis was inevitable. It could only be surmounted, if the President 'acted upon the carefully considered advice and unshakeable support of all his civilian and military advisors'.[105] It is clear from Acheson's memoirs that the very survival of the administration was believed to be at stake.

As Acheson also emphasised, the JCS played a crucial role in the MacArthur crisis. All Truman's civilian advisers agreed that the General must go, but the Pentagon had to be mobilised in support of this position. Without the active approval of the JCS, the removal of MacArthur would appear to be merely an act of political retribution. It would be more difficult for the Republicans to argue with the military judgement of the General's colleagues. A meeting of the chiefs could not be arranged until 8 April since only Bradley was in Washington. In the interim, he represented the military view. Bradley was plainly reluctant to take decisive action. Although the Great Debate had petered out on 2 April, he continued to fear a congressional assault on military programmes if MacArthur was recalled. Moreover, he hesitated to become associated with a political issue, fearing that the JCS would be accused of playing politics as much as MacArthur. Bradley wished the chiefs to remain non-partisan to protect their position in Congress.

His first instinct was to draft a letter to MacArthur, pointing out that he was embarrassing the administration. Since this was exactly what the General had set out to achieve, it is unclear what impact he expected it to have.[106] On 6 April he suggested another compromise. MacArthur should be recalled for 'consultation' before further action was taken. As Acheson noted, this was the road to political disaster: 'To get him back to Washington in the full panoply of his commands and with his future the issue of the day would not only gravely impair the President's freedom of decision but might well imperil his own future.[107] On 8 April, the chiefs were formally asked for their opinions on the relief of MacArthur. It was agreed that this was justified on military grounds. The JCS cited his lack of sympathy with limitation of the war and his failure to obey the presidential directive on public statements. The retaliatory bombing of Manchuria was also mentioned. It was noted that a directive could not be issued to MacArthur for fear that he would make 'a premature decision' in carrying it out.[108] This reveals the collapse of confidence which had occurred since December 1950. By the chiefs' own admission, the commander in the Far East was a soldier who could not be trusted. He might plunge the US into global war in pursuit of policies already vetoed by Washington.

On 9 April, with his civilian and military advisers in agreement, Truman directed the preparation of orders recalling MacArthur and replacing him with Ridgway.[109] These were completed on 10 April and transmitted over civilian lines to the embassy in Korea for Frank Pace, the Secretary of the Army, who was visiting the front. Pace was to fly to Tokyo and deliver the orders directly to MacArthur. It was decided that this method would save the General the embarrassment of direct communication through military channels with the 'inevitable leaks of such interesting news'.[110] Washington was anxious to save MacArthur's dignity for political reasons. It did not wish to worsen the inevitable political storm by appearing to insult a figure whom many regarded as America's greatest soldier. At the same time, the administration could not afford a premature leak which would allow MacArthur time to resign. This would give the General the initiative and deprive the President of the issue on which he intended to fight: civilian control of the military.

This fear led to a last-minute change of plan. It proved difficult to communicate with Pusan and in the early evening of 10 April, the White House picked up a press rumour that an 'important resignation' was expected in Tokyo. As the President's press secretary noted, if true, this would allow MacArthur to 'get [the] jump' on Truman and fight the President on the ground of 'serious blunders in foreign affairs'.[111] In order to avert this danger, the orders relieving the General were hastily transmitted direct to Tokyo and the press informed in the early hours of 11 April. As Truman informed Bradley, 'The son of a bitch isn't going to resign on me, *I want him fired.*'[112] The President had finally sacked MacArthur but had acted in a way which many regarded as precipitate and insulting.

6 Attrition

A political storm followed MacArthur's dismissal.[1] The Republicans seized on the issue as part of their strategy to discredit the administration before the presidential elections of 1952. MacArthur was portrayed as a martyr to Truman's appeasement of Asian communism.[2] On 11 April Republican leaders announced that the General had been invited to address Congress and called for an enquiry into US policy in the Far East. The tremendous popularity of the victor of Inchon made it difficult for the Democrats to resist.[3] The MacArthur hearings, which began on 3 May, vindicated Truman but at the expense of emphasising the collapse of bipartisanship. The committee split along party lines, the Republicans issuing a minority report, critical of US policy in the Far East.[4] In Western capitals, relief at Truman's decision was tempered by concern at the crisis which followed. The Canadians were worried by the 'tumultuous welcome' received by the General on his return and by the 'erratic and emotional atmosphere' in the US.[5] The British ambassador, Franks, warned London to expect a difficult few weeks.[6] MacArthur had made no secret of his distrust of Britain and his partisans charged London with complicity in his dismissal. Morrison, anxious to avoid British involvement in domestic politics, warned Labour MPs not to 'crow' over MacArthur's removal.[7] Only in the Far East was MacArthur missed. He had run Japan since 1945 and was an early advocate of a peace treaty. Dulles was quickly despatched to Tokyo to reassure the Japanese.[8] Jiang and Rhee, however, lost an outspoken champion. MacArthur's removal symbolised Washington's determination to limit the conflict in Asia and its reluctance to fight the Korean and Chinese civil wars on their behalf.

In his address to Congress and at the subsequent hearings, MacArthur defended his record while seeking public support for escalation. From the beginning, his position was uncritically endorsed by the Republicans. As Taft announced on 27 April, he had 'no difficulty whatever' in lining up with the General.[9] There was a strong element of opportunism in this alliance. MacArthur had always supported Truman's decision to intervene and quarrelled with the administration only because it was retreating from victory. Republican spokesmen, attempting to capitalise on disillusion with the war after November 1950, had not only condemned Truman for committing US troops but had called for evacuation. Only on the issue of unleashing Jiang had they displayed any consistency. This, however, was not allowed to impede Republican endorsement of MacArthur, who was a useful tool in election strategy. The party was less interested in defeating communism in Asia than in beating the Democrats in 1952.[10]

At the hearings, MacArthur launched an attack on the doctrine of limited war which he defined as 'appeasement'. According to the General, China was engaged in an all-out effort in Korea. By continuing to impose restrictions on American power, Washington was fighting on enemy terms. There were only three alternatives – victory, stalemate or 'yielding'. By opting for stalemate, the administration retreated in the face of aggression at great moral and physical cost. The war had no political objective and was thus difficult to justify. Its sole purpose was attrition, killing Chinese until Beijing tired of the struggle. MacArthur emphasised that this strategy worked both ways. By going on 'accordion fashion' with 'no mission for the troops except to resist and fight' the administration risked 'staggering' accumulative losses. The Chinese, with an unlimited pool of manpower, could afford attrition while the US could not. Washington would throw away lives and money only to be ultimately forced back on the two other alternatives which offered a definitive end to the war. There was no substitute for victory.[11]

MacArthur offered his own prescription for ending the agony of Korea. His strategy involved blockade, bombing and the use of Guomindong troops against the Chinese mainland. More Korean units would also be raised. This would ally American technology with Asian manpower. The US would no longer fight on enemy terms but would seize the initiative and carry the war to China. He had no doubts about Jiang's ability to defeat the communists. Guomindong forces were 'excellent'; 'It would have been a 100 per cent different picture if they had not been held in leash.' The General denied that it was a matter of choosing between Europe and Asia. It was simply a matter of dropping inhibitions and using the 'maximum force we have'. He offered a heady vision of liberated Asia, won at minimum cost in American lives and money.[12]

MacArthur claimed that the JCS agreed with his concept of broadening the war, citing the options list of 12 January brought to Tokyo by Collins and Vandenberg. He implied that the Pentagon had been overruled at higher civilian levels.[13] It is difficult to understand how MacArthur could have misread a document which pertained to future contingences and not to current policy as laid down in his directive and in the President's letter of 13 January. Both made it clear that the US would not escalate the war unless driven from the peninsula.[14] At times the chiefs had come close to endorsing his approach as an act of desperation. Sherman and Vandenberg in particular had flirted with the idea of an air and naval war against China in December 1950. The options list itself was drawn up when expulsion from Korea was not inconceivable.[15] At no time, however, had the JCS endorsed MacArthur. The whole thrust of the debate in January 1951 was to emphasise their reluctance to broaden the war except as a last resort. If MacArthur believed that his colleagues would support him at the hearings, he was to be disappointed. Truman had already secured the approval of the JCS for the recall of the General.

The administration's strategy at the hearings was to emphasise the risks of MacArthur's approach. While the polls showed widespread sympathy for the General, they also reflected public reluctance to become involved in global war. 'Belligerent escalation' had a quick appeal unless it was suggested that 'such a policy might have some undesirable side effects'.[16] As the Acting Secretary of the Army, Alexander, noted on 12 April, if the issue was defined in terms of limited or global war, 'between 80 and 82%' would support Truman.[17] Thus administration witnesses denied that MacArthur's strategy was the key to cheap and easy victory. Bradley doubted that air and naval power alone could defeat China. The US would have to invade, exposing itself to the exhaustive and inconclusive struggle which had faced Japan after 1937. If the US became bogged down in China, more important areas of the globe would be exposed to Soviet power.[18] This was a theme echoed by Vandenberg, who maintained that using the air force to 'peck at the periphery' was a poor strategy. He could 'lay waste' Chinese cities, but only at the cost of unacceptable attrition which would render his command incapable of deterring the Soviet Union. His 'shoestring' air force would not fight both Russia and China.[19] Vandenberg thus skilfully transformed his testimony into an undisguised appeal for increased appropriations. If the Republicans wished to fight China, they would have to will the means. If air and naval power proved indecisive, so also would the use of Guomindong and Korean troops. As Marshall remarked, committing a nationalist force would strip Taiwan of the 'core of its defense'. Nor were Guomindong troops likely to perform well in Korea. Their use against the mainland would only draw in the US: 'Chinese nationalist forces have not the ability to sustain an operation without getting so involved that we would be drawn into their support.'[20] Bradley stressed that the

first task was to equip Guomindong units to defend Taiwan. At present
their leadership and training was poor. As for Jiang, he had already
had 'a big chance to win in China' and could not do it. He was 'not in a
position to rally the Chinese people against the communists' even if
'we could get him ashore'.[21] MacArthur's argument that the Koreans
were 'very fine troops' was also dismissed. As Collins emphasised,
they had a dismal record in the field. Every time they were 'hit by the
Chinamen, they just plain run'.[22] On this subject, MacArthur had
displayed an ability to ignore his own recent recommendations. In
January 1951, he had opposed arming more Korean divisions because
of the weak performance of existing units.[23]

Administration witnesses emphasised the risks, not only of
becoming involved in an indecisive struggle with China but also of
provoking global war. According to Marshall, MacArthur's strategy
would have the US risk 'all-out war with the Soviet Union'. They
denied that China was engaged in total war. As Vandenberg
remarked, 'this sanctuary business . . . is operating on both sides'.
According to Bradley, the US was operating under 'rather favorable
ground rules'. The enemy had not committed his air power against 'our
front line troops, our ports . . . our bases in Japan or our naval forces.'
As long as the UN command was not 'suffering too much' from
restricting the war, it was best not to risk involving the USSR by
bombing Manchuria. A showdown with the communist bloc was
undesirable until the US had completed its rearmament. It was safer to
respond to limited aggression with limited force. Admittedly this
carried the risk of global war but it had yet to involve the US in
disaster.[24]

MacArthur's claim that a stalemate would produce an indefinite war
of attrition and staggering US casualties was also contested. While the
hearings were in session, Ridgway smashed two massive Chinese
offensives in April and May, rolling with the punch and exposing the
enemy to the crippling effects of air power and artillery. By 30 May he
could report a 'noticeable deterioration' in the fighting spirit of the
Chinese army. It was no longer capable of launching large offensives
south of the 38th parallel.[25] These successes supported official
confidence that an 'offensive defense' would bring the enemy to terms.
As Marshall argued, Beijing could not afford to go on losing
manpower at the current rate. According to Acheson, it was not a
question merely of manpower but of trained manpower and material
which China was using up at a tremendous pace. Beijing had already

sacrificed economic and social improvement to the demands of the war and could not continue to pay the costs indefinitely.[26]

Although testimony was censored, officials were dismayed by the amount of sensitive information they were asked to reveal. As the Deputy Secretary of Defense complained, the hearings were contributing to the enemy's knowledge 'in a shocking manner'. US security had been 'thrown . . . into a state of jeopardy never approached in our history'.[27] There was an element of exaggeration in this lament, since Moscow was doubtless already aware of the broad outlines of US policy. In some senses, the censorship which did exist operated to the political advantage of the opposition. The official view of Jiang and his forces was not published lest it assist the enemy. As Marshall remarked, such revelations would improve the prospects of the communists while 'wrecking' morale on Taiwan.[28] The Republicans could thus continue their pursuit of a mythical free China un-hampered by public knowledge of the real situation.

Whatever the threat of the hearings to national security, they offered the administration an opportunity to signal its position to the enemy. Acheson emphasised that Washington would be content with repelling aggression in the South. Neither the US nor the UN were committed to unifying Korea by force. At the same time, it was politically necessary to rule out any form of 'appeasement'. Marshall stressed that the US would never surrender Taiwan or concede a UN seat to China.[29] While his statement reflected established policy, its publication stripped the diplomatic camouflage from US support of the Five Principles. Beijing could no longer be lured towards a cease-fire by the diplomatic carrot of subsequent consideration of wider Far Eastern questions. The alternative, in Vandenberg's stark phrase, was to 'kill as many Chinese as possible', forcing a cease-fire on American terms.[30]

While the hearings were in session, the administration produced a major review of its strategy in the Far East. NSC-48/5 of 17 May 1951 defined as the long-term goal the elimination of Soviet influence in Asia. A series of current objectives included detaching China as an effective ally of the USSR, maintaining the security of the offshore defence perimeter and incorporating a rearmed Japan into the US global security system. In Korea, Washington sought as a minimum a settlement which would leave the ROK in charge of the south and allow the withdrawal of foreign troops. In default of such a settlement, a war of attrition would continue to impose maximum casualties on the enemy without extending the fighting or becoming committed to the forceful unification of the peninsula. Reliable Korean units were to be developed to assume a major role in the war and to deter further aggression from the north in the event of a ceasefire.[31] A start had already been made on improving the South Korean forces. Ridgway's successor at the Eighth Army, Van Fleet, had been selected partly because of his success with a similar programme in Greece.[32] On 4 May, he and Ridgway visited Rhee to complain about the 'grave lack of leadership' in the South Korean army. Rhee, who had been pressing for the mobilisation of ten more divisions, was warned that no equipment would be provided until the problem of leadership was solved.[33] The Americans envisaged the creation of US-managed military schools which would produce a new generation of professional Korean soldier.[34]

As for Taiwan, Guomindong forces were to be equipped and trained along 'somewhat austere lines' as earlier recommended by the JCS.[35] A mission under General Chase had already arrived on the island to oversee the programme and ensure that American assistance was not misused. This reflected ten years' bitter experience of nationalist corruption.[36] Jiang's forces were to be used to defend Taiwan and for other purposes if this proved necessary. NSC-48/5 argued that to prepare for Chinese aggression outside Korea and 'to protect the security of UN and US forces', plans should be prepared for an air and naval blockade of the mainland, military action against targets outside Korea and the use of nationalist forces either 'offensively or defensively'.[37] This represented the latest refinement of the JCS options list of 12 January and revealed unease with the costs of symmetrical response to aggression despite official faith in the continued validity of NSC-68. Washington did not intend to become bogged down in future indecisive ground wars which would drain its resources and divert its forces. In this respect, NSC-48/5 displayed a 'nagging suspicion that Republican critics might be right in charging that the US, by trying to respond symmetrically to proxy aggression, was losing control over the disposition of its own forces and over the expenditures necessary to sustain them.'[38]

NSC-48/5 included an interesting illustration of official thinking about China. While the document called for the detachment of China from the USSR and support for the development of 'an independent China which has renounced aggression', it was by no means clear what kind of regime the US had in mind. The JCS was firmly opposed to dealing with a Chinese Tito. Accepting national communism might be compatible with US interests in Europe but not in the Far East. The Pentagon argued on 15 May that 'An independent Communist China could not help but have a tremendous impact on South-East Asia and would undoubtedly foster the development of communistic governments in that area whether or not under the hegemony of China.'[39] There were hints in NSC-48/5 that Washington hoped to promote some kind of nationalist third force, between the political extremes of the Guomindong and the communists. It was precisely such a force that Roosevelt had attempted to encourage during the Second World War and which Washington regarded as the key to progress in other areas such as Indochina. The document talked about the need to 'expand and intensify . . . efforts to develop non-communist leadership and to influence the leaders and people in China to oppose the present Peiping regime and seek its reorientation or replacement.' Taiwan was to play an important role in this process. Washington was to encourage political changes in the Guomindong regime which would 'increase its prestige and influence in China proper'.[40] As early as April 1951 there were rumours that the US was attempting to promote liberal figures in the nationalist government.[41] This reflected the low official estimate of Jiang's appeal. As Rusk remarked, 'There were very few in Washington who expected that control of the mainland could ever be recovered by the Chinese Nationalists.' It was hoped that a new 'liberal' leadership in Taiwan would encourage the emergence of moderate anti-communists on the mainland. The future would lie in the political amalgamation of the two movements.[42]

Washington was less vague about the means necessary to detach China from the Soviet Union and foster alternative leadership. Force was to be used rather than negotiation. By deflating Chinese prestige, denying China Taiwan and the UN seat and imposing economic and physical attrition on Beijing, the administration hoped to discredit the Moscow faction. As Rusk argued as early as 13 February, the best way of 'unhooking' Beijing from Moscow was to make the Chinese aware of 'the cost of living with the USSR'. While the 'pro-Moscow' faction was currently 'on top' there was 'a strong nationalist element' which might gain ground if the strains of the war continued.[43] Washington attempted to increase the social and economic strains within China. As early as December 1950, the administration had talked about providing assistance to guerrillas on the mainland. Although Truman ruled out requesting UN support for such a programme in his letter to Attlee on 9 January, preparations went ahead for unilateral US action.

On 2 April, the JCS ordered the Pentagon to collaborate with other agencies on the issue. NSC-48/5 called for the US to 'foster and support anti-communist Chinese elements both inside and outside China'. By October 1951 the CIA, with military support, was providing assistance to guerrillas in south China on a high priority basis.[44] It also encouraged raids across the border by Guomindong armies which had taken refuge in Burma after 1949.[45] These were secret programmes, carried out without the official knowledge of the major UN allies, whose opposition was taken for granted.

This China policy suffered from several weaknesses. There was no social basis for a 'third force' in either China or Taiwan. The US mediation effort in the civil war had proved the bankruptcy of the whole approach. In this respect, it was not only the Republicans who were pursuing a mythical China. Even in Taiwan, where US influence was greatest, it proved impossible to take the first steps towards the creation of a liberal regime. Whatever the failings of Jiang as a leader, domestic politics made it impossible openly to contemplate ousting him from his position. Instead, the fiction that he represented the real China had to be maintained. Moreover, US aspirations in China were ultimately incompatible with a cease-fire in the Korean war. A settlement which left Beijing in control of the north was bound to increase the prestige of the regime both internally and throughout Asia. Whatever the costs in terms of Taiwan or domestic reconstruction, the Chinese communists could claim to have saved North Korea and repelled a Western force from their borders, reversing a century of military humiliation. In this respect, NSC-48/5 represented the triumph of hope over reality. Washington might will the end but it hesitated to will the means. The way out of Korea and back to a balanced global strategy lay in compromise with Beijing. At times, officials recognised this unwelcome fact. As Rusk remarked on 13 February, the US wished 'the existing regime in Peking to fall but . . . did not intend to undertake any overt commitment to bring it down.' Washington 'could, however, do something to confuse and impede its activities'.[46] Beneath a veneer of wishful thinking, this was essentially the approach laid out in NSC-48/5.

In the course of the MacArthur hearings, the desire to rebut Republican claims of a planned sell-out in the Far East and the wish to discredit the Moscow faction in Beijing led to a controversial public statement on China. On 18 May Rusk made a speech emphasising that the Guomindong regime represented the authentic views of the Chinese people. The Beijing group could not be regarded as legitimate, since it did not fulfil the first requirement of government, it was not Chinese. According to Rusk, China had become 'a slavic Manchkuo on a gigantic scale'.[47] As early as 13 February, Rusk had confided in the Canadian ambassador that continued recognition of the nationalists was a useful means of pressure on Beijing. The 'anti-Moscow' faction would not welcome derecognition of Jiang, since it would encourage the Stalinists to hope that the US was weakening and strengthen their position.[48] The speech was designed not only to appease domestic critics, but also to push home the fact that recent Chinese battlefield losses were the result of fighting for the USSR. According to Rusk, this might lead China to demonstrate its independence of Moscow.[49]

There was another audience to be considered, however – the Western allies. The speech was alarming since it came in conjunction with the appearance of a US military mission on Taiwan and the emotional political debate in the Far East. As one British official remarked, the statement was a 'bombshell'. Rusk had descended to the level of the MacArthurites 'and beat them at their own game'. His words implied that Washington would not deal with China until it had a regime acceptable to the West.[50] On 22 May Morrison complained that the speech raised forebodings of further action against China and set back the prospects of a settlement. The incident was the final spasm of an Anglo-American debate over the Far East which had continued despite the removal of MacArthur.

If Washington was under domestic pressure to adopt a tough political stance on China, London was equally subject to political pressures. The MacArthur crisis coincided with a major Cabinet row over the costs and implications of NSC-68 which ended with the resignation of the Minister of Labour, Nye Bevan, on 22 April. The ostensible cause was the imposition of prescription charges in Gaitskell's budget of April 1951. Behind this debate, however, lay continued unease about US global policy. A section of the Labour party was unhappy about the pace of rearmament demanded by the Americans and about the impact of US stockpiling on the British and world economies. It disliked German rearmament, accusing Washington of having 'bulldozed' London into accepting the principle in September 1950. It distrusted US policy towards China and moves to revive and rearm Japan. There was believed to be a real danger that American anti-communist hysteria would drag the world into war.[51] Bevan complained that Britain was becoming too subservient. He condemned Gaitskell for 'blindly' accepting an 'impossible rearmament programme'. The Chancellor was 'wildly pro-American and anti-Russian. He was an amateur foreign secretary'.[52] As in January 1951, the division was between those who wished to take an independent line within the Atlantic alliance and those who emphasised the need to maintain American friendship at any price. In April 1951, Crossman noted that the left and right of the party had never been further apart.[53]

In an effort to contain the split, the government pressed Washington to adopt a conciliatory line in the Far East despite the political crisis surrounding the recall of MacArthur. The British demanded a declaration of UN war aims which would offer China a means of ending the fighting without loss of face. London believed that a Five Power conference of Britain, France, the US, the USSR and India might provide the way forward. This group could request the president of the UN General Assembly to appoint a cease-fire committee representing the belligerents. With a cease-fire agreed, the conference could consider a peaceful settlement of the Korean problem, including the withdrawal of foreign troops, elections and unification. The way would then be clear to a discussion of wider Far Eastern problems.[54] The British scheme, which was supported by Australia and Canada, represented an attempt to reconcile the Five Principles with the Chinese note of 22 January. It was also a gesture to domestic opinion. As a British diplomat observed on 17 April, Morrison was under great pressure to make some declaration.[55] The idea, however, was anathema to Washington. As Rusk noted, the US was liable to be outvoted at any Five Power conference, particularly if India was a member. Nehru had long been regarded in Washington as an appeaser.[56] Quite apart from this consideration, any such statement would provide ammunition for MacArthur's Republican supporters, who claimed that the administration planned a 'sell-out' in the Far East.

This was not the only source of friction. Britain quibbled over the Japanese peace treaty, raising the issue of which government, communist or Guomindong, should sign for China.[57] It continued to dispute the need to concede in advance the right of the UN commander in Korea to bomb Manchurian airfields in the event of a heavy air attack against his forces.[58] It attempted to put a brake on the activities of the Additional Measures Committee, despite the failure of the Good Offices Committee to make any progress. Britain feared that a general embargo would split the UN, since India and the Arab–Asian bloc would refuse to comply. Moreover, it was reluctant to take any further step to alienate China.[59]

Acheson was infuriated with Britain. On 2 April he accused London of obstructing US policy and raised the possibility of 'real trouble' in Anglo-American relations. He asked Franks if the government was being 'blackmailed' by the Labour left. Acheson was particularly critical of the situation in Hong Kong. It was believed that the colony had become a major loophole in the Western embargo on the export of strategic goods to China. Trade with the mainland had risen since December 1950.[60] On 28 March the JCS noted 'with alarm' an increase in strategic exports to China and asked the State Department to press for the Western powers to deny all commodities which could be used in military operations.[61] Although Britain disputed the US figures and emphasised that the colony depended on the China trade, the administration remained dissatisfied. Acheson bitterly remarked that 'while we were losing people in Korea', Hong Kong was enjoying a 'boom'.[62] The political crisis caused by the recall of MacArthur increased US determination to bring Britain into line. Further foot-dragging would play into Republican hands by confirming doubts about the value of alliances and collective security. On 17 April Acheson argued that Washington must 'cash in' on the removal of MacArthur.[63] If Britain was being 'blackmailed' by the Labour left, he would invoke the danger of the Republican right.

The resignation of Bevan on 22 April cleared the way to accommodation with the US. The dominant group had always argued that a breach with Washington in the Far East would play into Republican hands and weaken the Atlantic alliance on which British security depended. Gaitskell had argued along such lines in January 1951. Similar fears moved Australia and Canada closer to the US position in the face of the 'extreme pressures' building up against the administration.[64] As the Canadian ambassador pointed out on 14 May, the 'leading figures' in the Departments of State and Defense were 'The victims and not the causes of domestic confusions . . . it is greatly in the interest of Canada and other countries of the free world not to add to their difficulties by furnishing ammunition to their domestic critics.'[65] It was not only a desire to appease American opinion that produced compromise in the Far East, but also the futility of straining the Western alliance on behalf of China. Since January 1951 Beijing had made no attempt to respond to the UN outside the battlefield. It was difficult to argue against additional measures or in favour of a UN declaration while China rejected compromise and continued its efforts to expel the UN from Korea. As Acheson argued on 30 April, it was difficult to see how the measures envisaged by Washington could make China more hostile to the West.[66] In a speech at Cardiff on 8 April, the British Minister of State, Younger, noted the difficulties of dealing with Beijing. Anglo-American differences existed over China but 'He felt bound to say that the Peking Government had not done much to help us convince our American friends that they were wrong.'[67] On 3 May the Foreign Office lamented Chinese xenophobia and Beijing's apparent determination to 'eliminate most trace of Western ideas and influence'.[68] In the British case, a final reason for compromise lay in the Middle East crisis which followed Iranian nationalisation of the oil industry on 2 May. While London favoured forceful measures, Washington advocated compromise. Ironically, Acheson adopted the argument employed by the British in the case of China, emphasising the need to appease nationalism, lest Iran be forced into the hands of the Soviet Union.[69] Morrison may have hoped to trade British support for the US position in the Far East for American support in Iran. He was to be disappointed.

By early May, Britain had conceded to the US position on a range of issues concerning China. At the beginning of the month, the government announced an embargo on further sales of rubber to China through Hong Kong.[70] At the same time, it accepted Acheson's argument that as long as China continued to fight, the UN must show no signs of weakness. On the understanding that a selective embargo on the export of war materials was not the entering wedge for a general ban, Britain supported such a recommendation by the Additional Measures Committee on 17 May.[71] Morrison also agreed that the UN commander should have the right to retaliate against Manchuria in the event of a sudden air attack. In this he bowed to the inevitable, since a directive along such lines had already been issued to Ridgway on 28 April. The Foreign Secretary, however, stressed that agreement in principle did not waive Britain's right to consultation. Bombing was an issue of war or peace and any decision must be cleared with the Prime Minister.[72] Washington refused to commit itself on this question which was allowed to die away in October, partly because the US might demand a similar right in the event of British action against Iran.[73] London also moved towards the US position on Taiwan and the UN seat. In order to counter MacArthur's claim that Britian wanted to hand the island over to the 'Red enemy', Morrison made a speech emphasising that while the government stood by the Cairo declaration, it did not favour conceding Taiwan as long as the Korean war lasted. Once the fighting was over, the question might be considered by the UN.[74] On 11 May Morrison expressed interest in an American suggestion that there should be a 'moratorium' on the problem of the UN seat.[75] Britain had always maintained that Beijing was entitled to representation as the legal government of China. In September 1950 it had voted in favour of an Indian resolution to seat communist delegates as Chinese representatives in the General Assembly.[76] As Morrison noted, however, while the legal position remained clear, he did not wish in present circumstances to display 'any enthusiasm' for the communist cause.[77] On 5 June Britain voted to postpone consideration of the issue at a meeting of the UN Trusteeship Council. According to Younger, this step was taken because Chinese action in Korea was 'inconsistent with the principles and purposes of the Charter'.[78]

In June 1951 the problem of the Japanese peace treaty was finally solved. It was agreed that neither China would be invited to sign, the question being left up to Japan to solve by subsequent bilateral agreement. As for Taiwan, Tokyo would simply renounce sovereignty, evading the question of which Chinese government was entitled to the island.[79] The government recognised that this was the best arrangement which could be made. As Dulles explained, the treaty would not be ratified by the Senate if it appeared to appease the Beijing regime. He assured London that Washington had no intention of forcing an alignment between Japan and Taiwan, which would raise the spectre of the Sino-Soviet pact of 1950. Morrison argued that dropping the inclusion of the Guomindong was a 'courageous decision' in view of the state of American politics. Britain must not let the chance of a compromise slip.[80] By the end of the spring, therefore, Anglo-American differences in the Far East had been put into 'cold storage'.[81]

While bringing its allies into line, the administration was attempting to establish contact with its enemies. A firm and unified stand by the Western powers was regarded as fundamental to the success of this effort. In May 1951 Charles Marshall, of the Policy Planning Staff, visited Hong Kong to establish contact with Chinese factions opposed to the war. Washington had picked up rumours of divisions between Mao and Zhou and hoped to drive in a wedge which might end the fighting.[82] In talks with shadowy Chinese intermediaries, he outlined American readiness to compromise in Korea, while emphasising the attractions of MacArthurism if the American people did not see quick results. This approach proved ineffective.[83] Contacts with the Russians, however, produced better returns.

On 2 May Malik, the Soviet ambassador to the UN, offered two junior US diplomats a ride into Manhattan. A general conversation occurred during which the Americans insisted that the US desired a peaceful settlement in Korea. Malik was non-committal but hinted that the issue might be settled by discussion. The terms would have to be acceptable to all the interested parties.[84] It was suggested at the State Department, however, that Malik's gesture might indicate a desire to improve relations. Washington should follow up the opening rather than continue to play 'blind man's bluff' with the Soviet Union. It was suggested that an approach be made by Kennan, who was on leave of absence from the State Department. Such a semi-official feeler could later be disowned if necessary.[85] The first meeting between Kennan and Malik took place on 31 May. Kennan emphasised the dangers of a 'collision' over Korea. Washington wished to avoid such a development but it might become inevitable if Beijing persisted with its present course. The best means of averting this danger lay in a cease-fire.[86] At a second meeting, on 5 June, Malik agreed that his government desired a peaceful settlement.[87] The terms which Moscow envisaged were made public in Malik's famous UN radio broadcast on 23 June which called for 'Discussions . . . between the belligerents for a ceasefire and an armistice providing for mutual withdrawal from the 38th Parallel.'[88] After enquiries by the US embassy in Moscow, Gromyko confirmed that the statement represented the official Soviet view.[89] It was an important breakthrough since it indicated that the Russians would not support Chinese demands for political preconditions on Taiwan and the UN seat.

Washington was determined to conduct negotiations through the commanders in the field. In this way it could guarantee control. At the UN, there was always a risk that political questions would be raised and that the allies would speak with different voices, offering openings to Soviet diplomacy. As Acheson remarked, the US experience in December 1950 convinced the administration that 'the UN was the worst of all places to conduct discussions'.[90] Moreover, a strictly military approach allowed Washington to avoid dealing with Beijing on an official basis. Chinese forces were technically 'volunteers', acting on their own responsibility. As Gromyko pointed out, however, their commander could speak for them.[91] The arrangement also protected the administration on the home front. It was less easy to characterise as appeasement than talks with China at the UN, conducted by the State Department. Acheson wished to avoid a repetition of the uproar which had followed US acceptance of the Five Principles. Washington experienced little difficulty with the UN allies over the field commander approach. It was welcomed as removing the political obstacles which had previously inhibited movement towards a ceasefire. The practical result was that the armistice talks were conducted by the UN Command on American instructions. 'Other governments . . . were kept informed of their progress, and . . . sometimes even consulted, but the United Nations itself played no active role.'[92] This was an arrangement which Britain in particular was later to question. For the moment, however, relief at the sudden breakthrough obscured all other considerations.

In acting on the Soviet suggestion that the UN command approach the Chinese and North Koreans, Washington was anxious to avoid any impression that it was suing for peace. From the beginning, the propaganda dimension of the issue was recognised. On 29 June, Ridgway broadcast a message to the enemy commanders noting that he had been 'informed' that they might desire an armistice: 'Upon receipt of word from you that such a meeting is desired I shall be prepared to name my representative [and] suggest a date at which he could meet with your representative. I propose that such a meeting could take place aboard a Danish hospital ship in Wonsan harbor.'[93] According to Rusk the message was phrased to put the idea across that it was the communists who had asked for peace, without humiliating them as MacArthur's abrasive message of 23 March had done.[94] On 2 July Beijing radio broadcast an acceptance signed by Kim Il Sung and General Peng Teh-huai of the Chinese People's Volunteers. The message stated that they were 'authorised' to hold negotiations and suspend military operations. A meeting was suggested at Kaesong on the 38th parallel. The fact that the North Korean leader, Kim, was 'authorised' to hold talks, showed where the real power lay following the Chinese intervention.[95] The North Koreans were indeed apparently stunned by Malik's broadcast and the move towards an armistice in what they regarded as a war of national liberation. There is evidence that the leadership was deeply divided on the issue. A similar phenomenon was evident in the south, where Syngman Rhee was to emerge as an obstacle to a cease-fire. As in 1945, both Koreas saw their destiny being defined over their heads by the great powers.[96]

If the North Koreans were dissatisfied with the Soviet decision, so

also were the Chinese. Soviet support for a simple cease-fire
decoupled the issues of Taiwan and the UN seat from the Korean
question, an association on which Beijung had always previously
insisted.[97] Moscow, however, had powerful levers in its relationship
with China. The Chinese relied upon the USSR for military equipment
and training, a dependence accentuated by the mauling some of its best
divisions had received in Korea at the hands of Ridgway. Beijing relied
upon the Russians to build up its air force and to defend the vital
province of Manchuria in the event of US attack. There was,
moreover, Russia's status as the leader of the communist bloc, a
position with which the Chinese leadership did not quarrel. As for the
Soviet Union, various reasons have been suggested for the sudden
endorsement of a cease-fire. Kennan believed that the Kremlin had
reached a stage where it must either take a greater role in the war, with
the dangers of an open clash with the US, or promote a compromise
settlement.[98] The Russians had already warned Washington in March,
through the columnist Joseph Alsop, that Russian forces would
intervene if UN troops again approached the Yalu border, a possibility
which could not be ruled out following the Chinese defeats of April
and May.[99] In recommending that Washington follow up the opening
offered by Malik, Kennan emphasised that the Russians stood at 'the
edge of the precipice'.[100] It has also been argued that the Soviet Union,
like the US, was prepared to sacrifice the Far East for Europe. If
Washington's priority was to integrate Germany into NATO,
Moscow's was to block German rearmament. A meeting at Paris on
this issue had collapsed on 21 June and the Kremlin may have pursued
a Korean cease-fire to lessen tensions with the West and improve the
prospects of its European diplomacy: 'The timing of Malik's speech
was apparently calculated to demonstrate the flexibility of the Soviet
Union, which might benefit its negotiating position in Europe as well
as Korea'.[101]

The American decision to halt the northward advance at the
Kansas/Wyoming line, a defensive position just north of the 38th
parallel, at the end of June and to wage an offensive defence has
sometimes been criticised. Brodie argued that it let the Chinese off the
hook, giving them time to rebuild their shattered armies. It also
allowed the communists to drag out the cease-fire talks.[102] Ridgway,
however, was not optimistic about the prospects of a further advance.
Although the Chinese had been badly hurt, he credited them with the
ability to defend strongly in the north on terrain well adapted for the
purpose. Moreover, the further the UN command moved north, the

less effective air power became, as enemy lines of communication shortened.[103] Lastly, in military terms the possible casualties had to be considered. An attack on an enemy fighting a defensive war from good positions was a different prospect from the flexible war which Ridgway had been fighting, allowing the Chinese to attack and destroying them primarily with air power and artillery. In such a struggle, US losses were likely to be heavy. Nor was there any visible end to such a war. If the Chinese were driven across the Yalu, they might well refuse to accept a settlement, forcing the US to carry the fighting into China itself. Beyond all this loomed the international political dimension. The UN allies would certainly protest, introducing new strain within the alliance and over all loomed the threat of Soviet intervention.[104] On all counts, the risks of a further advance far outweighed any possible benefits.

In June 1951, therefore, the Korean war entered a new phase. While the fighting continued it was on a reduced scale, at least as far as ground forces were concerned. There would be no further dramatic advances and retreats along the length of the peninsula. The fighting was now limited and directed to a narrow purpose, influencing negotiating positions at the cease-fire talks. It is unlikely that when this phase of negotiating while fighting began, any of the principles foresaw that it would outlast the earlier stages of the war. It soon became clear, however, that far from producing a quick settlement, the military armistice talks merely accentuated the political and ideological differences between the two sides.

7 Negotiating while Fighting

Despite the move towards an armistice in July 1951, it proved difficult to end the fighting. The armistice rapidly became the subject of bitter debate. Since it was recognised that a political settlement was unlikely and that a cease-fire would define future developments on the peninsula, compromise was difficult. Both sides sought to end the war, but not at any price. The problem was complicated, not only by the ideological gulf between the protagonists, but also by a racial and cultural divide. Ridgway condemned his opponents as 'treacherous savages', an attitude reciprocated by the Chinese and North Koreans, compensating for decades of humiliation at the hands of 'foreigners'.[1] Despite its distaste for Asian communists, Washington was anxious to avoid a breakdown and showed some flexibility. It was recognised that if talks collapsed, the administration would face public pressure to adopt MacArthur's recipe for 'ending the war and getting the boys home'. As General Bradley remarked, it was better to make concessions than to risk all-out war with China.[2] At the same time, there was concern lest negotiations be 'unduly prolonged'. In this case, the American people might prefer 'clear-cut victory' to an indefinite stalemate.[3] The case for limited war, propounded at the MacArthur hearings, depended for continued legitimacy on the achievement of results at the conference table.

It was believed in Washington that Moscow hoped to use the armistice talks to slow down Western rearmament and the integration of Germany and Japan into the US global security system.[4] The administration was determined to avoid this trap. The West must not lower its guard. The pattern of demobilisation which had followed the defeat of the axis in 1945 must not be repeated.[5] As Charles Wilson, the Director of Defense Mobilisation, argued on 6 July 1951, the rearmament programme demanded an annual expenditure of $50 billion: 'We must tell Congress and people that we must go forward regardless of developments in Korea.' General Marshall, the Secretary of Defense, agreed that the 'real trap ahead of us is the Let Down'.[6] In an effort to educate the public, Acheson delivered a speech in Detroit at the end of the month, cautioning his listeners against a Soviet peace campaign. The Russians were just as dangerous 'cooing

116

like doves' as 'growling like wolves'. The USSR would remain a menace as long as it built up its military strength and refused to work for world stability.[7]

The administration was determined to continue strengthening the Pacific defence perimeter while seeking an armistice in Korea. The communists were not to be allowed to use the cease-fire negotiations as a bargaining counter to block this process. Political issues such as Taiwan or the Japanese peace treaty were not to be considered in the talks.[8] Not only was Ridgway forbidden to discuss such issues, but he was also barred from providing his armistice delegation with political advisers, lest the communists use this as a wedge to raise non-military questions. His proposal to call in Sebald, his political adviser in Tokyo, was considered especially ill-advised. As Washington emphasised on 9 July, Sebald had been 'thoroughly connected with SCAP and strictly Japanese subjects; we are most anxious not to connect the Japanese Peace Treaty with Korean problems.'[9] Political advice was to be dispensed at long-range.

Washington did not expect a political settlement to follow an armistice. Nor did it believe that the communists would abandon their designs on the south. A cease-fire was regarded as an interim measure against the renewal of aggression, pending the completion of Western rearmament and the establishment of a position of strength in the Far East. As Acheson argued on 19 July, the 'best hope' was that 'An armistice might develop into a situation of enough stability so that, with the presence of some UN forces over a period of time and with the general increase in the strength of the West, including the development . . . of a friendly Japan, temptation toward renewed effort by the Communists in Korea might be removed by the obvious seriousness of such action'.[10] The terms envisaged by the administration reflected a desire to avert a new surprise attack. The armies were to disengage and a twenty-mile DMZ was to be established, based 'generally on the position of the opposing forces at the time the armistice arrangements are agreed upon'. No ground, air or naval reinforcements were to be introduced, although individual and unit replacements would be permitted. POWs would be exchanged on a one-for-one basis. The cease-fire would be policed by a military armistice commission, representing both sides. Observer teams would have 'free and unrestricted access to the whole of Korea'.[11] Effective inspection was regarded as vital since it would guard against communist cheating and allow the gradual reduction of US forces on the peninsula.

The armistice negotiations proved difficult from the beginning. As the chief UN delegate, Admiral Turner Joy, complained, they flowed 'with all the speed of a stiff concrete mix'.[12] There was an immediate dispute over the neutrality of the conference site. In his broadcast to the enemy commander on 30 June, Ridgway had suggested meeting on board a Danish hospital ship in Wonsan harbour. The communists, however, had countered by proposing Kaesong. Ridgway rapidly came to regret his agreement to this site. Although it was originally between the lines, the communists moved up troops to surround the town before discussions began. Since Kaesong lay south of the parallel and was the ancient capital of Korea, it possessed considerable propaganda value. The communists used their control of access to portray the UN as a defeated enemy, suing for peace. When the talks began, UN delegates were humiliated and harassed by Chinese guards. The Western press was excluded whilst communist newsmen 'exposed reels of film'.[13] Acheson accused the enemy of an 'arrogant and offensive propaganda demonstration'.[14] When Ridgway made it clear that the UNC would not continue discussions under these conditions, the communists agreed on 14 July to a five-mile neutral zone around Kaesong, unrestricted access for the UN delegation during daylight hours and the admission of the Western press.[15] With this issue settled, the conference proceeded to consider an agenda: 'The communist agenda was short and simple. Its main points were Establishment of the 38th Parallel as the military demarcation line between both sides and the establishment of a demilitarised zone as basic conditions for the cessation of hostilities. . . .' and withdrawal of 'all armed forces of foreign countries from Korea'.[16] The agenda thus attempted to define the terms of the cease-fire in advance and conceded a dominating position in post-armistice Korea to the communists. As a 'basic condition' of the cease-fire, Ridgway would have to withdraw from the Kansas line. As Acheson noted, the US had 'no intention of giving up the strong positions of the Kansas line; indeed, we hoped to improve them'.[17] The parallel could not be defended against an attack from the north. Moreover, the communist proposals contained no provision for policing the armistice. This was apparently considered unnecessary since all foreign troops were to withdraw. It soon became clear that the enemy envisaged a unilateral Western withdrawal. The Chinese attempted to define foreign troops as troops in Korea on the orders of their government, a definition which would have exempted Chinese forces which were technically volunteers.[18] Acheson believed that this approach reflected not only the continuing communist desire to control all Korea but was also part of a general strategy in Europe and Asia aimed at driving 'American troops back to North America'.[19] The communist agenda, therefore, was viewed in Washington as an attempt to gain at the conference table what could not be won on the battlefield.

After some wrangling, the communists agreed on 16 July to eliminate from the agenda specific reference to the parallel as the military demarcation line. They proved more obdurate, however, on the withdrawal of foreign troops, despite UN insistence that this was a political item which could not be considered as part of a military cease-fire. On 20 July Ridgway became impatient and suggested calling a recess until the enemy accepted the UN position.[20] This move was resisted by Washington which was unwilling to risk a break by directly engaging communist prestige on the issue. The enemy had already conceded on the neutralisation of Kaesong and might find it difficult to retreat under pressure for a second time. If talks were to collapse, the UNC must avoid responsibility. It was pointed out, moreover, that an enemy concession under pressure might work to the disadvantage of the UN. The communists would have made 'two major concessions to UN ultima', increasing the pressure on Ridgway to yield if an impasse developed over 'minimum UN terms for an armistice' such as the Kansas line and adequate inspection.[21]

There is no evidence that military operations were hampered by the truce talks. While Washington was more cautious in this respect than its field commander, Ridgway was never overruled as he was on tactics at the negotiating table. On 21 July he requested permission to launch a mass air attack on Pyongyang which would destroy supplies and strike a 'devasting blow at the North Korean capital'. The administration was at first reluctant, pointing out the 'far-reaching political implications, of the operation at this juncture.[22] When Ridgway argued military necessity, however, the raid was authorised on 25 July.[23] On 10 August Ridgway was allowed to bomb Rashin, previously exempt because of its proximity to the Soviet border.[24] A similar situation existed on the ground. On 18 August Ridgway proposed OPERATION TALONS, a limited offensive north-east of Kumhwa, to throw the enemy off-balance and use up his supplies. While it was felt that such an offensive would not be 'helpful' at Kaesong, Ridgway was once more allowed to proceed on the grounds of military necessity.[25] TALONS was later cancelled, not through political pressure, but because of the possible casualties involved.[26]

The impasse over troop withdrawal was finally solved by a

face-saving compromise. A final item was included on a five point
agenda entitled 'recommendations to the governments . . . on both
sides'. This was designed to allow the communists to raise the issue
without committing the UNC to withdrawal as part of the armistice
agreement. The other points on the agenda were:

1 Adoption of agenda
2 Fixing of a military demarcation line between both sides so as to
  establish a demilitarized zone as a basic condition for the cessation
  of hostilities in Korea
3 Concrete arrangements for the realization of cease-fire and
  armistice . . . including the composition, authority and functions
  of a supervisory organ for carrying out the terms of the cease-fire
  and armistice
4 Arrangements relating to prisoners of war.[27]

This represented considerable concession by the communists and
constituted a framework within which Washington could negotiate. It
soon became clear, however, that in their approach to key issues the
two sides remained far apart.

When negotiations began on item 2, the communists reverted to
their earlier demand for a demarcation line at the 38th parallel. The
UNC, however, insisted that the demarcation line must be in the
general area of the battlefront which mostly lay above the parallel. As
an initial negotiating position, it suggested a twenty-mile DMZ north
of the Kansas line, a proposal which would have involved a communist
withdrawal.[28] According to Burchett's account from the communist
side, the Chinese expected an early agreement on the parallel.[29] As
Acheson later admitted, this had been encouraged by his own careless
use of words. On 2 June, at the MacArthur hearings, he had stated that
a cease-fire at or near the parallel would be acceptable. While Kennan
had been vague about the final armistice line in his talks with Malik,
the Soviet ambassador had been 'very precise' in his broadcast in
calling for 'mutual withdrawal of forces from the 38th parallel'.
According to Acheson, Washington failed to understand the historical
significance of the parallel as the demarcation line between competing
spheres of influence: 'It had been a most important line to both
Imperial Russia and Imperial Japan.' It had again served this purpose
in 1945. Instead of the return to the *status quo* apparently suggested by
Acheson and accepted by Malik, the communists found the US
insisting upon 'A new line for our sphere of influence, not only more
militarily advantageous but involving considerable loss of prestige for

them'. The enemy found it difficult to accept that 'what appeared to be trickery' was 'wholly inadvertent on our part'.[30]

By early August, discussions on the military demarcation line had reached deadlock. Moreover, the neutrality of the conference site was again at issue. On 4 August, in full view of the UN delegation, a company of Chinese troops violated the neutral zone.[31] Ridgway's instinct was to make a firm stand. He argued that the communists were dragging out negotiations and building up their military position in the hope of forcing the UNC to accept their terms. They understood only strength. Ridgway wanted to refuse to return to Kaesong until the enemy had provided new guarantees or agreed to a different site. He also favoured an ultimatum on the demarcation line. Washington, however, was unwilling to risk a breakdown and Ridgway was overruled.[32] The UNC returned to Kaesong after the communists had described the troop incident as a 'mistake' and sought a compromise on the demarcation line by resorting to sub-delegation meetings. It was hoped that a more informal approach would allow the enemy to retreat without loss of face.[33] Subsequent discussion produced some evidence of movement on the part of the communists. On 20 August the North Korean delegate drew a distinction between 'the line of contact' and 'the general area of the battleline' and insisted that as long as the UN insisted on a DMZ 'in the latter area, no progress would be made'.[34] This was an important concession since the communists were abandoning their demand for a cease-fire on the 38th parallel and the withdrawal of the UNC from its existing positions. If the line of contact became the truce line, the UNC could continue to occupy the Kansas/Wyoming defences, considered vital to the defence of Seoul. The issue was taken up again on 22 August when the communists pressed for agreement on the principle that 'Adjustments could be made to the line of contact by withdrawals and advances by both sides in such a way as to fix a military demarcation line'.[35] Their interest in such a settlement was made public by calculated leaks through newsmen at Kaesong.[36] It was hoped that on this basis it might be possible for Ridgway to suggest a four kilometre DMZ with the line of contact as the median, thus solving 'one of the touchiest agenda items'.[37] It proved impossible, however, to explore the matter further since the talks were unilaterally recessed by the communists on 23 August.

The ostensible reason was UN violation of the neutral zone. It was claimed that an American aircraft had bombed Kaesong on the night of 22 August. Ridgway denied the charge, arguing that the enemy had fabricated the incident.[38] He replied to the recess by intensifying limited objective ground attacks in the east/central sector to maintain pressure on the enemy and to improve the forward defences of the Kansas line. It was suspected in Washington that the recess had been called to increase tension in the Far East on the eve of the Japanese peace treaty. The ceremony was to take place in San Fransisco at the beginning of September.[39] Although the Russians had not been consulted about the terms, they had announced their intention of attending to present their own proposals. Acheson believed that the Kremlin might attempt to wreck the proceedings by resort to 'shock tactics to reduce the number of signatories . . . or arouse Japanese fears'.[40] As Rusk remarked on 27 August, the Soviet Union might 'play upon the uncertainties' in Korea as part of this approach.[41]

The incident confirmed Ridgway's objection to Kaesong. He wanted to terminate the neutral status of the city and to insist on a new site for future negotiations.[42] The administration, however, wished to avoid responsibility for a breakdown. Ridgway was authorised to suggest a new location without issuing a categorical refusal to return to Kaesong.[43] If the recess was part of a larger strategy to disrupt events at San Fransisco, it failed. The Japanese peace treaty was signed on 8 September, after a Soviet walkout.[44] It was hoped in Washington that the communists might now reopen negotiations if it could be done without loss of face. On 10 September the accidental strafing of Kaesong by an American aircraft offered an opportunity to build a bridge to the enemy. The UNC accepted responsibility for the attack and apologised. The communist response was 'almost friendly'. On 20 September the enemy agreed to a meeting of liaison officers at Panmunjom, a village between the lines.[45]

The renewal of contacts with the communists intensified the debate between Ridgway and his superiors. The enemy pressed for a meeting of the full delegations but was unwilling to consider an alternative site. Ridgway refused to surrender on this issue.[46] Nor did he approve of the tactics which Washington intended to adopt if the full delegations met. The administration wished to make a concrete proposal based on the communist position on 22 August. It would suggest a four kilometre DMZ with the line of contact as the median. The proposal was important because it contained an element of reciprocity. Both sides would withdraw for two kilometres although neither would have to abandon its main defensive line. An early initiative would prevent a return to haggling over the 38th parallel.[47] Ridgway viewed the proposal as dangerous. He did not object in principle but believed that to start with a concession would give an impression of weakness. His initial position should be the twenty mile DMZ in the general area of the battleline on which the UNC had opened the talks.[48] There was concern in Washington at this evidence of divergence. Ridgway's superiors were unwilling to force his hand over Kaesong but were reluctant to risk a breakdown, particularly as the communists seemed eager to renew negotiations. On 28 September, at a State/JCS meeting, it was agreed that Bradley and Bohlen should visit Ridgway to discuss the situation. As Bradley noted, 'When you are close to those sons-of-bitches you have different views.' The mission was also to investigate the military position. There was some confusion in Washington as to how badly the UNC needed an armistice. Bohlen left for Tokyo convinced that the communist build-up was changing the balance in Korea and made an armistice a matter of urgency.[49]

The visit was reassuring on the military side. Ridgway and his commanders were confident of their ability to repulse any enemy offensive and believed that supply shortages would give the communists 'an extremely hard time when the cold weather begins'. On tactics at the conference table, Ridgway was prepared to accept an initial position based on a four kilometre DMZ. He remained resistant, however, on the issue of the site, arguing that he had made 'steady concessions . . . on procedural matters', thus creating 'an appearance of weakness' unjustified by the military situation. While Bohlen returned convinced that Ridgway's hand should not be forced, the question was only resolved when the communists proposed full delegation meetings at Panmunjom on 7 October. Unlike Kaesong, the village lay between the lines where its neutrality could be better guaranteed and the scope for incidents reduced.[50]

Washington's reluctance to go to the brink in the negotiations reflected an awareness that the alternative to an armistice was 'worse than an armistice'.[51] A breakdown would raise questions about the viability of limited war and might lead to an all-out conflict with China. The problems became clear when the military options were considered. On 13 July the JCS produced a list of actions which might be taken in the event of no armistice to increase military pressure on the enemy. These included a ground advance as far as the North Korean neck and the removal of restrictions against air attacks on the electric power complexes on the Yalu river. 'Hot pursuit' into Manchuria would be authorised: 'Such pursuit to include destruction of enemy planes after landing and neutralization of opposing anti-aircraft fire.' The paper also called for the commitment of additional forces by the UN allies and a naval blockade of the Chinese mainland.[52]

There was considerable debate within the bureaucracy about these recommendations, as State and Defense attempted to evolve an agreed position for the National Security Council. The State Department was doubtful if the allies, particularly Britain, would accept a blockade. Its own preference was for an economic embargo by the UN. It also had reservations about hot pursuit, pointing out the possible Soviet reaction to attacks on Manchuria. The State Department, moreover, wished to tailor the military response to the actions of the enemy. The JCS wished their measures to be adopted as a package if talks collapsed. The Pentagon was reluctant to risk the security of the UN command by leaving the initiative to the enemy. Nor did it believe that action should await consultation with allies which might forewarn the communists.[53]

In the course of the debate, it became clear that some of the JCS proposals were militarily untenable. On 3 November a continued build-up of MIGs in Manchuria led to the abandonment of hot pursuit. An extension of the air war would merely expose the FEAF to attrition and force the commitment of scarce modern jets to Korea.[54] The production figures were not encouraging. While the Soviet Union was building one hundred MIGs a month, US industry was producing eleven swept-wing Sabres, the only Western fighter aircraft which could match the Soviet interceptor. The air force did not expect production to 'really get rolling' until the autumn of 1952.[55] Attacks on Manchuria would divert scarce fighters from more important tasks such as the defence of SAC bases in Britain and the Continental Air Command. Moreover, Japan was vulnerable to communist retaliation. A request by Ridgway for increased air strength in the Far East, particularly to defend Japan, was turned down on 17 August because reinforcements could not be provided 'without reducing . . . forces in other vital areas below unacceptable levels'.[56]

The prospects of a ground advance were even less encouraging. Ridgway's operations to straighten the line in August/September 1951 cost the UNC 60 000 casualties, 20 000 of them American, and displayed the difficulties of an offensive against an entrenched and fanatical enemy. The losses in this fighting led Ridgway to cancel a larger offensive, OPERATION TALONS, which had been authorised that autumn.[57] On 23 September he informed the JCS that he was considering two possible operations if talks collapsed. The first was an amphibious assault at Wonsan coordinated with an advance from the

Kansas line. This, however, might provoke Soviet intervention and would provide an ideal target for an atomic bomb. A less risky alternative was a landing near Tongchon coupled with an advance from the Imjin. While this would inflict heavy losses on the enemy, however, he warned that there would also be a 'sharp rise' of the UN casualty rate to 10 000 per month.[58]

The JCS had long been sensitive to the prospect of losses on this scale. On 13 October, Pace, the Secretary of the Army, drew Ridgway's attention to adverse public reaction to recent losses. Questions were being asked about the value of assaulting 'one hill after another'. Ridgway must emphasise the concrete benefits gained by these attacks and not appear to be fighting a war of attrition. He must also abandon codenames such as KILLER and MEATGRINDER which 'did not find favor with the American people'.[59] On 3 November the Pentagon faced military realities and abandoned the idea of an advance to the neck. The losses involved would vindicate MacArthur and provoke demands for decisive action against China.[60]

On 20 December 1951 the NSC produced a final list of options if the armistice talks collapsed. Under NSC-118/2, Ridgway was to conduct ground operations on a scale consistent with the capabilities of his command while avoiding 'disproportionate casualties'. The Yalu power plants were to be attacked. Manchurian bases would be bombed if enemy air activity threatened the security of US forces. Since State and Defense were unable to agree over an economic embargo versus a naval blockade of China, the question was referred to the NSC staff for further consideration. It was recognised that increased military pressure would demand the commitment of considerable reinforcements. This was particularly true in the air. The impact on global strategy would be severe and would 'play into the hands of the Kremlin.'[61] The administration thus faced a frustrating conclusion. It could not afford negotiations to fail. Military realities demanded a flexible position at the conference table. As Nitze concluded on 26 September: 'If our position in the event of a breakdown isn't a very good one to radically change the position of the Commies, then there is greater pressure to try to get an armistice.'[62]

When negotiations resumed at Panmunjom, the communists abandoned the 38th parallel and moved towards acceptance of a demarcation line based on the line of contact. There was a dispute, however, about adjustments to this line. Ridgway wanted Kaesong, arguing that it would have fallen to UN forces but for its neutralisation. The communists, however, were unwilling to abandon the ancient capital of Korea which possessed considerable prestige value. A second issue was communist insistence on finalising the demarcation line, whatever military changes occurred, while other items were being discussed. Ridgway found such an inhibition on his military operations totally unacceptable.[63] Once again, however, his superiors were unwilling to go to the brink. Washington refused to risk a break over Kaesong, which was considered a minor issue by both the public and the UN allies. As for the demarcation line, it was prepared to accept the communist proposal 'qualified by a time limitation for completion of all agenda items'.[64] On 17 November the UNC proposed a provisional line of demarcation which would be included in any armistice reached within thirty days. By 26 November a mutually acceptable line had been mapped out.[65]

Controversy has attended this decision ever since. Ridgway opposed such an open retreat from his previous negotiating position and called for 'more steel' and 'less silk' in the UN approach.[66] The administration was subsequently accused of relaxing pressure on the enemy, allowing the communists to build up an unassailable military position and stretch out the talks.[67] This argument, however, overlooks the military realities. As Bradley noted, the Eighth Army was going nowhere with the advent of winter. Major ground operations had already ceased. Air and naval bombardment, the main means of military pressure, was not curtailed.[68] The enemy continued to be subject to artillery fire and harrassment by ground patrolling. Despite Ridgway's earlier fears, there was no de facto ceasefire during the thirty day period allowed for discussion of other items. There is no evidence to suggest that the UN conceded any military advantage by its tactics at Panmunjom.

If Washington was willing to compromise on the demarcation line, it was also prepared to adopt a flexible approach on item 3, supervision of the armistice. Once more it differed from Ridgway, who demanded a firm minimum position from which there would be no retreat. While willing to compromise on details, Ridgway insisted that his superiors stand by the principle of effective inspection. If they backed down on this question, it would be interpreted as a sign of weakness. Moreover, ineffective supervision would expose not only the UNC, but also Japan, to a surprise attack after the armistice.[69] The administration, however, recognised that inspection was likely to prove a sticking point for the enemy. The best security guarantee was not inspection but the realisation in Beijing that further aggression would provoke direct retaliation against China.[70] In November 1951 discussions began with the British about a statement threatening China with 'greater sanctions' if it broke the truce.[71] Washington believed that such a warning would permit considerable modification of Ridgway's initial position at Panmunjom which called for joint observer teams at points of entry and communication centres plus aerial inspection to ensure that reinforcement did not occur.[72]

The communists objected from the beginning to the concept of belligerent inspection. On 4 December they proposed supervision of the armistice by a group of neutral nations chosen by both sides. It became clear that the enemy wished to exempt airfields from inspection. They insisted on the right to rebuild all forms of communication and argued that airfields were an internal matter which could not be considered under item 3.[73] It was felt in Washington that since the UN planned an extensive programme of reconstruction in the south, it would be unrealistic to insist that the north remain in a state of devastation. While some reservation was necessary on airfields, this should not become a breaking point.[74] Nor should a collapse be risked on the issue of neutral inspection. Thus Ridgway was ordered to avoid freezing the UN position. Haggling over item 3 was continuing at sub-delegation level when the thirty day limit on the demarcation line expired on 27 December.

Global strategic considerations continued to influence tactics at the armistice talks. On 10 December the President summoned a meeting of his leading advisers to discuss the situation at Panmunjom. Truman complained that the UNC had been 'too conciliatory: Our demands had not been strong enough. His impression was that they had been making all the demands and we the concessions.' He was concerned that the communists would breach a weak armistice and drive to Pusan in 1952, presidential election year. The fall of Korea would encourage disillusion with foreign military commitments and thus endanger NATO. The President remained fearful of Republican neo-isolationism. His officials, however, denied that the balance of concessions lay on the UN side and emphasised the difficulties if talks collapsed. The new Secretary of Defense, Lovett, argued that the US was 'generally inadequate in air strength throughout the world'. An extension of the war would expose scarce resources to attrition in a peripheral area. Moreover, it would place an intolerable burden on allies such as Britain which were in 'bad shape both financially and regarding manpower'. Little additional support could be expected from this quarter. The Acting Secretary of State, Webb, emphasised that the main task was to strengthen Europe and Japan. The US must not be sucked deeper into Korea. These considerations demanded compromise at Panmunjom. As Bradley remarked, the choice was 'to give in on some of these things or to go all-out against China'. The consensus was that a 'greater sanctions' statement was the best means of avoiding a breakdown and guaranteeing the armistice.[75]

While the talks continued, Washington sought the continued support of its allies. The most troublesome was South Korea, the only one represented at Panmunjom. Rhee was bitter about the negotiations which he realised meant a new partition of his country. Korean representation at the discussions was purely symbolic. Once more the future of the peninsula was being decided by the great powers. He resented not only his subordinate role at Panmunjom but also Korean exclusion from the Japanese peace settlement and from the network of security pacts concluded between the US and Pacific nations such as Australia, New Zealand and the Philippines. Rhee's nightmare was that Washington would abandon the south after the armistice and lay it open to a new invasion. Despite reassurances from Truman, he continued to snipe at the negotiations.[76] Thus Washington continued to find Rhee an uncomfortable ally. Muccio complained about his failure to control inflation or corruption and his habit of treating three-quarters of the population as subversive.[77] From the US point of view, the most encouraging development was the modernisation of the Korean army. In December Collins expressed his optimism about progress towards a new professional officer corps under US tuition. He failed to predict the leverage over the truce talks which the programme would eventually give Rhee.[78] The greater the role of the ROK army, the larger Rhee's scope for sabotaging the armistice, a fact which became clear in 1953.

If the most troublesome ally was South Korea, the most important remained Britain. London was anxious to reach an honourable settlement in Korea which would allow the withdrawal of UN forces. Plagued by economic problems and the crisis over Iran, it viewed the war as a distraction and looked 'longingly towards the exits'. From the British viewpoint, Korea was a '*sale guerre*' and Rhee 'even less worthy and responsible a leader than . . . Chiang Kai-Shek'.[79] In July 1951, Morrison expressed concern at Rhee's opposition to an armistice, an attitude shared by his conservative successor, Eden.[80] Nor did Britain have unreserved confidence in American policy, despite the removal of MacArthur. In September 1951 Morrison visited the US to sign the Japanese peace treaty. His brief revealed a fundamental ambiguity towards American conduct of the cold war, particularly in the Far

East. Containment was defined as a success and Morrison was to maintain the alignment with the US on which British security depended. At the same time there was a danger of pushing the Soviet Union into preventive war. The risk was greatest in the Far East where, 'under the pressure of an excitable public opinion', US policy 'might go to unreasonable lengths'.[81]

On 11 September Acheson and Morrison discussed the situation if armistice talks collapsed. This occurred against the background of the recess at Kaesong. Morrison emphasised the need to avoid all-out war with China and British inability to reinforce the Far East. Korea must be regarded as merely one example of Soviet 'trouble-making'. Britain was reluctantly prepared to agree to measures such as a ground advance to the waist and the bombing of the Yalu electric plants. It had reservations, however, about some of the political measures proposed by Acheson. The US wished to expedite Japanese rearmament, a move which might alarm Moscow. Morrison warned against any dramatic action in this area and insisted that Japanese troops must not be used in Korea. This might lead to Soviet involvement under the terms of the Sino-Soviet pact and thus to global war. Political and economic sanctions by the UN were also unwelcome. Acheson's suggestion of an economic embargo policed by the UNC would in practice be indistinguishable from a blockade and would create the danger of a clash with the Russians over access to Port Arthur and Dairen. Hong Kong was vulnerable to retaliation and there was also Indian reaction to consider. As for political sanctions, these would be ineffective and merely drive Beijing further into the Soviet camp. China was not yet a 'slavish satellite' and it was important to maintain its 'window on the West'.[82] This 'familiar exegesis' irritated Acheson and represented the lingering reflection of Attlee's arguments in December 1950.[83] As long as the war continued, however, there was unlikely to be open friction with Washington over China. The situation in the event of a truce was a different matter. Britain did not believe that China could be excluded from the UN forever and had not wholly abandoned the dream of a general settlement in the Far East.[84]

In November 1951 the Labour government was replaced by a Conservative administration with Churchill as Prime Minister and Eden as Foreign Secretary. The new premier was anxious to restore the Anglo-American partnership of the Second World War. On his visit to Washington in January 1952, he went as far as to suggest the division of the free world into spheres of influence with the US dominant in Asia and Britain in the Middle East. He was fulsome in his praise for the decision to intervene in Korea, arguing that it was a turning point in the cold war. He agreed with Acheson's view that the continuing impasse at Panmunjom was part of a Soviet scheme to transfer the Korean problem to the UN where political issues could be raised. The allies must stand firm against this manoeuvre and publicise the real source of frustration at the armistice table. Churchill held no brief for the Chinese communists, an attitude shared by Eden who thought that it was pointless to look for signs of Titoism in Beijing. On the subject of Taiwan, the Prime Minister stated that it would be 'shameful' to surrender Jiang's nationalists, supporters of the West since the Second World War, to their communist opponents.[85]

In practical terms, however, this rhetoric meant little. The Churchill government was not going to withdraw recognition from Beijing or agree that Jiang represented the authentic voice of China. It shared the reluctance of its predecessor to take risks in the Far East which might provoke global war. Moreover, continuing economic strains and the crisis in the Middle East demanded a resolution of the Korean conflict. Churchill was convinced that until Britain had reasserted its economic independence it would not be treated as an equal by the US, a development which demanded the reduction of global tensions.[86] The essential caution of the British approach was revealed in its attitude to the 'greater sanctions' statement. American readiness to consult rather than to take unilateral action was regarded as important. It was a development which the government was anxious to encourage.[87] At the same time, however, the statement was regarded primarily as a means of smoothing the way towards an armistice and an exit from Korea. London insisted on changes in the wording to avoid any implication that the Soviet Union was being threatened.[88] Moreover, it refused to be committed in advance on the type of action to be taken if the warning was ignored. The US envisaged bombing and blockade. Churchill was not unduly worried by the former, viewing it in the light of a nineteenth-century punitive expedition. China was not a country on which war was declared but 'rather a country against which war was waged'. Eden admitted that bombing might present fewer problems than blockade; however, he was unenthusiastic about any form of retaliation.[89] The Sino-Soviet pact meant that military action carried the risk of global war. An economic embargo or naval blockade was viewed as particularly provocative. The British argued that such measures would mean a clash with Russia over access to Dairen and Port Arthur. They were also aware of the danger of Chinese retaliation on Hong Kong.[90] There was little sympathy in Washington for this argument. The JCS believed that despite the measures taken in the spring, trade between the colony and the mainland was increasing.[91] A dossier produced during the Churchill visit was hotly disputed by the British, who questioned the accuracy of the US figures.[92] Thus, under the new conservative government, Anglo-American relations in the Far East differed in tone rather than in substance.

The 'greater sanctions' statement to which Britain and the other UN allies subscribed did not solve the problem of post-armistice security. It was largely bluff, since the US lacked the resources to put it into practice. The JCS hesitated to attack Manchuria, which had been transformed into a hornet's nest by the Chinese air build-up, but argued that a naval blockade coupled with bombing and mining of transportation routes might be enough to end aggression and undermine the Beijing regime.[93] Ridgway condemned this as wishful thinking. US air power was incapable of inflicting lasting damage on China, particularly if the Russians provided fighter support: 'In my opinion, the retributive potential of UN military power against Red China would be non-effective unless the full results of precipitating World War 3 were to be accepted and the use of atomic weapons authorized.'[94] Ridgway was aware that any expansion of the conflict in the Far East was unlikely to be unilateral. An attack on China would lay Japan open to retaliation and its defences were weak. Both he and his predecessor had long recognised that the only defence of the home islands in the event of a wider war was unrestricted use of atomic weapons.[95]

Whatever the military realities, the decision to threaten China with retaliation outside Korea in the event of a new aggression represented a move away from the symmetrical response to aggression presumed by NSC-68. It symbolised a growing concern about the costs and consequences of this form of containment. The continued impasse at Panmunjom displayed the difficulties of managing limited war. Military intervention around the periphery of the Soviet bloc threatened to bog the US down and exhaust it in a series of indecisive conflicts. At a meeting in the Pentagon on 22 January 1952, the Secretary of the Army, Pace, complained that the State Department seemed 'obsessed with the view that we could fight Communism by a series of peripheral skirmishes, regardless of where they might break out next.' Bradley remarked that while the JCS were not unanimous, he agreed with Pace. The State Department must be educated: 'We could not continue militarily pecking away at the periphery subject to the whim of the Communists.'[96] Quite apart from the loss of control over force dispositions, the costs of symmetrical containment were growing beyond what the allies and perhaps even the US could afford. Lovett had expressed his concern at the financial condition of Britain and France in December 1951, a concern which Churchill had reinforced on his visit to Washington in January.[97] This was to lead to some scaling-down of NATO rearmament in 1952 to accommodate to economic realities. The military build-up was misdirected if it ended up by destroying what it was intended to protect.[98]

Although its prescriptions were questioned, NSC-68 was not repudiated. In his final year, Truman continued to express faith in the 'fundamental validity' of its programmes.[99] A new approach to containment, however, was being shaped by the frustration of Korea. It was made possible by government spending on atomic weapons under NSC-68. The US entered the Korean war with a limited number of 'city-busting' bombs, designed for strategic use in a global war. In January 1951, however, the first tests of tactical weapons took place. Military planners were not slow to grasp their potential. The USAF embarked upon an ambitious programme to make its fighter bombers capable of carrying atomic weapons. On 5 July 1951 the Army Operations Division produced a memorandum on the actions necessary to break the Korean deadlock if truce negotiations failed. It assigned a central role to the new family of atomic weapons: 'In the event of a stalemate in Korea in which the Communist forces pit manpower against our technological advantages, use of the atomic bomb to increase our efficiency of killing is desirable. In the event of a general emergency including the defense of Japan, the application of the atomic bomb is essential.' The planners recommended field tests to evolve a doctrine for the practical use of tactical atomic weapons, a demand accepted by the JCS.[100]

In September 1951, in extreme secrecy, a series of practical experiments involving dummy bombs was carried out in Korea, codenamed OPERATION HUDSON HARBOR.[101] By July 1952 military planners were emphasising the versatility of tactical weapons which could be carried by fighter-bombers and would soon be available in the form of artillery shells.[102] These technical developments offered an opportunity to break the stalemate in Korea without risking huge ground casualties or exposing the air force to unacceptable levels of attrition. Air bases, communications and defensive lines could be dealt a quick knock-out blow. This was to provide the basis of the approach adopted by the incoming Eisenhower administration. It threatened to end the deadlock with tactical atomic weapons and envisaged 'greater sanctions' in terms of atomic strikes on the Chinese mainland. By this stage, the truce talks had been stalled for a year in an unforeseen controversy over the repatriation of POWs.

8 The POW Issue

The POW issue almost destroyed the prospects of an armistice. What had at first seemed a simple matter became entangled in national prestige and ideology. In theory, the question was covered by the Geneva convention of 1949. Although neither Pyongyang nor Beijing were signatories, both declared their intention of observing the Geneva code, North Korea in July 1950, China not until July 1952. Washington, an original signatory, did not ratify the convention until 1955, but announced at the beginning of the war that POW policy would be based on the Geneva rules.[1] Article 118 of the convention called for the automatic repatriation of *all* POWs at the end of hostilities. This uncompromising language was originally endorsed by Washington as a weapon in the cold war. It was intended to embarrass the USSR, which continued to hold large numbers of axis POWs as forced labour for reconstruction after 1945.[2] At Panmunjom, however, an ironic reversal of positions occurred. The communists invoked article 118, displaying a legal literalism which was never applied to other sections of the convention, while the US proposed a new principle, 'non-forcible' repatriation. Article 118 assumed that all POWs would desire to return to their own side. By late 1951, however, it had become clear that substantial numbers of Chinese and North Koreans wished to refuse repatriation. The forcible repatriation of anti-communists was politically impossible and ideologically repugnant. Thus Washington was compelled to press for a flexible approach. Truman refused to yield on the issue. He would not purchase an armistice by 'turning over human beings to slaughter or slavery'.[3] The situation, however, was not as simple as the President supposed. While the non-repatriates were later regarded as symbols of moral victory, 'heroes behind barbed wire' who had opted for freedom, the reality was different. There was little freedom of choice in the compounds of Koje-Do, an island off the west coast, where the use of terror to secure political allegiance was routine. As Muccio later recalled, 'What went on within these camps was *never* known nor understood by the US military.'[4]

On 26 September 1950 the US army assumed control of POWs on behalf of the UN command. This was intended to ensure that all contingents observed the Geneva convention, particularly the ROKs who had 'a tendency to mistreat or kill POWs at the slightest provocation'.[5] Washington was anxious to prevent reprisals against captured UN personnel and to win North Korean hearts and minds as the prelude to unification. By November 1950, with the collapse of the NKPA, the US held over 137 000 prisoners. The Eighth Army lacked the manpower to guard this vast number. POWs were accommodated in makeshift compounds where they were allowed to run their own affairs. Camp security was almost non-existent. This laxity was encouraged by the passive attitude of the POWs and by the belief that the war was almost over.[6] Despite official emphasis on the Geneva convention, conditions in the camps were poor. The Eighth Army lacked the resources to provide adequate food and medical treatment for such large numbers of men. One POW recalled poor food and clothing and lack of water. Prisoners were anxious to serve on outside working parties in order to scavenge amongst the discarded garbage of the US army. American medical officers estimated that 50 per cent of the POWs in Pusan were suffering from malnutrition in January 1951.[7] Diseases such as dysentry were rife and the detaining authorities lacked the facilities to deal with them properly. As a result, 6600 prisoners had died in UN captivity by December 1951. Added to these problems was brutality by American guards, who often displayed their racist dislike of 'Gooks' by harsh treatment. One British officer later recalled that some GIs treated their prisoners like animals, showing little respect even for the wounded.[8]

When China intervened in November/December 1950, greater attention was given to control of POWs. It was feared that with the UN command in retreat, the poorly supervised prisoners might return to their old allegiance, joining up with guerrillas to cut Eighth Army lines of communication. In February 1951 Ridgway launched OPERATION ALBANY, evacuating all POWs to the island of Koje-Do.[9] This move was accompanied by great hardship. One POW, who sailed on the last evacuation ship from Inchon, recalled: 'If any cameraman had filmed what happened during this voyage . . . even Satan would be indignant at seeing it.' Into a small hold were crammed 4500 men: 'When two-thirds of the POWs [had been] put in the ship, the room of the ship was jammed with people. GI guards pushed them . . . [further in], but they found it of no use and they stabbed the men around them with jackknives.' The prisoners were jammed tightly and unable to move. Those who fell were trampled to death by their fellows.[10] On Koje, food and conditions improved once a permanent network of compounds had been established. Life as a prisoner, however, remained unpleasant.

The POW problem continued to grow. By May 1951 Koje was accepting 2000 new prisoners every day, the majority Chinese captured in the spring offensives. The island was already crowded with refugees and space was at a premium. The result was inevitable. Compounds designed to hold 4500 soon held twice that number and even the spaces between the cages were pressed into service.[11] The army continued to suffer from an acute shortage of manpower to guard the camps. The recommended ratio of guards to POWs was 1:20, the actual ratio on Koje 1:33. The majority were Koreans, drafted into POW service to free US troops for the front. There was only one American MP to every 188 POWs. Moreover the US personnel was of poor quality, often rejected by other units. Discipline was lax. Guards slept on duty and deserted their posts to visit prostitutes in the adjoining refugee camps. Morale amongst officers was low and there was a high turnover of camp commanders. In the Eighth Army, Koje was regarded as 'the end of the line'.[12]

The shortage of personnel forced the camp command to rely on prisoner cooperation. Compound representatives maintained discipline, distributed supplies and liaised with the administration. Guards rarely entered the POW enclosures.[13] Behind the wire, camp life was shaped, not by military discipline, but by political struggle. Both Korean and Chinese prisoners came from societies riven by civil war where allegiances were fluid. Some POWs were anti-communists, who had deserted to the UN at the first opportunity, some were convinced party members, and many were simply peasant conscripts with little political understanding. The camp command made no attempt to segregate communists from anti-communists when it established the compounds of Koje. As a result, a bitter struggle for political control took place within the cages. At stake was the allegiance of the disorganised mass of POWs. The process by which communist cadres consolidated their control has been well documented. Leadership was provided by a hard core of party members, later reinforced by special agents who allowed themselves to be captured in the guise of private soldiers. An elaborate system of communications linked the communist compounds to each other and, through refugees on Koje, with the high command in North Korea. Discipline was enforced by strong-arm squads and kangaroo courts which did not stop at murder to attain their ends.[14]

The situation in the anti-communist compounds, which ultimately contained the majority of POWs, has been less closely examined. Leadership in the Korean cages was exercised by self-styled 'youth leagues' which differed little in organisation and ferocity from similar para-military groups in South Korea. American guards reported the sound of nightly beatings in these compounds.[15] In the Chinese camps, the leaders were ex-Guomindong soldiers drafted into the PLA after 1949 and members of secret societies which had long been linked to Jiang's regime. According to Philip Manhardt, a US civilian official who spoke Chinese, this group used 'brutal force' to attain control and to force POWs to express their loyalty to the Guomindong.[16] Terror was reinforced by the manipulation of essential supplies which were distributed by compound leaders.[17] The choice for the average POW was often to conform or to starve. This situation was tolerated by the camp administration which relied on POW 'trusties' and was sympathetic to the anti-communist cause. It was clear to the individual Chinese that he could not rely on the authorities for protection against the 'patriotic societies'. The anti-communist compounds were linked with each other and with the regimes they supported. A special section of Rhee's War Ministry advised the 'youth leagues' which were also supported by the 'violently anti-communist' ROK guards.[18] The Chinese were in contact with Taiwan through Guomindong personnel in the camp administration.

Chinese nationalists appeared on Koje as the result of a POW programme sponsored by Washington. Both sides regarded POWs as tools in the ideological struggle between communism and capitalism. While the Chinese tried to convert UN prisoners in their camps along the Yalu, the US attempted to demonstrate the bankruptcy of communism and the virtues of the capitalist system. MacArthur's directive for the invasion of North Korea in September 1950 noted, 'Treatment of POWs shall be directed toward their exploitation for psychological warfare purposes.'[19] POWs were to be re-educated for a life of freedom in a unified Korea. Acting on this directive, MacArthur established a pilot programme, using 500 POWs chosen to represent a cross-section of the North Korean population. The scheme incorporated lessons learned during the denazification of Germany and the re-education of Japan. The POWs were to be instructed in the values of democracy and to learn through films and lectures the 'truth' about communism and Korean history.[20]

The project collapsed with Chinese intervention and evacuation of the camps to Koje. In April 1951 however, a new 'orientation and education program' was introduced for all POWs. Literacy classes and vocational training were combined with films and lectures designed to introduce prisoners to Western concepts of justice and democracy.[21]

The scheme went beyond the Geneva obligation to provide for the intellectual welfare of POWs and was in many respects 'patently a political indoctrination program'.[22] The communist compounds participated in the literacy and vocational training classes. The literacy drive continued a project already in force in the PLA. They boycotted the orientation lectures, however, sending representatives only to note the names of collaborators for future retaliation.[23] The scheme fell within the parameters of NSC-48/5 which called for the US to encourage anti-communism in China and amongst Chinese abroad. The aim was not to persuade POWs to remain in the West but to return them to their homes at the end of the war as a focus of popular opposition to the regime. The administration did not envisage wholesale resistance to repatriation.

In order to administer such an ambitious project, the Far East Command required Chinese speakers. A controversy later raged over the origins of the personnel involved. The British were informed that around 25 Chinese had been recruited in Hong Kong and Taiwan. Only 12 of these were from Taipei.[24] The files of the Far East Command, however, tell a different story. In January 1951 MacArthur requested 20 linguists from Taiwan who were selected by Jiang's Ministry of Defence. In February 1951 he asked for an additional 55 and despatched a staff officer to Taiwan to coordinate psychological warfare programmes with the Guomindong regime.[25] Muccio recalled that 75 personnel were recruited on Taiwan who were 'doubtless members of Chiang Kai-Shek's Gestapo'.[26] It seems likely, moreover, that Chinese recruited outside Taiwan would have had nationalist sympathies and the endorsement of the Guomindong authorities. This was the only way to guarantee 'reliable' personnel.

The presence of Guomindong officers reinforced the anti-communist leadership of the Chinese compounds and produced a particular emphasis in the orientation programme. Propaganda concentrated on repatriation to Taiwan, a campaign enforced by 'beatings, torture and threats of punishment'.[27] The role of US officials in this development is unclear. Psychological warfare officers, however, were the first to emphasise the propaganda advantages if large numbers of Chinese refused repatriation.[28] This suggests that certain elements in the FEC and at the Pentagon colluded with the Guomindong campaign on Koje. By late 1951, therefore, a situation had been allowed to develop in the camps which conflicted with the priority of securing a Korean armistice. It soon became clear that the communists would not accept a situation in which many of their men refused repatriation and opted for the regime on Taiwan. It was politically and ideologically impossible, however, for Washington to use force to break the hold of the anti-communist POWs. The result was deadlock at Panmunjom.

Before this position was reached in April 1952, there was a long debate on the POW issue in Washington. The question was a complex one, involving not only the future of the anti-communists at Koje, but also the welfare of UN prisoners in communist hands. On 10 August 1951 the JCS suggested voluntary repatriation as a means of protecting anti-communist POWs. The chiefs admitted the dangers to UN prisoners but justified departure from article 118 on humanitarian and political grounds. If the principle of asylum could be established, psychological warfare programmes would be strengthened and the US would enjoy an advantage in the global ideological struggle for 'the minds of men'.[29] The idea met with opposition, however, both at the highest level of the Defense Department and from the Department of State. According to Lovett, who had replaced the ailing Marshall at Defense, the communists would never accept voluntary repatriation and would retaliate against UN prisoners if the issue was forced. Acheson concurred, emphasising that the best hope of securing the safe return of UN POWs was to stand by article 118. He agreed, however, that those in danger of death for collaboration should be paroled and released. Nor should ROK citizens forcibly drafted into the NKPA in 1950 be deported to the north.[30] In his reluctance to return anti-communists in danger of reprisal, Acheson was supported by Truman. On 29 October, the President expressed his own aversion to returning collaborators to be 'done away with', even if this meant delaying an armistice indefinitely.[31]

Truman and Acheson were influenced by the experience of 1945, when under the Yalta agreement, all Soviet citizens in the Western zones were returned to Russia. Force had to be used and horrific scenes occurred on the transports where many committed suicide rather than accept repatriation. The remainder were either murdered or despatched to labour camps.[32] Humanitarian considerations, however, were influenced by political calculation. An attempt to return Chinese anti-communists would be seized upon by the Republicans as an invaluable weapon in a presidential election year. No better proof could be offered of McCarthy's charge that the Democrats were 'soft on communism'.[33] Acheson assumed an unrealistic position, however, in recommending that the US stand by article 118 *and* protect anti-communist POWs. The only way in which this could be achieved was if the communists agreed to a 1:1 exchange. Since the UNC held more POWs than the communists, it could both secure the return of its own men and protect collaborators in danger of reprisal. These could be withheld and subsequently paroled. It was unlikely, however, that the communists would agree to this solution. As Ridgway emphasised, they would probably insist on an all for all exchange. In order to secure the repatriation of UN prisoners and an armistice, he might have to return even hard-core anti-communists.[34] By November 1951 the JCS had abandoned its previous position and supported this argument. The chiefs admitted the risk to anti-communist POWs but could see no solution to the problem which would safeguard UN prisoners. Since the communists already knew, from lists supplied to the International Red Cross, the total number of men in UN hands, it would be impossible to withhold any substantial number without their knowledge.[35] The problem of protecting *both* the UN POWs *and* the anti-communists at Koje seemed insoluble, since resolution depended on enemy agreement to voluntary repatriation, a principle rejected out of hand when it was raised at Panmunjom in January 1952.

In order to speed the negotiations, it had been agreed to hold simultaneous sub-delegation meetings on items 3, 4 and 5.[36] Ridgway entered discussions on item 4 without any indication of Washington's final position on repatriation. On 15 January 1952 he was authorised to agree to an all for all exchange, provided 'no forcible return of POWs would be required'. He was warned, however, that this was not necessarily an irrevocable stand.[37] A final position was not worked out until the end of February. On 2 February U. Alexis Johnson, Under Secretary of State for Far Eastern Affairs, suggested a solution which would avoid forcing the communists to agree to voluntary repatriation. Johnson's idea was to screen the POWs. This involved interviewing the prisoners and segregating them into repatriates and non-repatriates. The non-repatriates would be removed from the POW lists and the communists offered an all for all exchange of the remainder. If the grounds for refusal were narrowly defined, a total might emerge which the communists could accept without loss of face. Johnson recognised that any deal depended on a high number of repatriates. By this stage, Washington was shifting its ground from *voluntary* to *non-forcible* repatriation. Only if a POW indicated a determination to resist exchange would he be removed from the POW lists.[38]

In early February Johnson was sent to Korea with General John E. Hull, Assistant Chief of Staff of the Army, to discuss such a solution with Ridgway and the UN truce team. Johnson suggested that the UNC offer to concede on airfield reconstruction in return for communist agreement to screening. If this bargain was rejected, the POWs could be screened without communist consent and the proposal brought forward again on the basis of the revised lists. The communists would have little legitimate excuse to criticise such a fait accompli, having already withheld large numbers of ROKs from their POW list on the grounds that these men had been 'released at the front'.[39] Doubts were expressed about this approach. Hull seemed 'almost embarrassed' and clearly shared the reservations of the JCS, who were worried about reprisals against American POWs. Nor was Ridgway enthusiastic, emphasising the irrevocable nature of screening.[40] The most outspoken critic, however, was Admiral Joy, who felt little sympathy for enemy POWs. They had surrendered, not for ideological reasons, but because they were 'hungry, poorly equipped and out of ammunition'. The demands for voluntary repatriation, which had been 'widely ballyhooed', could be traced to propaganda by 'Chinese Nationalist elements'. Screening without communist consent would inevitably endanger American POWs: 'We should sacrifice our men for a bunch of Chinese and North Koreans who were formerly our enemies and had shot at us.'[41] Despite these reservations, however, there seemed little alternative but prolonged deadlock. As Johnson explained, Truman felt 'very strongly' that some solution must be found which did not require forced repatriation. The UN stand must be defined within these parameters.[42] On 27 February the Johnson plan was approved by the President as the final and irrevocable position at Panmunjom. Every effort was to be made to secure communist agreement to screening before a fait accompli in order to protect UN POWs.[43]

In retrospect, the most remarkable aspect of the POW debate was the ignorance of all concerned about the situation in the camps. Nobody knew how many of the 132 000 prisoners in UN hands would refuse repatriation. On 2 April the Chinese suggested that since no progress was possible on the issue of principle, the talks should recess while lists were checked to produce a final figure for the POW exchange. This concession seemed to open the way to a compromise since screening could take place with tacit communist consent. Moreover, the Chinese seemed ready to accept less than a total exchange. When they pressed for an estimate of the total number likely to be produced when POW lists were checked, the UN team hazarded a guess of 116 000.[44] This was to prove unfortunate. The subsequent failure to produce such a number was viewed as a deliberate attempt by the US to score a propaganda victory at communist expense.

The communist concession at Panmunjom was viewed with 'cautious optimism' in Washington.[45] It was confidently expected that screening would produce a figure which the communists could accept without loss of face. The figure of 116 000 represented the total number of POWs in UN hands, less ROKs drafted into the NKPA, and not reclassified as civilians.[46] While it was felt to be rather high, the administration expected to have between 110 000 and 116 000 available for exchange. According to Johnson, the UNC held 9000 prisoners who did not appear on the official lists and could be used to replace non-repatriates. These were ROKs reclassified as civilians who had opted for the DPRK and guerrillas recently captured in OPERATION RATKILLER. The inclusion of this group would bring the repatriation figure to over 110 000.[47] According to Acheson, 'most of the Communist prisoners' would be 'quite ready to be repatriated'.[48] A State Department interrogation team, involved in an intelligence project using Chinese POWs, noted that despite Guomindong claims, only 25 per cent were unwilling to return and only 15 per cent genuine nationalists.[49] By even the most pessimistic estimate, 90 per cent of the Koreans and 40 per cent of the Chinese would be available for exchange.[50]

Such an outcome would remove the last major obstacle in the way of an armistice and secure the return of American POWs. Item 5, recommendations to goverments, had been settled on 19 February. A political conference was to be summoned within three months of the armistice to 'settle through negotiation the questions of the withdrawal of foreign forces' and the 'peaceful settlement of the Korean question etc.' The UN delegation agreed to this phrasing with the reservations that 'foreign forces' meant 'non-Korean forces' and that 'etc.' should not be taken as referring to questions such as Taiwan and the UN seat.[51] This left only the dispute over the rehabilitation of airfields and a new issue raised by the communists, the demand that the Soviet Union serve on the Neutral Nations Supervisory Commission. It was reckoned, however, that these were 'straw men' which could be used as bargaining counters.[52]

It was assumed in Washington that screening would take place in an atmosphere which guaranteed each POW freedom of choice. This, though, was far from the case. The communist compounds resisted screening. The camp command, lacking manpower, hesitated to use force. The anti-communist enclosures took steps to ensure a majority for non-repatriation. According to Chinese linguists with the US army, 'harrowing' scenes preceded the official screening, in which 'violent, systematic terrorism' occurred. Those who wanted repatriation were 'either beaten black and blue or killed'. As a result, when polled the majority were 'too terrified' to say anything but ' "Taiwan" repeated over and over again'. The figures produced by screening were 'by no means indicative of the POWs' real choice'.[53] It was clear that the situation on Koje was beyond the control of the military authorities. These developments were brought to the attention of officials only when it was already too late. A US civilian employee on Koje informed Muccio, who warned his superiors about the situation in the camps. Johnson, the author of the screening plan, admitted his own helplessness on reading Muccio's cable: 'All I can do now is to keep my fingers crossed and hope for the best.'[54] The army linguists complained to Joy, who approached Ridgway with their recommendation that the anti-communist compounds be broken up, the leadership removed and the POWs relieved of 'the terror which presently gripped them'. When Ridgway raised the matter with the Eighth Army, however, both Van Fleet and the camp command demurred. It was argued that the compounds could not be broken up without bloodshed. Moreover, removal of POW spokesmen would achieve little. They were merely figureheads and real power lay with a secret anti-communist council whose leadership could not be identified.[55] The flawed results of screening were allowed to stand.

The figure produced by the poll on Koje was fatal to the prospects of an early armistice. Of the 106 000 POWs screened, only 31 000 demanded repatriation. This number was brought up to 70 000 by counting the communist compounds which had not been screened. The majority of the Chinese had refused to be exchanged and demanded to be sent to Taiwan. This was a serious development, since it was already clear that Beijing would never accept such an outcome. Thus screening produced, not a solution, but a new problem. As Ridgway had warned, the results were irrevocable. When the communists were informed of the UN figure on 20 April, they were stunned. When Joy produced a package deal on 28 April, trading the UN position on airfields for communist acceptance of the revised POW list and the elimination of the USSR from the armistice commission, his offer was rejected. The communists were being asked to make two concessions to one by the UNC.[56] Moreover, the POW deal was based on figures regarded by the Chinese as both dishonest and humiliating. The armistice talks had reached deadlock.

Acheson had played a key role in the decision on non-forcible repatriation. The service chiefs were divided and the Defense Secretary, Lovett, had strong doubts. Nor were Ridgway and the truce team enthusiastic. Acheson's trump card, however, was his knowledge that he was telling Truman what the President wished to hear.[57] Truman had made his own repugnance to forced repatriation evident by the end of October 1951. It is unlikely that he then knew, or was ever subsequently informed, about the real situation at Koje. Once the President's views were known, Acheson never wavered and suppressed his earlier doubts. Truman's attitude assisted Acheson in the ensuing bureaucratic debate and discouraged doubters like Lovett, who was, in any case, new to his job. Both Acheson and Truman believed that humanitarian and ideological considerations were involved. Truman did not want to assume responsibility for a set of massacres such as followed Yalta. Moreover, in the struggle with Asian communism the non-repatriates were a useful propaganda weapon, demonstrating the illegitimacy of the regimes in Pyongyang and Beijing. For Americans, they would allow a military stalemate to end with moral victory, a conclusion with domestic political implications. Neither foresaw that the war would drag on for over a year on the POW issue.[58] This was, however, a risk they were prepared to take as part of the global struggle against communism.

The UN allies watched the evolution of POW policy with considerable misgivings. They were anxious both to secure a quick end to the war and to relieve the sufferings of their own men in enemy hands. There was some distrust of US motives, which was largely attributable to longstanding differences on China and Taiwan. This was particularly true of Britain, the major UN ally. As the Foreign Office remarked in January 1952, while there was an element of genuine humanitarianism in US policy, ideological considerations were also involved. The Americans 'with help from the Chinese Nationalists' had enjoyed 'some success in re-indoctrinating Chinese PWs in their charge'. These men were destined for Jiang's army. The longer the talks were bogged down over this issue, the longer British prisoners would be held by the communists. London had 'no interest at all' in seeing Guomindong forces built-up 'at the expense of additional suffering to British and Commonwealth prisoners'.[59] There was well-founded scepticism about the benefits of such a transfer to the

Chinese POWs themselves. It might be a case of leaping from 'the Communist frying pan into the Nationalist fire'.[60] Eden agreed with these sentiments. There was also a strong reluctance to depart from the Geneva convention, risking reprisals against UN prisoners and creating a precedent which might be used by the communists in future wars. These doubts, however, were overridden by countervailing pressures. Both Churchill and Eden had been party to the Yalta agreement on Soviet citizens and recalled the fate of those repatriated in 1945. The Prime Minister emphasised that the fate of the POWs involved considerations of 'honour and humanity'. They could not be turned over for execution or imprisonment.[61] Eden felt a similar concern. As he noted in February 1952, the legal grounds for non-repatriation might be poor 'but this doesn't make me like the idea of sending these poor devils back to death or worse'.[62] For both men, moreover, the Anglo-American alliance was of supreme importance. With Washington clearly moving towards non-forcible repatriation in early 1952, London hesitated to jeopardise relations by breaking step. Eden, however, continued to have private reservations. When the talks became bogged down on the issue, he emphasised that while there must be no departure from the principle of non-forcible repatriation, 'every possible means of circumventing the deadlock must be explored'.[63] This was to lead to friction with Washington later that year. The Australians displayed a similar mixture of public support and private doubt. The Prime Minister, Sir Robert Menzies, remarked that 'If the allied choice lay simply between continuation of the war and acceptance of forcible repatriation . . . he would have no hesitation in choosing the latter.'[64] He thus went further than Eden in criticising US policy. As Menzies recognised, however, other factors were involved. Australia, like Britain, did not wish to offend its major ally and encourage the communists by a public show of dissent. The ANZUS pact must not be endangered. Thus, during the final year of the war, 'Australian servicemen fought for a principle about which the Australian Government had major reservations.'[65]

The real victims of non-forcible repatriation were UN prisoners in communist hands who had to endure another year in their grim camps along the Yalu. In the spring of 1952 the Chinese admitted to holding 11 559 POWs, including 7142 ROKs, 3198 Americans, 919 British, 234 Turks, 40 Filipinos, 10 French, 6 Australians, 4 South Africans and one each from Canada, Greece and Holland. The figures for Koreans and Americans represented only a fraction of those recorded as missing in action. Many of the Americans had died of disease, malnutrition and ill-treatment in the winter of 1950/1, while 50 000 Koreans had been simply drafted into the North Korean army.[66] The position of the US personnel had featured in the early stages of the debate on repatriation and had influenced the views of the Pentagon, but they were ultimately sacrificed to the larger issues of the cold war. The fate of enemy non-repatriates was accorded a higher priority than the safety of captured UN soldiers. The POWs thus received a raw deal from their own side. As will be seen, their victimisation was to outlast the war.

On the communist side, POW policy was laid down by China. Western intervention surprised Pyongyang, which never had an opportunity to develop a coherent approach to POWs as the war swung from near victory to almost total defeat in November 1950. No preparations had been made to hold or exploit American prisoners. As a result, policy was made in the heat of battle. North Korean troops registered their resentment of UN intervention by brutal treatment. POWs were often shot, particularly if they were wounded and unable to walk. Those who survived capture were stripped of boots and uniforms and marched north, to be held in overcrowded civilian prisons or requisitioned schools.[67] At this stage, treatment improved. Although sanitary conditions and medical care remained poor, food became better. US prisoners in Pyongyang jail were fed on a diet of bread, rice, dried fish and fruit, with meat three times a week.[68] These changes coincided with the first concerted attempts to exploit POWs for propaganda purposes. Prisoners were invited to broadcast denouncing US intervention or to write statements supporting the North Korean case at the UN. General Dean, captured after the fall of Taejon, found his captors more anxious to secure this kind of concession than purely military information.[69] Such efforts at exploitation and propaganda, however, were short-lived. They collapsed with the Inchon landing and the imminent elimination of the North Korean state.

As MacArthur's advance began, the POWs were marched towards the Yalu and the onset of a savage winter, often without boots and in the remnants of their summer uniforms. Food was poor and scarce. There were no medicines and many died. Strafing by UN aircraft, fulfilling MacArthur's orders to destroy everything between the battleline and the Chinese border, added to the miseries imposed by brutal guards. Once more atrocities occurred. Philip Deane, an *Observer* correspondent captured in July outside Yongdong, was in a column commanded by Major 'Tiger' Kim of the Security Police, an officer who gained a well-merited reputation for brutality. Kim seems to have hated Westerners and took out his frustrated nationalism after Inchon on those in his charge. Kim executed one young American lieutenant for allowing sick and dying men to drop out of the column, contrary to North Korean orders.[70] Those who fell behind in this way were summarily shot. Deane later recalled: 'We heard many shots. At one point in the serpentine winds of the road, stopping because of dysentry, I looked down to the lower bend. The Tiger was pushing one of the dying with his foot into the ditch. When the GI was completely off the road, the Tiger shot him. I saw two more killed in this way . . . before the guard kicked me on.'[71] The worst mass atrocity took place north of Pyongyang, shortly after the city fell to Walker's Eighth Army. One hundred American POWs were taken from a train hiding inside a railway tunnel and shot by their guards, who then fled.[72] In the confusion of the North Korean collapse, such acts were committed by individual units acting out of panic or resentment over impending defeat. The remnants of the North Korean army were in a dangerous and desperate mood by November 1950. Deane talks of meeting 'small groups of ragged North Korean soldiers, battle-weary, wounded, dispirited and hostile.'[73] Some of those responsible for the November atrocities were captured by UN forces and identified by their surviving victims. They were never sentenced, however, because of fear of reprisals against UN prisoners in communist hands and were exchanged after the truce was signed in July 1953.

As the weary POWs reached the Yalu, they began to pass columns of Chinese troops moving south. Morale amongst the guards soared as news came in of new victories against MacArthur's forces. For the POWs, liberation, which had seemed so close, became once more a distant prospect. The Chinese brought with them a POW policy established during the civil war and the struggle against Japan. This was 'quickly and fairly consistently substituted for the brutal and non-political measures which the North Koreans . . . had applied to their captives'.[74] The so-called 'lenient policy' treated POWs as victims of the ruling classes, students who were to be educated and pointed towards the truth. Strict rules were laid down governing the treatment of prisoners. POWs were to be given food and medical treatment. They were to be neither robbed nor abused. Instead they were to be led towards an understanding of the true nature of the war and of their own societies. After such re-education, prisoners could either be released at the front to rejoin and demoralise their old units, or held for longer-term indoctrination. The first form was widely used against the Guomindong during the civil war. The longer-term manipulation of POWs was most evident in the treatment of Japanese captured in World War Two. These men were taken to special holding areas and any officers and NCOs were removed. The prisoners were then given lessons concerning 'the nature of the Chinese revolution and the character of Japanese society and of the war'. Novel ideas, questions and problems were presented 'with which the average Japanese was unfamiliar and unable to deal'. Promising students were given special privileges. The camps themselves were not closely guarded, language, appearance and the distance from the lines making it difficult for Japanese prisoners to escape. A similar pattern was to emerge in Korea. The purpose of this indoctrination was explained by the Japanese communist leader, Tetsu Nosaka, who argued that those who returned to postwar Japan with 'new ideas' would 'lead dozens or hundreds to work actively for a peaceful, democratic Japan and for its cooperation with the democratic world.' They would provide a guarantee against the revival of capitalism and militarism.[75] The Russians used similar tactics with German and Japanese POWs during the war. It was the apparent effectiveness of the policy in the case of the Japanese, which was to stimulate fears in the Pentagon about the ideological vulnerability of GIs in Korea.

The Chinese, therefore, regarded POWs as an asset and were anxious to take as many as possible, often at considerable risk to themselves. Non-American troops were a particular prize because they offered an opportunity to exploit tension between the US and its allies. The 'lenient policy', however, was not always strictly applied: 'During the early months of Chinese intervention, their claim to treat prisoners well was quite untrue.'[76] All soldiers loot and the PLA was no exception. POWs were quickly relieved of watches, rings and wallets. Nor were the Chinese in a position to practice what they preached.[77] The decision to intervene had been sudden and no preparations had been made to house and feed prisoners during the bitter winter of 1950/1, the worst in Korea for forty years. As a result, many died from exposure, wounds and poor food. Conditions did not improve until the summer of 1951, when a system of permanent camps took shape.[78] Atrocities continued to occur in the heat of battle, sometimes committed by North Korean rather than Chinese units. An NCO of the Northumberlands, captured at Easter 1951, witnessed two POW policies in force side by side. While the Chinese were distributing cigarettes and treating the wounded, the remainder of his section, which had fallen into North Korean hands, was being executed on the other side of the road.[79]

At the beginning, the Chinese exploited prisoners for short-term military advantage. POWs were given a meal and a political speech, before being released to their own lines. A group of Americans from Almond's X Corps, captured in November, were 'inspected by a Chinese officer who gave them cigarettes, a good meal of chicken, and told them they could rejoin their own forces. Then they were left to their own devices.' Others found themselves greeted by nurses who treated the wounded and distributed gifts of candy.[80] These tactics had an impact on troops who had been taught to think of the Chinese communists as 'brutal tyrants'.[81] In November/December 1950 the morale of many units was poor and the Pentagon took steps to prevent further demoralisation. Orders were issued to evacuate all released POWs through medical channels as quickly as possible. They were not to be returned to their units.[82] The Chinese soon abandoned the practice as UN morale improved with Ridgway's offensives in the spring. What had succeeded against the Guomindong and had shaken a beaten UNC, produced no returns against a revitalised and advancing army.

Thereafter, the Chinese concentrated on holding and indoctrinating POWs in camps along the Yalu. Unlike the German and Japanese camps of World War Two, these were relatively open: 'There was no barbed wire, no tiger boxes with machine gunes . . . and only a few guards stationed at strategic points. The Chinese hadn't bothered much about security. The vast expanse of territory between Chongsong and the UN lines was sufficient defence.[83] Escapes were few and unsuccessful. Escapers were instantly identifiable by language and appearance as Westerners and hence as the enemy. The country was inhospitable and the population hostile. Indeed the Chinese guards claimed to be protecting their 'students' from the wrath of the local population. There was some truth to this claim. The aerial destruction of the North did little to endear the West to Korean civilians. On occasion, POWs were spat upon and stoned.[84] Moreover, the extensive system of air raid warning posts throughout the area meant that all key points in the direction of the UN lines were thoroughly covered. No neutral state offered refuge. North Korea was bordered by China and the USSR, officially neutral, but unlikely to welcome and repatriate an escaping POW. Added to the risks and difficulties of escape was the fact that truce talks began in July 1951. In the circumstances, most prisoners concluded that it was sensible to await an armistice and a POW exchange.

Chinese methods of prisoner indoctrination became known as 'brainwashing', although neither drugs nor hypnotic techniques were employed. Rather, psychological pressure and calculated brutality was used within a totally controlled environment: 'Every activity of the prisoners, whether it was a sing-song or a private languages class, had to be censored and sanctioned beforehand if it were not to be branded as illegal and a hostile act calling for punishment.'[85] The process began by breaking down old forms of authority. Officers and NCOs were removed to special camps. The rest of the POWs were informed that although they could be considered war criminals, they would be given an opportunity to repent and learn the truth.[86] An educational programme began, explaining communism, capitalism and the origins of the war. Prisoners were encouraged to question and criticise the social and economic organisation of their own countries. They were expected not only to learn but also to confess past errors in self-criticism meetings.[87] Like born-again Christians, they were to give public testimony of repentance and repudiate past sins. The POWs were isolated from each other as well as from old forms of authority. Informing was deliberately encouraged to break down any kind of group solidarity and increase dependence on the Chinese. Where informers did not emerge, an illusion was created by inviting selected prisoners for long solitary walks or interviews with political officers. This was designed to produce distrust and ostracism which might eventually turn the selected prisoner into a real informer.[88] A special effort was made to play on racial and national antagonism. Blacks, Puerto Ricans and Filipinos were segregated from white Americans. An attempt was also made to single out Irish POWs.[89] It was hoped that these minorities would be particularly susceptible to indoctrination because of their victimisation by the US and British ruling classes.

The attempt to create a total environment, extended beyond study into leisure and recreation. Camp loudspeakers were tuned to the English language service of Radio Beijing. The few films shown were Soviet. One POW recalled that these mainly featured endless rows of combines, fighting the battle of production amongst a sea of grain. The Chinese also put on a showing of their epic revolutionary opera, 'The White-haired Girl'.[90] Contacts with the outside world were carefully controlled. The International Red Cross was refused access until just before the armistice. The only visitors from the outside were journalists sympathetic to the Communists, such as Alan Winnington of the *Daily Worker* and Wilfred Burchett of *Ce Soir*, or representatives of the World Peace Council.[91] The only English language reading materials were the *Daily Worker*, the *Shanghai Gazette* and a few Black American radical publications.[92] Mail was also manipulated to make POWs feel alientated and isolated. Letters from home were few and infrequent. Often only those containing bad news came through.[93] One British POW heard nothing from his mother for the duration of the war, although he received a letter from a girl accusing him of fathering her baby.

The education programme proceeded on a reward/punishment basis. Those who resisted or showed leadership qualities were removed. They were considered 'reactionaries', who had forfeited the right to 'lenient' treatment. Such men were subjected to beatings, confinement in latrine pits or 'sweat boxes' and deprivation of food and water. Everyone was made aware that Chinese patience was limited.[94] The full weight of Chinese brutality was used against air force prisoners in 1952 to secure germ warfare confessions. These were filmed and shown, not only to the world, but also to the POWs, to prove the evil of the UN side. Prisoners who showed a 'progressive' attitude were rewarded with special privileges and promoted to key positions in the 'Daily Life Committees' which ran the camps. They organised propaganda events such as the Inter-Camp Olympics of 1952, prepared study materials for other POWs and produced newspapers sympathetic to the administration.[95] The object of the whole education programme was to transform the prisoners into a force which would 'fight for peace' within their own societies upon release.

The POWs, however, also had an immediate propaganda role. They were encouraged to sign petitions condemning the UN role and to write letters home in praise of the Chinese. Since the communists did not produce a POW list until April 1952, collaboration in such efforts was the only way a prisoner could inform the world that he was still alive. Quite apart from a desire to reassure wives and relations, many POWs were anxious to publish the fact of their existence to make it harder for the Chinese subsequently to kill them or withold them from an exchange, a threat which was often made by political officers. The majority were guilty of such acts of technical collaboration, without ever becoming 'progressives'. The aim was to establish a modus vivendi with the Chinese in order to survive the war.[96] The families of POWs were also enrolled in the communist peace campaign. They were informed that the best means of securing the speedy return of the prisoners was to join the World Peace Council and 'fight for peace'. Like the petitions and letters, these appeals were part of an attempt to erode the will to fight on the home front, in order to secure concessions at Panmunjom. When repatriation became an issue, POWs were used in another propaganda role. Chinese 'lenient treatment' was contrasted to the brutality of the UN authorities at Koje. In 1952, the 'progressives' produced a pamphlet on the Inter-Camp Olympics, praising Chinese policy and emphasising the spirit of harmony and mutual understanding which characterised the relationship between the POWs and their captors.[97] Since the Chinese were insisting on a strict interpretation of article 118 of the Geneva convention, an insistence which contrasted sharply with their violation of other sections of the code, no attempt was made until the very end to encourage non-repatriation amongst the prisoners. In late 1952, however, the Chinese began to seek candidates who would refuse an exchange. Promises were made of a university education and a good job in China.[98] This effort eventually produced twenty-one Americans and one Scot, prepared to renounce their own countries.[99] 'The 22 Who Stayed' were to produce some agonised soul searching in the American bureaucracy and media about the supposed ideological vulnerability of GIs, which was out of all proportion to the numbers involved.

There was a great deal of concern in the Pentagon about Chinese policy. This was based partly on experience with returning Japanese POWs and partly on a low estimate of the average American's will to resist. It was heightened by the germ warfare confessions of flyers such as Enoch, Quinn and Schwable. If a senior marine officer with twenty years' experience, such as Colonel Schwable, could be broken, what hope had the average GI? In February 1953, the State Department noted:

> Defense is very much concerned over the effectiveness of the Communist campaign and sees in it very real dangers, not only to the morale of US combat troops but also the home front and to the very moral fiber of our American system. Defense is particularly concerned lest the Communists release a huge batch of prisoners who . . . would have to be allowed to go to their widely dispersed home towns, where, having been 'converted', they could do immeasurable harm.[100]

This linked into military concern that the war-weary American people might let down their guard after the armistice and, as in 1945, demand massive demobilisation. Released POWs 'fighting for peace' could contribute to such a development. The scale of military concern was revealed during the exchange of sick and wounded prisoners, OPERATION LITTLE SWITCH, arranged with the communists two months later. As Clark recalled, 'Someone in Washington was apparently paralysed with fright at the possibility of our boys spouting the Communist line.' The fear was that the Chinese would stack the exchange with 'progressives' who would immediately go to work on the American home front. Clark was ordered to 'segregate suspected pro-Communists and ship them back in isolated groups', a policy to which he objected as 'pure character assassination'.[101] While instituting such precautions, the Pentagon was wrestling with the problem of warning the American people of the dangers without causing undue alarm or a witch-hunt against returning POWs. As one study concluded, terms such as 'brain-washing' or 'conversion' should not be used. Any information programme must 'avoid the impression that our captured soldiers were or are easy propaganda targets and readily converted or reoriented. We should not encourage the impression that Communism or Communists are overly persuasive, nor that our men are unduly naive and easy marks.'[102] In the soul-searching which followed America's first draw in war, however, this was to be precisely what happened. For many returning prisoners, repatriation was to become a 'March to Calumny'.[103]

9 Deadlock at Panmunjom

The impasse at Panmunjom coincided with presidential election year in the US, a conjunction which worried the UN allies. The volatile state of American public opinion and its possible impact on the conduct of the war had long been a source of concern. In September 1951 Herbert Morrison, the British Foreign Secretary, remarked that it was as necessary to 'restrain the more impulsive elements in America as it was to avoid provoking the Soviet Union'.[1] In February 1952 the Canadian ambassador, Hume Wrong, noted uneasily that the leading contender for the Republican nomination, Senator Taft, was advocating the unleashing of Jiang and a US-sponsored nationalist landing on the Chinese mainland. The public response to such appeals was 'hard to assess': 'There is a powerful sentiment . . . for winding up of the fighting in Korea. . . . Coupled with it is a desire to make the Chinese Communists suffer for what they have done. Unless there is an armstice soon, this will be exploited for domestic reasons during the campaign. In an election year, amateur strategy and diplomacy can exercise an unusually powerful influence on policy.'[2] The UN allies, therefore, redoubled their efforts to contain Washington. They sought to break the POW deadlock and restrain the Americans from precipitate action, an effort which reached its height at the UN in the autumn. In the process, the relationship between the US and its partners was subjected to new stresses and strains.

As Wrong had predicted, foreign policy played a key role in the campaign. The Republicans had been gearing up for such an assault ever since the Great Debate. The prospects for the Democrats were not encouraging. The party was weakened by a series of unsavoury corruption scandals and the attacks of McCarthy. Its leadership was stale, tired and saddled with an unpopular war. The standing of the administration had hit rock bottom: 'Truman endured his last months in office with a popularity rating of 23 per cent, the worst for any president in the history of poll-taking.'[3] On 29 March the President announced that he would not seek another term. This confirmed a private decision taken some time previously but was doubtless encouraged by Truman's dim prospects of re-election.[4] At the party convention in June, Adlai Stevenson emerged as Democratic candidate. Stevenson had a liberal record as Governor of Illinois but little experience of national politics. He tried to turn this to advantage, however, emphasising his distance from the administration. Stevenson refused to run as Truman's candidate and dissociated himself from the 'mess in Washington'.[5] This independence, however, did not extend to foreign policy. Stevenson defended Korea and containment, arguing that Truman's decision to intervene had prevented further aggression and global war. Refusing to endorse either appeasement or escalation, Stevenson promised the American people more of the same. As Truman had predicted, on this issue at least, Stevenson was running on the record of the outgoing administration.[6] This fact was to be exploited by the Republicans.

Although Taft was the Republican front runner in early 1952, he lost the nomination to General Dwight D. Eisenhower, who resigned his NATO command in April to seek office. Eisenhower was firmly identified with collective security and Europe first, standing at the opposite pole to the military hero of the right, MacArthur. His candidacy was encouraged by the eastern wing of the party which distrusted Taft as a mid-Western 'isolationist' who would repudiate containment in favour of 'fortress America'. Eisenhower himself claimed that his bid was dictated by the desire to save the country from the disaster of a Taft presidency. This was an exaggeration. Eisenhower had long been grooming himself for political office. As his fellow soldier, General George Patton, remarked in 1943, 'Ike wants to be President so bad you can taste it.' Beneath his cheerful open manner, lurked a fierce political ambition.[7] Ike's strength lay in his personal popularity and his ability to appeal to a broad spectrum outside party ranks. Since the Republicans were a minority, it was important to find someone who could win the votes of independents and dissident Democrats.[8] At the convention in Chicago, the party listened to its head rather than its heart and nominated Eisenhower over Taft, 'Mr Republican'. It was clear that many party stalwarts regarded Ike merely as a vehicle for gaining office. As the General complained, they talked about using his popularity as if he 'hadn't a brain in his head'.[9]

It was widely assumed that Ike's nomination meant that foreign policy would not become a political football. Both candidates shared a consensus on containment. Indeed during the Truman period, Eisenhower was closer to decision-making than Stevenson.[10] He was prepared, however, to fight a partisan campaign, both to appease the right following Taft's defeat and to tap the deep public frustration with containment, a policy which was symbolised by the Korean war.[11] The Republican platform and the Republican ticket attempted to strike a balance between both wings of the party. The platform endorsed collective security and alliances, while condemning the Democrats for handing over free peoples to communist enslavement at the Yalta conference. It condemned containment as negative and immoral, erecting in its place the concept of 'liberation'.[12] This idea had first been floated by Taft but was taken up and elaborated by John Foster Dulles, the acknowledged Republican expert on foreign policy. Dulles resigned from the State Department following the ratification of the Japanese peace treaty and re-entered politics. He wasted no time in establishing his distance from the administration he had served. His criticisms reflected not only his genuine doubts about the viability of NSC-68 but also a desire to stand well with the right wing of the party. Dulles, like Eisenhower, was a man with an ambition. He wanted to become Secretary of State, a post which had escaped him when Truman defeated Dewey in 1948. He did not want to be thwarted by the objections of the 'primitives' who had hounded Acheson.[13]

Dulles developed his ideas in a *Life* magazine article in May 1952. Drawing on earlier statements by Taft, he repudiated containment in favour of a policy of 'boldness'. Instead of pursuing 'treadmill policies' which threatened national bankruptcy in an attempt to match Soviet moves around the globe, America should counter communist probes 'with weapons of our own choosing, against targets of our own choosing, at times of our own choosing.' If the USSR feared such a response, it would not commit aggression. Although Dulles did not openly advocate the use of atomic weapons, he clearly relied upon them to provide his deterrent, an approach known as 'massive retaliation'. He coupled this with 'liberation', an ideological crusade to stimulate freedom in the satellite states. According to Dulles, these policies would contain and roll back Soviet power. Deterred from expansion and sapped from within, the communist empire would crumble.[14]

Eisenhower had doubts about 'massive retaliation' and resisted an attempt to include it in the party platform. He protested that it was too 'isolationist', reflecting the fortress America concepts of Taft. He endorsed 'liberation', however, as the price of party unity. His choice of running mate reflected a similar desire to placate the right. He selected Richard Nixon, the prosecutor of Alger Hiss, who stood well with the Taft wing. Ike's strategy soon became clear. He would take the high road to the White House, enrolling the American people in a 'crusade for freedom'. The right would be allowed to pursue its own brand of politics.[15] Despite his personal dislike of figures like

1. President Harry S. Truman and Secretary of State Dean G. Acheson, October 1950. Truman was about to fly across the Pacific to meet General Douglas MacArthur, a pilgrimage from which Acheson begged to be excused.

2. President Harry S. Truman decorates General Douglas MacArthur at Wake Island, October 1950. This was the high spot in their stormy relationship.

4. General Matthew B. Ridgway. Ridgway saved the Eighth Army from disaster in January 1951 and went on to succeed MacArthur as UN commander.

3. The British Prime Minister, Clement Attlee, flies to Washington in December 1950. As China intervened in the war, he wished to assert the British point of view and contain the fighting.

5. The British Prime Minister Winston Churchill and his Foreign Secretary Anthony Eden visit Washington, January 1952. Their aim was to restore the Anglo-American relationship of the Second World War.

6. The British Defence Minister, Lord Alexander, and the Minister of State at the Foreign Office, Selwyn Lloyd, visit a POW compound after the Koje riots. They saw only what they wanted to see to reassure British public opinion.

7. Syngman Rhee visiting British troops. The Korean leader was often an embarrassment to the UN cause.

8. General Dwight D. Eisenhower visits the front, December 1950. During his election campaign, Eisenhower had pledged that he would 'go to Korea'.

9. General Mark W. Clark signs the armistice 'with a heavy heart', July 1953. Like his predecessor MacArthur, Clark wanted victory.

10. ROK recruits press-ganged from the streets of Pusan. These confused and demoralised men were thrown into combat within days.

11. North Korean POW at Taegu, July 1950. In September the US Army took over responsibility for POWs because of the tendency of the ROKs to 'mistreat or kill POWs at the slightest provocation'.

12. & 13. Political prisoners on their way to execution. This 'medieval spectacle' had been going on for months within yards of US Army HQ. The suppression of the *Picture Post* containing these photos caused a Fleet Street scandal.

14. ROK marines at Inchon, September 1950. ROK forces were responsible for many atrocities in the liberated city.

15. 'A roundup of Communist suspects at Inchon'. As James Cameron reported, Rhee's definition of subversion was a wide one.

16. Mass grave at Hamhung discovered by advancing UN forces. As the DPRK collapsed in the autumn of 1950, the political police took revenge on their prisoners.

17. Refugee children in the ruins of Seoul. By December 1950 much of the population was homeless.

18. North Korean POWs repatriated to the DPRK proclaim their loyalty to King Il Sung, July 1953. The flags had been stained with their own blood.

19. The US, UN and ROK flags welcome reinforcements at Pusan, July 1950. Despite the UN banner, the war was run by the Americans.

20. The first US troops at Pusan, July 1950. Poorly trained and overweight from occupation duty in Japan, these men were soon on the brink of defeat.

21. US Military Police at Taijon, July 1950. The exhausted faces of these men reflect the strain of combat and retreat.

22. A US marine at Inchon, September 1950. The tea-room sign contrasts grimly with the surrounding desolation.

23. Jubilant American troops liberate Pyongyang, October 1950. The occupation of the communist capital was to be brief.

24. British troops round up NKPA stragglers, November 1950. The North Koreans were 'totally defeated and only too willing to give up to the first people who would take them'.

25. The US marines escape encirclement in north-west Korea, December 1950. Both sides suffered badly from the bitter winter weather.

26. A British outpost on the Imjin, 1952. When the truce talks began, Korea became a static war waged from such defensive positions.

27. A wounded Canadian is helped to a casualty station, winter 1952. Despite the truce talks, the war continued to take its toll.

28. An American jet pilot describes a 'kill'. The fighter pilots regarded themselves as an elite and had a glamorous war.

29. A MIG pilot ejecting over the Yalu. Poor training made communist losses in air combat high.

30. US troops toast the armistice. Orders were issued against any fraternisation with the enemy as the guns fell silent.

31. Non-repatriate Chinese released by the Indian Custodial Force, January 1954. The dispute over the fate of these men had delayed the armistice for fifteen months.

32. An American POW returns from North Korea, August 1953. For many of these men, repatriation was a 'March to Calumny'.

McCarthy, Ike was prepared to share platforms with such men in the cause of party unity. The most notorious of these occasions occurred in McCarthy's home state of Wisconsin. In 1951 McCarthy had attacked Eisenhower's friend and sponsor General Marshall as a traitor, because of his association with the 'loss' of China. Eisenhower planned to defend Marshall from a platform shared with the Senator but omitted the passage from his speech at the last moment. The demands of politics outweighed old obligations.[16]

In choosing to preach 'liberation', Eisenhower avoided commitment to specific measures. The concept was kept carefully ambiguous, although Ike emphasised that the policy would be pursued by peaceful means. 'Liberation', however, threatened to boomerang in late August. After a militant speech at Buffalo, Dulles was rash enough at a press conference to offer a vision of revolution in Eastern Europe, armed and supported by the US. This raised fears of atomic war at home and abroad on which Stevenson was quick to capitalise.[17] It threatened to undercut Eisenhower's support amongst independent voters a key element in his campaign. Ike was furious with Dulles over the incident and after emphasising the peaceful nature of 'liberation', dropped the concept from the remainder of his campaign.[18]

His political advisers, however, were already working up a new issue – Korea. Polls showed that the war was the overriding concern of Americans. It was an issue on which Eisenhower could exploit his wartime record against the inexperience of Stevenson. The American people would be invited to place their faith in Eisenhower's ability to end the war. Ike had previously hesitated to exploit Korea. He had approved of Truman's decision to intervene and opposed escalation. Moreover, he felt a professional reluctance to undercut the men in the field who were struggling with the problems of the armistice. The lure of victory, however, drove Eisenhower on. Korea was the one issue which could really mobilise the Republican right, many of whom distrusted the General on the basis of his record and his defeat of Taft. It would also appeal to a wider electorate. In order to harness these constituencies, Eisenhower opted for ambiguity. He would imply an ability to change matters and condemn Truman, without endorsing specific measures. He would be all things to all men. He brought Korea into his campaign in mid-September in a speech at Cincinatti, attributing the war to the failures of the administration. American soldiers had been called upon to fight because of the mistaken policies of the politicians. On 3 October, capitalising on a new wave of US casualties as fighting flared up along the front, he called upon the ROK to assume a larger share in the war. It was to be 'Asians against Asians' with American support on 'the side of freedom'.[19]

These partisan attacks infuriated Truman. The President had originally admired Eisenhower and sounded him out about the Democratic nomination in 1951. He now believed that Ike had fallen into the hands of the isolationists and was busy repudiating everything he had previously stood for.[20] In private he was bitterly derogatory, claiming that Ike knew 'as much about politics as a pig knows about Sunday'.[21] Eisenhower's failure to defend Marshall was bad enough, but his exploitation of the Korean issue was downright disloyal: 'I will never understand how a responsible military man . . . could use this tragedy for political advantage.'[22] For Truman, it was the last straw, and in mid-September he embarked on a speaking campaign, less to support Stevenson, than to blast Ike. Eisenhower reacted badly, claiming that the President had lowered the dignity of his high office by 'undignified behavior' and low partisanship. The relationship between the two never recovered. When Eisenhower visited the White House in January 1953 to ride with Truman to his inaugural, the frigid atmosphere was obvious.[23]

Despite Truman's spirited intervention, Korea proved to be a winning issue. In a carefully timed speech on 24 October, designed to answer Truman's challenge that Eisenhower should make his remedy clear, Ike argued that the Democrats could not solve the problem they had created. If elected, he would make the war his first priority. He would 'go to Korea'. Ike had in fact promised no solution but had given the impression of a commitment to action.[24] The effect was electrifying. As newsmen informed his campaign chief, Sherman Adams, 'That does it – Ike is in.'[25] It was an appeal which the Democrats could not match. The party was inescapably entangled in an exhausting and endless war: 'Stevenson, trapped by Truman's record and convinced that there was no other way out, ended up a sacrifical lamb.'[26] Eisenhower won a landslide victory in November, performing better than his party which rode on his coattails to a bare majority in both houses of Congress. His triumph owed much to the popular belief that he could achieve an honourable settlement in Korea and end the frustrations of the Truman period.[27] It remained to be seen how he would execute his mandate.

It was against this political background that events in Korea unfolded. Truman's instinct in the spring was to be tough with the communists in an attempt to force them to terms. He would not concede anything on the repatriation issue, the only question that remained unresolved at Panmunjom. The President sought an armistice which would allow him to claim moral victory. The defection of large numbers of enemy POWs provided a useful weapon in the battle for Asian hearts and minds and might weaken the authority of the Beijing regime. Truman's combative instincts were merely confirmed by domestic politics. With the Republicans raising the cry of 'liberation', the return of defectors to communist tyranny was unthinkable, even had the President so wished. Truman was aware that the war constituted a formidable political handicap for the Democratic candidate in November. He would not consider, however, the smallest compromise to the communists simply for partisan political advantage. The truce had to be firm and viable. He hoped that an inflexible position in the talks, coupled with increased military pressure, would force the communists to an armistice on terms which would vindicate him and his party before the electorate and before history. If his decisions were influenced by domestic politics, it was in the direction of stepping up military action to bring the enemy quickly to a settlement. The last restrictions on military action within the parameters of limited war were swept away in the spring of 1952.[28]

The Chinese, however, pushed back, equally hoping to break the impasse at Punmunjom by military pressure. Their tactic was to stand firm on the POW issue in the hope of forcing a compromise as the US election campaign warmed up. Various means were used to embarrass the administration, including limited area ground attacks, timed to coincide with the final stages of the elections.[29] As the war flared up on the ground and in the air, the UN allies found themselves caught in the middle. A combination of Chinese intransigence and American inflexibility left a truce as far away as ever as the war entered its third year. As rumours spread that the US was considering a blockade of China and a request for further reinforcements from its UN partners, Eden wrote a minute which captured the mood of allied frustration and concern: 'I do not want to be further entangled in China, nor have we the forces to spare to relieve them of any part of their burden in Korea'.[30] As the Foreign Office noted, 'The last thing we want is tough resolutions pushed through merely from a feeling that something must be done.'[31]

The deadlock at Panmunjom was followed by trouble in the Koje camps. The communists claimed that force had been used to secure a majority in favour of non-repatriation. In support of this claim, the communist compounds kidnapped the camp commander, General Dodd, on 8 May. In return for his release, they demanded a public admission that the UNC had been guilty of brutality. Dodd's replacement, General Colson, seemed to concede these charges to secure the release of his colleague.[32] The incident coincided with the transfer of General Ridgway to Eisenhower's NATO post and the arrival of General Mark Clark as UNC commander. Clark was a militant anti-communist, who had been convinced by his experiences with the Russians in post-war Austria that communists only understood force.[33] His response to the Dodd affair was to take firm measures to restore order, backed by Washington, which was severely embarrassed by the whole incident.[34] Combat troops were drafted into Koje and camp personnel fired 'left and right'. Dodd and Colson were court martialled and reduced in rank. A new POW command was established. At the end of May, OPERATION REMOVAL cleared refugees from the vicinity of the camps to prevent communication between the POWs and the communist high command. This was followed by OPERATION BREAKUP, which dispersed the communist compounds into smaller units.[35] There was fighting and fatalities on both sides. Clark, however, was determined to impose discipline. The POW command instituted a 'shoot to kill' policy. 'POW threw rocks at UNC personnel: POW shot dead', was considered a satisfactory incident report.[36] Van Fleet, the Eighth Army commander, warned his subordinates: 'I will be much more critical of your using less force than necessary than too much.'[37] This crackdown occurred only in the communist cages. The non-repatriates collaborated with the camp command and were not affected. They were removed from Koje, the Chinese to the island of Cheju-do and the Koreans to the mainland.[38]

The Koje riots embarrassed the administration. They revealed that the camps were out of control and raised doubts about the screening process.[39] The UN allies felt that Washington had handled the situation badly and was attempting to share the blame. British and Canadian combat troops formed part of the UN force drafted in by Clark to impose order. Ottawa regarded the POW issue as a political hot potato and wished to avoid direct responsibility for the camps. The government protested against the use of Canadian troops, referring to the established principle that a Canadian force should not be broken up without the consent of Ottawa. The unfortunate Canadian liaison officer who had authorised the move was recalled from Tokyo and retired prematurely.[40] The Americans were furious at Canadian disloyalty in the crisis while Moscow Radio made the most of the affair.[41] Washington was forced to justify its position on POWs. On 20

May a meeting at the State Department agreed that for 'public consumption' there should be a 'frank statement' about the difficulties on Koje and an admission of past error. It was to be emphasised, however, that the US stood by the Geneva convention, while the communists were using the POWs for 'provocation and propaganda purposes'. The crackdown in the compounds had been provoked. The refusal of over 80 000 men to accept repatriation was to be stressed since it hit the communists 'in a most sensitive and vulnerable spot' while vindicating the US. There were, however, certain other facts 'about which there is some doubt as to the desirability of full public disclosure'. These included

a) Chinese Nationalist influence prior to the screening of the Chinese POWs

b) Prisoner-to-prisoner brutality preceding and during the screening. Paul Nitze, of the State Department, described these questions as 'the firecrackers under the table'. Thus the administration opted to cover up the flaws in screening. Instead a firm line against the communist compounds would be coupled with an emphasis on the moral victory represented by 80 000 non-repatriates.[42] This protected the administration on the domestic front while attempting to keep allied opinion in line.

The POW dispute coincided with the communist germ warfare campaign. The Americans were accused of dropping insects infected with typhus, bubonic plague and other epidemic diseases on North Korea and Manchuria. Although such charges had emerged at an earlier stage in the war, they were not developed into a coherent propaganda campaign until February 1952. China and the DPRK refused to allow either the International Red Cross or the World Health Organisation to investigate the situation on the grounds that these organisations were biased towards the West. Their case rested on confessions by captured airmen, such as Enoch, Quinn and Schwable, and on the findings of an international scientific commission sponsored by the World Peace Council, an organisation backed by Moscow. In the West, the germ warfare charges were dismissed as propaganda, designed to compensate for the humiliation of the repatriation figures and to discredit the US in Asia. It was also argued that they were a useful cover-up for the communists' own failure to safeguard public health.[43] While the charges were clearly manipulated, however, they should not be simply dismissed. The Japanese had experimented with bacteriological warfare against China between 1940 and 1942. The campaign was conducted by Unit 731, which used insects to spread

plague and conducted tests on POWs and political prisoners. The
Japanese scientists responsible were captured by the Americans in
1945 and promised immunity from prosecution in return for
cooperation.[44] Moscow and Beijing were aware that Japanese
experience and personnel had been incorporated in US bacteriological
warfare research programmes. The Chinese, therefore, had every
reason to fear that Washington might follow the Japanese example and
launch germ attacks. The evidence suggests that the communists took
their charges seriously. It was but a short step to connect the outbreak
of epidemic disease behind the front with American air activity.

While the communists had reason to believe their charges, however,
conclusive evidence has never emerged. The airmen retracted their
confessions on repatriation while the scientific commission could be
dismissed as a communist front, despite the presence of eminent
figures such as Professor Joseph Needham, a Cambridge biochemist.
It is known that Washington was conducting a germ warfare research
programme which was accelerated after 1950. It was argued that the
US must be in a position to retaliate against enemy first use of such
weapons.[45] It is also known that in the immediate aftermath of Chinese
intervention, the Pentagon considered employing nerve gas to stabilise
the situation.[46] This is not evidence, however, of germ attacks later in
the war. The UN command certainly displayed a strong interest in the
health of the enemy. Special operations were mounted to secure
detailed information on epidemics, which included attempts to kidnap
communist soldiers from military hospitals.[47] It could be argued that
such raids were necessary to secure knowledge which would safeguard
UN troops against the spread of disease across the lines. It could
equally be claimed, however, that such operations were intended to
monitor the results of a germ warfare campaign. It is possible that
while not launching a full-scale attack in Korea, the US experimented
with insect vectors as delivery systems, an explanation later favoured
by Wilfred Burchett, who covered the war from the communist side,
and by Professor Needham.[48] This hypothesis is also open to question.
Such tests would have revealed the progress of American research in
peripheral attacks against the communist 'second team', allowing the
Russians to develop counter-measures for use in a wider conflict. The
Pentagon felt that it was lagging behind the Russians in the area of
bacteriological warfare. In April 1952, the planners complained that if
the signal to retaliate were given in a war with the Soviet Union, the US
could 'make little more than a token effort'. Washington would lack a
significant BW capacity until 1954.[49] In the absence of convincing

evidence the case must remain open, although on balance it is unlikely that germ warfare was employed.

Whatever the truth about germ warfare, the impasse at Panmunjom forced Washington to consider new ways of putting military pressure on the communists. It was believed that ground offensives would incur heavy casualties for little tangible gain. American losses would have an inevitable effect on the domestic front where the presidential campaign was beginning. In May 1952 Mark Clark succeeded Ridgway as UN commander and instituted a review of options. This concluded that the most cost effective means of pressure was air power. Air warfare should be intensified and directed at targets of economic importance. This might bring home to the communists the crippling costs of the war and break the deadlock at Panmunjom. The most prominent targets of this type were the Yalu river power plants, which had been immune from attack since 1950. They provided electricity, not only to North Korea, but also to Manchuria and Soviet installations at Dairen and Port Arthur. Clark expected problems with Washington and was surprised to receive quick approval for his plan.[50] Truman was obviously gambling on tough action to force an end to the war. On 23 June, the biggest 'Air-Force-Navy air assault of the war' was launched against the key plant at Suiho. Altogether, thirteen installations were bombed. This ushered in a new strategy, 'air pressure' to force acceptance of UN truce terms.[51]

The escalation of the air war drew protests from Australia, New Zealand and India. The biggest political storm, however, occurred in Britain. London had supported Washington on the POW issue, although with increasing misgivings as it became clear that the results of the screening would be unacceptable to the Chinese. The deadlock in the talks, the Koje riots and rumours of Guomindong influence in the camps, raised questions about US policy which the government felt ill-equipped to answer. Its own private information, from the UN commission on Korea and other sources, suggested that terror was commonplace in both the communist and anti-communist cages. The situation had not been 'conducive to the delicate process of screening'. As the Foreign Office remarked apprehensively on 24 March: 'A deplorable state of affairs this seems. . . . If one half of this should reach the ears of Parliament there will be hell to pay.'[52] In order to reassure domestic opinion, Selwyn Lloyd, Minister of State at the Foreign Office, and Lord Alexander, Minister of Defence, were sent to Korea in June 1952. Eden emphasised the 'parliamentary value' of the exercise.[53] The ministers talked to the camp administration and visited a compound for Korean non-repatriates. Lloyd was disturbed by the presence of a strong anti-communist organisation amongst the POWs and reports of nightly beatings behind the wire. He was persuaded, however, that this was a cultural rather than a political phenomenon. Koreans were simply prone to violence. Alexander emphasised the violence in the communist compounds. Both pronounced themselves satisfied with the screening.[54] There is a strong suspicion that they allowed themselves to be persuaded rather than confront Washington on a sensitive issue. A reporter from the *Toronto Star*, who accompanied Lloyd, recorded a far different impression. The government was embarrassed when his report was picked up and published in Britain by the *Daily Worker*.[55] The ministers not only reassured Parliament on the POW issue, but also the Canadians. They returned via Ottawa and reported their favourable impressions of Koje to the Canadian cabinet.[56]

While in Korea the British visitors met Clark and raised the possibility of placing a British officer on his staff who could influence decisions and keep the government informed. This reflected a desire to avoid the fait accompli presented when British troops were sent to Koje. Alexander emphasised the political value of the appointment. It would help the government defend itself against Bevanite attacks. He also raised the question of British representation at Panmunjom While the US agreed to the appointment of a British Deputy Chief of Staff at the UNC, a British presence at the truce talks was unwelcome. It would stimulate demands from other allies and complicate the negotiations. Moreover, it would encourage the communists in the wake of the Canadian controversy by indicating lack of confidence in American leadership. In the light of this response the British did not pursue the issue.[57] The goal of the mission, to reaffirm public faith in the Anglo-American alliance, was undermined by the Yalu bombing. The British ministers had not been informed about the plan, probably because of US doubts about British security following the Burgess–Maclean spy scandal. It seemed a slap in the face, however, to launch the operation just after Lloyd and Alexander had left Korea. Attlee charged that the attack violated the Morrison–Acheson agreement in which London had agreed to such raids only if truce talks collapsed.[58] As the State Department admitted, the bombing represented a change of policy and 'consultation should have taken place'.[59] While Churchill defended the raids as legitimate military operations, he faced a storm in the Commons. As Lloyd emphasised, the Prime Minister would probably have agreed if consulted. Unilateral action made it difficult to defend US policy.[60] Eden asked Acheson to defuse the situation in a private address to MPs on 26 June, admitting that Britain should have been consulted and pledging closer cooperation in the future.[61]

When the Yalu attacks occurred, tentative contacts had been established with China on the POW issue through India. In early May, Zhou suggested to New Delhi that London use its influence to secure an armistice.[62] Although wary of a possible attempt to drive a wedge in the Anglo-US alliance, Eden was anxious to follow up this feeler.[63] The longer the war lasted, the greater the danger of escalation. In the emotional atmosphere of an election year the risk was particularly acute. It was therefore, important to break the deadlock at an early stage. While a formula was still under discussion with Washington, Pannikkar acted on his own, suggesting that POWs be rescreened by a belligerent commission with a neutral chairman.[64] On 15 June, Zhou responded favourably to this approach, adding his own modifications. He proposed that rescreening be supervised by a neutral commission and that it take place in a neutral zone with the POWs released from military control and the influence of Guomindong agents.[65] This initiative came to nothing. On 3 July the Chinese insisted that while the Geneva convention need not be applied to Koreans who were in their own country, all 'foreigners', that is Chinese, must be automatically repatriated.[66] Nehru blamed the Suiho bombing. This implied that a realignment of forces had occurred in Beijing in which Zhou was overruled.[67] It was by no means clear, however, how much the earlier scheme owed to Zhou and how much to the fertile imagination of Pannikkar. It was later suspected that the affair had been engineered by the ambassador who had put words into Zhou's mouth to inflate his own importance with the Indian hierarchy.[68] Whatever the reality, the Suiho attack was at best 'ill-timed'. As the Chinese Vice-Minister for Foreign Affairs informed the Indian embassy, Beijing would not be forced into concessions by 'gunboat tactics'.[69]

While Washington was dealing with the Koje riots and allied reaction to the Suiho bombing, it also faced a crisis with the ROK. Rhee had always been an unsatisfactory ally, sniping at the truce talks and demanding ever larger amounts of aid. He further embarrassed the Americans by his 'intense antipathy to anything Japanese'. Soon after Clark's arrival, he protested at the employment of Japanese technicians by the UNC and had his police harry and arrest them.[70] As if this were not enough, he provoked a political crisis in the ROK by proclaiming martial law in Pusan on 25 May. Rhee had been elected for a four year term in 1948, under a constitution which placed the

choice of President in the hands of the political assembly. He had since
alienated many politicians and was not guaranteed a second term in
1952. Rhee demanded that the assembly amend the constitution to
allow his election by direct popular vote. When this was resisted, he
proclaimed martial law and arrested several dissident assembly-men,
claiming that they had been corrupted by the communists. He
threatened to dissolve the assembly if it remained intransigent.[71]
Martial law raised questions about the status of the ROK army in the
UN command. Rhee might involve it in a civil war behind the front
without consulting Clark. Moreover, his action struck directly at the
basis of the US military training programme, which was attempting to
create an efficient force by reducing political factionalism in the officer
corps. Rhee threatened to purge the ROK Chief of Staff and impose a
figure more closely tied to his own political future. It was reported that
morale in the ROK forces was suffering as a result.[72]

American embarrassment was intensified by reaction abroad, which
was universally unfavourable. Rhee's action did not increase the
popularity of the war. As one Canadian diplomat complained, it was
difficult for the Western democracies to justify sending arms and
money to a regime which locked up the opposition.[73] Plimsoll, the
Australian head of the UN commission on Korea, warned Rhee that
public opinion throughout the world was shocked. This might have a
'bad effect' on support for the ROK at the UN.[74] A similar warning
was delivered by Lord Alexander at a meeting in Pusan. The British
people did not understand martial law 'and things like that'.[75] He had
only himself to blame if the ROK was misunderstood. The US joined
this chorus of condemnation and pressed for the repeal of martial law.
Washington went so far as to authorise planning for the arrest of Rhee
and the installation of an alternative government by the UNC.[76] Clark,
however, was reluctant to launch OPERATION EVERREADY,
except if Rhee directly threatened the safety of his command. With
truce talks at a standstill and combat troops committed to Koje, he
simply lacked the manpower to impose order behind the lines.[77] A
major weakness of EVERREADY was not merely shortage of troops,
but the growing realisation that there was nobody to whom the UNC
could hand over. Whatever his disadvantages, Rhee was the only Korean
figure who enjoyed widespread popular support. The alternative was a
weak government, totally dependent on UNC support. The removal of
Rhee would cause chaos and offend Korean nationalism. The only
beneficiaries might be the communists. As one State Department
official was forced to admit, 'We could be cutting off our nose to spite

our face if we took drastic action against Rhee.'[78] US action thus never went beyond veiled threats and psychological warfare. Rhee was aware of his strong position. He may have been further encouraged by the belief that Clark and Van Fleet would never move against him. Both were militant anti-communists who, whatever Rhee's other failings, sympathised with his position as a conservative patriot. The crisis was finally resolved in July when the assembly conceded popular election to the Presidency. On 24 August, Rhee gained his second term.[79] His capacity to frustrate and embarass the US, however, was not exhausted. In September 1952 he launched an undeclared naval war against Japan, harrying fishing boats off the Korean coast.[80] Clark was faced with the problem not only of dealing with the communists but also of maintaining the peace between two US allies within his theatre of operations. Rhee's stand during the martial law crisis, his stubborness, his brinksmanship and his resentment of foreign interference, set the scene for the even more dramatic events the following year on the eve of the armistice.

As the election campaign entered its final stages, Washington intensified the bombing. Truman, having weathered the crises of the spring, was in no mood to compromise. There were those who argued that the stick should be coupled with the carrot in dealing with Beijing. At the prompting of Kennan, now ambassador to Moscow, the State Department worked out a possible settlement during the summer. The repatriates would be exchanged and the problem of the non-repatriates left over for consideration by the political conference demanded by the armistice agreement. China would hesitate to renew the war if no solution was forthcoming and the question would be allowed to fade away.[81] This linked into a Mexican proposal that the non-repatriates be sent to neutral nations and allowed to work while a conference discussed their status. A postponement of the non-repatriate question until a political conference had been suggested by Vincent Hallihan, the Progressive Party candidate in the US elections and endorsed by the *Daily Worker*. It might therefore appeal to the communists.[82] The timing of any initiative was believed to be important. In August the US intensified 'air pressure', including the saturation bombing of Pyongyang. This coincided with a visit by Mao to Moscow. It was hoped that the destruction of the North Korean capital would increase Chinese demands on Russia, demands which Stalin might find unwelcome. A US initiative would offer the Russians a way out and save Chinese face, since Beijing would not be forced to subscribe formally to the principle of non-forcible repatriation.[83]

Acheson argued that even if the communists rejected the plan, it would have considerable propaganda value. Washington would have displayed its flexibility and could hold the allies in line at the UN General Assembly meeting in October.[84]

The Pentagon, however, opposed any compromise. It argued that a truce on the terms proposed would allow the communists to rebuild airfields and restore communications. The American people would be lulled into a sense of false security and demand that Washington 'bring the boys home'. A dispute over the POW issue at the political conference would be used by China as an excuse to renew the war against a weakened UN command. 'Air pressure' must continue until the enemy accepted the package proposal of April 1952.[85] The military argument begged the question. If the Chinese intended to break the armistice, they would not require the excuse of the POWs. Moreover, *any* truce would mean the reconstruction of North Korean airfields, a fact already conceded by the JCS. The 'greater sanctions' statement had been drawn up at military insistence precisely to meet this situation and deter any new attack. Behind these arguments lurked a determination to humiliate China. The Pentagon was convinced that it did not need to compromise. China could be forced by bombing to accept the POW figures.[86] There may also have been a political angle to military objections. The Pentagon was cultivating a tough image to ingratiate itself with a possible Republican administration. On the right, the role of the JCS in MacArthur's dismissal had been neither forgiven nor forgotten. It was not the time to become associated with a proposal which might be condemned as 'appeasement'.

Clark was particularly outspoken in his opposition to a compromise. He maintained that the destruction of enemy morale by bombing offered a better road to an armistice than the suggestion of a 'Commie sympathizer' (Hallihan) 'who had recently been in jail'.[87] Clark's own recommendation was to expand the war. On 29 September he called for reinforcements, the expansion of the ROK army, the employment of two Guomindong divisions, the bombing of Manchuria and the employment of atomic weapons in order to achieve a settlement on American terms.[88] He may have been influenced by the political situation and the prospect of a Republican victory. Liberation implied the end of restraints in waging the Korean war. By his own admission, Clark began planning for escalation at this point, in case Washington decided to 'go for victory'.[89] Thus Clark hoped to achieve the outcome which had eluded MacArthur, with whose frustrations he had always sympathised. Truman was not prepared to take dramatic steps which would mean further problems with the allies. The only one of Clark's recommendations which was accepted was an increase in the ROK army, agreed after Eisenhower had urged that 'Asians fight Asians' and the emergence of American casualties as an issue in the campaign.[90] He accepted the advice of the Pentagon, however, on the POW issue. On 24 September he ruled out the compromise suggested by the State Department. Military and psychological pressure on the enemy would continue. On 8 October, the UNC recessed the talks at Panmunjom as a symbol to Beijing of American determination.[91]

It has been argued that Truman's decision cost Stevenson the election.[92] Truman, however, would rather be right than popular. Even had his instinct not been for toughness over compromise, he was boxed in on this issue. A proposal which was opposed by the military stood little chance of acceptance at home, where discord within the administration was bound to leak out. Nor was there any guarantee that the communists would accept. Truman believed that any offer would be taken as a sign of weakness and that the enemy would hold out for more. He would be left open to Republican accusations of 'appeasement' without any compensating gain. Nor should the American people be encouraged to hope for easy solutions, an 'isolationist' appeal which he accused Eisenhower of employing. Stevenson would have to stand or fall on administration policy. As Acheson predicted, however, a tough stand created difficulties with the allies at the UN. Britain had supported the State Department compromise and was disappointed by its defeat. London was alarmed by the attitude of the Pentagon and Clark's hawkish preferences. Eden was determined not to be railroaded into fresh measures against China simply to please the US military and relieve the domestic pressures on the administration.[93] This attitude was shared by Lester Pearson of Canada, the President of the General Assembly. When the meeting began at the end of October, Pearson began to seek a compromise which would avert the danger of a wider war in Asia.[94] Eden's support for these moves led to another row within the alliance. As a result, the Eden–Acheson relationship was to end on a sour note.

The administration went to the UN determined to mobilise international support for its position at Panmunjom. It quickly secured allied support for the twenty-one-power resolution, designed to display solidarity on the POW issue in the face of an anticipated Soviet propaganda barrage. At the same time, however, some of the Western powers, led by the British were keen to explore all possible paths to a compromise. The opportunity was offered by India. On 27 October, Krishna Menon, a member of the Indian delegation, produced a plan which avoided forced repatriation while meeting Chinese insistence on the Geneva convention. He claimed that his government was in touch with Beijing and his scheme showed traces of the earlier formulas discussed by Zhou and Pannikkar. While the details were vague, Menon envisaged the removal of the POWs from military control to the custody of a neutral commission representing Sweden, Switzerland, Poland and Czechoslovakia. They would be held for an indefinite period while all means short of force was used to secure their return.[95] On 3 November he refined his idea to include an impartial chairman, perhaps India.[96] Britain and Canada saw advantages in this scheme. It would win over Asian opinion and might divide the Chinese from the Russians. If it failed, the position would be no worse. It would be clear that Beijing and not the UN was preventing a settlement. Neither was concerned about the indefinite detention of the non-repatriates. The men were former enemies whose fate was less important than that of UN personnel in communist hands. They should be given no inducement to stay and block a Korean armistice.[97]

The Indian plan, however, ran into adamantine opposition from Acheson. He regarded the plan as a dangerous distraction from the twenty-one-power resolution. It threatened to 'give us the words and the other side the decision'. POWs would be offered the choice of repatriation or indefinite detention. Many would choose repatriation in despair, opening the US to a stunning propaganda defeat.[98] Washington had invested too much symbolic importance in the non-repatriates since the Koje riots to take such a risk. He distrusted the influence of a commission which included communists, despite the arguments of Selwyn Lloyd who maintained that the Swedes and Swiss would prevent any 'hanky panky'.[99] Most of all, he resented the role of India, regarding Nehru as little better than an appeaser. Pearson's association with the scheme did little to balance this feeling. Acheson had resented the Canadian role since the Koje crisis in the spring. He was unmoved by arguments about the importance of Asian opinion and condemned what he regarded as a cabal against the US. Under attack by the Republicans at home, Acheson demanded loyalty of the allies.[100] He felt betrayed, and attacked their tendency to accept a lead from India which had 'contributed nothing' to the war. The US must take the decisions because it bore the major share of the burden.[101] Acheson went as far as to warn Eden that the American people regarded the issue as a test of collective security. If their allies let them down, they would question the value of foreign commitments, including NATO.[102] This was a tired echo of the threat deployed to secure British support in the crisis of December 1950.

A bitter struggle ensued over the Menon plan. Acheson was unwilling to accord it priority over the twenty-one-power resolution and insisted on amendments, always finding new arguments to withold approval. Eden found him unhelpful and 'irrational', a complaint which was echoed by Pearson.[103] The defeat of the Democrats in the presidential elections did nothing to soften Acheson. If anything, his attitude hardened. He intended to pass on to his successor, a firm position on the POW issue. The Republicans would be unable to claim that the last act of the Truman administration had been to appease communism. On 16 November the JCS were brought to New York to register their objections to an armistice which left the POW issue unresolved.[104] Pearson and Eden were unmoved. The intransigent attitude of the generals merely made them redouble their efforts. As Pearson noted, it was impossible to avoid the impression that the Pentagon opposed not only the Indian resolution, but also any kind of armistice.[105] Acheson, however, continued to use military objections to block progress. On a brief state visit to Ottawa on 21 November, he informed the Canadian cabinet that the US was bearing the main burden of the war, and the allies must defer to the judgement of American soldiers. He also maintained that since the Democrats had been defeated, they lacked a mandate to support new initiatives, particularly if opposed by the Pentagon.[106] In pursuit of this strategy, an attempt was made to secure Eisenhower's support. The President-elect, however, refused to be drawn. Acheson was increasingly frustrated by the erosion of support for the twenty-one-power resolution and Anglo-Canadian mobilisation of support for the Menon plan, which threatened to leave the US isolated.[107] At a private meeting on 19 November, his anger was vented on Lloyd and Pearson. The one was a little Welsh lawyer, the other 'an empty glass of water' who should be brought to heel by the United States. As Eden later noted, 'But for the knowledge that Mr Acheson had just come from a somewhat prolonged cocktail party in his own suite, I should have felt bound to take him up seriously.' It was 'sad to see the temporary disintegration' of Acheson's character 'under the stress of events'.[108]

Eden and Pearson refused to be browbeaten. Their position was strengthened by the results of the election, since Acheson lacked the power to implement some of his more extreme threats. In a series of private conversations, Eden found Eisenhower, although non-committal, more sympathetic to the Menon plan than Acheson once the position had been fully explained. He agreed on the necessity of retaining Asian goodwill and of not alienating the Indians. This attitude was reflected in the Republican press, which was generally supportive of the Indian scheme, thus containing attempts by the US delegation to bring pressure on Britain and Canada through inspired leaks to the newspapers.[109] While holding firm against Acheson's manouevres, Eden and Pearson were prepared to build bridges for the Americans to cross. As Pearson noted, the one hope of success was to produce an Indian resolution in a form which the US could support.[110] Menon was persuaded to consider changes which met some of the more substansive American objections particularly over the composition of the neutral commission and the length of time the POWs could be held in custody. The clear lack of support for his own inflexible position inside and outside the UN forced Acheson to compromise on 23 November, when he agreed to endorse the Menon resolution with amendments on these two points. The American concession was confirmed the next day when, following the condemnation of the Indian plan by the Soviet delegate Vishinsky, Acheson made a speech in its favour. It was, however, far from the enthusiastic welcome which Eden and Pearson had originally desired, being almost wholly concerned with legal analysis and the changes desired by the US.[111] Eden later felt that the Americans had lost the chance to give a lead to Asia. They had appeared to back Menon grudgingly and only after the Russians had made plain their disagreement.[112] Eden traced Acheson's attitude to an irrational dislike of India and a desire to project a tough image after years of McCarthyite attacks.[113]

The Indian resolution was finally passed on 3 December, opposed only by the Soviet bloc. As amended, it called for POWs to be handed over at the armistice to a neutral commission under an executive chairman. The prisoners were to be available for persuasion for ninety days after the truce after which the problem of those who remained could be taken up by the political conference. In default of a solution after a further thirty days, the UN would assume responsibility for their 'ultimate disposition'. This clumsy procedure was necessary to reconcile the US and Chinese positions on the problem. *All* POWs were to be made available for exchange, but the 'hard core' of non-repatriates would be offered an alternative.[114] The ambiguous phrase 'ultimate disposition' covered American determination to turn these men over to the ROK and Taiwan. On 15 December, Beijing followed Moscow's lead and rejected these terms. The only hopeful sign was that the Chinese reply was 'not in either abusive or even excessively belligerent terms'.[115] Nehru believed that Zhou had been overruled by the Russians.[116] It has been argued, however, that at this stage both Moscow and Beijing were prepared to wind down the war.[117] Both powers were perhaps reluctant to deal with the outgoing Truman administration, representing a party which had been repudiated at the polls. There was little point in endorsing a compromise which might be repudiated by the Republicans. A solution to the POW problem, therefore, awaited the inauguration of Eisenhower in January 1953.

10 Eisenhower: Peace with Honour

The immediate effect of the Republican victory was to encourage those who hoped for a military solution. Rhee had distrusted Truman ever since the removal of MacArthur. He disliked the truce talks which threatened his country with a new partition and hoped that Republican rhetoric about liberation would be translated into action. According to Rhee, Truman was a leader with 'cold feet' who had pursued a 'cowardly policy' in Korea. The only real alternatives were for the US to advance to the Yalu or else to withdraw. He hoped that Eisenhower would begin his first term by bombing Manchuria.[1] The possibility of escalation was also entertained by Clark, who had experienced his own frustrations since his appointment in April 1952. Clark inherited Ridgway's problem of maintaining pressure on the enemy without incurring unacceptable costs. He attempted to solve it by intensified bombing and by a larger Asian contribution to the ground war. In July 1952 he recommended the expansion of the ROK army beyond the ten divisions agreed in 1951 and the introduction of two Chinese nationalist divisions to the battlefront.[2] Guomindong forces were politically unacceptable, but in October 1952 the authorised strength of the ROK army was increased to twelve divisions – after US losses had become an issue in the election campaign.[3]

As Clark recognised, however, even an expansion of ROK forces to twenty divisions, a figure he favoured as an ultimate target, would not allow the US to disengage.[4] At most it would ease the strain on American resources while continuing to pin down a substantial proportion of US military strength in a peripheral area. A militant anti-communist, Clark was no enthusiast for an armistice and felt an increasing sense of frustration with the stalemate at Panmunjom. He favoured a decisive engagement with the enemy rather than an indefinite continuation of this situation. In October 1952, perhaps influenced by the rhetoric of liberation, he drew up contingency plans to expand the war in case a new administration decided to 'go for victory'.[5] Clark was in no doubt that such a development was vital to US security. The communists had to be 'decisively' defeated in their first test of arms with the free world. He was aware that casualties might be heavy but hoped to contain US losses by using sixteen ROK divisions, along with Chinese nationalist troops to increase his manpower. Clark also wished to increase US air and ground strength and to use tactical atomic weapons to overcome the formidable defence lines in North Korea. A key element in his plan was the destruction of Manchurian airfields to guarantee UN air superiority.[6] Clark was confident that such a blow would not provoke global conflict with the Soviet Union. Echoing MacArthur, he maintained that the Russians would only go to war 'on a time-schedule of their own choosing'.[7]

Clark's confidence was encouraged by the advent of the tactical atomic weapons incorporated in his plan. It was believed that they gave the US an important technological advantage which outweighed communist superiority in manpower. Ground offensives could be launched at an acceptable cost. Nor would strikes across the Yalu expose US airpower to heavy attrition. Atomic attacks could eliminate the MIG hornets' nest around Antung quickly and cheaply. As early as July 1951, Pentagon planners noted that in the event of a stalemate in Korea 'use of the atomic bomb to increase our efficiency of killing is desirable'.[8] By the summer of 1952 tactical weapons had been developed which could be delivered by fighter bombers, along with an atomic artillery projectile.[9] The Pentagon was clearly fascinated by the possibilities of the new technology. At a press conference in Tokyo in July 1952, Collins talked about the development of atomic cannon and emphasised that the US would use every means to defend its troops, a statement endorsed by Clark.[10] The new technology coincided with increasing military frustration at the Korean stalemate and emerging doubts about the value of a symmetrical response to aggression. It seemed to offer a means of exerting decisive military pressure and made concessions to the Chinese to secure an armistice less attractive. The feeling of power and confidence stimulated by these weapons was further encouraged by the successful test of a hydrogen bomb in November 1952. As Bradley later recalled, by 1953 the US possessed enough atomic ordinance to 'clobber the hell' out of the Chinese without reducing its capacity to wage global war.[11] By May 1953 the JCS had developed a plan of operations which incorporated the use of the new tactical weapons against North Korea and Manchuria.[12] The opposition of the Pentagon to a compromise at the UN in November 1952, which alarmed Eden and Pearson, reflected the growing belief that in the last resort the stalemate could be broken by military means.

Eisenhower had kept his options open throughout the campaign. He was committed to nothing beyond enlarging the Asian role in the war and visiting the battlefield. He continued to avoid decisions in the period before his inauguration in January 1953. When he visited Korea in mid-November, he confined himself to inspecting the front and did not consult Clark about escalation.[13] Rhee, who had hoped to use the occasion to symbolise a new unity between Washington and Seoul, was similarly disappointed and was snubbed by the President-elect.[14] As he returned across the Pacific on the USS *Helena*, Eisenhower learned that MacArthur had delivered a speech to the National Association of Manufacturers on 5 December in which he claimed to have a secret plan to end the war. MacArthur stated that he would communicate this scheme to the new President.[15] The two men were old political and military rivals, their relations coloured with considerable personal animosity. The demands of party unity and public relations, however, demanded a positive response, and before the inauguration, the two men met at the home of John Foster Dulles, who had been chosen by Eisenhower as Secretary of State. MacArthur suggested that Ike meet Stalin and demand the unification and neutralisation of Korea and Germany. If the Russians refused to agree, the US should 'clear' North Korea and bomb China. MacArthur advocated the use of atomic weapons and the sowing of a radioactive belt along the Yalu border to cut off the communist armies from their source of supply. Once the battlefield had been isolated, UN forces would land on both sides of the peninsula, while Jiang liberated the Chinese mainland. Communism in Asia would be defeated and US security guaranteed. Eisenhower did not openly reject this fantasy, although he emphasised the need to keep UN allies in line.[16]

As President, Eisenhower faced the problem familiar to Truman. China had to be persuaded to end the fighting on terms acceptable to the US. Washington had to find a means of pressure which did not damage the US more than it hurt the communists. Eisenhower rejected continuation of the stalemate. His political credibility depended on securing an honourable end to the war. His only option, therefore, was to threaten to remove existing restrictions on military action. In January 1953, in an act of symbolic escalation, Eisenhower 'unleashed' Jiang, announcing that the Seventh Fleet would no longer defend the communist mainland. This pleased the right and confirmed party unity. Jiang proclaimed the imminence of liberation and landing exercises were held in the spring.[17] The threat to China, however, was more symbolic than real. Whatever the illusions of the right, the administration realised that Jiang was a flawed instrument of liberation. As Vice-President Nixon remarked in November 1953, the Guomindong was no longer 'a positive force' in Asia. Jiang had become 'a liability rather than an asset'.[18] The public 'unleashing' was accompanied by private acts of restraint. US advisers were ordered to prevent 'precipitate action' which might provoke a wider war with China. Eisenhower's announcement was not to be acted upon. It was part of a 'larger psychological warfare effort' to end the Korean conflict.[19]

The main focus of this effort was in Korea itself. In the spring of 1953 Eisenhower studied the possibilities of a UN offensive, employing a strengthened ROK army and American reinforcements. In May 1953 Clark was authorised to increase ROK strength to sixteen divisions, and to mobilise a further four at his own discretion.[20] Atomic weapons occupied a key role in these military plans. As the strategic planners at the Pentagon complained to the JCS on 23 March, Korea remained a severe drain on US manpower and resources. The reason for the continued stalemate was that insufficient pressure had been exerted against China. Atomic weapons, however, offered a means of achieving this end with minimum losses and diversion of American strength. The planners believed that Manchurian airfields must be eliminated as a precondition for a successful offensive and regarded tactical atomic weapons as particularly valuable in this role: 'US atomic superiority provides one major means of increasing the capabilities of US–UN forces and reducing the growing Chinese Communist air threat to the US military position in Korea and Japan. The efficacy of atomic weapons in achieving greater results at less cost makes it desirable to plan for their use.' In any attempt to neutralise Manchuria employing only conventional means, 'the attrition rate would probably be exceedingly high', a possibility which had always deterred attacks in the past. The planners concluded that 'The efficacy of atomic weapons in achieving greater results at less cost . . . in connection with Korea, points to the desirability of re-evaluating the policy which now restricts [their] use.[21] The JCS endorsed this report in May 1953, noting that a new offensive would require the employment of atomic weapons to guarantee success.[22] It was a judgement which the President also endorsed. As Eisenhower later recalled, 'To keep the attack from becoming overly costly, it was clear that we would have to use atomic weapons.'[23]

It was important to let the enemy know what was under consideration in Washington. Eisenhower considered this a vital element in his plan to exert psychological pressure on Moscow and Beijing. The possibility that the new administration would 'move without inhibition' in its use of weapons was first raised at a press conference on 14 December, when Eisenhower returned from Korea. In a 'brief but pointed' reference, Eisenhower stated that the US faced an enemy 'whom we cannot hope to impress by words, however eloquent, but only by deeds – executed under circumstances of our own choosing'.[24] In hinting that he would abandon the old rules, Eisenhower paraphrased Dulles' call for 'massive retaliation' and employed a threat which Truman had avoided. The new administration continued to imply that escalation was being considered throughout the spring. Atomic weapons were moved to Okinawa. During a visit to India on 22 May, Dulles warned Nehru that if an armistice did not emerge, hostilities 'might become more intense.'[25] The President was aware of the dangers of atomic escalation. Japan was vulnerable to retaliation and difficulties would be raised by UN allies. Britain in particular would regard the employment of atomic weapons as a 'decision of the gravest kind'.[26] Such private reservations, however, were never revealed in public and it remains unclear how far Eisenhower would have gone, had psychological pressure proved unsuccessful.

Dulles was more hawkish. He was anxious to maintain the confidence of the Republican right and to avoid the political controversy which had surrounded Acheson. This made it important to appear tough on China. Moreover, he was doubtful about the value of a Korean armistice before Beijing had been taught a lesson. As he informed Eisenhower's assistant, Emmet John Hughes in April 1953, the US might regret a ceasefire: 'I don't think we can get much out of a Korean settlement until we have shown – before all Asia – our clear superiority by giving the Chinese one hell of a licking.'[27]

Chinese prestige would be inflated by a truce. Beijing could claim to have forced a draw with the most powerful nation in the world. This would strengthen the regime internally and encourage communism throughout Asia. Dulles was particularly concerned about the situation in Indochina where the French had been bogged down in a frustrating guerrilla war against the Vietminh since 1946.[28] Beijing, freed of any threat to the Manchurian border from UN forces in Korea, might switch its full attention to South-East Asia, an area Dulles considered strategically vital to Western interests.[29] He therefore wished to increase the pressures on the Chinese government and to reduce its prestige, with the ultimate aim of encouraging a non-communist alternative in Beijing. As part of this approach, he favoured military escalation in Korea and his reluctance to conclude an armistice was evident throughout the spring. Dulles was prepared to employ tactical weapons and insisted on the need to break down the 'false distinction' between atomic and conventional warfare.[30] Thus Eisenhower, the soldier, was less hawkish than Dulles, the civilian. While the President might regard the atomic bomb as just another weapon, he was less casual than his Secretary of State in envisaging its use. He appears to have regarded the atomic threat primarily as a means of diplomatic pressure and preferred accommodation in Korea to escalation. Indeed he sometimes became impatient with the overzealous militancy of his Secretary of State. As he sharply remarked to Hughes, 'If Mr Dulles and all his sophisticated advisers really mean that they can *not* talk peace seriously, then I am in the wrong pew. For if it's *war* we should be talking about, I *know* the people to give me advice on that – and they're not in the State Department.'[31]

By threatening 'massive retaliation' to end the war, Eisenhower embraced a concept which he had rejected before the election. He found atomic weapons attractive, however, on the grounds of cost. The President believed that spending on the scale of NSC-68 would bankrupt the United States: 'It would be impossible . . . to maintain military commitments around the world . . . did we not possess atomic weapons and the will to use them.'[32] The US could not afford the continued costs of the war. As the Secretary of the Treasury, George Humphrey, argued, a Republican administration committed to reduce taxation had to 'get Korea *out of the way*'. Beyond that, it had to 'figure out a *completely new military posture*'.[33] The US could not afford further limited wars in which it attempted to match Chinese manpower and allowed the communists to dictate the terms and duration of the conflict. The atomic threat could both end the fighting and provide a cheaper form of containment in the future. After Korea the US role in Asia would be based on an air force armed with atomic weapons. Ground forces would be provided by local allies, whose soldiers were cheaper and more expendable than the American GI. In Korea and Indochina the US would arm 'native' forces to handle local security. Overt aggression would be deterred by communist fear of an atomic response. This approach became known as 'The New Look' and formed the basis of Eisenhower's future policy in the far East. Within the military establishment, the main beneficiary was the air force, which could provide 'more bang for a buck' than an expensive standing army.[34]

The UN allies were concerned about the threat of escalation. Britain especially had long been sensitive on the issue. Churchill welcomed the election of Eisenhower, who was associated with the successful wartime alliance, and hoped to strengthen the Atlantic relationship in cooperation with the new President. Eisenhower's attitude to the Indian resolution at the UN in November was encouraging.[35] However, a strong distrust of the Republican right remained, coupled with increasing concern about the attitude of the Pentagon. There were rumours that the Republicans would 'unleash' Jiang and impose a naval blockade of China. Clark was known to favour a new offensive in Korea and the reluctance of the JCS to seek an armistice had been revealed at the UN in November.[36] Britain baulked at such MacArthurite possibilities. Its attitude was made clear in a speech by Churchill on 11 November, pledging cooperation with the new administration and emphasising Anglo-American solidarity on the POW question. At the same time, the Prime Minister revealed his opposition to escalation which would only pin down the US and benefit Russia.[37] The government hoped to work with 'moderates' in the new administration to keep the right in check.

This attempt to contain the US was not wholly successful. Although British reservations about 'unleashing' Jiang were made plain before the Eisenhower administration took office, London was not consulted about the decision to withdraw the fleet from the Taiwan straits. Eden was piqued by Eisenhower's failure to treat Britain as an equal in the first major act of his administration.[38] The new flirtation with Jiang as an instrument of liberation alienated India and worsened the political atmosphere with China.[39] It also had domestic political implications for a conservative government with a narrow majority, since Labour reacted strongly to any US move in support of the Guomindong.[40] As early as December 1952 Dulles had been informed that such action would merely 'exacerbate' British opinion, without leading to a final solution in Korea. Eden sent a strong protest to Washington and criticised the American action in Parliament in 'acid terms'.[41] Whatever its reservations about US China policy, however, London could not maintain a wholly intransigent attitude without arousing the fury of the McCarthyite right. In March the government announced further restrictions on trade with Beijing.[42] These represented little new and were intended to demonstrate that Britain was not colluding with the enemy. London, however, would not endorse military escalation. When Dulles raised the issue on 5 March he found Eden unenthusiastic. Dulles emphasised US determination to disengage from Korea. He believed, however, that it might be first necessary to expand the war. The UN command could drive to the Korean waist which could be fortified and largely turned over to the ROK. The communists would be left with a small northern rump. In order to achieve this result, it might be necessary to bomb Manchuria and blockade the Chinese coast. Eden raised questions about actions which were likely to provoke a clash with the Soviet Union and insisted that London must be consulted in advance before further military moves.[43]

The dangers posed for Britain by escalation had remained constant since 1950. If US actions involved Russia in the war, Britain might be the first to suffer. Hostilities in the Far East would have repercussions in Europe where US bomber bases in south-east England were natural targets for a pre-emptive Soviet atomic attack.[44] Whatever his Victorian contempt for China and his belief that Eden was too critical of the Americans in the Far East, the Prime Minister could never grant Washington a free hand against Beijing because of possible Soviet involvement. He felt 'grave anxiety' about the attitude of the US military, which seeemed to favour a showdown with the communists before the Russians could develop the H-bomb and build up a matching stock of atomic weapons: 'The whole concept of atomic or nuclear warfare filled him with horror.' The 'appalling nightmare' of 'mass destruction' was soon to lead Churchill to propose détente with the Soviet Union, a task which required a settlement of the Korean conflict.[45]

Thus Britain continued to urge the importance of negotiation. In January 1953, after a meeting with the President of the International Red Cross, Eden proposed an exchange of sick and wounded POWs.[46] Washington agreed and on 22 February Clark approached the communists through the liaison officers at Panmunjom, where talks had been in recess since October 1952.[47] Eden also asked the Russians to use their influence with Pyongyang to secure the release of civilian internees, including the British Minister to Seoul, captured in July 1950.[48] While these initiatives were justified on humanitarian grounds, they were also intended to revive the armistice talks before their future prospects were overtaken by military events. They were ultimately to produce a break in the stalemate and the first new progress towards a cease-fire.

It is unclear when the communists decided to compromise on the POW question. China had rejected the UN resolution of December 1952 after the Soviet bloc had voted against it in the General Assembly, claiming that it was not in accordance with the Geneva convention. The Indians believed that Zhou had been forced to surrender to Russian pressure.[49] It suited Moscow to pin the US down in Korea, while keeping China dependent on Soviet military and economic aid. Dulles later claimed that only the willingness of the Eisenhower administration to go to the brink of atomic war overcame communist intransigence and broke the stalemate.[50] Many subsequent writers endorsed this conclusion.[51] Others, however, maintain that the communists were preparing to wind the war down before the spring of 1953. When Zhou visited Moscow for the Party Congress in October 1952, he obtained Stalin's agreement to end the war. The Russian leader was about to embark on a new series of internal purges like those of the 1930s, a course which demanded that he 'disengage the Soviet Union from foreign entanglements'. Moreover, the conflict was providing a severe drain on Russian resources and was easing Washington's task in securing German and Japanese rearmament.[52] If Stalin took such a line, it strengthened the position of those in Beijing who wished to end the Korean struggle and switch resources to internal reconstruction. A decision to deal with the new Republican administration, therefore, may have been taken in Moscow and Beijing before the death of Stalin on 4 March 1953. Thus a perception of the political and economic costs of further hostilities persuaded both sides to return to the conference table.

Whatever Stalin's ultimate intentions, the process of disengagement 'accelerated dramatically' after his death. The new leadership sought some relaxation of international tension, while consolidating its domestic position. At Stalin's funeral, his successor, Georgi Malenkov, emphasised the possibility of peaceful coexistence with the US. On 15 March he returned to this theme in a speech before the Supreme Soviet, arguing that all disputes should be settled by peaceful means.[53] The implications were soon evident in Korea. On 28 March, two days after Zhou's return from Stalin's funeral, the Chinese and North Koreans agreed to an exchange of sick and wounded. They also proposed an early resumption of the armistice talks. On 30 March Zhou made a broadcast setting out a possible solution to the POW impasse. All prisoners who desired repatriation should be exchanged on the conclusion of a ceasefire. The remainder should be handed over to a neutral state 'so as to ensure a just solution to the question of their repatriation'. On 1 April Molotov, the Soviet Foreign Minister, endorsed this proposal, which was formally presented at Panmunjom the following day.[54] On 8 April the North Koreans freed the civilian internees, who returned to the West via Moscow.[55] The Russians had obviously used their influence, an action they had refused to take in the past. This was the first evidence that the communists would match words with deeds.

The thaw produced a new sense of optimism amongst the UN allies. As the Australian Foreign Minister remarked, for the first time 'top communists' had indicated publicly that they were interested in ending the war.[56] According to Churchill, Zhou's proposals were a 'welcome step' which might break the deadlock at Panmunjom. Eden heard the news with relief and pressed for an early resumption of talks to 'probe and test' communist intentions.[57] Eisenhower and Dulles, however, felt that an exchange of sick and wounded must precede any broader negotiations. The communists must prove their 'good faith'.[58] Beyond this, they were divided. Eisenhower felt compelled to make some public response to Malenkov and Zhou. Dulles believed that the President should take a firm line. The communist bloc was experiencing severe inner strains and should not be helped out of its difficulties by the West. He was suspicious of the communist desire for a Korean armistice, which he feared would free China to intervene in South-East Asia, and preferred military escalation to teach the Chinese a lesson. If Eisenhower mentioned the subject, Dulles wished him to make a Korean cease-fire conditional upon non-intervention in Indochina, a demand many of the President's advisers believed would be unacceptable to Beijing.[59] Dulles had already publicly implied such an approach in a joint communique issued on 29 March, following a visit by the French Prime Minister to Washington. Nor did he wish a Korean armistice to lead to the 'releashing' of Jiang, decreasing the strains on China and shattering the dream of the ultimate collapse of the communist government in Beijing.[60]

Eisenhower, however, dealt in more tangible factors. The most important of these was financial. If he did not end the war, he could not fulfil his pledge to cut the military budget and reduce taxation. Moreover, he believed that the American people were seeking a response to the communists which went beyond the tired rhetoric of the cold war.[61] His speech, delivered to the American Newspaper Association on 16 April, was purged of Dulles' more extreme demands. It emphasised the huge financial and social cost of the arms race and indicated US readiness to cooperate in the search for peace and disarmament. It called as a first step for the Soviet bloc to show evidence of good faith, at the Korean armistice talks and over the Austrian peace treaty.[62] Although this statement did not lead to an early summit conference with the new Russian leadership, as advocated by Churchill, Eisenhower had indicated his readiness for a

Korean cease-fire which did not breach the parameters established under Truman and which the Chinese would have found difficult to swallow.

The President had made a Korean armistice a test of communist good faith. It remained to be seen what would be delivered at Panmunjom. The initial signs were encouraging. The exchange of sick and wounded, OPERATION LITTLE SWITCH, was arranged within two days, a record for the negotiations. As Clark remarked, things had never 'moved so fast'.[63] On 26 April the armistice talks resumed. These, however, rapidly fell into the familiar pattern of wrangling over the POW issue. On the UN side, the atmosphere was worsened by the revelation that many wounded POWs had been held back from the exchange, a fact which roused suspicions of communist good faith.[64] For their part, the Chinese refused to acknowledge that the non-repatriates had made a free choice. They demanded that these men be transferred to a neutral country, freed from 'intimidation' and provided with 'explanations' by their own side which would persuade them to return home.[65] On 7 May the communists refined this vague proposal, and suggested that the neutral custodian should be a five power commission of Sweden, Switzerland, Poland, Czechoslovakia and India. It would be called the Neutral Nations Repatriation Commission and its troops would take charge of the POWs in Korea. It would hold the non-repatriates for four months of 'explanations' and would reach its decisions by majority vote. The fate of those remaining after this time would be discussed by the political conference called for in the armistice agreement.[66] This proposal was close to the UN resolution of December 1952, recently reaffirmed by the General Assembly but rejected by China and North Korea. For the first time, the communists abandoned their insistence on strict adherence to the Geneva convention and the automatic repatriation of all POWs at the end of hostilities.

The scheme, however, was unacceptable to Washington. The Americans objected to placing a final decision on POWs in the hands of a political conference. It might never be held, and even if it was, there was no guarantee that an agreement would emerge. The non-repatriates would thus be faced with the prospect of indefinite detention. The only road to freedom would be to accept communist 'explanations' and repatriation. As Clark complained, 'The plan . . . failed . . . to provide a clear path to political asylum for men who persisted in their refusal to return home.'[67] If large numbers defected to their old allegiance, US prestige would be damaged and China vindicated. Washington had vested too much symbolic importance in the non-repatriates to take this risk. A second problem was the abiding American distrust of India. Nehru's attitude to China was suspect and he was considered an 'appeaser'. New Delhi could not be trusted to take a robust stand against communism. Thus the Indians could not be considered 'neutral'. They might vote with the Czechs and Poles on the commission, providing the communists with a built-in majority.[68] Lastly, there was the problem of custodial forces. The idea of communist troops from Czechoslovakia and Poland at large behind the UN lines was unwelcome. Moreover, the anti-communist leaders of the cages might resist transfer to such a force, causing bloodshed and grave political problems for the administration at home.[69] The fundamental problem, however, was Washington's reluctance to relinquish control of the camps except under conditions which guaranteed non-repatriation. US officials even wished to use the term 'custodial' to refer to the neutral commission, in order to avoid the implication that its purpose was repatration. Since the communists insisted that this was its sole function, the two sides remained far apart.[70] Prestige was at stake. The US was unwilling to risk large scale defections, and hoped to use the POWs as tools of psychological warfare. The Chinese and North Koreans were equally unwilling to swallow the humiliation of the existing figures.

An additional threat to the armistice was emerging in the person of Syngman Rhee. As Clark recalled, while the negotiations 'bumbled on angrily, real trouble was developing in the rear'.[71] From this point, he was engaged on two fronts – with the communists at Panmunjom and with his ally at Pusan. By May 1953 Rhee was to appear the more dangerous. The Korean leader was infuriated by the progress towards a ceasefire which repudiated liberation and left his country divided. He suspected that once the fighting ended, South Korea would be abandoned, to become the ultimate victim of either China or Japan. Rhee considered both equally dangerous to Korean independence. On 9 April he wrote to Eisenhower expressing his determination to fight on as long as Chinese troops remained south of the Yalu. The President replied that the US sought an honourable truce. The issue of unification and Chinese forces would be dealt with at a political conference.[72] This message failed to reassure Rhee. On 24 April, as armistice talks resumed, he threatened to withdraw ROK troops from the UN command, if an arrangement was concluded which left Chinese troops on the peninsula.[73] By ordering his men to continue fighting, Rhee could veto a cease-fire. By the spring of 1953 the rebuilt

ROK army was holding two-thirds of the UN line. It was unclear how far Rhee was bluffing in an attempt to wring concessions from Washington. Clark was convinced, however, that on the question of the POWs at least, the Korean leader was deadly serious.[74] From the beginning Rhee adamantly refused to hand over Korean non-repatriates to the NNRC. He condemned the commission out of hand, arguing that it would bring a swarm of 'spies, saboteurs and agitators' into the ROK. As for the Indians, they were tools of Beijing: 'He would not permit any Indian troops on ROK soil as neutrals or anything else.' Rhee threatened to release the Korean non-repatriates unilaterally, rather than hand them over to the commission.[75] He had the power to execute this threat. While the Chinese non-repatriates were held on the island of Cheju-Do, the Korean cages were on the mainland. In the event of a break out, the POWs could quickly blend with the local population. While the camps were administered by Americans, the guard force was provided by the ROK, and it would be impossible to hold the POWs if it was withdrawn. Rhee's reaction on the prisoner issue was 'the first positive storm warning of what was to come'.[76] Clark believed that Rhee was less concerned about the Chinese non-repatriates and would not obstruct their transfer to neutral custody. In an effort to avert a crisis behind his lines, he recommended that only the Chinese be handed over. The Koreans should be freed as civilians when the armistice was signed.[77]

The UN response to the communist offer was delivered on 13 May. It displayed both a determination to minimise the risks of repatriation and to avoid a clash with Rhee. While accepting the neutral commission, the UNC insisted that it operate on the principle of unanimity, blocking any advantage to the communists if India voted with Poland and Czechoslovakia. 'Explanations' were to last for only sixty days, after which the POWs would be freed as civilians and the commission disbanded. The Korean non-repatriates would not be handed over but would be released on the conclusion of the armistice. The custodial force for the period of 'explanations' was to be provided by India alone.[78] The communists condemned these terms as a 'step backwards' and talks recessed for four days. They claimed that the unanimity rule would allow the UN nominees, Sweden and Switzerland, to paralyse the operations of the commission until the sixty day period had expired. The release of the Koreans was also unacceptable. Both amounted to forcible non-repatriation.[79] The UN terms somewhat mollified Rhee but at the expense of alienating the other allies. The deadlock at Panmunjom produced the most concentrated expression of alarm since the crisis of December 1950. Washington seemed to be repudiating UN policy on repatriation as expressed in the resolution of December 1952, in favour of a harsher line designed to appease Rhee and the Republican right. In the spring of 1953 nobody was willing to risk global war for the sake of an Asian dictator and the China lobby. The Eisenhower administration rapidly faced a major crisis with its allies over the terms on offer at Panmunjom.

The Canadians lobbied fiercely to secure concessions from the US. The Foreign Minister, Lester Pearson, was only 'with difficulty' dissuaded from publicly condemning the UN terms. He was particularly bitter because Canada had helped engineer the UN resolution of December 1952, which the communists now accepted as a basis of negotiation. The Americans had unilaterally rejected, in the name of the UN, terms which the General Assembly had endorsed.[80] Canadian officials warned Washington that Ottawa could not share responsibility for such a drastic departure 'when the alternative was the continuation of hostilities . . . potentially dangerous to world peace'.[81] Churchill, warned by Nehru that Zhou was threatening to withdraw all Chinese concessions, also protested. There was a strong feeling in Britain that US handling of the talks had been 'inept to a degree' and that Washington was too inflexible.[82] It was suspected that the American attitude was being dictated by the Republican right. Attlee gave voice to this concern during the foreign affairs debate on 12 May, when he asked whether Eisenhower or McCarthy was running US policy.[83] The Prime Minister had to take parliamentary feelings into account. Moreover, he wanted the war out of the way, in order to pursue his dream of detente with the Russians. He was impatient with Rhee, who threatened to block such an outcome: 'If I were in charge, I would withdraw UN troops to the coast and leave Syngman Rhee to the Chinese . . . Korea does not matter now. I'd never heard of the bloody place till I was seventy-four.'[84] Churchill felt frustrated by Eisenhower's attitude both to Korea and to the plan for a summit conference. On occasion he revealed his own private fears of the Republican right. As his doctor noted, 'At times he wonders whether Ike's election was a good thing for us – or for the world. Perhaps, after all, we should have been better off with Stevenson and the Democrats.'[85] Britain was prepared to accept Chinese terms without substantial modification. As long as the principle of non-forcible repatriation was observed, London was not disposed to quibble over details. As the Foreign Office argued, whether the POWs were repatriated, remained in indefinite detention or were liberated as civilians, was much less important than securing an armistice. If the non-repatriates faced the prospect of indefinite detention under the Chinese terms, they would be no worse off than thousands of displaced persons in European refugee camps.[86]

The crisis occurred while Dulles was visiting India. As a result, the situation was handled by Eisenhower and the Under-Secretary of State, Walter Bedell Smith, who had served as Ike's Chief of Staff during World War Two. This guaranteed a flexibility which might otherwise have been lacking. Both men had long experience of the compromises necessary to ensure the smooth operation of an alliance at war. They had to find a solution which would satisfy the UN allies and the Chinese, without raising a political storm at home. While the Republican right, under Senators Taft and Knowland, had reluctantly endorsed an armistice, it could not be pushed too far.[87] Zhou objected to the UN proposal on three main grounds: the demand for unanimity, the failure to refer the POW issue to the political conference, and the release of the Korean non-repatriates on the conclusion of the armistice. He had made his position clear both to Nehru and through the medium of the New China News Agency which listed the points of disagreement and remarked ominously that on a solution would depend 'whether there will be an early ending to the Korean War'.[88] On 18 May, with relations with the allies 'rapidly deteriorating', the administration produced a compromise. The NNRC was to reach its decisions by a majority of four. Korean as well as Chinese non-repatriates would be handed over, running the risk of 'an ugly situation' with Rhee. There would be ninety days of explanations and the question of POWs refusing repatriation after this period would be considered by the political conference. If no solution emerged, however, within one hundred and twenty days of the NNRC assuming control, the remaining prisoners would be released as civilians or the matter referred to the UN General Assembly. This amounted to the same thing, since the US secured pledges from its allies that in such an event, they would vote for release. The communists recognised the redundancy of the provision and it was not included in the final POW protocol. Washington remained firmly opposed to accepting communist troops in the camps. There were to be no Polish and Czech 'goon squads', uniformed thugs who would enforce repatriation on reluctant POWs. An Indian custodial force was to have sole control of the prisoners.[89] By making these concessions, Washington had returned to the substance of the UN resolution which it had seemed to repudiate on 13 May.[90] While guarding its own interests, it had displayed, under strong allied pressure, a willingness to meet the Chinese halfway.

When Clark presented these proposals on 25 May it was made clear that the UNC would consider no further concessions. The talks had reached the point of no return. This was emphasised in both Beijing and Moscow. On 22 May Dulles informed the Indians that, if an armistice was not speedily concluded, hostilities might become more intense, a veiled hint that Washington was considering the use of atomic weapons.[91] The irony of this evidently escaped him. In October 1950 Washington had dismissed as bluff Zhou's warning to Pannikkar that China would intervene if US troops crossed the thirty-eighth parallel. On 26 May Bohlen, the US ambassador in Moscow, was ordered to see Molotov and present an outline of the UN offer. He was to emphasise that rejection would mean the end of talks and the creation of a situation which the US would prefer to avoid.[92] Without pushing the Russians into a corner, Washington was raising the spectre of a wider war. While such hints were given to the enemy, the allies were informed that if the UN terms were not accepted within one week, the negotiations would be broken off. Clark would step up air and naval action against the north and denounce the agreement neutralising Kaesong and Panmunjom. He would unilaterally release the Chinese and Korean non-repatriates, presenting the communists with a fait accompli.[93] These were more modest measures than were being suggested to the communists at the time and displayed Eisenhower's awareness of allied sensitivity on the atomic issue. While the allies welcomed these developments, they were universally reluctant to break off talks if the terms were rejected. The entire armistice would be sacrificed over a narrow gap between the sides on the POW question.[94] The administration, however, made it clear that domestic politics left little room for manoeuvre. Moreover, to give an impression of flexibility would encourage the communists to stall and pin the UNC down in further wrangling.[95] There remained the problem of Rhee, whose objections were overridden in the UN terms. It was hoped to buy his approval by a pledge to maintain the ROK army at twenty divisions and to provide massive reconstruction aid. His fears for the future were to be further calmed by informing him about the greater sanctions statement against renewed aggression which was to accompany the armistice agreement. There were doubts, however, as to whether Rhee would fall easily into line, doubts which were to prove well-founded.[96]

On 4 June the communists indicated broad agreement with the UNC proposals, which were formally accepted four days later. The end of the war appeared to be in sight. As Dulles informed the President, 'Barring unforeseen developmennts, it appears that the POW issue has been solved.' Clark predicted that an armistice could be signed as early as 18 June.[97] This breakthrough is often hailed as a triumph of atomic brinkmanship, obscuring the fact that Zhou had played his own version of the game and that the UN allies, caught in the middle, had exerted great pressure for a compromise. China was not simply forced to accept terms dictated by Washington. The Americans made concessions on matters such as the Korean non-repatriates, which returned to the substance of the UN resolution on which the communist proposals of 7 May were based. Dulles' atomic bluster concealed the fact that *both* sides had retreated to avoid a wider war. His threat was made *after* Washington had decided to meet Beijing halfway, thus minimising the risk that he would have to back his words with action. If China wished to avoid an atomic attack, the US was aware that escalation would disrupt the global alliance system, basic to containment. Both sides compromised to end a struggle whose costs were out of all proportion to its benefits.

Washington had warned its allies that Rhee might react violently to the revised POW terms, a prediction borne out by events. In the following weeks it was sometimes difficult to remember that the enemy was in Beijing and Pyongyang rather than in the presidential lodgings at Pusan. An armistice which might have been signed within days of the POW compromise was delayed for weeks while Washington engaged in 'little truce talks', not with the communists, but with its Korean ally. In the process, relations with the ROK deteriorated to the point where the Americans contemplated a coup against Rhee. As the fighting dragged on and men continued to die, Eisenhower registered his personal disgust with Rhee in the privacy of his diary: 'It is impossible to attempt here to recite the long list of items in which Rhee has been completely uncooperative. . . . Of course the fact remains that the probable enemy is the communists. But Rhee has been such an unsatisfactory ally that it is difficult indeed to avoid excoriating him in the strongest of terms.'[98] At Cabinet, the President expressed the hope that the Korean people would 'overthrow' Rhee and replace him with 'a more moderate and sensible leader'.[99]

The crisis with the ROK began on 25 May, when Rhee was informed about the deal about to be tabled at Panmunjom. He felt betrayed by the sudden change in policy on POWs. He was humiliated at being informed of the new proposals only an hour before they were presented to the communists. Clark had never seen him so unstable and emotional. He condemned the terms as appeasement. The ROK would fight on alone, rather than accept an arrangement which left Chinese troops in the north. As for the NNRC, he repeated his pledge that 'no Indian soldier would be allowed to set foot in Korea'. His Foreign Minister, Pyun, who was also present, argued that to allow communists access to the prisoners for explanations was tantamount to forced repatriation.[100] Rhee had no faith in Eisenhower's reassurances. He suspected that once the war was over the US and UN would wash their hands of Korea. As he informed senior military commanders on 16 June, Koreans feared that 'their friends would abandon them with the enemy still in their country'.[101] This reflected bitter national experience. Rhee recalled that the US–Korean friendship treaty of 1882 had proved meaningless when Japan annexed the country. On 27 June the Foreign Minister cuttingly remarked to Clark that South Korea could not rely on US promises: 'The pledges of your Government, I have found in the past sometimes cannot be relied upon.'[102]

Clark believed that Rhee was exaggerating when he claimed that his attitude reflected the 'popular will'. By 1953 the Korean people were war weary, a fact revealed by the draft evasion rate which had reached one in four.[103] Nevertheless, Rhee was prepared to go to the brink in his opposition to an armistice. The ROK delegation was withdrawn from the truce talks, demonstrations were engineered in Pusan and Koreans working for the UN were terrorised by Rhee's police. In these circumstances, the threat to withdraw from the UN command had to be taken seriously. As Clark recalled, 'Since South Korean troops manned two-thirds of the front, a sudden decision by Rhee to remove them from my command presented all sorts of nightmare possibilities.'[104] Not least of these was the possibility that Rhee might ignore an armistice and continue to fight, in the hope of dragging the UN command into his support. On the eve of a final agreement with the communists, this did not bear contemplation. On 5 June, in an effort to buy Rhee off, Eisenhower offered him a mutual security pact after the conclusion of the cease-fire. This carrot was intended to reassure Rhee about the ultimate US commitment to the ROK. When Clark delivered this message, however, he found the Korean leader at his worst, alternating between 'despair and defiance'. He continued to

insist that the ROK would fight on, even at the cost of national suicide
He promised, however, to inform Clark before taking any steps to
withdraw Korean forces from the UN command.

The value of this pledge was revealed on 18 June when 'all hell broke
loose, by Rhee's order'. Early that morning, acting on the orders of the
Korean government, ROK guards released 27 000 Korean non
repatriates from their compounds. Clark had long been aware that
Rhee had the power to take such action. He lacked the manpower to
replace the ROK guards and was in any case reluctant to risk a clash
between the Korean army and other contingents of the UN command
In these circumstances, he had 'kept his fingers crossed' and relied on
Rhee's good faith to prevent unilateral action. The Korean leader
however, obviously regarded his coup as revenge for the humiliation of
25 May. Despite Clark's efforts, it proved impossible to recapture the
men, who were formed into labour battalions before being inducted
into the ROK army – perhaps not the type of freedom for which many
had hoped.[108] The Chinese compounds were not affected, although
some prisoners, in hospital at Pusan, were caught up in the breakout.
They were later smuggled out to Taiwan under the noses of the US
authorities.[109] The whole incident was an open gesture of defiance
which publicly flouted Clark's authority and demonstrated that Rhee's
wishes could not be ignored. It was a bombshell, since the articles of
the armistice had already been finalised. All that remained was to
'determine the date and arrangements for the signing ceremony'. Now
the 'fat was in the fire'. The communists immediately raised questions
about the ability of the UN command to control the ROK government.
If the South Koreans refused to sign an armistice, what guarantee was
there that they would live up to its terms. Rhee had already sabotaged
one of the armistice conditions by releasing the Korean non-
repatriates. As Clark ruefully remarked, he could not answer these
pointed questions because he did not know the answers himself.[110]

The Americans reacted strongly to Rhee's sabotage. Clark wrote to
the Korean leader expressing 'profound shock' at his unilateral action
in defiance of the UN command. This was the strongest official
criticism of Rhee ever made by an American and Washington insisted
on its publication.[111] Privately, Clark was even more cutting. While he
sympathised with Rhee's anti-communism, he was soured by his
obstructionism and breach of trust. According to Clark, Rhee was 'as
unscrupulous a dictator as ever lived. Anyone who raises his voice
against him is beaten up by thugs. . . . The sooner Rhee is told
irrevocably that we will go no further [with him], the more progress we

will make.'[112] Eisenhower also sent Rhee a message, warning that unless the ROK 'immediately and unequivocally' accepted Clark's authority, it might be necessary for the UNC to 'effect another arrangement'.[113] This openly hinted that Clark might call the Korean bluff and sign a separate armistice. Steps were taken to secure the remaining POWs. US reinforcements were rushed from Japan and Clark began to break up the Korean non-repatriate compounds into smaller cages, guarded by American troops.[114] He realised, however, that this programme was largely bluff. If Rhee attempted to free the 9000 Koreans who had not escaped in the mass breakout, he could only be stopped by force. The Korean leader was thought to have given the ROK Provost-Marshal authority to fire on US units which obstructed his forces. Clark ordered US camp commanders to back down, rather than risk bloodshed and fighting behind the UN lines.[115] In the event, Rhee did not push matters this far. The Chinese POWs, however, were more important to the armistice than the Koreans. While Beijing might accept the fait accompli which freed the Koreans, it was likely to react strongly to any interference with Chinese prisoners. It was difficult for the Chinese non-repatriates to escape since they were confined on the island of Cheju-Do. Nevertheless, US guards were increased while the American navy shadowed Korean warships off the coat. Jiang, who had shown signs of support for Rhee's position, was warned against any open demonstration of solidarity.[116]

These actions, however, did not solve the problem posed by Rhee. On 24 June the Assistant Secretary of State, Walter Robertson, was sent to Korea. The visit had been arranged on the eve of the breakout and postponed because of Rhee's action. Robertson's task was to assist Clark in bringing the Korean leader round.[117] While the talks dragged on, the US took steps to show that it was seriously contemplating 'another arrangement' as threatened in the President's letter. Supplies of petrol and ammunition to the ROK army slowed to a 'trickle'. There was a moratorium on activating new ROK units. It was made clear to ROK commanders that the UNC was prepared if necessary to sign a truce with the communists and withdraw. American teams began to survey evacuation routes to Pusan. This was intended to 'plant the seed' of insecurity.[118] It was known that ROK commanders were concerned by Rhee's stand and understood that without US support, they could not hope to hold the line.[119] It was hoped that they would either persuade Rhee to change his attitude or that 'influential ROK political and military elements would themselves take steps to bring about a situation in the ROK Government to assure its cooperation'.[120] In the last resort, therefore, Washington was prepared to encourage a military coup, although it refused to become directly involved. As early as 25 May Clark had revived his own emergency plan, EVERREADY. If Rhee endangered the safety of the UN command, he was to be arrested and a military government installed with the assistance of reliable ROK units. Washington baulked at the idea of such direct action against the regime. On 30 May it ruled against the establishment of a military government by the UNC while authorising Clark to act as necessary to guarantee the safety of his forces.[121] While these events were occurring, the US was heavily engaged on the diplomatic front, both with Rhee and with its allies. Before Robertson arrived in Pusan, a possible compromise had emerged. At a meeting with Clark, Rhee implied that while he would not sign an armistice, he might not oppose one. Nor did he openly reject a suggestion that the Chinese and Korean non-repatriates should be delivered to the NNRC in the demilitarized zone, established by the armistice agreement, to obviate the necessity of Indian troops and communist 'explainers' entering the ROK.[122] It proved difficult, however, for Robertson to pin Rhee down to any concrete arrangement. The Korean leader continually slipped away from compromises and raised new demands. His intractable stand was supported by the Foreign Minister Pyun, who was consistently unhelpful, pointing out new areas of disagreement to Rhee as soon as old ones had been resolved. Such was his role in the talks that Robertson speculated that he was a communist agent, deliberately driving a wedge between the US and the ROK.[123] The most serious areas of disagreement were over the political conference to be summoned after the armistice and the timing of the mutual security treaty on offer by Washington. Rhee demanded not only a strict time limit on the conference but an American pledge to renew the war if it produced no agreement. As for the defence pact, he demanded that the US sign the treaty *before* the conclusion of the armistice.[124]

Clark was convinced that Rhee was deliberately stalling to delay an armistice. Every day brought further losses as the communists intensified operations to improve their military position before the truce was finalised. On 16 June the heaviest artillery barrage of the war fell on UN positions in the central sector. By 29 June Rhee's obstruction had cost Clark 1700 casualties.[125] In this situation, Clark wished to call Rhee's bluff and sign an agreement with the communists: 'I am convinced that the sooner we sign an armistice, with or without Rhee's support, the better will be our position to handle

Rhee when we are not worried about a Communist attack.'[126] On 30 June he was authorised to reopen talks with the communists and to intensify psychological warfare in the south to reinforce the impression that the UNC would sign a separate cease-fire. His instructions, however, made it clear that this was largely bluff. Eisenhower emphasised that such preparations were for appearances only. There was 'No intention to withdraw from Korea'.[127] It was believed that there were grave dangers in presenting Rhee with a fait accompli. As Robertson emphasised, the Korean leader was a 'zealous, irrational and illogical fanatic' who might well 'call our bluff'. Since Washington could not simply abandon Korea to the communists after three years of bitter fighting, Rhee 'had us over an A-frame'.[128] The UNC could not withdraw, nor did the threat to do so seem likely to produce political change within the ROK. As even Clark was forced to admit by the beginning of July, no alternative leadership seemed likely to emerge from the ROK army.[129] The experience of the two weeks since 18 June confirmed the experience of the previous year. Rhee dominated Korean politics. The choice lay between his flawed leadership or a political vacuum and chaos. In these circumstances, there was little alternative but to continue bluffing, while making further concessions to buy Rhee off. At the same time the UN allies had to be held in line. All were seriously alarmed by the situation in Pusan and public sentiment began to emerge in Britain and Canada for the question to be considered by the UN General Assembly. The administration was anxious to avert such a development which could undermine Robertson's quiet diplomacy. Rhee had always distrusted the role of the UN allies, particularly the British, whom he accused of manipulating American policy in the cause of appeasement. A vote of censure by the General Assembly would merely throw fuel on the flames and increase his irrationality. Pressure was brought to bear on Ottawa and London to delay action. The allies agreed but emphasised the need for a speedy solution. They had their own public opinion to consider. Beleaguered on all sides, the Eisenhower administration intensified its efforts to reach an agreement with Rhee.

By 12 July a solution had emerged. The US agreed to support an ROK army of twenty divisions and to withdraw from a political conference after ninety days if no 'concrete achievements' emerged. Washington would consult on joint objectives before the conference opened. Rhee accepted a security pact after the armistice but only after Dulles had taken the unprecedented step of securing a pledge from the Senate that such a treaty would be ratified. In return, Rhee agreed not to obstruct the armistice and to assist in the delivery of the non-repatriates to the DMZ where the Indian custodial force would take charge.[131] The British had agreed to help transport and land the Indians directly from the sea to the DMZ to avoid offending Rhee by bringing them through Korean territory. In the end, both Rhee and the Americans had been bluffing. Rhee, however, had been willing to go further towards the brink and had secured considerable concessions. Eisenhower had retreated from the demand for an unequivocal commitment to the UN command. The agreement contained no clear-cut statement about the future relationship of the ROK to the UN command. Rhee merely promised not to obstruct the armistice. Nor did it spell out the action to be taken if a political conference failed. It later became clear that Rhee had not abandoned his rhetorical demand to renew the war. As Dulles noted, though ambiguous as it was, the agreement was the best the US was likely to obtain.[132] It was necessary to save Rhee's face in order to allow him to retreat gracefully. As Robertson emphasised, he had to be 'led as well as pushed'.[133] It was hoped that once the fighting ceased, it would prove difficult for Rhee to whip up any enthusiasm for renewing the war.[134] Nevertheless, the US continued to take precautions. When he visited Korea in September, Dulles stressed the importance of keeping ROK petrol and ammunition supplies low, multiplying the difficulties of launching a march north.[135] Thus in US–Korean relations, the war ended where it had begun, with a marked US distrust for the nationalist aspirations of Syngman Rhee, aspirations which could only be fulfilled by mobilising American power in their support.

The cost of saving Rhee's face was high. As Clark complained, American prestige suffered. Rhee had held the most powerful nation on earth to ransom. Not only did the US lose face, it also lost lives: 'The war at that time was costing us an average of nine hundred UN casualties a day, and the maddening part of it was that we had been virtually in complete agreement with the Communists . . . when the prisoners were released.[134] Washington also paid a financial price. Quite apart from the direct costs of the war, Rhee's refusal to allow the NNRC into the existing camps forced the UNC to bear the additional costs of transporting the POWs to the DMZ and constructing new compounds there, a price calculated by Clark at over $7 000 000. Lastly, there was a political price to be paid with the allies.[137] Rhee's attitude called into question the validity of the 'greater sanctions' statement which was to accompany the armistice. Nobody wished to be committed to renewing the war on behalf of Rhee or to give him any encouragement to wreck the truce. The Americans, however, continued to view the statement as an integral part of the armistice. The greatest problem was with the British, who had raised questions about the statement even before Rhee's release of the POWs. Churchill did not want to undermine the prospects of detente which might follow an armistice by issuing an open threat. Moreover, he had a slender parliamentary majority and opposition reaction to consider. Washington, however, had already made it clear that it regarded the matter as fundamental to the Atlantic alliance. After the Under-Secretary of State, Lord Salisbury, visited Washington in July, a compromise emerged. Dulles made it clear that 'greater sanctions' would apply only to unprovoked communist aggression and not to any incident engineered by Rhee. The statement would not be issued after the armistice but contained in Clark's final report on the war to the UN Secretary-General.[138] This had the advantage for the Conservative government of occurring during the parliamentary recess when the political repercussions could be minimised. At the same time, London refrained from adopting firm military commitments. The steps to be taken if the 'greater sanctions' threat were ever implemented remained ambiguous.

. Although the problems of Rhee and the allies were solved, one final obstacle remained – the communists. While the Chinese proved willing to sign an armistice without the Korean non-repatriates released by Rhee, they stalled the talks while they launched one final massive military operation. On 14 July an offensive was launched against ROK divisions in the Kumsong area. By 20 July the ROK Capitol division and much of the Third division had been practically destroyed. The operation displayed many of the continuing weaknesses of the ROK army despite two years of American training. While the Chinese operation may have had military objectives, its main purpose was undoubtedly political. It was directed against the Korean army and designed to underline the consequences of any attempt to break the truce and march north. It may also have been intended to reassure Pyongyang on the eve of the armistice. When the UNC moved up American troops to contain the situation, the advance halted. Eisenhower speculated that the Chinese wished to avoid a clash with US troops.[139] On the American side also, there was little inclination to renew large-scale fighting. As the Chinese offensive gathered momentum, Dulles telephoned Collins, the Army Chief of Staff, to express his concern. Dulles did not want China to finish the war with a victory. He emphasised the political dangers of allowing the communists 'the last word' in the fighting: 'If we have any reasonable chances of [a] counter-offensive it would have advantages.' Collins, however, was unenthusiastic: 'It was unfortunate, but the only people who could do it would be us, and we have to weigh the angle of the cost. If it fell down, we would have to go after it, but if we can stabilise, the actual terrain is not very significant.'[140] Nobody, it appeared, was willing to die for the ROK in the final stages of the war.

After Rhee had been taught a lesson, the communists proceeded with the armistice talks, obtaining assurances on 19 July that if the ROK attacked and they resisted, the UNC would continue to observe the armistice and that the UNC would not provide Rhee with supplies if he launched an operation against the north.[141] With these questions out of the way, work began on 23 July to draw up a final demarcation line as the basis for a DMZ. The date of the signing of the complete armistice was arranged for 27 July. At the last moment, however, the communist commanders refused to come to Panmunjom. They refused to sign an agreement with a representative of the ROK present. The reasons for this are obscure, although perhaps the communists feared some ROK provocation within the DMZ. As a result, Clark never met his adversaries face to face. Instead the truce documents were signed at Panmunjom by the armistice delegations and subsequently by the commanders at their respective headquarters. The final instrument was initialled by Harrison and Nam-Il at 10.00 a.m. on 27 July.[142] Twelve hours later the guns fell silent. It had taken five days for the United States to become involved in a ground war on the Asian mainland. It had taken two years to conclude a satisfactory armistice. The war had cost the US 142 091 casualties and had ended in a draw. For the first time in its modern history, America had failed to leave the battlefield victorious.

PART II
The Problems of Limited War

11 The War on the Ground

Intervention in Korea involved the US army in a type of war for which it was unprepared. Limited war was foreign to the American military experience in the twentieth century in which wars were global and involved the total mobilisation of resources to defeat the enemy: 'The prevailing axiom among the American Military at the time the Korean War began, existing since World War I and reinforced by World War II was: modern war is total war.'[1] The decision to intervene in Korea was taken to allow the US to 'resist aggression' while building up its forces for a possible global war against the Soviet Union. Because the commitment to Korea was limited, Washington was ultimately prepared to accept less than total victory rather than pour resources indefinitely into a peripheral struggle or risk involving the Russians. This was something which those engaged in the war found hard to accept, particularly after China intervened.

MacArthur was not the only general in the Far East to demand a total war with China rather than preparation to fight a theoretical future war against the USSR in Europe, he was merely the most outspoken. As his Chief of Staff, General Edward M. Almond, complained, Korea was never a 'police action' to those engaged in the fighting. The US had lost an opportunity to deal a 'death blow' to expanding communism by defeating China. This opinion was also shared by one of MacArthur's successors at Far East Command, General Mark Clark.[2]

If many professional soldiers found the constrictions of limited war frustrating and believed that there could be 'no substitute for victory', it also produced problems of morale and motivation amongst the troops. The war seemed to lack any clear political aim and its purpose was sometimes questioned. It was difficult to ask men to die to preserve a military stalemate in an obscure corner of North-East Asia. This was only solved by fighting a largely defensive ground war after June 1951, leaving offensive operations to the FEAF. Korea became a *Sitzkrieg* along fortified lines similar to those of World War One. This anachronistic approach was designed to keep losses low, preserve morale and prevent demands for escalation or withdrawal from the home front where Korea had become 'a sour little war'. An army with a doctrine of aggression and mobility was pinned down in static defence which left the initiative in ground operations with the enemy.

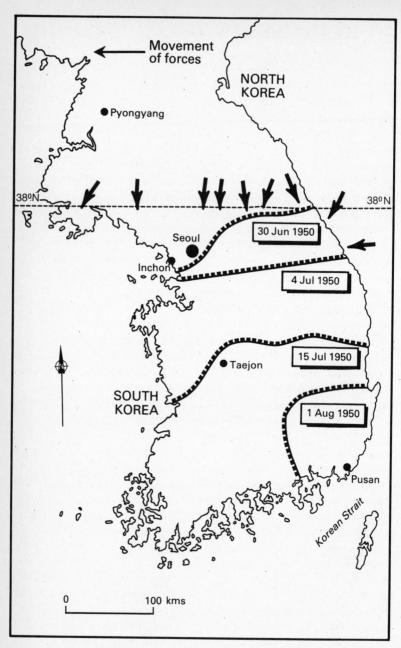

3. STAGES OF NKPA ADVANCE, JUNE–AUGUST 1950

The burden of the initial fighting fell on the four US divisions in Japan which constituted the Eighth Army under General Walton Walker. This was an occupation and not a fighting force. The troops lacked knowledge of basic infantry skills. There had been no large scale manoeuvres or live firing exercises. Many of the men were more familiar with the beer halls and brothels of the Japanese cities than with the basics of soldiering. As one critic later complained, it was a 'cream puff army': 'If these guys had spent more time on the firing range and less time in the PX snack bar . . . they might be alive today.'[3] In an era of low defence budgets and atomic deterrents there had been strict limitations on expensive military manpower. MacArthur's occupation forces had been particularly badly hit. His divisions were 30 per cent under authorised strength and had been forced to reduce the number of battalions in each regiment from three to two to maintain a functioning organisation. The personnel who were sent to the Far East were often those who were not wanted elsewhere. Under prevailing strategic priorities, the best troops were retained in the US or sent to Europe. Of the enlisted men who first fought in Korea, '43 per cent were ranked within the army's two lowest intelligence classifications. In other words *almost half* tested below what the army normally considered *acceptable*.'[4] At a time of high civilian wages the army had to take what it could find. There was also a shortage of competent officers. The best tended to be creamed off by the headquarters organisation in Japan while the infantry received what was left. Indeed the whole organisation was top heavy with military bureaucracy and rear echelon troops inevitable in a peacetime army of occupation.[5] In addition to a lack of trained infantry and professional leadership there were critical supply shortages. When the war began there were only three serviceable tanks in the Far East Command.[6] Thus the Eighth Army went to war 'short of everything from men to machine guns'. It was 'understrength, poorly trained, physically unfit and extremely badly armed and equipped'.[7] This force was set against the NKPA which contained a high proportion of veterans of World War Two and the Chinese civil war. Its deficiences were soon to emerge on the battlefield.

The US Army, however, went to war in the expectation of a quick victory. The confidence of both the troops and FEC headquarters amounted to arrogance. While MacArthur privately admitted that his men were 'flabby' from good living in Japan, he had no doubts about their ability to defeat Koreans.[8] He planned to use two divisions. The 24th Division would brace the ROKs while the First Cavalry landed in the enemy rear at Inchon, cutting the supply lines of the NKPA and catching it in a trap from which there would be no escape. As he informed the journalist Marguerite Higgins at the beginning of July, the ROKs only needed 'an injection of ordered American strength. . . . Give me two American divisions and I can hold Korea.'[9] The amphibious operation, code named BLUEHEARTS, had been conceived by MacArthur on his first visit to the front on 29 June.[10] On 6 July his headquarters staff briefed the First Cavalry on the plan. It was urged to 'expedite preparations to the utmost limit because if the landing is delayed all the First Cavalry will hit when it lands will be the tail end of the 24th Division as it passes north through Seoul.' One officer ruefully recalled that this prophecy proved incorrect. The First Cavalry did 'hit the tail of the 24th Division on 20th July 1950 but it was not moving north'.[11] The confidence of MacArthur's headquarters was shared by the men on the spot. General John Church, who was sent to Korea in the first days of the war to assess the situation, believed that what was required was 'some men up there who will not run when they see tanks'.[12] General George Barth, who arrived with the first troops from the 24th Division, informed newsmen on 5 July that 'Those Commie bastards will turn and run when they find they're up against our boys. We'll be back in Seoul by the weekend.'[13] The only sceptics were the officers of the Korean Military Advisory Group [KMAG] who had seen the NKPA in action. They watched with bitter anticipation as the first US troops started towards the front, brashly predicting a speedy end to the fighting. These men were the self-conscious heirs of the victorious armies of 1945. The NKPA might be able to rout other Koreans but Americans were a different matter: 'They were . . . going to kick some gooks and get out.' The pleasures of garrison life in Japan would be renewed within a few days.[14] The thought of defeat did not enter anyone's head. From MacArthur to the lowliest GI there was a disastrous underestimation of the strength and tenacity of the advancing enemy.

   The first clash occurred at Osan on 5 July between forward elements of the 24th Division, Task Force Smith, and NKPA tanks and infantry. The American artillery, with only six armour piercing rounds, was unable to stop the tanks, which also proved impervious to bazooka fire. They rolled through the American position which was then outflanked by infantry.[15] Its ammunition running low and threatened with encirclement, Task Force Smith withdrew: 'The stragglers came bootless and beaten and without guns across the hills and splashing through the paddi fields. Gunners pulled the breech blocks out of their guns and hurled them away.'[16] As the news came in, there was consternation at rear headquarters. The incredible had happened. The US Army was in retreat. The first American to die in Korea was killed at Osan: 'His name was Private Shadrick and his friends carried him out with a respect for the dead that was forgotten in the days ahead.'[17] For those engaged, the Korean 'police action' rapidly became a bitter and bloody war.

The defeat of Task Force Smith began a month of retreat. An attempt by General William F. Dean's 24th Division to hold the Kum river line failed. On 20 July the city of Taejon fell. The 24th Division lost 30 per cent of its men and much of its equipment. Dean himself was captured after the battle, the highest ranking American to fall into enemy hands during the war.[18] By the beginning of August, the Eighth Army under General Walton Walker had been pushed behind the Naktong river into the Pusan perimeter and was struggling desperately to maintain a toe-hold in Korea. MacArthur was forced to cancel BLUEHEARTS. By mid-July both the 1st Cavalry and the 25th Division had been committed to the fighting under Walker's command. Reinforcements were rushed from the US and Okinawa. At the beginning of August the 1st Provisional Marine Brigade and the 2nd Division landed at Pusan. At the end of the month they were joined by the British 27th Brigade from Hong Kong. The shortage of infantry, however, remained critical. With the exception of the Marine Brigade and the British, many of the new units were filled out by line of supply troops, PX clerks and typists. Some of these men were not even given the chance to adjust their rifle sights before being thrown into combat. The President's military aide, General Frank E. Lowe, noted that between 1 July 1950 and 1 March 1951 60.6 per cent of all replacements were non-combat soldiers. He met one unfortunate who had spent his training as a company clerk and never fired a rifle.[19] In an attempt to solve the manpower shortage, Koreans were drafted into US units. These men were simply pressganged by the police. As the Americans themselves admitted, the methods of recruitment were 'a bit rough': 'Many recruits were simply picked up from the streets of Pusan and Taegu. Schoolboys still carried their schoolbooks when they arrived in camp. . . .'[20] These bewildered and often demoralised people received their training in action. On 14 July Rhee placed his army under Walker's command but it was weak and unreliable. While some units fought well, many had disintegrated in the first week of the war when 24 000 went missing. ROK headquarters was in confusion and Walker complained about the 'inept' leadership of the Koreans.[21]

The average GI was bitter about the lack of ROK support and felt that the South Koreans should be doing more in their own defence. One officer called the performance of Rhee's forces 'a major scandal'. The US army should not be held to blame for the reverses in Korea.[22]

The Eighth Army itself, however, was not without faults. It proved difficult to hold a line with understrength units which were continually being outflanked and attacked from the rear.[23] An additional problem was infiltration. NKPA troops often passed through the lines disguised as refugees or were mistaken for retreating ROKs. Marguerite Higgins was caught in one such attack on a rear area headquarters. This 'was only one of the hundreds of cases in which confusion in identifying the enemy cost us lives. It is, of course, part of the difficulty of being involved in a civil war.'[24] The Americans were particularly vulnerable to these tactics. They were reluctant to leave the roads and often panicked when cut off from their vehicles. Lacking basic infantry skills they were unwilling to counter-attack in the absence of massive air and artillery support. Some units broke and fled at the first hint of encirclement. This was known in the US Army as 'bugging out'. Straggler points had to be established outside Pusan. On 9 August the Eighth Army complained that 'The abandoning of weapons and other equipment by our front line forces . . . has reached such a point that the impact is being felt on our supply system.'[25] Morale suffered and troops began to lose faith in their weapons, particularly the bazooka which proved ineffective against tanks. During the battle for Taejon, General Dean had led a 'tank hunting' party to prove to his men that enemy armour was not invulnerable.[26] The situation was serious enough to warrant an emergency airlift of a new and more powerful anti-tank weapon from arsenals in the United States.[27] Other senior officers made a point of appearing at the front to rally their men and white lies were told about the military situation.[28]

Walker 'smarted' at the performance of his forces. An aggressive commander who had served under Patton in Europe, his instinct was to attack. As his forces moved into the Pusan perimeter he made it clear that there must be no further retreat. On 29 July he informed the staff of the 25th Division, 'I am tired of hearing about lines being straightened. There will be no more retreating . . . our soldiers must . . . stand or die.' There would be no Dunkirk or Bataan in Korea.[29] The Pentagon blamed the GI for the situation. A high-level meeting on 9 August complained that the American soldier lacked 'an aggressive fighting spirit'. He was 'not up to World War Two standards'.[30] The Army Chief of Staff, General Joseph Collins, attributed this to the 'softening influences to which our youngsters have been exposed from birth on'.[31] The socioeconomic groups from which the troops were drawn, however, had had little experience of the good life in America. Whatever 'softening influences' had entered their lives had come with occupation duty in Japan. Walker was also criticised. He was accused of poor leadership and there was talk of replacing him with General Matthew Ridgway, a paratroop officer in World War Two who was being groomed for high office at the Pentagon.[32] The Army was really seeking scapegoats. The failures of the GI in Korea reflected the lack of training for which the Army was to blame rather than any character defect in the American soldier. As for Walker, his crime was to be associated with an embarrassing defeat in an army with a cult of winning. It is difficult to believe that any other general could have done better. Although he mounted an inspired defence of the Pusan perimeter in August 1950, shuttling his slender reserves to successive danger points, he was never forgiven for the early performance of his forces. Walker was to become the forgotten commander of the Korean War.[33]

In August 1950 the NKPA launched a series of 'desperate' assaults on the Pusan perimeter in an attempt to win the war before the American build-up was complete.[34] In the process it was exposed to savage attrition. The high command had planned a four week campaign against the ROK and had to mobilise additional divisions to deal with the new American enemy. Like Walker, the North Koreans faced a shortage of trained infantry. By mid-August the Army had been diluted by troops who had received only seven days training before being sent to the front lacking proper uniforms and even weapons. Each battle further reduced the professional cadre of officers and NCOs with which the NKPA had entered the war. It proved impossible to replace losses of heavy equipment such as tanks and supplies began to run low because of American interdiction bombing.[35] Meanwhile Walker's forces were becoming stronger as men and munitions poured into Pusan. By the beginning of September, the Eighth Army outnumbered the enemy by 2:1 and held a 5:1 superiority in tanks. Despite the changing balance of power, however, the NKPA continued to fight with fanatical determination.[36] The great Naktong offensive, which began on 27 August, penetrated the front at several points. The North Koreans, however, were unable to maintain their momentum and wilted in the face of determined counter-attacks and the combined weight of American firepower from the air and from the ground. Walker correctly described the offensive as the 'last gasp' of the NKPA.[37] By mid-September 'the People's Army had almost shot its bolt. Less than 30% of the old China hands remained, and these were dirty, tired, hungry and in rags. . . . Only frequent summary executions and the threat of death could hold the newly drafted trainees in line.'[38] In the NKPA 4th Division, the desertion rate rose to 40 per cent.[39] Exhausted by the Naktong battles, the NKPA was about to receive its death blow in the counter-attack which MacArthur had been planning since early July.

Despite the cancellation of BLUEHEARTS, MacArthur continued to believe the war could be won by an amphibious operation. By 23 July he had evolved a new plan, CHROMITE, for a two division landing in the enemy rear coupled with an offensive by the Eighth Army.[40] MacArthur badgered a reluctant Pentagon to supply the 1st Marine Division without which he argued his scheme could not succeed. The formation was hurriedly composed from recalled reservists and drafts on the fleet. By the end of August it had reached Japan, where it joined the 7th Infantry Division in the X Corps under MacArthur's Chief of Staff, General Edward N. Almond.[41] The plan called for X Corps, led by the marines, to land at Inchon in mid-September. This seemed a risky choice of site. The port was approached by narrow twisting channels with a tidal range of thirty-two feet. US forces could be cut off in a city which might be transformed into a fortress. As one naval officer recalled, 'We drew up a list of every conceivable and natural handicap – and Inchon had 'em all.'[42] At the Pentagon, the plan evoked uneasy memories of Anzio. A defeat would mean expulsion from Korea and the humiliation of the US. The JCS were only won round by the lack of alternatives. As MacArthur argued at a crucial meeting with JCS representatives on 23 August, a landing further south would not produce a decisive result. It was a choice between Inchon and a bloody war of attrition as Walker tried to force his way up the peninsula. He stressed the value of surprise, recalling Wolfe's victory at Quebec in 1759. While Washington remained doubtful, MacArthur was allowed to go ahead.[43]

His gamble proved justified. When the marines landed on 15 September, one unit suffered more casualties from naval covering fire than from the NKPA which had left the city largely undefended.[44] The following day, Walker began his breakout from Pusan. Despite some initial delays, the Eighth Army made good progress and enemy resistance on the Naktong collapsed. A junction between X Corps and Walker's forces was effected on 27 September near Suwon.[45] The objective of the Inchon landing was Seoul which MacArthur considered of vital political and military importance. He insisted that the city must fall by 25 September, three months after the war had begun.[46] This meant a direct frontal assault on NKPA positions in Seoul rather than the flanking movement favoured by the commander of the 1st Marines, General Oliver P. Smith. Almond angered the Marines by urging speed and threatening to bring in the 7th Infantry to do the job.[47] In the event, FEC headquarters announced the fall of the city on 25 September while fighting was still raging in the streets. The ROK capital was not secured for three further days.[48] Ordnance was expended recklessly to reduce US casualties, with fearsome results on the civilian population. Two-thirds of the city was destroyed. A huge pall of smoke hung over the Han river. Rutherford Poats of United Press reported the scene in liberated Seoul: 'Telephone and power lines festooned the streets or hung from shattered poles which resembled grotesque Christmas trees. . . . A tiny figure . . . stumbled down the street. Her face, arms and legs were burned and almost eaten away by the fragments of an American white phosphorous shell. She was blind, but somehow alive.'[49] On 28 September, in the war damaged capitol building, with the smell of death wafting through the empty windows and shards of glass dropping from the shattered rotunda, MacArthur offered a prayer of thanksgiving and formally returned the city to Syngman Rhee.[50] He had won his greatest triumph. Unknown to MacArthur, however, he also stood on the verge of his greatest defeat.

On 9 October MacArthur's forces crossed the 38th parallel to complete the defeat of the NKPA. The Army advanced along the roads riding on anything that would move. The slightest resistance was met by air strikes and artillery while the troops awaited the results in their vehicles. Villages were destroyed to flush out single snipers.[51] The process shocked many who witnessed it. As Reginald Thompson of the *Daily Telegraph* remarked, 'few people' had 'suffered so terrible a liberation'.[52] Civilians also suffered in other ways. The advancing army adopted a racist attitude towards Koreans which had been evident from the earliest days of the conflict. The people amongst whom the troops were moving were treated as things, 'gooks' who deserved little consideration. Army drivers played 'chicken' with North Korean villagers and refugees. Reginald Thompson recalled, 'They didn't bother to look where they were going . . . driving the peasants into the gutters, and even tight back against the mud walls of the dwellings. . . . This seemed to amuse them.' The vehicle in which he was travelling 'managed to knock down two children more than three feet off the road. Blood poured from the mouth of a boy of four or five years, his face clotted with blood and dust as he lay unconscious, and another appeared badly hurt in the body.'[53] Thompson reported incidents of mindless vandalism and looting along the line of advance. He came across one group of soldiers bombarding peasant houses with bricks. They were not 'angry' or 'nasty', 'they were simply bored, thoughtless undisciplined children, stuck by the roadside in a Gook village. . . . Gook was a shroud with which they covered human beings and pretended that they were not human beings.'[54] An army chaplain, a veteran of World War Two, later complained to General Ridgway that 'poor discipline' and the refusal to investigate serious crimes 'made murder, rape and pillage easy for the criminally inclined'. One soldier in his unit had slit the throats of eight civilians near Pyongyang. Seven men caught in the act of rape in the city itself were released unpunished. The divisional commander had stated that one American life was worth any number of Koreans: 'The men took him at his word. [Koreans] who were anxious to serve our cause and to destroy Communism were regarded as enemies and treated as such.'[55]

Pyongyang, abandoned by the NKPA, fell largely undamaged to the Eighth Army on 20 October. It became the only liberated communist capital to host a production of the Bob Hope Show. While sightseers gawped at Kim Il Sung's private office, special intelligence teams descended on the files of the government ministries. Task Force Indianhead had to compete with looters and souvenir hunters to obtain information.[56] The Counter-Intelligence Corps, with the assistance of the ROKs, hunted out any surviving 'communists' who were consigned to the central prison. Thousands of POWs were rounded up, 'They were bewildered men, totally defeated and only too willing to give up to the first person who would take them.'[57] Many changed into civilian clothes and hastily acquired ROK flags which they waved hopefully at Walker's advancing columns.[58] On 24 October Mac-Arthur ordered his forces to make full speed towards the Yalu, hoping to complete the campaign before the onset of winter. Many discarded steel helmets, entrenching tools and even ammunition, in order to travel light.[59] The 1st Cavalry planned a victory parade in Tokyo while ammunition ships en route from the US were turned back, their cargoes considered unnecessary.[60] The entire army, from generals to GIs, assumed that the war was almost over. A major new enemy, however, was about to intervene.

On 2 October China threatened to enter the conflict if US forces crossed the parallel. This was dismissed as bluff by both Washington and Tokyo. According to MacArthur's intelligence chief, General Charles Willoughby, Chinese threats were 'diplomatic blackmail'. Neither Beijing nor Moscow would commit resources to a 'lost cause'.[61] MacArthur was dismissive of China and confident that he could deal with anything sent against him. As he boasted to Truman at Wake on 14 October, his air force would destroy any troops who crossed the Yalu: 'if the Chinese tried to get down to Pyongyang there would be the greatest slaughter'.[62] The PLA might have defeated other Chinese in the civil war but would be unable to withstand a modern Western army. Chinese capabilities and intentions were underestimated. It was another example of the 'gook syndrome', the arrogant misjudgement of Asians which almost led to disaster in July. The consequences in November were to be even more serious. As MacArthur was talking at Wake, the Chinese were crossing the Yalu undetected. The PLA was a phantom which left no shadow. It moved by night, carrying its own supplies, and hid by day. There were no vehicle parks or ammunition dumps to betray its presence. By November 1950 300 000 troops were across the Yalu.[63] This was a technologically backward force. It was a peasant army equipped with a mixture of aging Japanese and American weapons. There was 'an extreme shortage' of artillery. Below divisional level, communications were conducted by runner and bugle.[64] The PLA commanders, however, were determined to negate the US technological advantage by fighting on their own terms. The Chinese were preparing a vast ambush across the Chongchon river which was to deny MacArthur victory and to administer a stunning reverse to American arms.[65]

MacArthur advanced towards this new enemy with his forces divided. In September 1950 he had decided to maintain X Corps as a separate command. While the Eighth Army pushed up the west coast, X Corps would be brought out through Inchon and sent round the peninsula, landing at Wonsan in the east and pushing down the only lateral valley in North Korea to link up with Walker's forces at Pyongyang.[66] This plan was resented by Walker and his staff. It was believed that Almond was MacArthur's 'blue-eyed boy' and that the Eighth Army, which had done most of the fighting, was being neglected as victory approached. MacArthur's decision was thought to display a lack of faith in Walker. The Eighth Army, however, was determined to seize the glory of liberating Pyongyang and during the advance across the parallel, Walker urged his forces on lest his rival Almond arrive first in the communist capital.[67] MacArthur, however, had sound military reasons for his plan. He argued that both forces could not be supplied through Pusan and Inchon. It was essential to capture a port on the east coast and to envelop what remained of the NKPA. In the circumstances, coordination of the two widely separated commands was best effected through his own headquarters in Tokyo rather than by Walker's staff.[68]

MacArthur's instructions from Washington for the march north were that as 'a matter of policy' no non-Korean troops were to be used in the sensitive border provinces adjoining China and the USSR. Only ROKs were to advance beyond the narrow Korean neck. The rest of his forces would halt approximately eighty kilometres north of the line Pyongyang–Wonsan. If MacArthur had stuck to his original plan, the Chinese would have had little choice but to carry the war to a united American command deployed along this line. They would have been forced into the open and exposed to the full effects of air power and artillery. On 24 October, however, MacArthur breached these limitations by ordering an advance to the Yalu.[69] He was not overruled by Washington. X Corps, which had been delayed by mines at Wonsan and was unable to land until 25 October, after the fall of Pyongyang, was given a new mission to clear the north-east while Walker advanced across the Chongchon river.[70] This meant that MacArthur's forces met the Chinese under the worst possible conditions, divided from each other by the towering Taebek mountains and forced to advance along narrow valleys where they could be cut off by enemy troops poised on their flanks. The situation was ideally suited to Chinese tactics of ambush and encirclement.

The Chinese presence was first revealed at the end of October when the 6th ROK Division was destroyed at Onjong. FEC headquarters, however, refused to accept the presence of major Chinese units until the 8th Cavalry was mauled at Unsan in the first days of November. Walker was forced to halt his advance and retire behind the Chongchon river. At Sudong, in the north-east, the marines also ran into trouble.[71] MacArthur refused to abandon his offensive. On 5 November FEAF was ordered to destroy the Yalu bridges and every means of communication between the border and the battleline. The Chinese were to be weakened by air interdiction and finished off by the advancing ground forces. Although Washington complicated this strategy by insisting that only the Korean ends of the international bridges should be attacked, MacArthur was confident that it had produced results.[72] The Chinese vanished from the battlefield and on 21 November leading elements of the 7th Infantry Division reached the Yalu at Hyesanjin in the north-east.[73] On 17 November

MacArthur predicted that it would require a ten day campaign to clear the remainder of Korea. He would then repatriate Chinese POWs and withdraw the Eighth Army to Japan.[74] This wishful thinking was encouraged by faulty intelligence. While Willoughby registered some concern at the situation he consistently underestimated the number of Chinese opposing MacArthur's forces. He calculated that there were 70 000 on the Korean side of the Yalu, an error of 75 per cent.[75] MacArthur himself believed that there could be no more than 30 000, arguing that a larger number could not have escaped detection.[76]

McArthur was later accused of rushing blindly towards his fate like Custer at the Little Big Horn.[77] According to the Chinese he treated their military potential with contempt.[78] Yet in his own terms, MacArthur was taking a calculated risk as at Inchon, assuming that air power could compensate for any weakness in his ground forces.[79] As he later argued, he had no alternative but to advance: 'If I went forward, there was a chance that China might not intervene in force and the war would be over. If I remained immobile and waited . . . [the Chinese] had enough divisions to surround the army . . . and every day would increase their force by fresh divisions from Manchuria. This would mean the utter anihilation of our entire command.'[80] Unlike Inchon, however, the element of surprise was on the enemy side. Afterwards MacArthur claimed that the offensive had been merely a 'reconnaisance in force' to test the strength of the Chinese.[81] At the time he described it as a 'decisive effort'.[82] As the advance began on 24 November, he visited Walker's headquarters where he pledged that if the operation was successful, the boys would be 'home by Xmas', a statement which was to later prove embarrassing.[83] With the exception of his favourite, Almond, his subordinate commanders were less optimistic. General Oliver P. Smith of the Marines had reservations about a plan which strung out his men along narrow mountain roads in the face of unknown numbers of Chinese. A strategy suited to mopping up operations against the NKPA was ill-advised against a dangerous new opponent. Smith took precautions to ensure that he was not cut off from the coast. Walker respected the Chinese after Unsan and refused to move until his supply situation eased.[84] Nobody, however, predicted the extent of the impending defeat.

Within days MacArthur's command was faced with disaster as strong Chinese forces attacked American units strung out 'from hell to breakfast' along narrow dirt roads.[85] At X Corps headquarters, Almond was stunned. As Smith recalled, his superiors could not believe 'that the Chinese had attacked in force.'[86] There was a similar

214

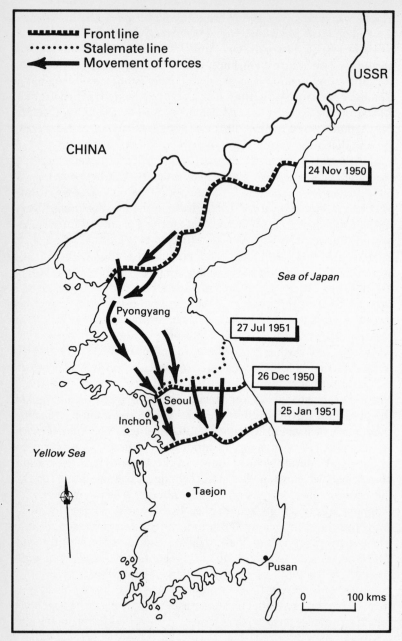

4. THE CHINESE INTERVENTION, NOVEMBER 1950–JANUARY 195

sense of unreality in Tokyo. Not until 28 November did MacArthur summon Walker and Almond to Japan and admit that his command would have to retreat.[87] The pattern of the fighting resembled the early clashes with the NKPA. The ROK divisions, painfully rebuilt since July, broke and fled. There were fresh examples of 'bugging out' amongst American troops both at the front and behind the lines. Old problems re-emerged. As a Chinese intelligence report, based on the earlier clash at Unsan, remarked, American troops relied on machines and were unhappy in a classic infantry battle: 'Cut off from the rear, they abandon all their heavy weapons . . . They become dazed and completely demoralised. They are afraid when the rear becomes cut off. When transportation comes to a standstill, the infantry loses the will to fight.'[88] The American reaction to encirclement was often to attempt to drive out, a recipe for disaster against an enemy who held the hills. Withdrawing from Kunuri, the 2nd Division, Eighth Army, lost one third of its men and most of its equipment attempting to break through enemy roadblocks against heavy flanking fire. Blazing vehicles soon blocked the evacuation route and the troops fought in isolated groups, unable to concentrate their available firepower against the Chinese. The pass on the Kunuri road was described as 'the valley of death': 'Wounded and dead clogged the ditches. Some lay apathetically while others ran along in the column's dust, desperately trying to hitch a new ride. Officers had not anticipated trouble and now, committed, they could only bore ahead, trying to bring through the few men riding in the same vehicle with them.'[89] Amongst Walker's troops only the British and the Turks were fully trained as infantry and formed the rearguard on the retreat south. In the north-east, the marines, displaying their traditional professionalism, fought their way down the roads to Hungnam, inflicting large casualties on Chinese forces attempting to cut them off from the sea. This did nothing to endear them to army officers who had long resented their self-appointed elite status.

Walker was forced to fall back through Pyongyang, pursuing a scorched earth policy as he went. Villages were evacuated and burned. Public buildings and utilities in Pyongyang were blown up and supply dumps put to the torch to keep them out of enemy hands. The retreating forces scrounged what they could find before engineers detonated mountains of food and winter clothing.[90] By Christmas the Eighth Army, deprived of its victory parade in Tokyo, was back across the parallel. Walker believed that he might have to retreat to the old Pusan perimeter for a last stand.[91] His retreat had been precipitate and outran the Chinese pursuit. This was caused by a haunting fear of encirclement. There were no reliable troops on the Eighth Army flank until January 1951, after X Corps had been evacuated from Hungnam by sea and brought into line in the South. The troops were weary and dispirited. There was widespread speculation in the 24th Division that the unit faced another Taejon. Its commander was forced to issue a reassurance that the division would never again be placed in a situation from which there was no escape. There would be no Bataan in Korea.[92]

Discipline, which had become lax during the victorious advance of the autumn, worsened in retreat. There was an outbreak of disorder in Seoul which was quashed only by the imposition of a curfew and firm action by the military police. It took the form of looting, rape and assaults on civilians.[93] The 'gooks' were resented and blamed for the rout beyond the Chongchon. The President's military aide, general Lowe, complained that 'as a dependable military force' the ROKs were 'almost non-existent'. They were 'cowardly and in no wise to be depended upon. Their faults, military and otherwise, may be glossed over.' Many had abandoned their American advisers to the enemy.[94] As allies, the Koreans were distrusted. On 10 January, the 1st Cavalry issued a warning of increased guerrilla activity which displayed strong suspicion of the local population: 'It may be expected that if the enemy makes further advances, many Koreans now appearing friendly will jump on the bandwagon.[95] Contingency plans for total evacuation were kept secret from the ROKs, lest they provoke defections and clashes with US troops.[96] This attitude of suspicion and resentment was often reciprocated. A colonel in the ROK 2nd Division who became drunk, chased his KMAG adviser with a pistol, threatening to kill him. The unfortunate American captain was reassigned to another unit.[97]

The resentment of Koreans was only one aspect of the general ill-feeling within MacArthur's command. If the Americans blamed the ROKs, many British soldiers blamed the Americans. The British had a tradition of fighting retreats and did not understand an approach which broke contact with the enemy in an attempt to hold a line far to the rear. Caught up with an 'unfamiliar American army in retreat', British troops felt 'bewildered and half ashamed of this curious method of waging war'.[98] Officers of the 29th Brigade complained that Walker's forces had withdrawn too precipitately.[99] Their attitude of superiority, which sometimes amounted to contempt, was shared by many ordinary soldiers. As one of them wrote to his wife in January 1951,

'We would be winning if only the Yankees would stand, but they won't.' The troops were 'fed up with this farce out here'.[100] The Turks, who suffered heavily in the fighting beyond the Chongchon, were similarly aggrieved. They complained that they had been 'let down' by their American allies who had provided no fire support and had failed to advise the Brigade of withdrawal plans.[101]

MacArthur rightly accused the press of exaggerating the scale of the defeat. The Chinese failed to encircle his armies which lived to fight another day.[102] At the same time, however, total disaster clearly threatened in December 1950. Two-thirds of the US Army faced destruction.[103] In these circumstances, the Pentagon speculated about the use of the atomic bomb.[104] There was particular concern about the fate of X Corps, caught in the icy mountains of the north-east. Plans were made to rush equipment to Japan to rebuild Almond's divisions if they were faced with a Dunkirk. There was even speculation about the emergency deployment of the 82nd Airborne Division, the only unit remaining in the strategic reserve.[105] Following military logic, MarArthur called for retaliation against China. He wanted to bomb Manchuria and to unleash Jiang's nationalist divisions against South China. He did not rule out employment of atomic weapons against the new enemy. He also demanded reinforcements. Japan was protected only by civilian police and his divisions in Korea were on average 5000 men understrength.[106] MacArthur was given fillers but no major new organised units. Nor was he allowed to widen the war. Washington was unwilling to change the strategic axis of containment by pouring indefinite resources into a fight against the communist 'second team'. Although fresh divisions were completing their training in the US, they were destined for Eisenhower in Europe. Since it was believed that Russia might risk war, it was considered of cardinal importance to proceed with these European deployments. Preparation for global war took precedence over MacArthur's peripheral struggle in the Far East. Washington was ultimately prepared to settle for a draw in Korea rather than attempt to unify the country against the new Chinese opponent. While MacArthur was eventually sent two National Guard Divisions, these were intended to defend Japan against *Russian* attack. He was forbidden to move them to Korea or to milk them for replacements without the permission of the JCS.[107] MacArthur found the restrictions imposed by global strategy intolerable. It was immoral to ask American soldiers to die in a stalemate when an opportunity existed to crush Asian communism. There could be 'no substitute for victory'. His attempt to force a change by appealing to the domestic front led to his recall on 11 April 1951.[108] Like McClellan in the civil war, he had overstepped the bounds of military propriety by interfering in politics. By that stage, General Mathew Ridgway was proving him wrong.

On 22 December, at the nadir of his professional career, Walton Walker was killed in a road accident. Ridgway was rushed to Korea to replace him, taking charge of an Eighth Army which absorbed X Corps as soon as it was evacuated from Hungnam. Ridgway had long been dissatisfied with the performance of the GI in Korea. He was determined to introduce changes and determined to attack.[109] A member of the dominant Europe first group at the Pentagon, he recognised the importance of forcing China to accept a draw with the forces available. The Eighth Army must overcome its awe of the Chinese 'hordes' and become an effective fighting instrument. His first priority was to infuse the troops with the will to fight. He was quick to fire incompetent commanders and tightened up on discipline, insisting on strict observance of the uniform regulations. The troops had to shave and wear their helmets. Loss of equipment was treated as a serious offence. With the shelves stripped bare at home, the army could not afford to waste weapons and vehicles which would be utilised by the Chinese.[110] In an attempt to motivate the men, Ridgway emphasised the importance of the war to national security. The question 'Why are we here?' was discouraged.[111]

Most important of all, Ridgway moved the Army out of its vehicles and onto its feet. He favoured a broad front approach which used American firepower to 'bleed China white'. There would be no more romantic dashes along the roads but a slow methodical advance using technology to negate the Chinese advantage in manpower. Every hill was to be cleared: 'We must clean out everything on the way whether it is a company or a battalion.'[112] His goal was to push the enemy back, ridge by ridge, 'killing as many as possible in the process'.[113] He fought a flexible campaign, pulling back when the Chinese attacked and subjecting them to the withering effects of US airpower and artillery. When the enemy ran out of steam, he would advance behind a curtain of fire. These tactics were accompanied by a psychological warfare campaign which invited the Chinese to count their dead. By March 1951, Ridgway's forces were back across the parallel and had reoccupied Seoul, abandoned in December 1950. In April and May, rolling with the punch, he defeated two Chinese counter-offensives, imposing fearful losses on the enemy.[114] In April alone the Chinese lost 70 000 men, a rate of attrition which was unendurable. By the end of May, the army which had crossed the Yalu was falling back in confusion. Ridgway was able to report a 'noticeable deterioration' in the morale of the enemy troops. The invincible opponent of December 1950 was 'on the run'.[115]

While imposing maximum attrition on the enemy, Ridgway was careful not to risk large losses amongst his own men. This would have political repercussions at home. He was particularly sensitive about the fate of allied units. The use of the British and the Turks as rearguards in December had caused ill-feeling and risked unwelcome questions in the British and Turkish parliaments at a crucial point in the cold war.[116] Ridgway issued strict instructions that in future no foreign unit was to be used as a rearguard for Americans or given a sacrifice mission. When he discovered that a British group had been left behind during the evacuation of Seoul, he ordered a maximum effort to rescue it, short of losing an equal number of men. The rescue would have a 'most electrifying effect on the 8th Army and particularly upon our relations with the British'.[117] He also attempted to quell dissension within his international command by condemning 'comments . . . regarding the alleged unreliability of any particular nationality; all troops we have are necessary and we must do the best with what we have.'[118]

The order against 'sacrifice missions' was breached by the last stand of the Glosters at the battle of the Imjin (22–5 April 1951). The Battalion destroyed the Chinese 63rd Army but was itself overrun, earning a Presidential Unit Citation.[119] The award covered some political embarrassment. Ridgway admitted that the unit had fought well and inflicted grievous losses on the enemy but blamed the Corps and divisional commanders for not pulling it out quickly enough from its exposed position: 'I cannot but feel a certain disquiet that down through the channel of command the full responsibility for realising the danger to which this unit was exposed, then for extricating it when that danger became grave, was not recognised nor implemented. . . . There are times when it is not sufficient to accept the judgement of a subordinate commander that a threatened unit can care for itself.' Colonel Carne of the Glosters, 'a most gallant officer', should have been ordered to withdraw. As Ridgway reiterated, 'We must not lose any battalion, certainly not another British one.'[120]

The Eighth Army, having broken the Chinese spring offensives, halted in June 1951 along the best defensive line beyond the parallel. By this stage, Ridgway had been promoted. On 11 April he replaced MacArthur as head of the UN command and FEC. Eighth Army was taken over by General James Van Fleet, an aggressive disciplinarian in the Ridgway mould. Washington was prepared to settle for a draw rather than commit further resources to a peripheral struggle. With the enemy expelled from South Korea it could be claimed that the US had achieved its aim and defeated aggression. Ridgway agreed with this decison. As he argued, a pursuit to the Yalu risked full-scale war and the dissipation of American military strength in the 'bottomless pit' of the Asian mainland.[121] On 10 July 1951 truce talks began at Kaesong. It proved difficult, however, when negotiations stalled, to use the army as an instrument of political pressure. The transition from a war of manoeuvre to positional warfare meant that ground action took the form of frontal assaults on defended hills. The enemy was well dug in, developing a bunker system which was proof against the heaviest artillery barrage. This negated the American technological advantage, employed by Ridgway in the spring to kill large numbers of Chinese advancing in the open. The enemy was now dispersed and protected. While the Eighth Army could still impose disproportionate losses, it risked unacceptable attrition of its own men and repercussions on the home front. There was also the question of morale to consider. The troops were not fighting for victory but merely to influence negotiating positions at the talks. It was hard to ask men to die in a remote corner of North-East Asia when national survival was not at stake and equal sacrifices were not asked from other sections of the armed forces or the home front. They felt that they were a forgotten army in an increasingly meaningless war. The result was a move away from labour intensive ground fighting to capital intensive air pressure, which hit the enemy while minimising American casualties.

The implications of positional warfare became evident in August/October 1951 when Van Fleet launched a limited attack in the Iron Triangle area to improve his line and bring pressure on the enemy. In an assault on 'Bloody Ridge', the 36th ROK Regiment was destroyed. The 9th US Infantry, committed in support, also suffered heavy losses and had to be reinforced by the 23rd Regiment. Despite the expenditure of 451 979 rounds by American artillery the enemy fought on: 'The only way to reduce the long ridge was bunker by bunker at close range, with rifle and grenade. It was horrible, bloody work.'[122] When the NKPA pulled out on 5 September, it had lost 15 000 men. The US 2nd Division, however, had taken 3000 casualties to seize 'three insignificant knolls amongst the hundreds along the line'.[123] In the struggle for an adjoining feature, 'Heartbreak Ridge' (13 September/15 October), the US 2nd Division lost 5600 men. Once again the territorial gains were meaningless. The enemy merely fell back on the next ridge line. After these battles 'everyone was sick to death of casualities'. Ridgway cancelled further offensive plans. In future all assaults above battalion size required the permission of FEC headquarters.[124]

The Eighth Army was committed to a *Sitzkrieg*. The main offensive effort was in the air. The war settled down to a routine of patrolling and sniping, punctuated by larger battles for hills with more political than military importance. These incidents were usually initiated by the enemy, who was prepared to expend manpower recklessly to improve his position at the truce negotiations. If the US could use air power, China had no option but to employ its ground forces, rearmed with Soviet weapons and increasingly effective artillery. In these actions casualties were heavy. In October 1952, to make a point during the US Presidential elections, the Chinese assaulted White Horse Hill. Van Fleet replied with an attack on enemy positions in the Triangle Hill complex, designed to relieve Chinese pressure. The battle began to suck in units at a furious pace as prestige became involved. The US 7th Division was soon committing a battalion a day to the fighting. When the struggle ended with parts of the position in US hands, Van Fleet had suffered 9000 casualties.[125] In the spring of 1953 his successor, General Maxwell Taylor, initiated a survey of the outpost line and decided to evacuate positions which were not militarily essential. The costs of defending them were out of all proportion to the benefits derived. Pork Chop Hill, held throughout the spring against a series of assaults, was abandoned in July, shortly before the truce was signed.[126] This sensitivity to losses kept the average yearly rate below that of the first twelve months of the war. The cumulative total, however, was high. Of American casualties, 45 per cent were incurred after the truce talks had started.

While holding the line in Korea, the US attempted to turn over a larger share of the ground war to the ROKs. The lull in the fighting was employed to rebuild this twice-shattered force into a functioning military organisation. An officer cadre was created, trained at new military schools and in the United States. This was to be free of the political favouritism and corruption which had plagued the old army. A club was held over Rhee's head to achieve reform. He was informed that his army would not be expanded and re-equipped until changes were made.[127] At the same time, attempts were made to educate the US forces out of their prevailing 'gook attitude', in order to boost the morale and self-respect of the Koreans.[128] Neither programme was an unqualified success. Many Americans remained 'guilty of trampling under their thoughtless booted feet the very rights of man for which [they] were avowedly fighting. . . . The American Army at war is not the world's best behaved, despite what Mom and Pop may smugly believe.'[129] As for the ROKs, it proved impossible to eradicate political favouritism and corruption completely.[130] A force born out of Japanese colonialism could not be made to identify with the Korean people it was meant to defend. While the ROKs held two-thirds of the line by 1953, weaknesses remained which were only camouflaged by the static nature of the war. Many Americans continued to ponder the mystery of why 'their' Koreans continued to fight better than 'ours'.

Officers continued to neglect their men and to misuse military equipment, a trait which could not be eradicated by civics lectures and American training. The ROKs depended for supplemental rations beyond a basic minimum on a cash allowance paid to regimental commanders. This was often misappropriated and the men went hungry. Inflation, endemic during the war, undermined the value of army pay. A houseboy employed by the Americans earned as much as a Korean general. Officers made up the difference by dealing on the black market, an option not open to the unhappy conscripts. The officer corps remained a privileged caste which imposed its will on the peasant conscripts by brutal discipline.[131] The continuing weakness of the ROKs was revealed in July 1953 when the Chinese launched a final offensive against the ROK 11 Corps in the East/Central sector of the front. The operation was intended as a warning to Rhee who had been threatening to sabotage a ceasefire agreement. On 17 July General Mark Clark reported that the situation was 'not good'. Some units had fallen back in confusion. The Americans had been 'too optimistic' about the capabilities of officers who performed well in a static war but could not respond to sudden emergencies.[132] When the offensive was over, two ROK divisions had suffered heavy losses and supporting American artillery units had been overrun: 'These men, those who survived, would never afterward be admirers of President Rhee.'[133] The war ended, as it had begun, with resentment about the military performance of America's Korean ally.

By this stage, there had been changes in the American Army which differed in many respects from the force which had entered the fighting in July 1950. In May 1951, to improve morale, a rotation system was introduced. This maintained the spirit of the men but at the price of efficiency. The Eighth Army lost its cohesion. Generals had no permanent staff, while at a lower level the composition of companies and platoons was constantly changing. Rotation also took a toll in other ways. The troops lost their aggressive edge. They were mainly interested in surviving long enough to accumulate sufficient points to qualify for rotation out of Korea. There was a reluctance to take risks on patrol or to provoke the enemy. By 1953 there were doubts about the capacity of the Eighth Army to launch an offensive without a period of extensive retraining.[134] Other changes also occurred. The Army was racially integrated and lost the all black units which had characterised American military organisation since the civil war. It was argued that blacks fought better in integrated units. This was reinforced by the manpower shortage. Black units were often overstrength in 1950 while white rifle companies were undermanned. It made no sense to keep black recruits in the rear because no vacancies existed in segregated regiments. By the end of the year, a large amount of de facto integration had occurred under commanders desperate to use every resource available. The practice was unpopular amongst traditionalists like Almond, who tried to reverse the situation in X Corps. In July 1951, however, Ridgway officially integrated FEC, a move soon followed by other commands.[135] Despite these changes, one factor remained constant throughout the war – a chronic shortage of high quality infantry. When Taylor took over, he was shocked to find that 10 per cent of his command were illiterates.[136] The best educated were still being drawn off along the pipeline for specialist jobs in the military bureaucracy.

Behind the front some of the problems emerged which were to plague the US Army in future Asian wars. The black market was endemic and by 1952 the loss of supplies had become serious. FEAF estimated its losses alone at $33 000 per month. The worst offenders were the ROKs who made unauthorised raids on American dumps. On one occasion they managed to divert the entire contents of a supply ship in Pusan harbour. US troops in the supply branches were also involved. It was difficult to prevent the theft of supplies because of the chronic manpower shortage. As the US Army complained, 'Lack of necessary numbers of trained military police has been a long-felt situation . . . and the high rate of pilferage and loss of property can be largely charged to that shortage.'[137] Since the ROK was a sovereign state and touchy about its prerogatives, it was difficult to recover stolen goods.[138] A move against the black market depended on the cooperation of the very authorities which derived the most benefit from its existence. The police in particular derived a flourishing income from supplying stolen American vehicles to the black marketeers and levying protection money from a sub-economy flourishing at US expense.[139]

A similar impasse existed in relation to prostitution and drugs. At the time, because of the high incidence of VD, Korea was defined as the most venereal war in American history.[140] Behind the lines and in Japan, there was a flourishing trade in girls to serve the needs of the US army. The brothels were considered undesirable by the high command, not only because they were a source of infection, but also because they supplied narcotics. By 1952 the Army was becoming increasingly concerned about drug abuse, particularly by troops on rest and recreation leaves in Japan. Drugs were regarded as a threat to ideological as well as physical health. It was suspected that the brothels were at the centre of an international communist conspiracy to subvert American youth. 'Every drug addict' was 'a potential communist.'[141] It proved difficult to act against the brothels, though, without the assistance of civil police. This was not forthcoming in Korea, where the police themselves supplied the refugee girls and took a proportion of the profits. Nor was there much enthusiasm in Japan to eradicate a flourishing part of the local economy.[142] When the issue was raised with the Japanese police in 1952, they pointed out that responsibility for much of the drug traffic rested with the Americans. A great deal of the heroin entering Japan was landed by an American airline, Civil Air Transport, at US bases not open to Japanese customs inspection.[143] The meeting broke up with the issue unresolved. CAT was a CIA proprietory airline which was hauling drugs for its Chinese nationalist 'assets' who occupied the opium-growing golden triangle in Burma and were supported as a possible guerrilla threat to the Chinese communists.[144] Whatever ideology might suggest, therefore, it turned out to be 'our' Chinese and not 'theirs' who were helping to subvert American boys.

Whatever the attitude of the troops, the *Sitzkrieg* was unpopular with their commanders. Only Ridgway adapted comfortably to the demands of a limited war, regarding Korea as but one element in a global struggle with Soviet communism. His successor at FEC, Mark Clark, believed that the US should seize the opportunity to defeat Asian communism. It made no sense not to strike directly at China and secure a decisive outcome. Clark favoured a general offensive coupled with the use of tactical atomic weapons against North Korea and Manchuria. At the Eighth Army, Van Fleet was frustrated by the tight political controls on his military operations. He called the static war 'a canker slowly eating at the morale of his troops' and was endlessly devising plans for offensives which were rejected on the grounds of casualities.[145] He retired in disgust in early 1953, earning the reputation of a 'mini-MacArthur'. Both Van Fleet and Clark had hoped that the election of Eisenhower in November 1952 would change the course of the war. It was soon clear, however, that like his predecessor Eisenhower was anxious to avoid expending resources and manpower in a peripheral war against the communist 'second team' if it could be avoided. While he threatened to extend the conflict, he rapidly settled for a draw when the opportunity occurred. In July 1953 Clark signed an armistice with 'a heavy heart'. He became the first US field commander in the twentieth century to end a war short of total victory, a distinction which he did not covet. His sympathies then and later lay with MacArthur. The demands of limited war remained foreign to his military experience and training: 'It was beyond my comprehension that we should countenance a situation in which Chinese soldiers killed American youths in organized formal warfare, and yet fail to use all the power at our command to protect these Americans. . . . I was still unable to understand this situation after I succeeded to the command of United Nations Forces. . . . I was convinced that in the long run we should save American lives by making sacrifices for victory in Korea.'[146]

Korea confirmed a military prejudice which had always existed against ground wars on the Asian mainland. In 1954, as US Army Chief of Staff, Ridgway argued strongly against intervention to save the French in Indochina. According to Ridgway, air power alone would be insufficient. The US would have to become involved on the ground and fight to win. The administration must weigh the costs involved and not make the kind of unthinking decisions which had typified the response to the Korean crisis in 1950.[147] Clark was similarly reluctant to repeat the frustrations of Korea. 'Never, never again should we be mousetrapped into fighting another defensive ground war. . . . Never should we commit numerically inferior American troops . . . against numerically superior forces of the enemy's second team unless we are prepared to win.'[148] Clark, like Van Fleet, believed that the future in Asia lay with local armies trained and equipped by the US and backed by American air and naval power. It was one of the ironies of history that within twelve years the US Army was once more to find itself pinned down in an unpopular war on the Asian mainland. That time it was to emerge without even the doubtful satisfaction of a draw.

12 The War in the Air

The Air Force, like the Army, was unprepared to fight a limited war on the Asian mainland. Air Force planning focused on global war with the Soviet Union in which atomic bombs delivered by the Strategic Air Command were the decisive weapons. The USAF justified its independence from the Army in terms of its leading strategic role and fought the Navy to maintain its position as custodian of the atomic deterrent. According to W. Stuart Symington, the Secretary of the Air Force, the strategic bomber carrying atomic weapons was the surest deterrent to war and 'the one means of unloosing prompt, crippling destruction on the enemy if war broke out'.[1] The joint strategic war plan in force when the Korean conflict broke out, OFFTACKLE, gave a central role to atomic bombing. Any Soviet invasion of western Europe was to be answered by prompt air retaliation on Russian industrial cities, destroying the Soviet capacity to wage war.[2]

The viability of OFFTACKLE, approved by the Joint Chiefs of Staff in December 1949, was questionable from the beginning. In 1950 Strategic Air Command was equipped with nineteen wings of piston-engined aircraft, many of them B-29s of World War Two vintage, which would operate from British bases in the event of war. These airfields lacked fighter protection and were vulnerable to Soviet air strikes. Without the bases there could be no offensive, since SAC relied for over 86 per cent of its planned attacks on B-29s which could not strike Russia from US airfields.[3] The only intercontinental bomber, the B-36, had been the subject of bitter controversy in Congressional hearings in 1949, when its performance was questioned by the Navy, which argued that funds would be better spent on aircraft carriers. Although the USAF won the debate, questions remained about the capabilities of the B-36. Only thirty-four had been delivered by May 1950 and these were plagued by maintenance problems.[4] When the Korean crisis began, SAC clearly felt itself in a poor position to wage global atomic war. The SAC commander, General Curtis LeMay, ordered the priority development of a long-range jet bomber to replace the unreliable B-36. Production of atomic weapons was also stepped up to place the US in a better position to launch a devastating air offensive against the USSR.[5]

If the Strategic Air Command seemed a hollow threat in 1950, other parts of the Air Force were in an even worse state of preparedness. In an era of tight budgets the USAF had invested its resources in the strategic bomber at the expense of other commitments. Tactical air power, which was to play a vital role in Korea, had been neglected since 1945. Despite the panic over the Soviet acquisition of the atomic bomb, the air defence of the United States was almost entirely lacking. In addition to these problems there was an acute shortage of skilled manpower, a serious weakness in an increasingly technological service.[6] The implementation of NSC-68 eased the financial restrictions on the expansion of the USAF and led to the construction of a more balanced force. Modern aircraft, however, could not be produced overnight. It took time to gear up for mass production. The most advanced fighter aircraft of the period was the F-86 Sabre, but only 180 were produced in 1951.[7] The Air Force command was obsessed with supply problems and expressed grave concern when the national steel strike of 1952 threatened production schedules. As one memorandum complained, if the strike lasted, aircraft procurement would be as much as 20 per cent behind schedule by the end of the year: 'It is imperative that every action to be taken to insure reopening of the mines and resumption of steel production at the earliest possible moment to prevent complete disruption of the aircraft production program.'[8]

The main aim of the expansion programme was to fill out existing deficiences and to place the USAF in a better position to wage a global war against the Soviet Union. This was a priority with which the demands of the air war in Korea often conflicted. The Air Force embarked on the Korean adventure expecting a short decisive war and instead became involved in a long inconclusive struggle. The result was a desperate juggling of resources to meet both Korean and global requirements. Before the Korean war the FEAF was already under strength. Since the major targets in the event of war were in European Russia, MacArthur's command had a low priority. As early as 1948, he complained in strong terms about the transfer of aircraft to Europe during the Berlin crisis: 'It no longer appears to be realistic to consider the Far East as a . . . secure flank in the military contest with communism.'[9] Not only was FEAF under strength in June 1950 but it also lacked the basic resources to fight even a limited war in Korea. There was a shortage of bombs, maps and target intelligence. Pilots had been trained for the air defence of Japan and not in ground attack, their main task in the Korean fighting. Everything had to be hastily improvised. Bombs and fuses were recovered from wartime stockpiles or ordered from the Japanese, who also proved an invaluable source of intelligence on their former colony.[10] The Japanese had built the Korean industrial base, the rail and road network and the important bridges, all of which became targets for FEAF bombs. Air crew learned their new tasks in combat and errors inevitably occurred. There was an initial tendency to attack indiscriminately in the vicinity of the front:

> The results . . . were often disastrous. American pilots attacked a column of thirty ROK trucks, killing two hundred South Korean troops. An American officer working with an ROK unit said he was attacked by 'friendly' aircraft five times in one day. . . . 'The fly boys really had a field day: they hit friendly ammo dumps, the Suwon airstrip, trains, motor columns, and KA (Korean Army) HQ'. Four Australian planes blew up an ammunition train heading *north* to supply ROK units. Nine boxcars of vital ammunition were destroyed.[11]

On the Pusan perimeter in August a platoon of the Argylls was napalmed by US planes. It was later calculated that, 'Of the fifteen war correspondents who died in this war, seven were killed by the air force.'[12] Such incidents became fewer as the pilots learned their new jobs and air ground liaison improved. There had been no joint exercises in occupied Japan.[13]

The USAF met the emergency by calling up the reserves and raiding stocks of aircraft allocated to the Air National Guard.[14] These were hastily taken out of storage and rushed to Japan aboard an aircraft carrier. The Navy also provided valuable direct support in the air war from carriers stationed off the Korean coast. Naval and Marine air played a vital role although inter-service relations were not always smooth. The Air Force wished to vindicate its independent existence, the Navy to justify its pre-Korea insistence on the importance of carriers. Although FEAF was given 'coordination control' of the entire Korean air effort, it accused the Navy of maintaining an independent line which undermined this principle. FEAF headquarters complained in April 1951 that it had 'resorted to time consuming suggestion, cajolery, request and conference' with the Navy and was still 'seldom certain that air tasks requested will be accomplished'.[15] Such friction was inevitable and was part of a struggle between the services for appropriations and power at the Pentagon. The Air Force took its public relations seriously and early smuggled a public relations man into Korea. This had to be done surreptitiously because of MacArthur's well-known insistence that all publicity be centred directly on himself.[16]

FEAF entered the war with a mixture of ageing equipment. Its most modern aircraft, the F-80 Shooting Star, had been the first jet fighter to enter service and was obsolete by 1950. The F-51 Mustang was propeller-driven and began life as an escort fighter in World War Two. The twin-engined B-26 bomber was of a similar vintage. By the end of the Korean War it was only kept flying by cannibalising existing machines and scouring wartime dumps for spares. These aircraft performed well in a ground attack role once the pilots had mastered the unfamiliar techniques. An early discovery was the adaptability of jets to this task. The small number of moving parts in a jet engine made it less vulnerable than a piston engine to ground fire, while the absence of propeller torque increased the accuracy of bombing and strafing.[17]

FEAF was reinforced at the beginning of the war by the four-engined B-29s of the Provisional Bomber Command under a SAC officer, General Emmett O'Donnell. This consisted of three SAC groups transferred from the US and one from the Thirteenth Air Force. The SAC squadrons were low priority units scheduled for early conversion, to the B-36 and their aircraft were not capable of carrying atomic bombs. The SAC commander, General Curtis Le May, was unwilling to whittle too much from a club which might have to be used against the real enemy, the USSR.[18] By 1950 the B-29 had begun to look 'tired and not a little obsolete'. Its 'useful life was clearly nearing its end.'[19] Only the lack of serious opposition allowed all these aircraft to be employed at low cost in the summer of 1950. Counter-air operations in July quickly eliminated the North Korean Air Force of Russian-built war surplus Yak fighters and Stormovik ground attack aircraft. FEAF operations were not impeded from the air and met only light resistance from the ground. Flak was weak and inaccurate allowing leisurely bombing runs from low altitudes. The Americans ruled the skies, a position which was not threatened until China entered the war.

Despite the increasing demands of the war after Chinese intervention in December 1950, and a new threat to air superiority in the shape of the MIG which outclassed the aircraft with which FEAF had entered the fighting, Washington continued to employ obsolescent stock as far as possible. In the first two years only the minimum number of modern jets necessary to maintain air superiority was despatched to Far East Command. These were grudgingly conceded because they had to be diverted from other areas and impeded the build-up towards readiness for global war.[20] This situation was resented at FEAF headquarters. The commander, General Stratemeyer, naturally accorded the war he was fighting a higher priority than readiness for a theoretical future war against the Soviet Union. In May 1951 he complained that the Air Force was treating Korea as a 'minor skirmish'. An opportunity existed to deal a 'serious blow to Red China and to Communism in Asia' and 'all-out assistance' should be given to the forces engaged there.[21] The USAF Deputy Chief of Staff replied that global war plans must come first: 'Our . . . war plan envisions an air effort from an area closer to major targets than if launched from Korea or Japan. We must follow this strategy. . . . The fact is that industry is not producing sufficient aircraft to increase your strength. . . . You have got to conserve aircraft. Crew or unit augmentation with our other commitments is not possible.'[22] For the same reasons the Air Force high command was unwilling to expand the war into Manchuria when China intervened. Although O'Donnell favoured the use of atomic weapons against Manchuria, his superiors disagreed.[23] At the MacArthur hearings General Vandenberg argued that such a move would divert resources from the main task of deterring the Soviet Union. While his bombers could lay waste Chinese cities, they would be exposed to heavy attrition against a secondary enemy. As long as the US possessed a 'shoestring' Air Force, it must conserve its resources.[24] Vandenberg thus combined an argument for caution with an appeal for funds. It was only in the winter of 1952/3 when the supply situation eased that FEAF was completely re-equipped with modern Sabres and Thunderjets. Until that point the command remained 'short of everything'.[25]

Shortage of modern aircraft was only one aspect of a general lack of resources in FEAF. There was a lack of suitable bases in the Korean theatre. It was soon clear that efficient prosecution of the war required the transfer of much of the 5th Air Force from Japan to Korea where facilities were primitive and scarce. A construction programme was necessary to rehabilitate existing airfields and to provide new ones. There was, however, a shortage of engineers and construction equipment which delayed completion of reconstruction until the summer of 1952.[26] In the interim, facilities were makeshift and uncomfortable. Airfields were seas of mud in the winter and covered with dust clouds in summer.[27] These conditions complicated the task of maintenance, already difficult because of Korea's position at the end of a long supply line from the US. Aircraft had to be parked in the open where they invariably deteriorated. In the early months of 1951 technical problems and lack of spares grounded 45 per cent of Sabres.

In the summer of 1952 dust damage to engines reduced the availability of ground attack aircraft.[28] In the case of the older types, many spare parts came from World War Two stockpiles and were themselves defective. New aircraft often required extensive repair before becoming operational, since they crossed the Pacific on carrier flight decks and despite waterproofing were exposed to corrosive spray and salt air. This problem was not overcome until 1952, when the perfection of mid-air refuelling allowed aircraft to fly direct to Japan from the United States.[29] Ground crew efficiency as well as weather conditions affected the availability of aircraft. One veteran recalled that 'The biggest problem was . . . that many maintenace personnel were unadapted to the type of aircraft [they serviced], and even officers and NCOs were not up to par on maintenance.'[30] Ground crew specialisation was important because of the increasing complexity of the equipment with which they had to work. As *Fortune* noted in February 1952, in World War Two a mechanic could handle both aircraft engines and electrical systems: 'Now it takes an electronics specialist with years of background in radio to keep the Sabre's electrical system in tune.'[31]

At the beginning of the war the Air Force had to make good shortages of personnel by calling up the reserves, veterans of World War Two. Some of these men naturally resented being snatched away from peacetime occupations to serve in a war in an obscure corner of Asia. As one reservist, recalled to fly ageing B-26s, remembered: 'We were just given planes of a sort and told where to strike. We had no idea why we were fighting in Korea.'[32] Morale, however, did not become a major problem until the Chinese entered the war in November 1950. Until that point fighter opposition and anti-aircraft defences were negligible and it was possible to foresee an early end to the war. Chinese intervention changed this situation dramatically. Air operations intensified as MacArthur ordered crews flown to the point of exhaustion to stem the Chinese advance. This had a marked effect on the morale of aircrew who a month before had expected to return to peacetime duties in Japan and the United States. On 2 December 1950, Stratemeyer wrote to Vandenberg, pointing out that many of his men had already flown 140 missions. Combat exhaustion was having a bad effect on morale, which would continue to decline as long as aircrew saw only one guaranteed exit from Korea – 'to be killed'.[33] The crisis was surmounted by the introduction of a rotation system which released aircrew after a certain number of operations, varying according to combat mission. This restored morale and allowed Korea to be used as a large-scale training ground but also raised problems, most notably a drop in efficiency.[34] In general it was easier to maintain morale in the fighter units, which regarded themselves as the elite of the profession, than in the ground attack squadrons which faced an unromantic task against increasingly effective enemy flak. The routine, the danger and the lack of immediate results on the Chinese war effort made it difficult to convince fighter-bomber pilots of the value of their work and it was found advisable to vary their missions as much as possible.[35]

Korea was the first test of air power since 1945 but it was not the war for which the USAF had armed and trained. In the beginning the Air Force experienced considerable frustration. Prevailing doctrine assigned a decisive role to strategic bombing but political limitations on the conduct of the war ruled out a real strategic bombing campaign. North Korean industry was peripheral to enemy capacity to wage war. The sources of production and supply lay not within Korea itself but across the border in China and the Soviet Union. China could not be attacked without widening the war, an outcome Washington was anxious to avoid. As Vandenberg explained, this forced FEAF to use its power inefficiently, destroying supplies not at source nor along the extended lines of communication through Manchuria to the USSR, but only after they had crossed the border into North Korea.[36] The emphasis was thus on tactical air operations which had been neglected since 1945. The early expectation that air power alone could halt the North Korean advance rapidly proved mistaken, to the embarrassment of the Air Force, whose previous rhetoric about its decisive role in modern war rebounded. Doctrine maintained that ground forces were helpless without air cover, yet the North Koreans continued to advance despite total American air superiority.[37] In the beginning considerable publicity was given to the deployment of SAC B-29s to Korea and to the speedy destruction of the enemy Air Force. The failure of air power to achieve decisive results, however, gave rise to press criticism of previous concentration on the strategic bomber at the expense of other types and newspapers concentrated on the failures of tactical air power.[38]

In this respect, the USAF was more open to criticism than the other services. The Navy considered its contribution to the war justified its arguments in favour of a large navy which allowed the United States to project its power to distant quarters of the globe. The contribution of naval aviation in particular was held to support the position taken in the B-36 debate of 1949 on the need to maintain military flexibility by building aircraft carriers. The Army could criticise the curtailment of research and development funds for ground forces since 1945 and emphasise the need to maintain a capability to intervene quickly and decisively in peripheral wars.[39] The USAF experienced more difficulty in finding a limited war role than the other services. It was anxious to prove the decisive nature of air power, not least to maintain and increase its share of the defence budget, but the nature of the Korean war meant that aircraft were used largely as an adjunct of the ground forces. The FEAF Deputy Chief of Staff for Operations, General Smart, complained in June 1952 about 'the opinion so often expressed or implied that the Eighth Army is responsible for winning the Korean War and that the role of the other services is to support it in its effort'.[40] MacArthur and his successor Ridgway were held to be particularly guilty of 'ground force thinking'. From the perspective of the Air Force, Korea threatened to force air power back into the position of adjunct of the Army from which the doctrine of strategic bombing had originally freed it. Its commanders aspired to an independent role not dictated by army officers. The expansion of the commitment to NATO in 1951 made the USAF especially anxious that the pattern of ground force dominance should not be repeated in Europe.[41] To justify the leading role which the Air Force ascribed itself in the military establishment, both to Congress and the public, and to break the growth of 'ground force thinking', air power in Korea had to be seen as the decisive force.

The search for a decisive role, however, occurred within a context which not only limited the war to Korea but also circumscribed the use of air power within Korea itself. Restrictions covered both targets and methods of attack. An early blow to the proponents of air power was the decision of the National Security Council to ban mass incendiary bombing of population centres, a move designed to spare the civilian population of North Korea unnecessary casualties. FEAF planning staff wished to use O'Donnell's B-29s to launch a knock-out blow against the north, destroying industrial centres and civilian morale in a series of mass fire raids. The scheme was vetoed by Washington on the grounds that it would alienate Asian opinion, particularly in India, and cause problems at the United Nations.[42] Advocates of the 'big bomber' such as General LeMay, commander of SAC, believed that this decision cost the United States the chance of an early, and by implication cheap, victory.[43] It is difficult to see, however, how the destruction of the cities could have halted an army which at the time looked likely to push US forces off the peninsula. MacArthur himself

took this view and insisted that air power, including Bomber
Command, be used primarily to support the ground forces. As one
officer recalled, Vandenberg was reluctant to argue because of his
concern that 'if Eighth Army did get clobbered and he was using the
mediums to bomb . . . some . . . remote industrial area, it would have
been pretty unfavorable publicity for the Air Corps.'[44] When a
campaign was launched against industrial areas it was based on
precision attacks and certain targets were exempted for political
reasons. Najin (Rashin) gained immunity after one raid in August 1950
because of its proximity to the sensitive Soviet border. In September
attacks on the North Korean hydro-electric power system were
suspended after one strike on Fusen.[45] Originally this was because the
early conquest of the north was expected and subsequently because of
the importance of the power system to China.

   In the course of the war, however, all these restrictions were lifted.
By 1953 only the ban on violation of the Chinese and Soviet borders
remained. The catalyst for change was Chinese intervention in
November 1950 to which the United States responded by escalating
the air war. The first restriction to collapse was the ban on mass fire
raids. On 5 November MacArthur ordered FEAF to destroy the Yalu
bridges and southward to the battle line 'every means of
communication, every installation, factory, city and village.'[46] This
amounted to a scorched earth policy. The JCS at first baulked at the
order but then agreed that the air offensive could go ahead, provided
that only the Korean ends of the Yalu bridges were attacked. The first
major city to be razed under the new policy was Sinuiji.[47] Population
centres behind enemy lines were henceforth assumed to house troops
and all movement on the roads was defined as military. Only family
groups with children were to be spared, a distinction hard to make
from an aircraft approaching its target at over 300 mph.[48] From the
beginning napalm had been used extensively against troops and tanks,
but its employment was now extended to area raids on population
centres. In one raid on Pyongyang in July 1952, 2,300 gallons were
dropped.[49] The scale of these attacks caused some concern in Britain.
The Archbishop of York, the Methodists and the Free Church of
Scotland all questioned the indiscriminate use of napalm. Several
prominent personalities signed a letter to the *Times* condemning the
weapon. Churchill himself privately admitted qualms: 'I do not like
this napalm bombing at all. A fearful lot of people must be burned, not
by ordinary fire, but by the contents of the bomb. We should make a
very great mistake to commit ourselves to approval of a very cruel form

of warfare. . . . No one ever thought of splashing it about all over the civilian population. I will take no responsibility for it.'[50] The matter was not pursued, however, and there was no sustained public campaign against the bombing in the cold war atmosphere of 1952. The Americans attempted to avert criticism by arguing that only military targets were being attacked, ignoring the fact that any distinction between civilian and military had long since vanished. Before one raid on Pyongyang in 1951, the JCS emphasised that no publicity should be given to the mass nature of the attack which should be reported as 'a normal operation against persistent enemy build-up'.[51] In order to avoid controversy and to harass the enemy, FEAF launched a psychological warfare strategy to accompany the raids. Leaflets were dropped over several cities warning the population that one of them was to be attacked and inviting them to leave. This operation, PLAN STRIKE, was designed to disrupt production, lower morale and secure the US 'a favorable world press'. It could be argued that FEAF was displaying a humanitarian concern for civilian lives. The North Koreans would prevent an evacuation and would be held to blame at home and abroad for civilian casualties.[52] It is doubtful if this strategy worked as intended against the population of the North. Such was the scale of destruction that it seems unlikely that civilians were reassured by leaflets emphasising the military nature of the targeting.[53] According to General Dean, who spent the war as a POW in the DPRK, 'The civil population became so inflamed that a downed airman had virtually no chance of getting away from his wrecked plane or parachute.'[54]

The lifting of the ban on mass fire raids was accompanied by the erosion of other restraints as Washington attempted to force a settlement on its own terms through air power. Najin (Rashin) lost its protected status in August 1951. In July 1952 the power complexes were bombed. In April 1953 air attacks were extended to the irrigation dams which supported rice production. By May 1953 the JCS was contemplating the use of tactical atomic weapons to force a decision on the enemy.[55] It was a process of escalation which was to be repeated in Vietnam. Until the latter conflict, Korea set new records for the scale of destruction from the air. The bombing was heavy and continuous. In relation to its population and resources, the DPRK suffered more than Japan during World War Two. As General Curtis LeMay recalled, 'We burned down just about every city in North and South Korea both . . . we killed off over a million civilian Koreans and drove several million more from their homes.'[56] It is ironic that much of the napalm

employed in this task was produced in Japan, the power from which
Koreans were liberated in 1945.[57] Population and production were
forced underground and by the end of the war, Pyongyang had become
a city of cave-dwellers. In September 1952 Clark argued that air attack
had reduced civilian morale to breaking point, a judgement echoed in
subsequent accounts.[58] Such claims were probably exaggerated,
despite evidence of war weariness and indiscipline. General Dean
observed no signs of impending collapse during his captivity: 'These
people had been hurt by bombing and still were being hurt by it, but it
looked to me as if their countermeasures were improving faster than
our measures of destruction.'[59] According to former civilian internees,
the bombing merely stiffened the national will to resist and increased
hatred of the West.[60] Whatever the true state of morale in the DPRK,
it was in any case the will of China and the Soviet Union to support the
war which really counted. While both had to provide increasing
amounts of aid to the war ravaged North, they could be affected only
indirectly by the enormous destruction on the other side of the Yalu.

It was during the process of escalation that FEAF developed a
doctrine defining the role of bombing in limited war which became
known as 'air pressure'. Before the idea was fully developed, however,
two years were spent searching for a decisive role. In the process, the
Air Force and the Army became embroiled in a dispute about the
proper use of tactical air power. The debate became so bitter as to be
common knowledge even to the enemy.[61] Many Army officers felt that
the USAF had neglected tactical air power since 1945 and that its
concept of tactical air operations ignored the needs of the ground
forces. They wanted air power concentrated at the front in close
support of troops. This conflicted with tactical air doctrine which
attached greater importance to the attainment of air superiority and to
interdiction – that is, weakening the enemy by attacks on supply dumps
and lines of communication. Withholding air power until enemy
supplies and troops had been dispersed along the front was regarded as
a waste of resources.[62] An argument raged over control of close
support. The USAF defended the existing system in which under the
theatre commander, co-equal air and ground commanders decided in
consultation the allocation of aircraft to various tactical roles. This had
been established after the debacle in Tunisia in 1942 when the dispersal
of aircraft in penny packets under the control of ground forces had
allowed the Luftwaffe to concentrate its resources and seize control of
the air.[63] Many Army officers, however, felt that under existing
arrangements, the Air Force defined what was required in terms of

close support and were dubious about the benefits of distant interdiction. It was argued that the Army should adopt the Marine system in which specialised close support aircraft were controlled by the ground commander. According to General Almond, only then would 'the young men who must meet a numerically superior enemy be assured of that degree of fire support to which their losses entitle them.'[64] Criticism of the Air Force was not confined to Korea. In November 1950 General Collins, the Army Chief of Staff, advocated the attachment of a fighter bomber group under ground force control to each American division in NATO. He also wanted the Army to be consulted about the design of close support aircraft. These views were justified by reference to the Korean experience.[65]

The Collins proposals were regarded as a threat to the integrity of the Air Force. Although the Army denied any intention of creating a separate force, competing with the USAF for funds, the recommendations seemed to be a long step in that direction. The Air Force prepared to defend its position in the military establishment and if necessary, in Congress. Although the challenge never ultimately developed, the Air Force remained suspicious about Army designs on tactical air power and was particularly wary of its interest in helicopters.[66] In the 'Great Debate' over close support, officers such as Almond often exaggerated Air Force 'neglect'. Around 30 per cent of Air Force missions during the war were flown in close support which represented a generous allocation of air power made possible only by the lack of any real challenge to American air superiority.[67] There was an element of scapegoating about the entire argument which tended to surface when the war was going badly, most notably in the summer of 1950 and again following Chinese intervention in the winter of 1950–1. Neither service wanted to be blamed for defeat.

In its disputes with the Army, the Air Force always argued that interdiction paid greater dividends than close support. In this area, however, the impact of air power on the course of the war was ambiguous. While air power contributed along with land and sea power to the defeat of the North Korean forces in 1950 and to the containment of the Chinese offensives of 1950–1, it is difficult to claim that it played the decisive role, although the official history attempted to argue this point. It proved difficult to defeat an Asian army by bombing. Interdiction never isolated the battlefield. The most sustained interdiction campaign of the Korean war, codenamed STRANGLE, was launched against the North Korean road network in June 1951 and extended to the railway system in August. Between the summers of 1951 and 1952 100 per cent of the carrier effort and 70 per cent of Air Force operations were devoted to the attack on lines of communication. STRANGLE was regarded by General Ridgway as a means of preventing the Chinese from building up an offensive capacity during the truce talks which began in July 1951. It was a way of carrying the war to the enemy while avoiding the casualties inherent in large-scale ground fighting.[68] Zealots at FEAF headquarters, however, claimed that STRANGLE could isolate the battlefield and force the Chinese to withdraw to the North. It was believed in these quarters that the suspension of ground operations during the talks offered an opportunity to display the decisive impact of air power. General Weyland, Stratemeyer's successor at FEAF, and General Vandenberg were more cautious, believing that as long as the ground front remained static, the Chinese and North Koreans would be able to maintain their positions, since they could dictate the rate at which available supplies were expended. Both groups, however, were disappointed by the results of the campaign and the codename itself became an embarrassment.[69]

Planners underestimated the ability of the enemy to repair bomb damage by the reckless use of manpower. As one Air Force intelligence report remarked, the performance of the North Korean Railroad Bureau in repairing bridges, primary targets in the rail interdiction campaign, was 'little short of phenomenal'. The repair organisation went along with a primitive early warning system along the lines of communication, using sentries to warn of the approach of hostile aircraft. By the middle of the campaign FEAF officers were expressing grudging admiration for the ability of the Chinese to maintain a functioning logistics system under massive air attack.[70] A similar pattern was to emerge in Vietnam where bombing inflicted great damage but failed to prevent the movement of supplies. Moreover STRANGLE planners had overlooked the possibility that while interdiction would impose attrition on the enemy, it might also lead to unacceptable losses for FEAF. The enemy responded to the campaign by improving defences. By February 1952 there were 398 heavy anti-aircraft guns and 1482 automatic weapons in North Korea, mostly concentrated along the lines of communication, and the performance of their crews increased with practice.[71] FEAF lost 343 aircraft in STRANGLE and 290 were damaged whilst only 131 replacements were received. This was 'an unacceptable toll'.[72] One solution was to increase bombing altitudes but this reduced accuracy. By 1952 it was becoming clear that the operation was straining FEAF resources and producing a stalemate in which the effort of the Air Force to cut supply lines was balanced by the capacity of the Chinese and North Koreans to repair them.

STRANGLE was a controversial operation which was condemned by many as a failure. It did not succeed in isolating the battlefield as air-power enthusiasts at FEAF headquarters had predicted. According to Ridgway, the campaign proved that there was 'simply no such thing as choking off supply lines in a country as wild as North Korea'. It was 'self-delusion' to believe that Asian armies could be defeated from the air.[73] Apart from anything else they had a lower supply requirement than Western armies. The average Chinese division required only 50 tons of supplies per day, the average US division 610.[74] The Air Force history maintained, however, that too much emphasis had been placed on the rhetoric at the expense of the real aim of the operation, which was to prevent the enemy from accumulating enough supplies to launch a general offensive.[75] Judged by this standard, STRANGLE was a success. This begs the question of enemy intentions. It is debatable if a general offensive was ever planned. If the Chinese were seeking a compromise settlement at the truce talks, a ground attack was unnecessary. It was enough to guarantee military stalemate by establishing a strong defensive line and to launch local offensives, designed to influence the negotiations. Interdiction was unable to prevent this and merely made it more expensive. The official history, moreover, could not resist speculating that with improved night intruder capacity and a wider range of specialised interdiction weapons, STRANGLE might indeed have forced the Chinese to withdraw further north despite the static ground front. By this argument the zealots in FEAF were not so much wrong as premature in their expectations.[76] In fact in Vietnam it once again proved impossible to inflict decisive damage on an Asian army by bombing, despite the application of improved technology. In the end Korean interdiction operations merely confirmed existing positions. The Army emphasised the limited effectiveness of interdiction, while the Air Force 'refused to recognize or admit the significance of negative evidence on bombing effectiveness'.[77]

By 1952 FEAF headquarters was seeking new ways to employ air power, recognising that STRANGLE was producing a stalemate and trading 'coolies' for aircraft at an uneconomic rate. There was also a feeling that the campaign tied air power too closely to the defensive needs of the army. Planners sought a more offensive, independent and decisive role for FEAF.[78] What emerged from their deliberations was 'air pressure'. The aim was to attack selected targets of economic value to the USSR and China to bring home to their leaders the cost of continuing the war. Attacks on supply lines would also continue in an attempt to use up enemy resources. Air power was to be a political weapon. The most obvious target for testing the new doctrine was the North Korean hydroelectric system which was closely tied to Chinese and Soviet industry in Manchuria, Siberia, Dairen and Port Arthur. The most important plant was Suiho on the Yalu river. In February 1951 the Joint Intelligence Group of the JCS noted that destruction of Suiho would cause 'serious attrition of electric power resources available . . . to the USSR and China'. The most effective form of attack would be to breach the dam because of the extensive collateral damage which would be caused by flooding. The massive structure at Suiho, 295 feet thick at the base tapering to 58 feet at the crest, was, however, impervious to anything short of an underwater atomic explosion. This left as the main target the power houses on the Korean side of the Yalu. FEAF had long desired to bomb Suiho and the remainder of the hydroelectric plants but had been overruled for political reasons. While truce talks were making progress, no risk was to be taken of the Chinese breaking off negotiations. Moreover, precisely because of the importance of the plants to Manchurian industry, there was strong opposition from UN allies, particularly Britain, to an attack.[79] In June 1952 with negotiations at Panmunjom deadlocked on the POW issue, General Mark Clark, who replaced Ridgway in the Far East on 12 May, seized on the air pressure doctrine offered by FEAF as a means of forcing the Chinese to terms without incurring heavy casualties and political problems on the home front. This form of capital intensive warfare seemed to offer maximum returns for minimum losses. Previously an object of suspicion in Air Force circles because of his support of Collins' proposals on tactical aircraft, Clark was now hailed as an air power strategist. Somewhat to his surprise, Clark found his recommendations on air warfare, including attacks on Suiho, accepted by Washington as the administration attempted to end the deadlock at Panmunjom before the Presidential elections of November 1952.[80]

The Suiho plant was first raided by naval aircraft on 23 June while FEAF struck at other parts of the complex. Intelligence claimed dramatic results. Chinese electricity production was cut to 23 per cent of requirement and 30 out of 51 key industries in Manchuria and Dairen failed to meet their production targets. Despite the storm over Suiho which followed in Britain, air pressure continued both on the hydroelectric complex and other targets. On 11 July and 29 August there were new mass attacks on Pyongyang, codenamed OPERATION PRESSURE PUMP. Other targets selected for air pressure were cities on the Soviet or Chinese borders such as Hoeryong and Aoji, gold, silver and monzanite mines, and any other industrial target which had escaped damage or been reconstructed. Many of these produced materials valuable to the USSR, such as the monzanite mines which supplied the Soviet atomic bomb programme.[81] Clark was confident of success and opposed any compromise on the POW issue. According to his information, civilian panic in the North was becoming a threat to public order.[82] Both Clark and the planners failed to predict the ability of the enemy to adapt to the new strategy and to endure its effects. Despite Clark's expectations no compromise emerged at Panmunjom and the talks were indefinitely recessed in October 1952. This coincided with the exhaustion of air pressure targets in North Korea. Almost everything which remained to be bombed in June 1952 had been destroyed without result.

A fresh search began for the elusive 'decisive' target system, and in the spring of 1953 FEAF planners recommended an attack on the irrigation dams which provided water for North Korean rice production. The objective was to destroy the rice crop and to strain the Chinese economy by forcing the diversion of large quantities of rice to Korea. The original plan called for a knock-out blow against twenty essential dams. This was ruled out by Clark and Weyland in favour of a graduated attack on the irrigation system, perhaps to increase the pressure on the Chinese, perhaps because the attacks were potentially sensitive. German destruction of the Dutch dykes in 1944 had been condemned as a war crime. The reservoirs chosen for initial strikes lay close to military lines of communication and the bombing could be described as an attempt to destroy them by flooding. The first raid took place at Toksan on 15 May and successfully eliminated the dam. Four other reservoirs were subsequently hit.[83] Chinese acceptance of the UN position on POWs on 8 June was defined as a victory for air pressure. The dams were regarded as the decisive target system which had eluded FEAF planners since the beginning of the war.[84] This simplistic explanation ignored political factors and maintained that the complex negotiation at Panmunjom could have ended on UN terms at any time since June 1951 simply by dropping sufficient bombs on the proper targets. It ignored evidence that bombing might have prolonged the war. Optimistic predictions about the effects of air pressure in the summer of 1952 led officials to reject a compromise on the POW issue and voided tentative negotiations with China being carried out through the Indians.[85] Moreover the impact of the bombing on the irrigation system was not as decisive as some accounts suggest. The Chinese and North Koreans quickly learned that reducing the water level behind the dams minimised damage and of the five attacked only two were breached. At Toksan a temporary replacement was erected within two weeks. This was the familiar pattern of stalemate which had characterised STRANGLE. The ingenuity of FEAF in devising new methods of knocking out enemy targets was outmatched by the Communists' ingenuity in patching them up.[86]

The ambiguous record of bombing was obscured by the public attention focused on the fighter war, where American victory was clear-cut. The appearance of the MIG-15 in November 1950 rendered obsolete the aircraft then flying in Korea. Intelligence on Soviet aircraft development was poor and the appearance of a high performance swept-wing jet created a shock in the West similar to that produced by the Japanese Zero in 1941.[87] The Russians supplied aircraft and instructors to China under an agreement of February 1950 and during the war Beijing built up a powerful air force much of it concentrated in Manchuria. By June 1951 there were 445 MIGs behind the Yalu, a figure which had grown to 830 by 1953.[88] This force threatened American air superiority for the first time in the war. Its full potential became obvious in October 1951 when the main victims were the ageing B-29s of Bomber Command. In a series of raids over north-west Korea, Bomber Command suffered unacceptable losses. In a 'violent and desperate action' over Namsi on 23 October, 150 MIGs pressed home attacks against the bombers, despite the efforts of the fighter escort. While three MIGs were destroyed, FEAF lost three B-29s and five were seriously damaged. It was decided to discontinue daylight B-29 attacks in north-west Korea because of the difficulties of providing adequate fighter protection.[89] China had done what the Luftwaffe had failed to do: 'It had stopped precision daylight bombing by the USAF over an important part of enemy territory.'[90] Bomber Command was thereafter restricted to night raids. Despite the use of electronic counter-measures, radar controlled flak and searchlights were beginning to increase B-29 losses by the end of the war. Only the failure of the Chinese to acquire a radar-equipped night fighter kept them at an acceptable level.[91]

The experience of Namsi alarmed an Air Force already perturbed by the appearance of the MIG. After visiting Korea, Vandenberg warned that the area between Pyongyang and the Yalu was in danger of becoming 'No Man's Air'. The Russians had proved themselves capable of technological excellence and the US now faced 'a serious challenge'.[92] This language was partly designed to secure extra funds from the Congress and partly to divert blame from the USAF if air superiority in Korea was suddenly lost. Although the Chinese never mounted a sustained counter-air offensive, the MIGs remained a lurking threat for the remainder of the war. The 'hornet's nest' around Antung was also a powerful deterrent to the expansion of the air war into Manchuria. Such operations were likely to result in heavy attrition of US bombers and to undermine the capacity of the USAF to fight a global war with the Soviet Union.

The American reply to the MIG was the Sabre. It was another of the ironies of the war that both aircraft were powered by a version of the Rolls-Royce Nene, which Britain had supplied to the Russians under licence in 1947.[93] One Sabre wing was sent to Korea for combat evaluation in December 1950. A second arrived at the end of 1951, following Vandenberg's visit to the front. It was activated by diverting aircraft from other commands, a symbol of the seriousness with which the USAF viewed the MIG threat.[94] Air superiority thereafter rested largely with this small group of 150 jets. The Sabres were employed in a blocking role, flying patrols along the Yalu in what became known as 'MIG alley', to prevent interference with interdiction operations further south. On the surface the odds against the Sabre were unfavourable. It was a general purpose aircraft matched against a specialised interceptor fighter at the limits of its range. It had to battle against strong prevailing winds to reach its operational area and had a short combat endurance before lack of fuel forced a return to base. The MIG had a faster rate of climb and a higher combat ceiling and was operating close to home.[95] The advantage of protected air space across the Yalu, however, has often been exaggerated. In the interests of survival, US pilots routinely broke the order against violation of Chinese air space, a fact which caused a flurry of concern amongst the UN allies when it leaked out late in the war.[96] Despite the balance of advantage in favour of the MIG, the Sabre claimed a kill ratio of 10:1, destroying 792 MIGs for the loss of 78 Sabres.[97]

The survival odds were thus much higher than in the air war against Nazi Germany. The dominance of the Sabre was attributed to superior pilots and better armament. The MIG, armed with three slow-firing cannon, was poorly equipped for fighter combat. As one report noted, 'Experience has shown that, with the "snap shot" tactics required in [fighter action] . . . a high cyclic rate is mandatory to increase hit probability.' At the high closing speeds of modern jet combat, the first burst was decisive and accounted for 65 per cent of the kills.[98] In this respect the six .50 calibre guns of the Sabre proved superior. The sole tactical success of the MIG was against the large slow-moving B-29s, where its cannon were lethal.[99]

Despite the high kill ratio achieved by the Sabre, US pilots admired the MIG which they regarded as a simple aircraft, uncluttered by the gadgetry of American machines which often malfunctioned. Many revolted against technological sophistication and became known as the 'chuck it out brigade'. A leading spokesman of this group was the fighter ace Lieutenant-Colonel 'Gabby' Gabreski, who argued that 'We'd be better off without all this stuff'. He recalled the loss of one Sabre because the pilot forgot to cut the emergency fuel switch after take off. This resulted in a melted engine and 'We chalked up another casualty – not to enemy action but to profusion of gadgets in our planes.'[100] In the summer of 1952 fourteen aces petitioned the Air Force to remove the radar gunsight from the Sabre which often malfunctioned because of Korean dust and replace it with the older gyro computing model. One ace claimed that he would rather use a piece of chewing gum stuck to the windshield than the unreliable new sight.[101] The myth of the MIG as a clean and simple aircraft was encouraged by the fact that it remained a mystery for most of the war. As Air Force intelligence complained in April 1952, 'Our knowledge of this well-designed Russian fighter had not kept pace with the continuing development of engine and airframe.'[102] FEAF placed a high priority on securing a MIG for combat evaluation. A major problem, however, was that the Chinese never flew across the lines or out to sea where a crash would fall into American hands. FEAF intelligence operated a special unit which attempted to salvage parts from crashes behind enemy lines and which on one occasion captured a Chinese pilot, only to lose him when surrounded by North Korean troops. In April 1951 some engine parts were recovered from a wreck by a special team which was helicoptered to the crash and blew the remains apart with grenades, salvaging what was possible in fifteen minutes.[103] It was only in July 1951, however, that FEAF intelligence had a stroke of luck which improved its knowledge about the enemy machine. A MIG pilot ejected over north-west Korea and his aircraft flew out to sea, coming to rest on a coastal sandbar exposed at low tide. A special task force was hurriedly put together, consisting of the

British carrier, HMS *Eagle*, the cruiser HMS *Birmingham*, small craft from the ROK navy and a special lifting barge procured in Japan, to recover the machine before it was washed away or destroyed by the enemy. The scale of the force assigned to OPERATION MIG is an index of its importance to American intelligence. Quite apart from the need for FEAF to know more about the MIG, it was likely to provide the main opposition to SAC bombers over Russia in the event of war. The task force successfully recovered the crashed machine and brought it to Pusan where it was dismantled and sent to Wright-Patterson Air Force base for testing.[104]

A further step in the intelligence operation against the MIG was taken in 1953 at the suggestion of a newsman in Korea. Noting that in the past Chinese armies had been notoriously susceptible to 'silver bullets', he put forward the idea of offering a reward for the delivery of a MIG to UN lines. This was written up as the suggestion of an Air Force officer and submitted to Washington for approval.[105] It was regarded as a shrewd step in psychological warfare, playing on communist paranoia and making the Chinese distrust their own pilots. In April 1953 reward leaflets were dropped along the Yalu and the offer was broadcast in Russian, Chinese and Korean. FEAF intelligence claimed a drop in enemy air activity following OPERATION MOOLAH and speculated that enemy pilots had been grounded for security checks.[106] No MIGs appeared, however, until after the armistice, when a North Korean defector landed at Kimpo airfield. This was something of an embarrassment since it could be regarded as a violation of the spirit of the cease-fire. Moreover, President Eisenhower disliked the idea of paying bribes to defectors, believing that it was more important to encourage ideological conversion. He wished to return the aircraft to North Korea. A compromise was worked out by Walter Bedell Smith under which the pilot rejected the $100 000 bribe on the basis that 'his action was because of his own convictions and not for money'. He became a ward of the Committee for Free Asia, a CIA front, and was provided with technical education and financial support equal to the value of the reward. As an ironic footnote, it emerged that the Korean pilot, Captain Ro, had in any case been unaware of OPERATION MOOLAH. His decision had been dictated by resentment of the Russians.[107] In October 1953 there was a counter defection by Captain Bae of the ROK Air Force who flew a Mustang to Pyongyang. Bae, like Ro, was moved by resentment. He had been restricted to ground duties for disciplinary reasons and found North Korea attractive because it possessed MIGs.[108] The Americans had supplied the ROK only with outdated propeller-driven aircraft.

Despite the poor performance of the MIGs, the growth of Chinese air power preoccupied FEAF throughout the war. It was feared that the enemy might attempt to seize air superiority by a surprise attack on Korean airfields, destroying the small force of Sabres on the ground.[109] Standing patrols were maintained at dawn and dusk over the main bases to guard against this possibility. The Chinese, however, never committed their resources to large-scale offensive operations. Attacks were confined to night heckling raids by small PO-2 biplanes, which flew low to avoid radar and dropped light bombs almost at random. On occasion these scored lucky hits, destroying one Sabre on the ground and damaging eight in June 1951.[110] In general, however, they were no more than a nuisance. Chinese air concentrations across the Yalu were defensive and the war seems to have been used as a training exercise. As FEAF intelligence noted in February 1953, the failure to break UN air superiority 'is not so much a proof of inefficiency as an indication of a program designed to give as many units as possible this taste of combat'.[111] Pilots were rotated every six weeks which ensured that the majority of MIGs encountered in combat were flown by novices. Poor gunnery, lack of teamwork, low skills and at times sheer panic, kept the Sabre loss rate low.[112] The best enemy pilots, the 'honchos', were popularly supposed by the Sabre squadrons to be Soviet instructors with World War Two flying experience although this was never proved. The Chinese appear to have been training to defend Manchuria against SAC bombers, sacrificing quality for quantity in an attempt to build a large airforce in the shortest possible time.[113] This emphasis on defence was encouraged by the type of equipment and training provided by the Russians. The majority of the aircraft supplied to China were interceptor fighters, small numbers of jet bombers appearing only towards the end of the conflict.[114] Political factors probably helped dictate this policy. It must have been known in Moscow and Beijing that a sustained air offensive would be followed by counter air attacks on Manchurian bases. The United States had discussed the issue extensively with its UN allies in the spring of 1951. The air superiority gained in Korea was thus 'political air superiority' based on self-restraint by both sides. Manchuria remained inviolate and the Chinese in return did not attack air bases in South Korea and Japan. In this limited air war the Sabres prevailed.

Both sides used the war like the Spanish Civil War, to test equipment and to provide experience. Marine, Navy and British pilots were rotated through Sabre squadrons to provide a pool of personnel who had experienced modern jet combat. The war also provided training for bomber crews in radar bombing techniques.[115] It is debatable which side gained the most in technical intelligence. As the war moved into North Korea in 1950, special teams followed the troops to collect samples of Soviet-supplied radar and anti-aircraft guns. The bulk of this, however, proved to be surplus stock from World War Two.[116] The most important advance was the technical intelligence gained about the MIG-15 which must have been incorporated in SAC war plans. The Chinese, and through them the Russians, had an advantage in the field of technical intelligence collection. Since the UN was pursuing an air offensive, most crashes occurred on their side of the lines. This allowed the systematic examination of wrecks for information on electronics, radar and jet engine technology.[117] Knowledge was gained at a heavy cost. The Chinese and North Koreans lost 976 aircraft, FEAF 1466, with Navy, Marine and allied aircraft accounting for an additional 420. The majority of UN losses were from ground fire or accident, only 147 being claimed by MIGs.[118] The war was thus costly in terms of personnel and equipment, a fact sometimes overlooked: 'The results that were achieved must be weighed against the fact that . . . the Americans lost the equivalent of 20 combat groups . . . roughly a quarter of the USAF's first line strength as it stood in June 1950.'[119]

Despite the success claimed for air pressure, it was clear that the USAF did not wish to become involved in future protracted, indecisive and limited wars in Asia. The lesson drawn from Korea was that the experience must never be repeated. This was not a plea for disengagement but for improved technology and ground rules which allowed it to be used. In future communism in the Far East was to be contained not by conventional means but by direct atomic retaliation on China, in effect an application of global war policy on a limited scale. As the FEAF history noted, 'forward thinking' USAF officers had been dealing with this concept for some time but were hampered by policymakers who had 'never thought in terms of other than a ground warfare'.[120] In future Asia was to be held by native armies backed by American air power. This confirmed the thrust of weapons development since 1950 which had produced tactical atomic bombs capable of being carried by fighters. The tactical air command was built around this concept. As General Weyland defined its role in

1956, the task of the tactical air force was to complement SAC by allowing the United States to respond to aggression along a sliding scale. The Air Force had developed 'a limited atomic strategy' for use in peripheral wars.[121] This concept of the future relegated the Army to the role of strategic reserve and rejected 'ground force thinking'. It fitted the needs of the Eisenhower administration which was anxious to reduce military spending in the interests of balancing the budget. As one Air Force memorandum shrewdly noted, politically it was 'exceedingly important' for the President to appear as a champion of air power.[122] The USAF, therefore, welcomed the doctrine of massive retaliation which matched the ideas of those 'forward thinking' officers mentioned in the FEAF history. Thus the USAF, the major beneficiary of NSC-68, consolidated its position with the New Look. Korea confirmed the atomic obsession which had existed in 1950. The response to limited conventional war was to seek means of waging limited atomic war which would prevent the United States from being bogged down in a series of inconclusive struggles around the periphery of China. It was an irony of history that when the Air Force again found itself engaged on the Asian mainland, in Vietnam, it was once more in an indecisive interdiction and air pressure campaign, rather than in the decisive blow against 'aggression' predicted by the theorists of atomic air power.

13 Conclusions

At 10.00 p.m. on 27 July a sullen silence fell over the front. After thirty-seven months the Korean War had ended. The opposing armies disengaged and fell back on their main defence lines behind the DMZ. The outposts in No Man's Land were left 'deserted and quiet except for the rats'.[1] There was little rejoicing. For the first time in its modern history, the US had failed to win. The war had ended in a draw. This was an uncomfortable outcome for Americans. The public was in a dark mood, inclined to compare the costs of the war with its inconclusive result: 'There were no victory celebrations, no cheering crowds in Times Square, no sense of triumph', only relief that a 'sour little war' was finally over.[2] Eisenhower had fulfilled his campaign pledge and considered the armistice his greatest achievement. He had brought a settlement which avoided either 'appeasement' or an escalation which would have risked global war and strained the US alliance system. The terms were the best which could be obtained and reflected his belief that 'unlimited war in the nuclear age was unimaginable, and limited war unwinnable'.[3] Others, however, remained unconvinced. Clark signed the armistice with 'a heavy heart'. He continued to sympathise with MacArthur and believed that the war should have been carried to the Chinese mainland, eliminating Beijing as a permanent threat to US interests in Asia. The ceasefire merely increased Chinese arrogance and prestige. The price of a draw in Korea would be trouble in the future: 'I had grave misgivings that some day my countrymen would be forced to pay a far higher price in blood than it would have cost if the decision had been made to defeat the Communists in Korea.[4] For Clark, as for MacArthur, there could be 'No substitute for victory'. On the Republican right there were grumblings about 'appeasement'. These never grew into the kind of sustained political attack which had faced Truman. Eisenhower's prestige as a soldier and his vast personal popularity made him immune to such an assault. He was perhaps the only figure who could have forced through such a settlement and made it stick without a bruising political struggle. His achievement in Korea has been compared with De Gaulle's solution of the insoluble in Algeria nine years later.[5]

The armistice left two questions unresolved – the ultimate fate of the non-repatriate POWs and the political future of Korea. Both provided a fertile source of disagreement and recrimination. After the cease-fire, repatriate POWs were exchanged in OPERATION BIG SWITCH and the non-repatriates turned over to the NNRC and the Indian Custodial Force in the DMZ for 'explanations'. The Americans recognised that they had gambled to secure an armistice. Once outside UNC control there was no guarantee that large numbers of POWs would not opt for repatriation. US anxiety on this score reveals that officials were not as certain as their rhetoric implied about the real commitment of the mass of POWs to the regimes in Taipei and Seoul. Their main worry was that the prisoners would somehow be separated from the anti-communist leadership which had imposed order in the compounds. This emerged as early as 29 June when disturbing reports from the Counter-Intelligence Corps on Cheju-do reached U. Alexis Johnson at the State Department. The CIC warned that the Guomindong compound leaders might instigate 'active or passive resistance' to Indian troops and attack communist explainers. There had also been new outbreaks of violence between 'pro and anti-repatriation Chinese POWs'. Johnson noted that the situation raised unpleasant possibilities: 'These circumstances may necessitate the use of force by the Neutral Commission to maintain control. Under such conditions pro-Communist elements within the camps may come to the fore and lead a majority of the present non-repatriates to accept repatriation. This would provide a convincing propaganda opportunity to the Communists.[6] In order to avert such an outcome an intensive propaganda campaign was mounted in the camps with the assistance of the Guomindong regime.[7] The rules of the NNRC were explained and the prisoners were promised that after ninety days they would be liberated to Taiwan. Compounds would not be broken up for transfer to the DMZ, guaranteeing that the anti-communist leadership remained in control. The leaders took their own precautions, holding screenings to weed any 'communist elements' which remained.[8]

The POWs thus entered Indian custody under tight political control. This immediately caused problems for the NNRC. As the Indians complained on 15 October: 'There is an appreciable minority among the prisoners of war who desire to be repatriated. In view of the tightly knit internal organization of the prisoners of war, however, prisoner group leaders have great power over the prisoners and frequently resort to intimidation and coercion. Some of the prisoners of war wishing to go home have therefore had to indicate and exercise their choice surreptitiously.[9] The Americans did not deny the fact of political organisation but denied that coercion occurred. It was argued that those who went over the wire to seek repatriation were communist agents bugging out because they had failed to suborn fellow prisoners.[10] Despite these confident claims, Washington remained concerned about the outcome of 'explanations'. It objected strongly to the rules of procedure adopted by the NNRC, suspecting that India was bowing to Chinese pressure and voting with the Czechs and Poles, stacking the odds in favour of the communists. In particular, the Americans objected to rules which allowed repeated explanations to groups and individuals and provided for the segregation of prisoners who had received explanations from those who had not. The last was considered extremely dangerous. As US news correspondents at Panmunjom warned, 'If the Communists succeed in separating anti-Communist leaders from [their] respective compounds, then very appreciable numbers of prisoners may switch and elect repatriation.[11] The leaderless prisoners might be subjected to long sessions of indoctrination and bombarded with written and broadcast propaganda. On the wilder shores of the imagination, it was even feared that the communists would bring in strippers and prostitutes to tempt sex-starved POWs.[12]

These nightmares never came true. An early victory was scored when the POWs refused to appear for explanations if they were to be segregated after screening.[13] When the NNRC conceded this point, the hard-core anti-communists could appear at the beginning of the explanation process and disrupt the proceedings, secure in the knowledge that they were not surrendering political control of their compounds. Thus explanations were marked by abuse and violence which the Indians were hard pressed to contain. The communists were by no means blameless. While they did not resort to some of the more colourful methods feared by the Americans, they did abuse the spirit of the rules, dragging out the sessions to wear down and confuse prisoners and employing threats of retaliation against families.[14] The POWs used these tactics as an excuse to refuse further explanations and remained in their compounds.[15] The Poles and Czechs demanded that the Indians use force to secure POWs for interview, but the Indians refused. They had insufficient men to control the camps without the assistance of the compound leaders. Moreover, they feared attack by the ROK, which mounted a sustained propaganda campaign against India. Such was the violence of this rhetoric that India threatened to withdraw its forces unless their safety was guaranteed by the UNC.[16] As a result, the mass of POWs was never interviewed. There were only nine explanation days between 15 October and 5 November when the process broke down. Of the Chinese 2085 out of 14 700 were screened and of the Koreans, 1277 out of 7900. In all 440 Chinese and 188 Koreans opted for repatriation.[17] The NNRC blamed the breakdown mainly on the political leadership of the POWs. It complained in January 1954 of its 'serious doubts' that the anti-communist organisations in the compounds were of a wholly voluntary nature. The 'main object' of these organisations was 'to resist repatriation and prevent such prisoners as desired repatriation from exercising that right. . . . The state of affairs within the camps was certainly not conducive to the implementation of . . . the terms of reference.'[18] This condemnation did not merely reflect the influence of the Poles and Czechs who had a vested interest in discrediting the outcome of the explanations. In a separate report, the Swedes and Swiss agreed that 'The attitude of the prisoners of war in respect of explanations has . . . been influenced and coordinated by organizations of a political nature . . . acts of violence and even murders have been committed.[19] The communists attempted to turn the deadlock to advantage by insisting that the ninety day period *for* explanations meant ninety days *of* explanations, an outcome which would have faced the POWs with indefinite detention. This was not accepted.[20] The only remaining danger was that in the absence of a political conference, which it was soon clear would not take place, the Indians might continue to hold the POWs until the UN decided what was to be done. This might cause disorder and rioting in the camps of which the communists could take advantage.[21] In the event, the NNRC voted to dissolve after ninety days and the Indians relinquished control of the prisoners on 20 January 1954. Eighty-six opted to remain with the Indians. The remainder were repatriated to Taiwan and the ROK amid a barrage of propaganda.[22] A statement prepared for Dulles by the Psychological Strategy Board proclaimed: 'These men are much more than anti-communist. As strong as their resentment against communism and its way of life may be, their yearning for freedom has been much more intense and has sustained them during their long period of detention.' The significance of the UN stand on principle would not be lost on the communists in planning future aggressive action: 'They will remember that freedom is the popular choice, and the desire for freedom can overcome even the most intense indoctrination and brutal discipline. We in the free world have a special right to feel proud today. We have stood by a principle and won.'[23]

As has been argued, the real situation was by no means as clear-cut.

The degree of freedom of choice in the camps, even under Indian control, was always in doubt. US officials were aware of this when they defended the principle of non-forcible repatriation. The war was prolonged by fifteen months, at a cost of 2,500 American casualties a month, less to uphold a principle than to score a point in the cold war and weaken China. The non-repatriates were a symbol of US commitment to 'rollback' in a war which could not be won by traditional military means. As a British diplomat remarked in December 1952, the Americans began only by opposing repatriation at the point of a bayonet. By the end of 1952, however, they were demanding guarantees of non-repatriation as part of any solution to the POW impasse: 'It rather looks now as though the prisoners [are] being offered an inducement to refuse to return home instead of the scales being weighted the other way.'[24] Perhaps Washington had little choice but to embrace non-forcible repatriation in the circumstances of the time. The alternative in 1952 was to use force against the anti-communist compounds to secure a majority for non-repatriation. This would have caused problems with the ROK and Taiwan, not to mention political trouble at home. It was in any case ideologically unacceptable and was never seriously canvassed. By subsequently vesting such ideological significance in the non-repatriates, Washington helped block a settlement. As the British representative at the UN, Gladwyn Jebb, remarked in December 1952, if the US was only concerned with non-forcible repatriation, there could be little objection to informing non-repatriates that they were liable to remain in camps for the rest of their lives.[25] The Americans; though, were seeking more. The POWs must be liberated and seen to embrace the Guomindong and ROK regimes. Thus Washington insisted on cast-iron guarantees of early release from international custody which were wholly unacceptable to the communists.

The victims of this approach were UN prisoners in communist hands who were sacrificed in the wider interests of the cold war. The world was soon to witness the curious spectacle of Americans praising the conduct of enemy POWs on Koje while condemning its own returning prisoners for collaboration with communism. If the 'anti-communist heroes' were useful propaganda material in Asia, US POWs became 'the subjects of another type of propaganda – propaganda by Americans, about Americans, directed by Americans'. The theme was that there had been 'wholesale collaboration by the American prisoners . . . and that this unprecedented behavior revealed alarming new weaknesses in our national character'.[26] According to the

journalist Eugene Kinkaid, whose book *In Every War But One* was
written with the assistance of Defense Department officials, Korea
was an exceptional conflict. In no previous war had there been such 'a
wholesale breakdown of morale and . . . collaboration with captors'.[27]
In a series of lectures an Army psychiatrist, Major W. E. Mayer,
emphasised that the POWs had displayed no sustained resistance to
enemy indoctrination, despite conditions which were not as bad 'as in
Japanese and most German camps' during the Second World War.[28]
The conduct of the Americans was compared unfavourably with that
of other national groups such as the Turks and the British. For the US
prisoners, the return from North Korea was a 'march to calumny'.

The Pentagon had been concerned about the success of communist
indoctrination even before OPERATION BIG SWITCH. At that
stage, however, officials were concerned to limit controversy and not
to overrate the success of communist 'brainwashing'.[29] After the
armistice, this approach was replaced by agonised debate over the
ideological weakness of American soldiers. Two main accusations
were levelled at the POWs. The first was that they had lacked
discipline. Unlike other groups of POWs, the Americans lost all
organisation and solidarity. Morale was low and many died because
they refused to eat the unfamiliar rations offered by the communists.
According to Kinkaid, the army felt its losses were due not so much to
the Communists' disregard . . . of the Geneva Convention . . . as to
the breakdown of discipline among the prisoners themselves'.[30] One
officer attributed this to a 'new failure in the childhood and adolescent
training of our young men – a new softness'.[31] The second was that
these weaknesses had aided communist indoctrination. There had
been wholesale collaboration in the Yalu camps where over one-third
of the prisoners cooperated with the enemy. The fact that not a single
POW had escaped was taken as particularly damning evidence of a
lack of will to resist.[32] In the wake of the POW controversy, the Army
introduced a new code of prisoner conduct, emphasising that each
soldier must resist the enemy and refuse to collaborate beyond
supplying his name, rank and number as required by the Geneva
Convention.[33] According to the Army Chief of Staff, General
Ridgway, it was no longer enough to 'condition the soldier's body and
his spirit by subjecting him to the sights and sounds of simulated
battle'. He had also to be prepared to resist 'a new technique of war
. . . the technique we have come to know as brain-washing'.[34]
Attempts were made to improve the ideological awareness of the GI
and calls were heard for tougher discipline and better leadership.

The critics of American POW conduct did not go unchallenged and were later accused of misrepresentation and distortion. The sociologist, Albert Biderman, attacked the negative popular image of the prisoners. He did not deny that there had been weaknesses in leadership and morale but denied that the American record was any worse than that of other groups in Chinese captivity. In common with other nationalities, American POWs observed rituals such as group study and self-criticism. This signified no inner commitment and was the minimum necessary to avoid physical coercion, which the Chinese did not hesitate to employ. In terms of minimal acts of collaboration like signing a peace petition, the American record was no worse than that of other nationalities such as the British. While twenty-one Americans refused repatriation and embraced communism, this was one half of one per cent of US prisoners in communist hands and contrasted with the large numbers of Germans and Japanese converted during the Second World War.[35] The deaths and morale problems of the early period were due less to lack of will, than to the harsh winter conditions of 1950–1. The majority of Americans fell into enemy hands when the weather was at its worst and before a proper system of camps was organised. The other groups were captured in the spring when the chances of survival were higher. Moreover, the subsequent opening of truce talks buoyed their morale, since the prospect of an early exchange was opened up, a prospect not open to American POWs earlier in the year. The talks also had a bearing on the question of escape. Korea was unique in that armistice talks covered two-thirds of the war.[36] In these circumstances, POWs of all nationalities preferred to await an exchange rather than attempt the difficult feat of escape to the UN lines.

Despite Biderman's work, however, POW misconduct remains one of the facts which everyone knows about the war, where they know anything at all. In some respects the POWs were scapegoats for an unpopular result. In the view of the American right, the retreat from victory in Korea was the product of the failure of national will, which was blamed on the New Deal system. The POWs, representatives of the New Deal generation, became the symbols of this national degeneration. In this view, Americans collaborated while Turks did not, because a decade of social welfare had sapped the traditional Yankee values of self-help and rugged individualism.[37] In another sense, the prisoners were the victims of guilt by association common in domestic McCarthyism. Their detention in communist hands, indeed their very act of surrender, made them ideologically suspect. They had been exposed to contamination by a system which many believed capable of almost superhuman feats of indoctrination and mind control. The 'anti-communist heroes' of Koje had by contrast cleared themselves by struggle in the camps and by their determination to continue the fight against communism in the armies of the ROK and Guomindong. The Pentagon may have had its own reason for instigating, through Kinkaid and others, a domestic psychological warfare campaign utilising the experience of the POWs. It prevented an erosion of the will to fight, which the military had always feared would follow the war and emphasised the need for continued psychological as well as military mobilisation to resist communism. The enemy was a perverted system which would stop at nothing to dominate the world. The price of freedom was continued vigilance and a heightened ideological awareness. It is notable that the debate over POW conduct was an American phenomenon. It was little evident in Britain, which followed the US in numbers of prisoners in communist hands. The special branch was ordered to keep a discreet eye on ex-progressives but there was no national soul searching.[38] Perhaps the British were more aware of their limited power to transform the world and less uncomfortable that the outcome in Korea had been a draw.

Despite the provision in the armistice agreement for a political conference, the unification of Korea remained as distant after the war as before. On the UN side there was much wrangling over who should attend the political talks. Australia, Britain and Canada were anxious to appeal to Asian opinion and to show that a real attempt was being made to solve the problems of the Far East. They wished to invite India to the conference as the leading non-communist Asian power.[39] The Americans, however, insisted that only belligerents should be represented. They continued to distrust India as dangerously sympathetic to China and feared the reaction of Rhee, to whom Nehru was anathema.[40] When it became clear that American opposition would defeat a commonwealth resolution in the General Assembly, calling for the inclusion of India, New Delhi requested that it be withdrawn.[41] The Americans did agree, however, that North Korea and China could include the Soviet Union in their delegation if they so desired. This would confirm Soviet responsibility for the war and commit Moscow to any solution which emerged.[42] In the event, the debate over the composition of the UN delegation proved to be wasted effort. When the US, acting as the agent of the UN, opened talks with the communists at Panmunjom in October on the date and location of the conference, a deadlock rapidly occurred. The main question at issue was the communist demand that Russia attend as a neutral, an evasion of past and future Soviet responsibility that Washington was unwilling to concede. After a series of sterile and vituperative meetings, the US representative walked out on 12 December.[43]

Korean unification was not discussed until the Geneva conference of April 1954. By that stage, however, few had any illusions that a settlement would emerge and the great powers devoted more time and effort to the crisis in Indochina which was the main reason for the meeting. With the armistice holding, it was in Indochina rather than in Korea that a local struggle threatened to involve great power confrontation. There was an early agreement on this issue between the British and Soviet co-chairmen of the conference, Eden and Molotov. As Eden later recalled: 'I did not think that Korea was so urgent. After all there was no fighting there and matters could be allowed to remain for the time being in their present state, if we could not agree on further steps. But the situation in Indo-China had very dangerous possibilities. Molotov fully agreed.'[44] Once more, Korean unification had been deferred to suit the convenience of the great powers. The armistice line became what Acheson had predicted as early as 1951, the symbol of a tacit spheres of influence agreement between the blocs. For Koreans, the war had solved nothing.

Although UNCURK survived until 1972, Korea rapidly became a forgotten issue. The commission was powerless in the north and had little influence in the south. It was only kept going after the war at the insistence of Washington, which wished to preserve a facade of UN interest on the peninsula.[45] The major allies withdrew their troops as quickly as possible for financial and strategic reasons. By 1957, only a British liaison officer remained as Commonwealth representative on the UN command. The US also redeployed its troops. In 1954, the JCS decided to withdraw all but two divisions. Ultimately only 30 000 Americans remained as a symbol of American commitment to ROK security.[46] In the north, the Chinese also began withdrawing, a process completed in 1958. This did not mean the demilitarisation of Korea. On the contrary, the peninsula became the most heavily militarised area on earth. The NNSC was powerless to prevent this development. In the north, the communists began rebuilding airfields and flying in jets as soon as the armistice was signed.[47] The NKPA was re-equipped and a navy created. In the south, Washington fulfilled its pledge to sign a security treaty and to support an ROK army of twenty divisons.[48] As American troops withdrew, they turned over their equipment to the

Koreans. In 1957 Washington formally announced that it would no longer observe the restrictions on the introduction of new weapons. Thereafter US troops were equipped with Honest John tactical missiles and atomic cannon. Airfields were improved to accommodate a new generation of American jet aircraft. The ROK, backed by the US, became the first line of defence for Japan, the key to the American position in the Far East.[49] The build-up may also have been intended to restrain Beijing from intervention in Indochina, where American interest became concentrated in the wake of the Korean armistice.

The conflict was a disaster for Korea. An unparalleled degree of destruction was visited on the peninsula in the course of what the West called a 'limited war'. The employment of US technology had devastating consequences. As the journalist, James Cameron, observed: 'The soldiers [were] preceded at all times by air and artillery attack on a scale that assumed terrific resistance. If a village stood in the line of advance it must be obliterated *before* examination; the elimination of communities of civilians was inevitable because amongst them there might be sympathizers, if not active participants, of the other side.' From the moment that Korea was selected for an experiment in limited war, 'Korea was doomed'.[50] This was confirmed by no less a figure than General MacArthur at the hearings on his dismissal in 1951: 'The war in Korea has almost destroyed that nation . . . I have never seen such devastation . . . I have seen . . . as much blood and disaster as any living man, and it just curdled my stomach, the last time I was there. After I looked at that wreckage and those thousands of women and children and everything, I vomited.'[51] According to his bomber commander, General O'Donnell, the whole peninsula was a 'terrible mess. . . . There is nothing standing worthy of the name'.[52] The destruction was particularly severe in the North which had suffered both invasion and three years of concentrated bombing. According to General Zimmerman, chief intelligence officer of FEAF: 'The degree of destruction suffered by North Korea, in relation to its resources, was greater than that which the Japanese islands suffered in World War Two.'[53] Communist sources support this judgement. Indeed the devastation of North Korea was one of the few things about the war on which both sides agreed. In July 1951 Wilfred Burchett crossed the Yalu to cover the truce talks at Kaesong. The carnage he witnessed travelling South was worse than any he had experienced in the recent world war: 'Not even the smallest hamlet had been spared. . . . Villages could be recognised only as level black patches . . . whole towns had moved into primitive cave shelters. In

Pyongyang there were still a few buildings intact when I first passed through. But there was no hospital, school, church, temple or any public building standing along the entire road from the Yalu to Kaesong.'[54] Note that this account dates from 1951, *before* the UN command increased 'air pressure' on the North.

The human costs of the war were enormous. It 'decimated Korea, the very nation that the United States was theoretically attempting to save.' Millions died or were turned into refugees. The North suffered the worst losses: 'The DPRK has not released overall figures but a plausible estimate is that at least twelve per cent of the population and possibly fifteen per cent were killed – A higher proportion than in the USSR in World War Two.'[55] Many of the survivors ended the war as refugees in the ROK. These people were hailed by the West as further evidence of the illegitimacy of the Pyongyang regime. In fact many fled simply to escape the fighting or were forced out by the effects of UNC policy. The war diary of the 24th Infantry noted that during the retreat of December 1950 'It became necessary for units to screen entire villages and in many cases evacuate the entire male population of military age. . . . Razing villages along our withdrawal routes and destruction of food staples became the order of the day.'[56] As part of its blockade, the US Navy waged an unpublicised campaign against the Northern fishing fleet, seizing ships and crews and taking them South. The effects along the coast, where the population relied on fish, was dramatic. As the official history dryly remarked, 'The principal reason for so many North Korean refugees was simply starvation.'[57] Korea became the first Asian peasant society to suffer the horrendous effects of modern war. It was not to be the last.

The destruction of Korea was directed from American bases in the former colonial power, Japan, a country feared and hated by both Korean regimes. The war which devasted its former colony boosted the Japanese economy as US money poured in for supplies and armaments: 'There is some irony in the fact that one of the first stimuli to rebuilding the Japanese economy should come from the production of napalm bombs to be used to destroy towns and industries (many of them built by the Japanese) in newly-liberated Korea.'[58] Japan became a silent partner in the UN effort, supplying civilian manpower and shipping as well as supplies. The Japanese were even involved in minesweeping along the Korean coast, a fact kept secret at the time because of the Sino-Soviet pact. The war completed the economic reconstruction of Japan and its political rehabilitation.[59] Without the war, a Japanese peace treaty might have been a more difficult prospect. As things were, the fighting completed the integration of Japan into the US containment system in the Far East. After the war, as before, this implied a Japanese economic presence in Korea. This was a development which Rhee resisted throughout the war but which ultimately could not be prevented by the ROK.

It is arguable that Japan did better out of the war than any of the main protagonists. Another major beneficiary was the Guomindong regime on Taiwan which contributed little during the war beyond rhetoric and sporadic commando raids on the Chinese mainland. On the brink of eclipse in 1949, Jiang received a new lease of life as an instrument of containment. American military and economic aid was pumped into Taiwan and a US military assistance group arrived. At the UN, Washington supported the fiction that the Guomindong was the real representative of China. The situation did not change for another two decades. As in Korea, US intervention prevented the defeat of the right in a civil war and permanently institutionalised the conflict in two separate regimes. To Jiang's disappointment, however, Washington would never reconquer the mainland on his behalf. That impossible dream vanished in 1951 along with MacArthur. Whatever the rhetoric of the Republican administration, it was as anxious as its predecessor to keep Jiang in check.

China emerged from the war with increased prestige. Beijing had defeated a modern army in December 1950, administering the worst reverse to American arms since the civil war. Despite the setbacks which followed, it forced Washington to accept a draw. This reversed a century of humiliation at the hands of the West and signalled the emergence of a new China. UN economic sanctions and American paramilitary warfare in South China had failed to shake the regime. As early as January 1951, the CIA predicted that, 'For the foreseeable future the Chinese Communist regime will probably retain exclusive governmental control of mainland China. Although there is undoubtedly much dissatisfaciton with the Communist regime . . . it does enjoy a measure of support and acquiesence and is developing strong police controls. . . . There are no indications that current anti-Communist efforts can achieve a successful counterrevolution.[60] Nothing in the following years of the war changed this estimate. China emerged as a powerful force in Asia which had to be taken seriously by Washington. It had become a regional power in opposition to the US rather than in association with the US, an ironic reversal of Roosevelt's wartime vision. The cost to Beijing had been contained by fighting in another country. It was the cities and industries of North Korea which were destroyed. There was, however, a price to be paid. China suffered at least 900 000 casualties. It was excluded from the UN and lost any chance of ending the civil war by taking Taiwan. Economic reconstruction was impeded by the demands of the war and the regime accumulated a huge debt to the USSR for economic and military assistance. As the Chinese later complained 'no free aid was ever offered by the Soviet Union'. Not only did the Russians demand money for their weapons but they also collected interest.[61] There were rumours throughout the conflict of tension between Beijing and Moscow. If this existed, however, it was never revealed in public. While China sought an accommodation with the US after the armistice, it continued to 'lean to one side' in the cold war.[62] The Sino-Soviet split lay a decade ahead.

The Soviet Union, like Japan, was officially neutral. In fact, the Russians contributed supplies, training and political support to China and North Korea. Soviet advisers, pilots and anti-aircraft troops served behind the front. Moscow paid a high price to maintain the status quo on the peninsula. The results of the war were unwelcome and there was evidence of Russian displeasure at the outcome of North Korean 'adventurism'. Whatever Stalin's part in the origins of the conflict, it was used by Washington to 'sound the tocsin', reinforcing the containment system around the Soviet periphery. In the atmosphere of crisis produced by the fighting, the Truman administration was able to increase American military strength and build-up NATO, a programme already envisaged in NSC-68. It was also able to promote West German and Japanese rearmament, threatening the USSR on two fronts. Russia had to meet this development while assuming the burden of supplying its Chinese ally. These facts outweighed the advantages of any strains in the Western alliance caused by the war. Moscow responded in two ways. The first was by building up its own forces, both conventional and atomic. The second was to launch a peace campaign designed to avert the rearmament of West Germany. This effort was intensified by Stalin's successors. Ultimately, however, Moscow was unable to prevent the military revival of the West German state.[63]

The war marked a new phase in the relationship between the US and its major allies. Previously, particularly in Britain, the main priority had been to overcome the legacy of isolationism and commit Washington to a Western security system. After 1950 there was a new desire to contain the US and limit the exercise of American power. The MacArthur crisis and the rise of McCarthyism underlined the volatile influence of domestic politics on US policy. In London, Ottawa and Canberra, it became clear that a third world war 'could be caused not only by Communist aggression but also by American desires to make an example of China.'[64] Britain, where US air bases were a natural target, was especially at risk. It was clear to both Labour and Conservative governments that an American–Soviet clash over China was unlikely to be confined to the Far East. Britain would be the first to suffer. The significance of the bases was brought home to Attlee in December 1950 and obsessed his successor. Churchill 'blamed the late Labour Government for inviting the Americans to put atom bomb launching aerodromes in East Anglia, which he said would invite devastating reprisal bombing in the event of war.'[65] This sense of being in the front line, produced a strong element of caution in British policy. While defining the Anglo-American alliance as the basis of British security, both Attlee and Churchill attempted to contain the United States. By 1953 Churchill was arguing in favour of detente with the Soviet bloc and viewed Korea as a dangerous distraction.

The facts of power, however, constrained British influence. There is no evidence that allied pressure prevented the Americans from adopting any course which they might otherwise have taken. It is a myth that Attlee's visit prevented a wider war with China in December 1950. It was Ridgway's stabilisation of the front and not British diplomacy which finally kept the war limited. Britain was too reliant on American support elsewhere to push disagreement with Washington over Korea, a fact evidenced by the cabinet decision to avoid a confrontation at the UN in January 1951. Britain, in common with the other allies, realised that in the last resort it would have little option but to back Washington if the Americans widened the war. As the Australian Foreign Minister warned in February 1952, domestic pressures might make an American move against the mainland irresistible: 'Although we and the United Kingdom have asked for consultation before any such action is taken, America might take that action against our and the United Kingdom wishes. In that case we would probably find it very difficult to refrain from associating ourselves tangibly with the American action and might easily slide into a global war or at the very least into a war of large proportions.'[66] Thus the war was a frustrating experience, accentuating British dependence on the United States while increasing the need to control the Americans. This was a tension which was never satisfactorily resolved.

In the US. Korea became a forgotten war. Unable to celebrate victory, Americans preferred to forget the uncomfortable episode.

However, the war had permanent effects. It was used by Washington to stimulate rearmanent and round out the system of containment. The implementation of NSC-68 militarised the cold war. Korea also raised questions about the economic and political costs of limited war. Instead of a decisive outcome in 1950, the US found itself bogged down in a frustrating and interminable struggle on the strategic periphery. Korea ultimately discredited NSC-68 and produced the Republican revolt which assisted Eisenhower in 1952. It led to the 'New Look' which placed greater emphasis on local forces and nuclear deterrents to contain communism.[67] Despite the trimming of the military budget under Eisenhower, however, the US never returned to the austerity of the pre-Korea period. It remained in a permanent state of semi-mobilisation.

The war helped shift American attention towards the Far East, a tendency which accelerated in the following years. It froze the relationship between Washington and Beijing. Despite Chinese overtures in the mid-1950s, the US remained committed to non-recognition and Taiwan. Eisenhower and Dulles, like Truman and Acheson, believed that the best way of discrediting the Soviet alliance and the pro-Russian group in Beijing was to maintain economic and political pressure on China.[68] At the same time, China could no longer be dismissed as a power factor. In the future, Washington was careful to avoid provoking Beijing. Eisenhower preferred to concede North Vietnam to the communists in 1954, rather than risk another Korea. The ROK became a model for US policy on the Asian mainland, as it had been before 1950. Washington attempted to contain China by establishing stable nationalist regimes around the Chinese periphery, based on a third force which was neither communist nor colonial. In this process, the military assistance programme occupied a central role: 'The ROK Army had become by 1953 the primary model for the US military assistance program in Indochina' as well as in Taiwan and the Philippines.[69] It was the collapse of the Vietnamese experiment in the 1960s which was to bring back US troops to the Asian mainland in a new war of containment, as much against radical nationalism as against communism. This time, though, care was taken not to involve China. There was to be no invasion of North Vietnam no rollback which might lead to a wider war. This much at least had been learned from the Korean experience.

In the West, the war was officially regarded as a triumph for collective security over aggression. It was argued that the UN had been saved from the fate of the League of Nations and that further armed expansion by the communists had been deterred. In a longer perspective, an argument which centres on the lessons of the thirties is hard to sustain. In fact the mechanism of the UN had been employed by one bloc in the cold war against another and a local incident viewed in global perspective. It was not *collective* security but *selective* security which had been upheld. There was 'not a communist power' amongst the sixteen nations which intervened and 'scarcely evidence even of the non-aligned'. The whole enterprise had 'a character very different from the one anticipated for such cases by the founders of the UN Charter'.[70] At the height of the cold war, Western statesmen assumed that their own security interests were synonymous with international order. This approach allowed the UN to become the tool of American diplomacy. In retrospect, the Korean conflict seems less an exercise in collective security than an example of intervention against a Third World revolution which threatened to disturb the global status quo. From 1945 onwards, Washington was determined to contain the Korean left as well as the Soviet Union, assuming that all change would favour the Russians. In this respect, the war was the logical extension of US occupation policy. The UN role in Korea was to legitimise the American position. When China entered the war, the UN role was extended to containing the Chinese revolution and the rise of China as a regional power. In allowing itself to be manipulated in this way, the UN undermined its role as a peacemaker. China could not accept as disinterested an international body which excluded Beijing and which through the US was waging war on its borders. Through the conflict the General Assembly vacillated unhappily between the roles of belligerent and mediator. The essential decisions, however, were taken in Washington. Despite the wide claims made for the UN, Western leaders were aware that armed intervention by the organisation was the product of unique circumstances which were unlikely to be repeated. It would be more difficult in future to mobilise the moral authority of the organisation behind great power self-interest. As Eden conceded during the Suez crisis of 1956: 'The world knew that approval by the United Nations of action by the United States in Korea was an accident, due to Soviet absence from the Security Council and the non-application of the veto.'[71] In future confrontations between the blocs, the UN would prove irrelevant except as a sounding board for propaganda.

Notes and References

1 The Cold War and Counter-Revolution

1. Bruce Cummings, *The Origins of the Korean War, Liberation and the Emergence of Separate Regimes* (Princeton, NJ, 1981) p. 3.
2. Richard Storry, *Japan and the Decline of the West in Asia, 1894–1943* (London, 1979) pp. 24–7, 53–104.
3. Ibid, pp. 112–56.
4. Cummings, pp. 12–25.
5. Robert T. Oliver, *Syngman Rhee. The Man Behind the Myth* (London, 1955) pp. 138–42.
6. Gregory Henderson, *Korea, The Politics of the Vortex* (Cambridge, Mass., 1968) pp. 79–80.
7. Cummings, pp. 181–2.
8. Oliver, pp. 159–84.
9. James I. Mattray, 'An End to Indifference. America's Korean Policy During World War 2', *Diplomatic History* 2 (Spring 1978) pp. 183–5.
10. Cummings, pp. 33–8.
11. Mattray, pp. 181.
12. Oliver, pp. 132–55.
13. Joseph C. Goulden, *Korea, The Untold Story of the War* (New York, 1982) pp. 8–9.
14. Cummings, pp. 101–17.
15. Ibid.
16. Ibid.
17. Michael Schaller, *The United States & China in the Twentieth Century* (New York, 1979) pp. 38–61.
18. Warren I. Cohen, *America's Response to China* (New York, 1980) pp. 172–5.
19. Ibid.
20. Russell D. Buhite, *Soviet–American Relations in Asia, 1945–1954* (Norman, Oklahoma, 1981) pp. 5–36.
21. Bruce Cummings (ed.), *Child of Conflict, The Korean-American Relationship 1943–1953* (Seattle, 1983) pp. 12–13.
22. Mattray, pp. 181–96.
23. Ibid, pp. 181–96; Cummings, *Origins*, pp. 106–7.
24. Schaller, p. 107.
25. Ibid, p. 113.
26. Ibid, pp. 109–21.
27. John Lewis Gaddis, 'Korea in US Politics', in Yonosuke Nagai and Akira Iriye (eds) *The Origins of the Cold War in Asia* (Tokyo, 1977) pp. 281.
28. Merle Miller, *Plain Speaking, Conversations with Harry S. Truman* (London, 1974) p. 289.
29. Cohen, pp. 202–3; Buhite, pp. 126–36.
30. Gaddis, 'Korea in US Politics', pp. 284–5.

31. Dean G. Acheson, *Present at the Creation* (London, 1969) p. 432.
32. Cummings, *Origins*, pp. 115–18.
33. Mark Paul, 'Diplomacy Delayed: The Atomic Bomb and the Division of Korea', in Cummings (ed), *Child of Conflict*, pp. 77–8.
34. Ibid.
35. Ibid, pp. 88–9.
36. Cummings, *Origins*, pp. 120–1.
37. Ibid, p. 131.
38. Paul, pp. 90–1.
39. Cummings, *Origins*, pp. 81–91.
40. Ibid; Henderson, p. 119.
41. Cummings, *Origins*, pp. 382–426.
42. Robert A. Scalapino and Chong Sik Lee, *Communism in Korea*, Vol. 1, *The Movement* (Berkeley & Los Angeles, 1972) pp. 326–7.
43. Cummings, *Origins*, pp. 437–8.
44. Ibid, pp. 135–213.
45. Mark Gayn, *Japan Diary* (Tokyo, 1982) p. 398.
46. Gavan McCormack, *Cold War, Hot War* (Marrickville, New South Wales, 1983) p. 41.
47. Cummings, *Origins*, p. 441.
48. Buhite, pp. 148–9.
49. Ibid; Scalapino and Lee, pp. 277–8.
50. Cummings, *Origins*, pp. 238–9.
51. Gayn, p. 428.
52. Cummings, *Origins*, pp. 351–81.
53. Ibid, pp. 253–64.
54. Buhite, pp. 150–6.
55. William Whitney Stueck, *The Road to Confrontation, American Policy Toward China and Korea, 1947–1950* (Chapel Hill, NC, 1981) pp. 84–95; Gaddis, 'Korea in US Politics', pp. 282–3; Cummings, *Child of Conflict*, pp. 18–21.
56. Robert J. Donovan, *Tumultuous Years* (New York, 1982) pp. 94–5.
57. Stueck, pp. 94–5.
58. Shirley Hazzard, *Defeat of an Ideal, The Self-Destruction of the United Nations* (London, 1973); McCormack, pp. 74–5.
59. Stueck, p. 95.
60. Dennis Stairs, *The Diplomacy of Constraint Canada, the Korean War and the United States* (Toronto, 1974) pp. 18–22; McCormack, pp. 40–3.
61. McCormack, p. 41.
62. Ibid. pp. 43–6; Stairs, pp. 22–6.
63. Henderson, p. 156; Stairs, p. 25.
64. Stairs, pp. 25–6.
65. Stueck, p. 103.
66. Kim Chum-Kon, *The Korean War* (Seoul, 1973) pp. 109–10.
67. McCormack, pp. 50–3.
68. Report to the National Security Council, NSC-8, *Foreign Relations of the United States*, *1948*, Vol. 6, pp. 1164–70. Hereafter *FR 1948*.
69. Buhite, p. 168.
70. NSC-8, *FR 1948*, pp. 1164–70.

71. Stueck, pp. 102–5.
72. Ibid., pp. 105–9.
73. JCS Memo, 23 June 1949, JCS1483/74, RG 218, Box 25, Modern Military Records, National Archives, Washington DC. Hereafter MMR.
74. Stueck, pp. 108–9.
75. Ibid., p. 159.
76. Robert J. O'Neill, *Australia in the Korean War* (Canberra, 1981) p. 12.
77. Gaddis Smith, *Dean Acheson* (New York, 1972) pp. 175–6; Acheson, pp. 355–8.
78. Stueck, pp. 109–10.
79. Ibid.

2 The Korean Decisions

1. Robert J. Donovan, *Tumultuous Years* (New York, 1982) p. 141.
2. The position of the US with Respect to Asia, NSC-48/2, 30 December 1949, in Thomas H. Etzhold and John Lewis Gaddis (eds), *Containment, Documents on American Policy & Strategy, 1945–1950* (New York, 1978) pp. 252–76.
3. Franks to Bevin, 17 December 1949, FE/49/40, FO800/462, Public Record Office (PRO), Kew, London.
4. NSC-48/2, 30 December 1949; Robert M. Blum, *Drawing the Line, The Origins of the American Containment Policy in East Asia* (New York, 1982) pp. 175–7.
5. Cummings, *Child of Conflict*, pp. 32–8.
6. NSC-48/2, 30 December 1949.
7. Gaddis Smith, *American Diplomacy during the Second World War* (New York, 1985) pp. 91–2.
8. Buhite, pp. 91–8; Stueck, p. 139.
9. Buhite, pp. 94–5.
10. Blum, pp. 172–7.
11. Donovan, p. 87.
12. Ronald J. Caridi, *The Korean War and American Politics. The Republican Party as a Case Study* (Philadelphia, 1968) pp. 2–4.
13. Donovan, p. 136.
14. Ibid., pp. 61–2, 86.
15. William Manchester, *American Ceasar, Douglas MacArthur 1880–1964* (Boston, 1978) pp. 149–52.
16. Ibid., pp. 478–83.
17. John Gunther, *The Riddle of MacArthur* (London, 1951) pp. 1–12.
18. David Detzer, *Thunder of the Captains* (New York, 1977) pp. 25–7.
19. Gunther, pp. 55–8; Roger Morris, *Haig, The General's Progress* (London, 1982) p. 24.
20. Stephen Pelz, 'US Decisions on Korean Policy, 1943–1950. Some Hypotheses', in Cummings, *Child of Conflict*, p. 121.
21. FO Memo, 13 September 1949, F14109/1023/G, FO800/462, PRO.
22. Warren I. Cohen, 'Cold Wars and Shell Games', *Reviews in American History* (September 1983) p. 431.
23. Donovan, pp. 84–5.

24. Stueck, pp. 131–3.
25. FO Memo, 13 September 1949, F14109/1023/G, FO800/462, PRO.
26. Elisabeth Barker, *The British between the Superpowers, 1945–1950* (London, 1983) pp. 169–74.
27. Acheson, pp. 355–8; Gaddis Smith, *Dean Acheson* (New York, 1972) pp. 175–6.
28. Franks to Bevin, 8 March 1950, US50/8, FO800/517, PRO.
29. Donovan, pp. 158–9.
30. Gaddis & Etzhold, pp. 28–30.
31. Report to the National Security Council, NSC-68, *The Foreign Relations of the United States 1950*, Vol. 1, pp. 234–90. Hereafter *FR 1950*.
32. John Lewis Gaddis, *Strategies of Containment* (New York, 1982) pp. 95–106.
33. Ibid.
34. Ibid.
35. Cummings, *Child of Conflict*, p. 35.
36. Walter LaFeber, *America, Russia & the Cold War 1945–1984* (New York, 1985) p. 97.
37. Samuel F. Wells, 'Sounding the Tocsin. NSC-6 8 & the Soviet Threat', *International Security*, Vol. 4 (Fall 1979) pp. 124–5.
38. Acheson, p. 374; Donovan, pp. 61–2.
39. Wells, p. 124.
40. Ibid. p. 136–9; Acheson, pp. 376–9.
41. Pelz, pp. 121–5.
42. Ibid. pp. 125–6; Stueck, pp. 145–6.
43. Draft Memo, 30 May 1950, *FR 1950*, Vol. 6, pp. 349–51; Memo by Deputy Special Assistant for Intelligence, 31 May 1950, ibid., pp. 347–9.
44. John Lewis Gaddis, 'The Rise and Fall of the Defensive Perimeter Concept', in Dorothy Borg and Wald Heinrichs (eds), *Uncertain Years* (New York, 1980) pp. 86–8.
45. Leonard Mosley, *Dulles* (New York, 1978) p. 256.
46. Stueck, pp. 150–1.
47. Acheson, p. 352.
48. Stueck, pp. 162–4.
49. Memo of Conversation, 3 April 1950, *FR 1950*, Vol. 7, p. 42.
50. Mosley, p. 256.
51. Douglas MacArthur, *Reminiscences* (New York, 1964) p. 371.
52. Stueck, pp. 165–6.
53. Memo of Conversation, 10 May 1950, *FR 1950*, Vol. 7, pp. 78–9.
54. Ibid., p. 81.
55. Harry S. Truman, *Years of Trial and Hope* (New York, 1956) pp. 332–3.
56. LaFeber, pp. 100–1.
57. But see Karunker Gupta, 'How did the Korean War Begin?', *China Quarterly* 8 (October–December 1972) pp. 699–716; *Documents and Materials Exposing the Instigators of the Civil War in Korea*, Ministry of Foreign Affairs, Pyongyang, 1950.
58. *Krushchev Remembers* (London, 1971) pp. 332–3.
59. John Merrill, 'Internal Warfare in Korea, 1948–1950. The Local Setting of the Korean War', in Cummings, *Child of Conflict*, pp. 133–55.

60. Robert R. Simmons, *The Strained Alliance, Peking, Pyongyang, Moscow & the Politics of the Korean Civil War* (New York, 1975) pp. 102–10.
61. Cummings, *Child of Conflict*, pp. 49–50; Simmons pp. 110–16; Joyce and Gabriel Kolko, *The Limits of Power* (New York, 1972) pp. 577–8.
62. Scalapino and Lee, p. 394; Simmons, pp. 116–17.
63. Cummings, *Child of Conflict*, pp. 50–1.
64. Stueck, pp. 177–8.
65. Allen S. Whiting, *China Crosses the Yalu, The Decision to Enter the Korean War* (Stanford, 1968) pp. 45–6.
66. Krushchev, p. 333.
67. LaFeber, p. 101; Whiting, pp. 34–38.
68. Simmons, pp. 120–1; Krushchev, p. 335.
69. Wilbur Hitchcock, 'North Korea Jumps the Gun', *Current History* (20 March 1951) pp. 136–44.
70. 'Soviet Controlled Areas, Military Situation', No. 2730, 1 March 1950, MacArthur Papers, RG 6, FECOM, Box 49, Intelligence Summaries, February–March 1950, MacArthur Memorial Library (hereafter MACL), Norfolk VA.
71. Ronald K. Betts, *Surprise Attack* (Washington DC, 1982) pp. 53–4.
72. Frank Heller (ed.); *The Korean War, A 25 Year Perspective* (Lawrence, Kansas, 1977) p. 11.
73. *FR 1950*, Vol. 7, pp. 84–5.
74. 'Soviet Controlled Areas. Military Situation', No. 2753, 24 March 1950, RG 6, FECOM, Box 49, Intelligence Summaries, February–March 1950, MACL.
75. Donovan, pp. 143–6.
76. Stueck, p. 169; 'General Orientation for the Secretary of Defense & General Bradley', Selected Records Relating to the Korean War, Korean War File, DOD Pertinent Papers on the Korean Situation, 18 June 1950, Harry S. Truman Library (hereafter HSTL), Independence, MO.; Memo on Formosa, 14 June 1950, *FR 1950*, Vol. 7, pp. 161–5.
77. Goulden, p. 41.
78. Truman, pp. 331–2; Acheson, pp. 402–4; J. Lawton Collins, *War in Peacetime, The History and Lessons of Korea* (Boston, Mass., 1969) pp. 2–11.
79. Manchester, pp. 548–9.
80. Glen D. Paige, *The Korean Decision, June 24–30 1950* (New York, 1968) p. 86.
81. Kirk to Dept, 25 June 1950, *FR 1950*, Vol. 7, pp. 139–40.
82. Sebald to Acheson, 25 June 1950, ibid., p. 140.
83. Truman, p. 332; Miller, p. 273.
84. Webb to Snyder, 25 April 1975, Webb Papers, General Corr-S, 1973–5, Folder 2, Box 456, HSTL.
85. Truman, pp. 332–33; Ernest R. May, *Lessons of the Past, The Use and Misuse of History in American Foreign Policy* (New York, 1973) pp. 70–8.
86. Pelz, pp. 127–32.
87. See *FR 1950*, Vol. 7, p. 128.
88. Donovan, pp. 219–24.

89. Memo of Conversation, 25 June 1950, *FR 1950*, Vol. 7, p. 158.
90. Stueck, pp. 177–81.
91. McCormack, pp. 74–5.
92. O'Neill, p. 48; Stairs, pp. 29–30; Barker, p. 204.
93. Stairs, pp. 68–9; Collins, p. 34.
94. JCS to CINCFE, 12 July 1950, RG 319, Army Operations, 091 Korea, Box 121, Modern Military Records (hereafter MMR), National Archives, Washington DC.
95. Memo of Conversation, 26 June 1950, *FR 1950*, Vol. 7, pp. 178–83.
96. John W. Spanier, *The Truman–MacArthur Controversy and the Korean War* (New York, 1965) pp. 38–9.
97. JSPC Report, 14 July 1950, RG 218, JCS 1924/20, Box 26, MMR.
98. Truman, pp. 338–9.
99. Barker, p. 204.
100. Memo of Conversation, 25 June 1950, *FR 1950*, Vol. 7, pp. 157–61; Memo of Conversation, 26 June 1950, ibid., pp. 178–83.
101. Gaddis, 'Korea in US Politics', p. 299.
102. Memo of Conversation, 30 June 1950, Dean Acheson Papers, Box 65, HSTL.
103. Donovan, p. 206.
104. Truman, p. 343.
105. State/Defense Mtg, 25 June 1950, *FR 1950*, Vol. 7, p. 143.
106. Memo of Conversation, 26 June 1950, ibid., pp. 178–83.
107. Paige, pp. 230–1.
108. Memo of Conversation, 25 June 1950, *FR 1950*, Vol. 7, pp. 157–61.
109. State Dept Circular, 26 June 1950, ibid., p. 166. NSC Meeting 28 June 1950, Acheson Papers, Box 65, HSTL.
110. Acheson to Kirk, 25 June 1950, *FR 1950*, Vol. 7, p. 148; Acheson to Kirk, 26 June 1950, *FR 1950*, Vol. 7, pp. 176–7.
111. Kirk to Acheson, 29 June 1950, ibid., pp. 229–30.
112. Goulden, p. 99.
113. Donovan, p. 212.
114. GHQ, General Distribution, 30 June 1950, RG 6, FECOM General, Folder 1, Box 4, MACL.
115. Memo of Conversation, 25 June 1950, *FR 1950*, Vol. 7, p. 158.
116. Donovan, p. 211.
117. Truman to O'Mahoney, 28 June 1950, PSF Korean War File, Korean War Data General Folder, Box 243, HSTL.
118. MacArthur, pp. 379–80; Donovan, pp. 215–17.
119. Frank Pace Jnr, Oral History, HSTL.
120. MacArthur, p. 378.
121. Ibid., pp. 372–5.
122. Eben Ayers Diary, 1 July 1950, Ayers Papers, Box 27, HSTL; Stueck, pp. 154, 169.
123. Donovan, p. 223.
124. US Congress, Senate, Foreign Relations and Armed Services Committees, *Military Situation in the Far East*, 82nd Congress, 1st Session, p. 948.
125. Lucius Battle, Oral History, HSTL.

3 Across the Parallel

1. John E. Mueller, *War, Presidents and Public Opinion* (New York, 1973) pp. 48, 198–9; Caridi, pp. 68–70.
2. Donovan, pp. 242–7.
3. Gaddis, p. 114.
4. Donovan, pp. 320, 365.
5. Ibid., pp. 244–7.
6. Memo of Conversation, 14 July 1950, *FR 1950*, Vol. 1, pp. 344–6.
7. Donovan, p. 243.
8. Report to the NSC, 30 September 1950, *FR 1950*, Vol. 1, p. 400.
9. Acheson, p. 421.
10. Samuel F. Wells Jnr, 'The Origins of Massive Retaliation', *Political Science Quarterly* (Spring, 1981) pp. 116–51.
11. Hume Wrong to Lester Pearson, 1 August 1950, Lester B. Pearson Papers, MG 26 N 1, Vol. 35, The Public Archives of Canada, Ottawa.
12. Matthew B. Ridgway, *The Korean War* (New York, 1967) pp. 14–15.
13. Historical Record, June/July 1950, Matthew B. Ridgway Papers (hereafter MRP), Army War College, Carlisle Barracks, Carlisle, Pa.
14. Acheson to Truman, 11 September 1950, *FR 1950*, Vol. 7, pp. 721–2; Truman pp. 346–7, 383.
15. Roger Dingman, 'Truman, Attlee and the Korean War Crisis', *International Studies* (1982/1), International Centre for Economics and Related Disciplines, London School of Economics; Elisabeth Barker, *The British Between the Superpowers 1945–1950* (London, 1983) pp. 206–7.
16. Gaddis and Etzhold, pp. 324–34.
17. Harry R. Borowski, *The Hollow Threat, Strategic Air Power and Containment Before Korea* (Westport, Conn. 1982).
18. Bolte, Memo for Gruenther, 25 July 1950, RG 319, Army Ops, 091 Korea, Box 34A, MMR; Bolte to Collins, 13 July 1950, ibid.; MacArthur's suggested target list included Pyongyang, Wonsan and *all* the other major cities of the North. See Telecon, 24 June 1950, RG-9, Messages-Telecons, Box 113, MACL.
19. Stairs, pp. 71–6.
20. Ibid., pp. 76–8; O'Neill, pp. 85–6; Barker, pp. 208–10.
21. D. C. Watt, 'Britain and the Far East', in Nagai and Iriye, p. 109; Barker, pp. 204–5.
22. Cabinet, 6 July 1950, CAB128/18/CM 43 (50), PRO.
23. Chiefs of Staff, 27 June 1950, DEF4 COS (50) 96, PRO.
24. Stairs, p. 80.
25. BJSM to Ministry of Defence, 16 August 1950, FK1202/10, FO371/84159, PRO.
26. Stairs, p. 71; US/UK Discussions, 20–24 July, *FR 1950*, Vol. 7, pp. 462–5.
27. Cabinet, 25 July 1950, CAB128/18/CM 50 (50), PRO.
28. Tokyo to Ministry of Defence, 14 August 1950, FK1202/9, FO371/84159, PRO; BJSM to Ministry of Defence, 16 August 1950, FK1202/10, FO371/84159, PRO.
29. Ministry of Defence to GHQ FE Land Forces, 17 August 1950,

FK1202/10, FO371/84159, PRO; FO Memo, 14 August 1950, FK1202/6, FO371/84159, PRO.

30. Dingman, pp. 11–12.
31. O'Neill, pp. 75–6; Stairs, pp. 84–6.
32. Minute by Dixon, 19 August 1950, FK1202/18, FO371/84160, PRO.
33. McCormack, p. 131.
34. Jon Halliday, 'Anti-Communism and the Korean War (1950–1953)', in Ralph Miliband, John Saville and Marcel Liebman (eds) *Socialist Register 1984. The Uses Of Anti-Communism* (London 1984) pp. 142–3.
35. James Cameron, *Point of Departure* (London, 1978) p. 110.
36. Halliday, pp. 142–3; John Gittings, 'Talks, Bombs and Guns. Another Look at the Korean War', *Journal of Contemporary Asia*, Vol. 5, No. 2 (1975) pp. 205–17; William F. Dean, *General Dean's Story* (New York, 1954) pp. 84–5. On North Korean atrocities in Seoul see: Drumright to Dept, 29 June 1950, *FR 1950*, Vol. 7, pp. 240–1; Drumright to Dept, 19 October 1950, 695 A.95B26/10–1950, Box 3029, Dept of State Decimal File (hereafter DS), National Archives, Washington DC.
37. Memo by Muccio, 5 May 1951, *FR 1951*, Vol. 7, Pt 1, pp. 416–19.
38. McCormack, pp. 128–9.
39. Alan Winnington, *I Saw the Truth in Korea* (London, 1950) p. 6.
40. Philip Deane, *Captive in Korea* (London, 1953) pp. 80–4.
41. Dean Hess, *Battle Hymn* (New York, 1956) pp. 132–3.
42. Cameron, pp. 132–3.
43. Ibid., pp. 131–2.
44. Ibid.
45. UNCURK, Report on Atrocities, 17 February 1951, FK1681/27, FO371/ 92848, PRO.
46. FO Memo, 25 July 1950, FK1661/2, FO371/84178, PRO.
47. FO Memo, 13 September 1950, FK1661/2, FO371/94178, PRO.
48. Acheson to Muccio, 22 August 1950, *FR 1950*, Vol. 7, pp. 630–1.
49. Marguerite Higgins, *War in Korea* (New York, 1951) pp. 162–6.
50. Stueck, pp. 150–1.
51. Acheson to Douglas, 28 July 1950, *FR 1950*, Vol. 6, pp. 396–8.
52. Bevin to Acheson, 15 July 1950, *FR 1950*, Vol. 7, pp. 396–9; Stairs, pp. 93–7.
53. Barker, pp. 172–3; Watt, pp. 110–11.
54. Memo by Younger, 19 July 1950, US50/25, FO800/517, PRO.
55. COS, 6 July 1950, DEF4 (50) 103.
56. Loy Henderson, Oral History, HSTL; Lord Franks, Oral History, HSTL.
57. Sarvepalli Gopal, *Jawaharlal Nehru. A Biography*, Vol. 2 (London, 1979) pp. 101–3.
58. MOD to Rickett, 21 July 1950, Clement Attlee Papers, Bodleian Library, Oxford.
59. Memo by Bevin, 30 August 1950, CAB129/41 CP50/200, PRO; Cabinet, 4 September 1950, CAB128/18/55 (50), PRO.
60. Barker, pp. 204–5.
61. Stairs, pp. 93–7.
62. Dingman, pp. 8–9.

63. Truman to Acheson, 18 July 1950, Selected Records Relating to the Korean War, Box 6, Department of State, Neutralisation of Formosa 1, HSTL; Acheson to Douglas, 28 July 1950, *FR 1950*, Vol. 6, pp. 396–8.
64. Statement by Truman, 19 July 1950, *FR 1950*, Vol. 7, pp. 383–4.
65. Truman, p. 348.
66. DS to British Embassy, 23 August 1950, *FR 1950*, Vol. 6, pp. 444–6.
67. Truman, p. 355.
68. Memo of Conversation, 24 July 1950, SRRKW, Box 6, Neut. Formosa 1, HSTL; Johnson to Acheson, 29 July 1950, *FR 1950*, Vol. 6, p. 401.
69. Strong to Acheson, 14 July 1950, ibid., p. 375; Acheson to Tapei, 21 July 1950, ibid., p. 385.
70. Acheson to Johnson, 31 July 1950, ibid., 402–4.
71. Stueck, pp. 209–10.
72. Donovan, pp. 259–60; Acheson, p. 422.
73. Acheson, p. 422; 'Command and Staff Visit to Formosa, 31 July–1 August 1950', RG 6, FECOM Box 1, Series 1, General Files A, General Correspondence 2, MACL.
74. Acheson, p. 422; Strong to Acheson, 3 August 1950, *FR 1950*, Vol. 6, pp. 410–11.
75. Sebald to Acheson, 3 August 1950, ibid., p. 415.
76. Strong to Acheson, 3 August 1950, ibid., pp. 411–12.
77. Johnson to MacArthur, 4 August 1950, ibid., p. 423.
78. Memo by Harriman, 20 August 1950, ibid., pp. 427–30.
79. John W. Spanier, *The Truman–MacArthur Controversy and the Korean War* (New York, 1965) pp. 73–7.
80. Donovan, pp. 263–7; Memo of Conversation, 26 August 1950, Acheson Papers, Box 65, HSTL.
81. Truman, pp. 355–6.
82. Eben Ayers Diary, 26 August 1950, Ayers Papers, HSTL.
83. Truman, p. 356; Donovan, p. 365.
84. Memos by Marchant, 28 and 29 August 1950, *FR 1950*, Vol. 6, pp. 464–8; Memo by Bevin, 31 August 1950, CAB 129/41 CP(50) 194, PRO; Memo by Matthews, 31 August 1950, *FR 1950*, Vol. 6, 473–6.
85. Acheson to embassy, 14 August 1950, ibid., p. 438.
86. Johnson to Acheson, 11 September 1950, SRRKW, Neutrality of Formosa 3, Box 6, HSTL; Acheson to Johnson, 13 September 1950, Ibid.
87. Stueck, pp. 207–8.
88. MacArthur, pp. 394–9.
89. Report by NSC to the President, 9 September 1950, *FR 1950*, Vol. 7, 712–21.
90. James F. Schnabel and Robert J. Watson, *The Joint Chiefs of Staff and National Policy*, Vol. 3, *The Korean War*, Pt 1, p. 230; Microfilm, MMR.
91. Buhite, pp. 233–4.
92. Acheson, p. 445.
93. Caridi, pp. 84–5.
94. Collins, p. 144.
95. Stueck, p. 219; 'Position Paper for USUN, 19 September 1950, *FR 1950*, Vol. 7, pp. 736–7.
96. Marshall to MacArthur, 29 September 1950, ibid., p. 826.

97. Memo by Bancroft, 23 September 1950, ibid., pp. 759–62; Minutes of 6th mtg of US delegation to UN, 25 September 1950, *FR 1950*, Vol. 7, pp. 768–9; Spanier, pp. 101–2.
98. Goulden, p. 239.
99. Dingman, p. 12.
100. Bevin to Attlee, 25 September 1950, UN/50/11, FO800/511, PRO.
101. Attlee to Bevin, 21 September 1950, UN/50/6, FO800/511, PRO.
102. Stairs, pp. 121–2; Minutes of 6th mtg of UN Delegation to UN, 25 September 1950, *FR 1950*, Vol. 7, pp. 768–9.
103. Gopal, pp. 105–6.
104. Memo by Marchant, 27 September 1950, *FR 1950*, Vol. 7, pp. 793–4; Rusk to Webb, 28 September 1950, ibid., pp. 797–8.
105. Webb to Henderson, 28 September 1950, ibid., pp. 819–21.
106. Memo by Battle, 28 September 1950, ibid., pp. 811–12.
107. Spanier, pp. 97–8.
108. Ibid., pp. 86–7.
109. Holmes to Acheson, 3 October 1950, *FR 1950*, Vol. 7, p. 839.
110. Truman, p. 362.
111. UKHC to Commonwealth Office, 9 October 1950, FK1022/422, FO371/84101, PRO.
112. Memo by Allison, 4 October 1950, *FR 1950*, Vol. 7, pp. 868–9.
113. Truman, p. 362.
114. Joint Logistic Plan Committee, 1 July 1950, JLPC 460/D, RG 218, Box 25, MMR.
115. Bevin to Foreign Office, 4 October 1950, FE50/38 FO800/462, PRO; COS, 3 October 1950, DEF4 COS(50)160, PRO; COS, 4 October 1950, DEF4 COS(50)161, PRO.
116. Stairs, p. 124.
117. Memo by Allison, 4 October 1950, *FR 1950*, Vol. 7, pp. 868–9.
118. COS, 5 October 1950, DEF4 COS(50)162, PRO.
119. Stairs, pp. 124–5.
120. David Rees, *Korea: The Limited War* (London, 1964) p. 100.
121. Cabinet, 9 October 1950, CAB128/18/CM63(50)67, PRO.
122. Stairs, pp. 124–5.
123. Dingman, p. 12.
124. *The Times*, 5 October, 1950.
125. Donovan, p. 276.
126. Report by NSC, 9 September 1950, *FR 1950*, Vol. 7, p. 720.

4   Disaster

1. Acheson, p. 456.
2. Donovan, p. 287.
3. Ibid., pp. 284–5.
4. Substance of Statements made at Wake Island Conference, 15 October 1950, *FR 1950*, Vol. 7, pp. 948–62; Major-General Charles A. Willoughby and John Chamberlain, *MacArthur 1941–1951 Victory in the Pacific* (London, 1956) pp. 360–1.

5. CIA Memorandum, 12 October 1950, *FR 1950*, Vol. 7, pp. 933–4.
6. Stueck, pp. 236–7.
7. MacArthur, p. 415.
8. Acheson, p. 462.
9. Ibid.
10. Stueck, pp. 219–20.
11. Ibid., p. 239.
12. Collins, p. 180.
13. Donovan, pp. 298–9.
14. Acheson, pp. 454–5.
15. Spanier, pp. 90–1.
16. Civil Affairs Directive, 28 October 1950, *FR 1950*. Vol. 7, pp. 1007–10.
17. Peter Farrar, 'Britain's Proposal for a Buffer Zone South of the Yalu in November 1950: Was it a Neglected Opportunity to End the Fighting in Korea?', *Journal of Contemporary History* 18 (1982) p. 331.
18. US Department of the Army, *The United States Army in the Korean War*, Vol. 1, *South to the Naktong, North to the Yalu*, Roy E. Appleman (Washington DC, 1961) p. 699.
19. *The Times*, 5 October 1950; Collins to MacArthur, 27 October 1950, RG 319, Chief of Staff, 091 Korea.
20. *The Times*, 2, 3, 5, 9 October 1950; Drumwright to Department, 19 October 1950, 695A, 95 B26/10–1950, DS; UNCURK Report, February 1951, FK1661/27, FO371/42848, PRO.
21. Henderson, p. 167; See also *Kim Il Sung. Short Biography* (Pyongyang, 1973) p. 20; Halliday, p. 145; René Cutforth, *Korean Reporter* (London, 1952) pp. 38–9, 50–2.
22. 21st Infantry, Report on Attached ROKs, 26 October 1950, 24th Infantry Division, Message File, Box 3513, Army Command Reports, RG 319, Federal Records Center (here after FRC), Suitland, Maryland.
23. McCormack, p. 116.
24. Acheson to Seoul, 8 November 1950, 795B.00/11–850, DS.
25. *The Times*, 9 October 1950.
26. Acheson to Seoul, 8 November 1950, 795B.00/11–850, DS.
27. Cameron, pp. 143–5.
28. Halliday, p. 146.
29. FO to Korea, 2 November 1950, FK1661/15, FO371/94178, PRO; Jebb to FO, 15 November 1950, FK1661/28, FO371/84179, PRO.
30. Memo by Rusk, 28 October 1950, *FR 1950*, Vol. 7, pp. 1004–5.
31. MacArthur to Truman, 16 October 1950, ibid., pp. 963–4; O'Neill, p. 128.
32. O'Neill, p. 128
33. Memo by Rusk, 28 October 1950, *FR 1950*, Vol. 7, pp. 1004–5.
34. Substance of Statements at Wake, ibid., p. 960.
35. Memo by Emmons, 16 October 1950, ibid., pp. 970–2.
36. Drumright to Acheson, 16 October 1950, ibid., p. 964; Memo by Emmons, 16 October 1950, ibid., pp. 970–2.
37. Muccio to Acheson, 20 October 1950, ibid., pp. 984–6; Muccio to Johnson, 5 November 1950, 795G.00/11–550, DS; Emmons to Johnson, 27 December 1950, 795a.00/11–1950, DS.

38. O'Neill, p. 134.
39. CINCFE to Hong Kong, 9 October 1950, RG 9, Outgoing Misc June–Oct 1950, Box 51, MacL; G-2 SCAP to Chief of Staff, 22 February 1951, RG 6, FECOM General Files, Folder 11 Corr-Gen Jan–Apr, Box 1, MACL.
40. CINCFE to 8th Army and X Corps, RG 9, War Out, Misc–16–31 Oct 1950, Box 50, MACL.
41. John Costello, *The Pacific War* (London, 1985); Richard Lewin, *The Other Ultra. Codes, Ciphers & the Defeat of Japan* (London, 1982); F. W. Winterbotham, *The Ultra Secret* (London, 1974); Edward Van Der Rhoer, *Deadly Magic* (New York, 1978).
42. JCS to CINCFE, 20 March 1951, RG 9, Messages JCS, 30 June 50–5 April 51, Box 43, MACL.
43. US Department of the Army, *Handbook on the Chinese Communist Army*, Dept of the Army Pamphlet 30–51, September 1952.
44. S. L. A. Marshall, *The River & The Gauntlet* (New York, 1953) pp. 1–7.
45. Drumright to Acheson, 29 October 1950, *FR 1950*, Vol. 7, p. 1014.
46. Rees, pp. 124–8.
47. Stueck, p. 240.
48. Farrar, pp. 323–3; COS, 13 November 1950, DEF4/37 COS(50)178, PRO; COS, 15 November 1950, DEF4/37 COS(50)180, PRO; COS, 20 November 1950, DEF4/37 COS(50)182, PRO; Cabinet, 13 November 1950, CAB128/18/CM73(50)139–141, PRO; Bevin to Franks, 16 November 1950, FK1023/1084, FO371/84114, PRO.
49. Bevin to Franks, 16 November 1950, ibid.
50. Collins, pp. 205–6; JCS1776/156, 8 November 1950, RG 319, Army Ops, 091 Korea, Box 33A, MMR.
51. Memo for the President, 10 November 1950, PSF Subject File NSC Meetings, Box 220, HSTL; Truman, pp. 378–80.
52. Acheson to USUN, 13 November 1950, *FR 1950*, Vol. 7, pp. 1143–5.
53. Memo by Rusk, 13 November 1950, ibid., pp. 1141–2; Editorial Note, 15 November 1950, ibid., p. 1158; Memo by Matthews, 17 November 1950, 795.00/11–1750, DS.
54. Perkins to Chubb, 9 October 1950, *FR 1950*, Vol. 7, pp. 916–17. MacArthur, however, rejected any suggestion of a public statement; see Acheson to Muccio, 21 October 1950, ibid., p. 987; MacArthur to JCS, 22 October 1950, ibid., pp. 991–2.
55. Truman, pp. 378–80; Acheson, p. 467.
56. MacArthur to JCS, 9 November 1950, *FR 1950*, Vol. 7, pp. 1107–9; Truman, p. 379.
57. Stueck, p. 250.
58. Ibid., p. 246. Franks to FO, 14 November 1950, FK1023/99, FO371/84113, PRO.
59. Collins, pp. 199–201; Truman, pp. 374–6.
60. Memo by Acheson, 10 October 1950, *FR 1950*, Vol. 7, p. 922.
61. Collins, pp. 199–201; Acheson, pp. 463–6; Truman, pp. 374–6.
62. Stueck, p. 257.
63. See Marshall's statement in Memo by Jessup, 21 November 1950, *FR 1950*, Vol. 7, pp. 1204–8.

64. Acheson to Douglas, 13 November 1950, ibid., pp. 1144–45.
65. COS, 15 November 1950, DEF4/37 COS(50)180, PRO; Bevin to Franks, 17 November 1950, *FR 1950*, Vol. 7, pp. 1172–5.
66. Stueck, p. 248.
67. Acheson, p. 466.
68. Memo by Muccio, 17 November 1950, *FR 1950*, Vol. 7, pp. 1175–6.
69. Franks to FO, 10 November 1950, FK1022/85, FO371/84113, PRO.
70. Franks to FO, 24 November 1950, FK1023/165, FO371/84118, PRO.
71. Jebb to FO, 22 November 1950, FK1023/152, FO371/84117, PRO.
72. Farrar, pp. 345–6.
73. Collins to MacArthur, 24 November 1950, *FR 1950*, Vol. 7, pp. 1222–4.
74. Franks to FO, 23 November 1950, FK1023/161, FO371/84118, PRO.
75. MacArthur to JCS, 25 November 1950, *FR 1950*, Vol. 7, pp. 1231–3.
76. Farrar, p. 345.
77. Ibid., p. 347.
78. Acheson, p. 468.
79. Farrar, pp. 346–7; Hutchinson to Bevin, 22 November 1950, FK1023/150, FO371/84117, PRO.
80. MacArthur, pp. 426–7.
81. Ibid.
82. Manchester, pp. 596–9; Michael Straight, *After Long Silence* (London, 1983) p. 250. For a full account of this spy ring see, Andrew Boyle *The Climate of Treason* (London, 1980).
83. Manchester, pp. 596–9.
84. Whiting, pp. 134–6.
85. Melvin B. Vorhees, *Korean Tales* (London, 1953) pp. 104–5.
86. MacArthur to JCS, 28 November 1950, *FR 1950*, Vol. 7, pp. 1237–8.
87. Manchester, pp. 616–17.
88. Collins, Memo for JCS, 8 December 1950, JCS1176/169, RG 218, Box 29, MMR.
89. CIA memo, 2 December 1950, *FR 1950*, Vol. 7, pp. 1308–10; Memo by Jessup, 28 November 1950, ibid., pp. 1242–9; Acheson, pp. 471–2.
90. Memo by Jessup, 3 December 1950, *FR 1950*, Vol. 7, pp. 1323–34; Truman, pp. 387–8.
91. Ibid., p. 388.
92. Ibid., p. 428–9.
93. Acheson, p. 471.
94. Memo by Jessup, 1 December 1950, *FR 1950*, Vol. 7, pp. 1276–81.
95. Bolte to Collins, 13 July, 1950, RG 319, Army Ops, 091 Korea, Box 34A, MMR; Bolte, Memo for Gruenther, 25 July 1950, ibid, MMR.
96. Memo by Collins, 20 November 1950, RG 218, JCS2173, Box 29, MMR.
97. Memo for Joint Strategic Survey Committee, 28 November 1950, RG 218, 383.21 Korea (3–19–45), Box 29, MMR.
98. Goulden, pp. 396–7; Gregg Herken, *The Winning Weapon* (New York, 1980) pp. 332–3.
99. Acheson, pp. 471–2; Donovan, pp. 315–16.
100. Truman, 388.
101. Acheson, 471.
102. NSC Meeting, 28 November 1950, PSF–Attlee Mtgs, Dec. 1950, Box

171, HSTL; Memo by Jessup, 1 December 1950, *FR 1950*, Vol. 7, pp. 1276–81.

103. MacArthur to JCS, 3 December 1950, ibid., pp. 1320–2.
104. Memo by Jessup, 3 December 1950, ibid., pp. 1325–34; First mtg of President Truman and Prime Minister Attlee, 4 December 1950, ibid., pp. 1361–74; Acheson, p. 474.
105. Acheson, p. 482.
106. Memo by Jessup, 3 December 1950, *FR 1950*, Vol. 7, pp. 1325–34.
107. Ibid.
108. Truman/Attlee Mtg, 4 December 1950, ibid., pp. 1361–74; Cabinet, 12 December 1950, CAB128/18/CM84(50) PRO.
109. Truman/Attlee Mtg, 5 December 1950, *FR 1950*, Vol. 7, pp. 1392–1408.
110. Cabinet, 29 November 1950, CAB128/18CM79(50), PRO; COS, 20 November 1950, DEF4/37 COS(50)182, PRO; COS, 30 November 1950, DEF4/37COS(50)189, PRO; COS, 1 December 1950, DEF4/37 COS(50)191, PRO; Holmes to Acheson, 3 December 1950, *FR 1950*, Vol. 3, 1698–1703.
111. Margaret Gowing, *Independence and Deterrence. Britain and Atomic Energy 1945–52*, Vol. 1, *Policy Making* (London, 1974), pp. 308–10.
112. Ibid., pp. 310–13; John Baylis, *Anglo-American Defence Relations* (London, 1984), pp. 39–41.
113. FO Memo, 2 December 1950, FE58/47, FO800/462, PRO.
114. Cabinet, 29 November 1950, CAB129/18/CM79(50), PRO.
115. Lester Pearson, *Memoirs*, Vol. 2, *The International Years* (London, 1974) pp. 180–3.
116. Truman, pp. 411–13.
117. Truman/Attlee, 4 December 1950, *FR 1950*, Vol. 7, pp. 1361–74; Truman Attlee, 5 December 1950, ibid., pp. 1392–1408; British Record, 5 December 1950, PSF Conferences, Dec. 1950–2, Truman–Attlee, Box 164, HSTL.
118. Truman/Attlee, 4 December 1950, *FR 1950*, Vol. 7, 1361–4; Truman/ Attlee, 7 December 1950, ibid., pp. 1449–61.
119. Truman/Attlee, 7 December 1950, *FR 1950*, Vol. 7, p. 1451.
120. Ibid.
121. Meeting with Congressional Leaders, 1 December 1950, PSF, Subject File Foreign Affairs, Attlee mtg, Dec 1950, Box 171, HSTL.
122. Attlee exaggerated his achievement on his return – see Cabinet, 12 December 1950, CAB128/18/CM85(50), PRO.
123. Acheson, pp. 480–1.
124. Ibid., p. 484.
125. Gowing, pp. 314–19; Baylis, p. 41.
126. Memo by Battle, 7 December 1950, *FR 1950*, Vol. 7, pp. 1430–2.
127. Donovan, p. 320.

5   A Crisis of Confidence

1. Donovan, p. 323.
2. Ibid., pp. 323–4; William J. Sebald, *With MacArthur in Japan* (London, 1965) pp. 260–2.

3. US Joint Chiefs of Staff, *The History of the Joint Chiefs of Staff*, Vol. 4, *The Joint Chiefs of Staff and National Policy*, Walter S. Poole. Microfilm, MMR.
4. Acheson, pp. 512–13.
5. Caridi, pp. 109–40; Gaddis, pp. 118–21.
6. Donovan, pp. 322–3.
7. Ibid.
8. Caridi, p. 127.
9. Ibid., 116–23.
10. Report by Malcolm MacDonald, 26 November 1953, FC10345/13, FO371/105221, PRO.
11. Acheson to Douglas, 5 January 1951, *FR 1951*, Vol. 7, Pt 1, pp. 27–8.
12. NSC Mtg, 28 November 1950, PSF Attlee Mtgs, Box 171, HSTL.
13. Acheson, p. 513.
14. Stairs, p. 158.
15. Ibid., pp. 160–1.
16. Ibid.
17. O'Neill, p. 174.
18. Ibid., pp. 174–6.
19. Stairs, pp. 162–3.
20. Acheson, p. 513.
21. Ibid.
22. Duff to Collins, 15 January 1951, RG 319, Chief of Staff, 091 Korea, MMR.
23. Stairs, pp. 164–5.
24. Ibid., pp. 165–6; Acheson to Douglas, 24 January 1951, *FR 1951*, Vol. 7, Pt 1, pp. 123–4.
25. Stairs, p. 165; Caridi, pp. 121–5.
26. Stairs, pp. 166–8.
27. O'Neill, pp. 181–2.
28. COS, 8 January 1951, FK1022/23, FO371/92756, PRO; Jebb to FO, 1 January 1951, FK1022/5, FO371/92756, PRO; COS, 12 January 1951, DEF4/39COS(51)10.
29. Attlee to Truman, 8 January 1951, *FR 1951*, Vol. 7, Pt 1, pp. 37–8; Truman to Attlee, 9 January 1951, ibid., pp. 39–40.
30. Cabinet, 29 January 1951, CAB128/19(51) CM10, PRO; Gifford to Acheson, 29 January 1951, 795.00/1–2591, DS.
31. Cabinet, 18 January 1951, CAB128/19(51) CM4, PRO.
32. Muccio to Acheson, 20 December 1950, *FR 1950*, Vol. 7, pp. 1579–81; Muccio to Acheson, 21 December 1950, ibid., pp. 1586–7.
33. FO Memo, 29 January 1951, FK1661/21, FO371/92857, PRO.
34. US Memo, 20 December 1950, FK1661/4, FO371/92847, PRO.
35. Webb to Muccio, 18 December 1950, *FR 1950*, Vol. 7, 1567; Webb to Muccio, 19 December 1950, 795.00/12–1950, DS.
36. Muccio to Acheson, 20 December 1950, *FR 1950*, Vol. 7, 1579–81.
37. UNCURK Report, 17 February 1951, FK1661/27, FO371/42848, PRO.
38. 'Dalton Diary', 31 December 1950, Dalton Papers, LSE.
39. Rickett to Bevin, 23 January 1951, Attlee Papers, January 1951, Bodleian Library, Oxford.

40. Bevin to Attlee, 12 January 1951, US/51/5, FO800/517, PRO.
41. Strachey to Bevin, 2 January 1951, US51/1, FO800/517, PRO.
42. Memo by Younger, 1 January 1951, FK1022/66, FO371/92756, PRO.
43. Cabinet, 25 January 1951, CAB128/19(51)CM8, PRO.
44. Phillip M. Williams, *Hugh Gaitskell* (London, 1979) pp. 242–9.
45. Matthew T. Connelly, Notes on Cabinet Mtgs, 26 January 1951, Post Presidential File, Set 1, Box 1, Matthew T. Connelly Papers, HSTL.
46. US Memo, 22 January 1951, FK1022/27, FO371/92756, PEO; Franks to FO, 18 January 1951, FK1023/24, FO371/92762, PRO.
47. Acheson to Douglas, 27 January 1951, *FR 1951*, Vol. 7, Pt 1, pp. 142–3.
48. Stairs, pp. 174–5; Cabinet, 29 January 1951, CAB128/19(51)CM10, PRO.
49. John Edward Wiltz, 'The MacArthur Hearings of 1951: The Secret Testimony', *Military Affairs* (December 1975) p. 170.
50. Truman, pp. 432–3.
51. JCS to MacArthur, 29 December 1950, *FR 1950*, Vol. 7, pp. 1625–6.
52. MacArthur to JCS, 30 December 1950, ibid., pp. 1630–3; JCS to MacArthur, 29 December 1950, ibid, pp. 1625–6; Acheson, pp. 514–15.
53. MacArthur to JCS, 30 December 1950, *FR 1950*, Vol. 7, 1630–3.
54. JCS to MacArthur, 9 January 1951, *FR 1951*, Vol. 7, Pt 1, pp. 41–3; MacArthur to JCS, 10 January 1951, ibid., pp. 55–6.
55. Donovan, pp. 346–7.
56. Truman, pp. 435–6.
57. JCS to MacArthur, 12 January 1951, *FR 1951*, Vol. 7, Pt 1, 69.
58. Memo by Jessup, 12 January 1951, ibid., pp. 68–70. Memo by Rusk, 12 January 1951, ibid., pp. 66–7.
59. Truman, pp. 435–6.
60. Manchester, p. 625.
61. JCS to Marshall, 12 January 1951, *FR 1951*, Vol. 7, Pt 1, pp. 71–2.
62. Wiltz, p. 170; Acheson, p. 516.
63. Wiltz, p. 170.
64. Ibid.
65. Manchester, p. 625; Donovan, pp. 348–9.
66. Acheson, p. 512.
67. Schnabel and Watson, pp. 437–8.
68. Acheson, p. 517.
69. Schnabel and Watson, pp. 437–8.
70. Acheson to USUN, 17 February 1951, *FR 1951*, Vol. 7, Pt 1, pp. 178–80.
71. Collins, pp. 263–7.
72. Goulden, p. 460; Acheson, p. 517.
73. Marshall to Acheson, 1 March 1951, *FR 1951*, Vol. 7, Pt 1, pp. 202–6.
74. Memo by Barnes, 20 February 1951, 795.00/2–2051, DS.
75. Goulden, p. 462.
76. JCS to Ridgway, 31 May 1951, *FR 1951*, Vol. 7, Pt 1, pp. 487–93.
77. Acheson to USUN, 3 April 1951, ibid.
78. Truman, pp. 339–40.
79. Acheson, p. 518; Donovan, p. 349.
80. MacArthur, pp. 441–2.
81. Truman, p. 442; Acheson, pp. 518–19.

82. MacArthur, pp. 440–3; Manchester, p. 636.
83. Manchester, p. 637.
84. Ibid., p. 617.
85. Minute by Scott, 5 March 1951, FK1094/7, FO371/92812, PRO; Jebb to FO, 24 March 1951, FK1096/7, FO371/92813, PRO.
86. Cabinet, 22 March 1951, CAB128/19(51)CM22, PRO; FO Memo, 3 April 1951, CAB129/45CP(51)100, PRO; Stairs, pp. 220–1.
87. Cabinet, 22 March 1951, CAB128/19(51)CM22, PRO.
88. Morrison to Franks, 24 March 1951, FK1096/8, FO371/92813, PRO.
89. Stairs, pp. 226–7.
90. Franks to FO, 24 March 1951, FK1096/9, FO371/92813, PRO.
91. Franks to FO, 6 April 1951, FK1022/37, FO371/92757, PRO; Memo by Nitze, 6 April 1951, *FR 1951*, Vol. 7, Pt 1, pp. 307–9.
92. Morrison to Franks, 7 April 1951, FK1022/37, FO371/92757, PRO; Morrison to Franks, 9 April 1951, ibid. COS, 9 April 1951, FK1022/42, FO371/95758, PRO.
93. Minute by Scott, 5 April 1951, FK1022/36, FO371/92757, PRO; COS, 6 April 1951, DEF4/41COS(51)59, PRO.
94. COS, 30 March 1951, DEF4/41COS(51)55, PRO.
95. Memo by Rusk, 5 April 1951, *FR 1951*, Vol. 7, Pt 1, pp. 296–8; Morrison to Franks, 9 April 1951, FK1022/37, FO371/92757, PRO.
96. Truman, pp. 443–4.
97. Memo of Conversation, 24 March 1951, Acheson Papers, Box 66, HSTL.
98. Ibid.
99. Truman, p. 443.
100. Acheson, pp. 519–20; Truman, pp. 445–6.
101. Truman, p. 447.
102. 'Truman Diary', 5 April 1951, PSF Diaries, Box 278, HSTL.
103. Truman, p. 443–4.
104. Acheson, p. 521.
105. Ibid.
106. Bradley, Memo for the record, 25 April 1951, 795.00/4–551, DS; Schnabel and Watson, p. 539.
107. Acheson, pp. 521–2.
108. Bradley, Memo for the record, 25 April 1951, 795.00/4–551, DS.
109. Acheson, p. 522.
110. Ibid., pp. 522–3.
111. Donovan, p. 356.
112. Merle Miller, *Plain Speaking. Conversations With Harry S. Truman* (London, 1974) p. 305

6 Attrition

1. Donovan, p. 358.
2. Caridi, pp. 148–75.
3. Ibid., pp. 146–7.
4. Ibid., pp. 163–4.
5. Stairs, pp. 230–1.
6. Franks to Morrison, 13 April 1951, AU1015/9, FO371/90907.

7. US Embassy, 13 April 1951, Weeka 15 England, RG 84, FRC.
8. Acheson, p. 523.
9. Caridi, p. 154.
10. Ibid., p. 175.
11. Rees, pp. 264–75; Goulden, pp. 514–31.
12. Goulden, pp. 514–31.
13. Ibid., pp. 515–16.
14. JCS to MacArthur, 9 January 1951, *FR 1951*, Vol. 7, Pt 1, pp. 41–3; Truman, 435–6.
15. Memo by Rusk, 19 December 1950, *FR 1950*, Vol. 7, 1770–3; Wiltz, p. 170.
16. John E. Mueller, *War, Presidents and Public Opinion* (London, 1973) p. 103.
17. Memo by Alexander, 12 April 1951, RG233, SecDef CD092 Korea 1951, Box 232, MMR.
18. US Congress, Senate, Foreign Relations & Armed Services Committees, *Military Situation in the Far East*, 82nd Congress, 1st session, 3–31st May 1951, pp. 729–1182. Hereafter *Military Situation*.
19. Ibid., pp. 1393–9, 1379–90.
20. Wiltz, p. 171.
21. Ibid.
22. Ibid., p. 169.
23. Marshall to Acheson, 19 January 1951, JSPC853/81/D, RG 218, Box 29, MMR.
24. *Military Situation*, pp. 729–1182; Wiltz, p. 168.
25. Ridgway to JCS, 30 May 1951, CCS383.21 Korea (3–19–45) Sec 49, RG 218, Box 32, MMR; *Military Situation*, pp. 321–724.
26. *Military Situation*, pp. 1782–3.
27. Connelly, 14 May 1951, Notes on Cabinet Mtgs – Post Presidential File, Box 1, HSTL. See also Truman, pp. 451–2.
28. Connelly, 20 April 1951, HSTL.
29. *Military Situation*, pp. 321–724; Acheson, p. 531.
30. *Military Situation*, p. 1385.
31. NSC48/5, 17 May 1951, *FR 1951*, Vol. 6, Prt 1, pp. 33–63.
32. US Dept of the Army, *The United States Army in the Korean War*, Vol. 3, *Truce Tent and Fighting Front*, Walter G. Hermes (Washington DC, 1962) pp. 62–7.
33. Muccio to Acheson, 6 May 1951, *FR 1951*, Part 1, Vol. 7, pp. 419–20.
34. Henderson, pp. 352–3.
35. NSC48/5, 17 May 1951, *FR 1951*, Vol. 6, Part 1, pp. 33–63; Bradley to Marshall, 16 March 1951, 'Courses of Action Relative to Communist China & Korea–Anti-Communist Chinese', RG 233, SecDefCD098 (Korea) 1951, Box 232, MMR.
36. Ibid.; *The Times*, 15 May 1951.
37. NSC48/5, 17 May 1951.
38. Gaddis, p. 123.
39. JCS, Memo for SecDef, 15 May 1951, RG 330, SecDef CDO92 (China) 1951, Box 228, MMR.
40. NSC48/5, 17 May 1951.

41. US Congress, House of Representatives, Foreign Relations Committee, Sub-Committee on Far East, *US Policy in the Far East*, Pt 1 (Washington DC, 1980) pp. 128–9.
42. Wrong to Pearson, 16 February 1951, Lester Pearson Papers, HG26N1, Vol. 10, File Korea, Canadian Policy 1950–51, CNA.
43. Ibid.
44. NSC48/5, 17 May 1951; Poole, pp. 403–4.
45. FO Minute, 2 January 1952, FC1015/3, FO371/99231, PRO.
46. Wrong to Pearson, 16 February 1951.
47. Rees, p. 204; Cohen, p. 216.
48. Wrong to Pearson, 16 February 1951.
49. Franks to FO, 21 May 1951, FC10345/4, FO371/92246, PRO; Franks to FO, 23 May 1951, FK10345/5, FO371/92246, PRO.
50. FO minute on FK10345/5, FO371/92246 PRO.
51. Michael Foot, *Aneurin Bevan* (London, 1973) pp. 312–40; Kenneth Harris, *Attlee* (London, 1982) pp. 473–80; Rees, p. 230–42.
52. 'Dalton Diary', 6 April 1951.
53. Ibid;, 11 April 1951.
54. British Embassy to Dept of State, 10 April 1951, *FR 1951*, Vol. 7, Pt 1, pp. 328–9. Morrison to Acheson, 17 April 1951, ibid., pp. 351–2.
55. Memo by Emmons, 17 April 1951, ibid., pp. 344–51.
56. Johnson to Rusk, 10 April 1951, ibid., pp. 329–30; Memo by Rusk, 14 April 1951, ibid., pp. 346–7.
57. FO Memo, 20 March 1951, CAB129/45 CP(51), PRO; Memo by Acheson, 2 April 1951, Acheson Papers, Box 66, HSTL.
58. Franks to Morrison, 13 April 1951, FK1022/39, FO 371/92757, PRO; Morrison to Franks, 30 April 1951, FK1022/48, FO371/95758, PRO; Memo by Nitze, 12 April 1951, *FR 1951*, Vol. 7, Pt 1, pp. 338–44; State/JCS Mtg, 18 April 1951, ibid., pp. 353–62.
59. FO Memo, 3 April 1951, CAB129/45 CP(51), PRO; Morrison to Harvey, 30 March 1951, FK1086/15, FO371/92813.
60. Memo by Acheson, 2 April 1951, Acheson Papers, Box 66, HSTL.
61. Bradley, Memo for Marshall, 28 March 1951, RG 330, SecDef CDO92 (Russia) 1951, Box 235, MMR.
62. Memo by Acheson, 2 April 1951, Acheson Papers, Box 66, HSTL.
63. Acheson to Embassy, 17 April 1951, *FR 1951*, Vol. 7, Pt 1, pp. 352–3.
64. O'Neill, pp. 218–19.
65. 'Current State of Relations between Canada & the US', 14 May 1951, Hume Wrong Papers, Vol 8, File 43, MG30 E101, CNA.
66. Acheson to Morrison, 30 April 1951, *FR 1951*, Vol. 7, Pt 1, pp. 390–4.
67. *The Times*, 9 April 1951.
68. FO memo, 3 May 1951, CAB129/45 CP(51), PRO.
69. Acheson, pp. 505–7.
70. Cabinet, 7 May 1951, CAB128/19(51) CM34, PRO; Morrison to Acheson, 10 May 1951, *FR 1951*, Vol. 7, Pt 1, pp. 427–31.
71. O'Neill, pp. 218–19.
72. Morrison to Acheson, 10 May 1951, *FR 1951*, Vol. 7, Pt 1, pp. 427–31.
73. Memo by Tomlinson, 29 September 1951, FK1022/70, FO371/92758, PRO.

74. Cabinet, 7 May 1951, CAB128/19(51)CM34, PRO; *Economist*, 19 May 1951, p. 1148.
75. Morrison to Acheson, 10 May 1951, *FR 1951*, Vol. 7, Pt 1, pp. 427–31.
76. Evan Luard, *Britain & China* (London, 1962) pp. 205–6.
77. Morrison to Acheson, 10 May 1951, *FR 1951*, Vol. 7, Pt 1, pp. 427–31.
78. Luard, pp. 206–7.
79. Ibid., pp. 202–3.
80. FO Memo, 9 June 1951, CAB129/46 CP51, PRO; FO Memo, 19 June 1951, CAB129/46 CP51, PRO.
81. *Economist*, 19 May 1951, p. 1148.
82. Acheson, p. 532; Memo of Conversation, 6 and 7 January 1951, 12 and 13 January 1951, *FR 1951*, Vol. 7, Prt 2, 1476–1503. Memo by Marshall, 30 January 1951, ibid., pp. 1533–5.
83. Memo by Marshall, 9 May 1951, ibid., pp. 1655–64.
84. Memo of conversation, 3 May 1951, ibid., Pt 1, pp. 401–10.
85. Davies to Nitze, 8 May 1951, ibid., pp. 421–2.
86. Memo by Kennan, 31 May 1951, ibid., pp. 483–6.
87. Memo by Kennan, 5 June 1951, ibid., pp. 507–11.
88. Editorial Note, ibid., pp. 547.
89. Acheson, p. 533.
90. Ibid., pp. 533–4.
91. Ibid.
92. Stairs, 237.
93. Broadcast by Ridgway, 29 June 1951, *FR 1951*, Vol. 7, Pt 1, 587.
94. Memo by Heidemann, 29 June, 1951, *FR 1951*, ibid., pp. 592–5.
95. Memo by Lockhart, 3 July 1951, ibid., pp. 613–18.
96. Muccio to Acheson, 30 June 1951, ibid., pp. 604–5; Simmons, pp. 198–99.
97. Simmons, p. 199.
98. Memo by Kennan, 5 June 1951, *FR 1951*, Vol. 7, Pt 1, pp. 507–11.
99. Memo by Barbour, 16 March 1951, ibid., pp. 235–8.
100. Memo by Kennan, 5 June 1951, ibid., pp. 507–11.
101. Simmons, pp. 198–9.
102. Bernard Brodie, *War and Politics* (New York, 1973), pp. 95–7.
103. Ridgway to JCS, 30 May 1951, CCS 383.21 Korea (3–19–45) Sec 49, RG 218, Box 32, MMR; State/JCS Mtg, 15 March 1951, *FR 1951*, Vol. 7, Pt 1, pp. 232–4.
104. Matthew B. Ridgway, *Soldier: the Memoirs of Matthew B. Ridgway* (New York, 1956) pp. 219–20.

7 Negotiating while Fighting

1. Ridgway to JCS, 7 August 1951, *FR 1951*, Vol. 7, Pt 1, pp. 785–9. Kenneth T. Young, *Negotiating with the Chinese Communists* (New York, 1968) pp. 349–50.
2. Austen to Hickerson, 23 May 1951, *FR 1951*, Vol. 7, Pt 1, pp. 447–8; Memo by Bohlen, 4 October 1951, ibid., pp. 990–4; Memo for Truman, 10 December 1951, ibid., pp. 1290–6.
3. NSC 118, 20 December 1951, PSF 216, HSTL.

4. Joint Intelligence Committee, 'Aims of Communists in Peace Negotiations', 15 August 1951, CCS383. 21 Korea (3–19–45) Sec 58, 218, Box 33, MMR.
5. Ridgway to JCS, 4 July 1951, CCS 383. 21 Korea (3–19–41), Sec 51, RG 218, Box 32, MMR.
6. Connelly, Notes on Cabinet Mtgs, 6 July 1951, Post Presidential File, Box 1, HSTL; Memo of Conversation, 6 July 1951, Acheson Papers, Box 66, HSTL.
7. *Economist*, 28 July 1951, p. 200.
8. JCS to Ridgway, 30 June 1951, *FR 1951*, Vol. 7, Pt 1, pp. 598–600.
9. JCS to Ridgway, 9 July 1951, ibid., p. 640.
10. Acheson to Morrison, 19 July 1951, ibid., pp. 698–701; Acheson, pp. 536–7.
11. JCS to Ridgway, 30 June 1951, *FR 1951*, Vol. 7, Pt 1, pp. 598–600.
12. C. Turner Joy, *How Communists Negotiate* (New York, 1955) pp. 18–20.
13. Ibid., pp. 4–6.
14. Acheson, p. 535.
15. Rees, pp. 290–1.
16. Acheson, p. 535.
17. Ibid.
18. Goulden, p. 565.
19. Acheson, p. 535.
20. Ridgway to JCS, 20 July 1951, *FR 1951*, Vol. 7, Pt 1, pp. 711–13.
21. JCS to Ridgway, 21 July 1951, ibid., pp. 716–19.
22. Ridgway to JCS, 21 July 1951, ibid.
23. JCS to Ridgway, 25 July 1951, ibid., pp. 730–1.
24. JCS to Ridgway, 10 August 1951, 383.21 (3–19–45) Korean Documents, MMR.
25. Memo by Matthews, 21 August 1951, 795.00/8–2151, DS.
26. Memo for Diary, 5 September 1951, Ridgway Papers, Special File, Apr 1951–Jan 1952, Box 20, MRP.
27. Rees, p. 292.
28. Ridgway to JCS, 27 July 1951, *FR 1951*, Vol. 7, Pt 1, pp. 739–45.
29. Wilfred Burchett, *At the Barricades* (New York, 1981) pp. 164–5.
30. Acheson, pp. 535–6.
31. Rees, p. 292.
32. Ridgway to JCS, 7 August 1951, *FR 1951*, Vol. 7, Pt 1, pp. 785–9; Ridgway to JCS, 11 August 1951, ibid., p. 801–10; JCS to Ridgway, 6 August 1951, ibid., pp. 789–80; JCS to Ridgway, 11 August 1951, ibid., pp. 811–12.
33. Ridgway to JCS, 15 August 1951, ibid., 819–20.
34. Ridgway to JCS, 20 August 1951, ibid., pp. 844–5.
35. Ridgway to JCS, 22 August 1951, ibid., pp. 847–8.
36. Burchett, p. 166.
37. General Hull, Briefing for NSC, 22 August 1951, Army Ops 091 Korea, RG 319, Box 38, MMR.
38. Rees, p. 398. For the PRC/DPRK version see Burchett, pp. 166–7.
39. Memo by Rusk, 15 August 1951, *FR 1951*, Vol. 7, Pt 1, pp. 817–19.
40. Acheson, pp. 542–3.

41. Memo by Heidemann, 27 August 1951, ibid., pp. 855–7.
42. Ridgway to JCS, 3 September 1951, ibid., pp. 875–7; Ridgway to JCS, 11 September 1951, ibid., pp. 900–1.
43. JCS to Ridgway, 5 September 1951, ibid., pp. 882–3; JCS to Ridgway, 12 September 1951, ibid., pp. 902–3.
44. Acheson, pp. 546–7.
45. JCS to Ridgway, 12 September 1951, *FR 1951*, Vol. 7, Pt 1, pp. 902–3; Memo by Marchant, 17 September 1951, ibid., pp. 917–19; Ridgway to JCS, 21 September 1951, ibid., 925–7; Schnabel and Watson, p. 600.
46. Ridgway to JCS, 25 September 1951, ibid., pp. 937–8.
47. JCS to Ridgway, 21 September 1951, ibid., pp. 924–5; State/JCS mtg, 26 September 1951, ibid., pp. 955–62.
48. Ridgway to JCS, 24 September 1951, ibid., pp. 933–5; Ridgway to JCS, 26 September 1951, ibid., pp. 952–5.
49. State/JCS Mtg, 26 September 1951, ibid., pp. 955–62; Memo by Bohlen, 4 October 1951, ibid., pp. 990–4.
50. Memo by Bohlen, ibid.; Advance HQ, UNC to Ridgway, 7 October 1951, ibid., pp. 1005–5.
51. Memo by Treumann, 26 November 1951, ibid., pp. 1177–80.
52. JCS to Marshall, 13 July 1951, ibid., pp. 667–8.
53. Schnabel and Watson, p. 630; Memo by Hickerson & Merchant, 3 August 1951, *FR 1951*, Vol. 7, Pt 1, pp. 771–4; State/JCS Mtg, 29 August 1951, ibid., pp. 859–64.
54. JCS to SecDef, 3 November 1951, ibid., pp. 1107–9.
55. State/JCS Mtg, 25 September 1951, ibid., pp. 939–44; Memo for President, 10 December 1951, ibid., pp. 1290–6.
56. JCS to Ridgway, 17 August 1951, 383.21 (3–19–45), Korean Documents, MMR; Hermes, pp. 58–61.
57. Schnabel and Watson, pp. 610–23.
58. Ridgway to JCS, 23 September 1951, CCS383.21 Korea (3–19–45) Sec. 64 RG 218, Box 34, MMR.
59. Pace to Ridgway, 13 October 1951, Ridgway Papers, Special File, Apr 1951–Jan 1952, Box 20, MRP.
60. JCS, Memo for SecDef, 3 November 1951, CCS383.21 Korea (3–19–45) Sec 68, RG 218, Box 35, MMR; Memo by Johnson, 7 November 1951, *FR 1951*, Vol. 7, Pt 1, pp. 1093–5.
61. NSC118/2, 20 December 1951, ibid., pp. 1382–99.
62. State/JCS Mtg, 20 December 1951, ibid., pp. 955–62.
63. Schnabel and Watson, pp. 614–19.
64. Draft Message to Ridgway, 5 November 1951, CCS 383.21 Korea (3–19–45) Sec 68, RG 218, Box 35, MMR; JCS to Ridgway, 6 November 1951, *FR 1951*, Vol. 7, Pt 1, pp. 1092–3.
65. Rees, pp. 300–1.
66. Ridgway to JCS, 13 November 1951, *FR 1951*, Vol. 7, Pt 1, pp. 1128–30.
67. Rees, pp. 300–1; Joy, p. 129; Goulden, pp. 580–2.
68. State/JCS Mtg, 12 November 1951, *FR 1951*, Vol. 7, Pt 1, pp. 1122–4; JCS to Ridgway, 13 November 1951, ibid., p. 1126; Schnabel and Watson, p. 622.
69. Ridgway to JCS, 24 November 1951, *FR 1951*, Vol. 7, Pt 1, pp. 1173–6.

70. Collins to Ridgway, 19 November 1951, ibid., pp. 1148–50.
71. Memo by Matthews, 21 November 1951, ibid., 1156–8.
72. Webb to Acheson, 30 November 1951, 795.00/11–2951, DS.
73. Ridgway to JCS, 4 December 1951, *FR 1951*, Vol. 7, Pt 1, pp. 1239–40; Ridgway to JCS, 7 December 1951, ibid., 1279–81.
74. JCS to President, 8 December 1951, ibid., pp. 1281–2.
75. Memo for President, 10 December 1951, ibid., pp. 1290–6.
76. Muccio to Acheson, 10 July 1951, ibid., pp. 644–5; Muccio to Acheson, 28 July 1951, ibid., 745–7; Muccio to Acheson, 22 December 1951, ibid., p. 1418.
77. Memo by Muccio, 5 May 1951, ibid., 416–19.
78. Memo for President, 10 December 1951, ibid., pp. 1290–6.
79. Ringwalt to Emmons, 11 October 1951, 795.00/10–1151, DS.
80. Memo by Johnson, 14 July 1951, *FR 1951*, Vol. 7, Pt 1, pp. 675–8.
81. Memo by Attlee, 30 August 1951, CAB129/47 CP(51), PRO.
82. Second Mtg of US/UK Foreign Ministers, 11 September 1951, *FR 1951*, Vol. 7, Pt 1, pp. 893–900; Memo by Morrison, 22 October 1951, CAB129/47 CP(51), PRO.
83. Acheson, p. 538.
84. Holmes to Acheson, 3 August 1951, 795.00/8–351, DS.
85. Memo of Dinner Mtg on SDS *Williamsburg* on the 5th of January 1952, 6 January 1952, PSF General File, Box 116, HSTL; Talks between the President and PM Churchill, 8 January 1952, ibid., Truman–Churchill Talks, 9 January 1952, ibid.
86. Franks to FO, 27 January 1952, AU1051/31, FO371/97593, PRO; Cabinet, 17 January 1952, CAB128/24CC16(52), PRO. Churchill raised the economic issue in Washington – see Truman–Churchill talks, 8 January 1952, First Formal Session, PSF General, Box 116, HSTL.
87. Eden to FO, 29 November 1951, FK1022/75, FO371/92759, PRO; Brief for Eden, 28 November 1951, FK1022/77, FO371/ 92759, PRO.
88. Gifford to Acheson, 8 December 1951, *FR 1951*, Vol. 7, Pt 1, pp. 1221–3.
89. British Embassy to Dept of State, 3 December 1951, ibid., pp. 1221–3; COS, 30 November 1951, FK1022/76, FO371/92759, PRO; David Carlton, *Anthony Eden* (London, 1981) pp. 302–3.
90. British Embassy to Dept of State, 3 December 1951, *FR 1951*, Vol. 7, Pt 1, pp. 1221–3; Brief for Eden, 28 November 1951, FK1022/77, FO371/ 92759, PRO.
91. Memo by Barnes, 28 November 1951, *FR 1951*. Vol. 7, Pt 1, pp. 1189–93; British Embassy to Dept of State, 3 December 1951, ibid., pp. 1223–4.
92. Stephen Jarika Jnr (ed.), *From Pearl Harbor to Vietnam. The Memoirs of Admiral Arthur W. Radford* (Stanford, 1980) pp. 276–7.
93. Elliot to COS, 20 December 1951, FK1022/98, FO371/92760, PRO.
94. Ridgway to JCS, 7 January 1952, CCS 383.21 Korea (3–19–45) Sec 78, RG 218, Box 36, MMR.
95. JCS to Ridgway, 11 July 1951, 383.21 Korea (3–19–45), Korean Documents, MMR; Clark to JCS, 23 June 1952, Selected Records Relating to the Korean War, DOD Vol 7, Box 17, HSTL; CINCFE to Dept of Army, December 1950, RG 9, Messages Personal For, July 1946–Mar 1951, Box 112, MACL.

96. Memo for Foster, 22 January 1952, RG 330, SecDef CD O92(Korea), Jan–Feb 1952, Box 319, MMR.
97. Memo for President, 10 December 1951, *FR 1951*, Vol 7, Pt 1, 1290–6.
98. Gaddis, pp. 123–4.
99. Ibid.
100. Memo by Operations Division, 5 July 1951, RG 319, Korea 091 Army Ops, Box 38A MMR.
101. Memo for SecDef, 14 August 1951, Selected Records Relating to the Korean War, DOD Korean War File, DOD Vol. 8, Box 17, HSTL; Schnabel and Watson, pp. 613–19.
102. R & D Report, 16 July 1952, RG 233, SecDef CD 38k (War Plans–NSC114), Box 262, MMR.

8 The POW Issue

1. Hermes, pp. 135–8.
2. Ibid.
3. Truman, p. 461.
4. Muccio, Oral History, HSTL.
5. Dept of the Army, *The Handling of POWs during the Korean War* (hereafter *Handling of POWs*), Military History Office, Office of the Assistant Chief of Staff, G-3, June 1960, pp. 4–5.
6. Ibid., pp. 5–10.
7. William C. Bradbury and Samuel M. Meyers, 'Socio-political Behavior of Korean and Chinese. A Historical Analysis', in William C. Bradbury, Samuel M. Meyers and Albert D. Biderman (eds), *Mass Behavior in Battle and Captivity. The Communist Soldier in the Korean War* (Chicago, 1968) pp. 232–3.
8. US Army Unit Diaries, Histories & Reports, RG 319, 8th US Army in Korea, Reports Command Judge Advocate, December 1950, FRC; Report by Commander Peterforce, August 1952, FK1553/86, FO371/ 99640, PRO.
9. *Handling of POWs*, pp. 11–12.
10. Bradbury and Meyers, pp. 240–1.
11. *Handling of POWs*, pp. 13–14; Report by Commander Peterforce, August 1952, FK1553/86, FO371/99640, PRO.
12. *Handling of POWs*, pp. 13–20.
13. Bradbury and Meyers, pp. 244–56.
14. Among many accounts see Robert Leckie, *Conflict* (New York, 1962) pp. 285–92; Rees, pp. 322–3; Mark Clark, *From the Danube to the Yalu* (London, 1954) pp. 55–70.
15. Lloyd to FO, 19 June 1952, FK1551/119, FO371/99634, PRO.
16. Muccio to Johnson, 19 March 1952, 795.00/3–1952, DS.
17. UNCURK Report, 15 May 1952, FK1553/11, FO371/99638, PRO.
18. Interim Report of the Neutral Nations Repatriation Commission', 22 January 1954, Korean Documents, MMR.
19. NSC 81/1, 9 September 1951, *FR 1950*, Vol. 7, pp. 712–21.
20. Kenneth K. Hansen, *Heroes Behind Barbed Wire* (New York, 1957) pp. 42–52.

21. Ibid., pp. 53–71, 80–8.
22. *Handling of POWs*, pp. 105–16.
23. Hansen, pp. 55–7, 60–1.
24. Franks to FO, 29 May 1952, FK1551/84, FO371/99633, PRO; Steel to FO, 24 June 1952, FK1551/116, FO 371/99634, PRO; Washington itself was confused about the numbers involved – see Memo for Major Dwan, 28 May 1952, 611.95a 24/5–285, DS.
25. CINCFE to US Consul, 2 January 1951, RG 9 China Jan–Feb 1951, Box 13, MACL; CINCFE to US Consul, 3 February 1951, ibid.; CINCFE to US Consul, 18 February 1951, ibid.
26. Muccio, Oral History, HSTL.
27. Muccio to Johnson, 19 March 1952, 795.00/3–1952, DS.
28. Barton Bernstein, 'The Struggle over the Korean Armistice: Prisoners of Repatriation?', in Bruce Cummings (ed.), *Child of Conflict* pp. 276–7.
29. JCS memo, 8 August 1951, *FR 1951*, Vol. 7, Pt 1, pp. 792–4.
30. Acheson to Marshall, 27 August 1951, ibid., pp. 857–9; Lovett to JCS, 25 September 1951, RG 330, SecDef CD383.6 1951, Box 271, MMR.
31. Memo by Webb, 29 October 1951, *FR 1951*, Vol. 7, Pt 1, p. 1073.
32. Nicholas Bethell, *The Last Secret* (London, 1976); Nikolai Tolstoy, *Victims of Yalta* (London, 1978).
33. Acheson, p. 653; Bernstein, p. 280.
34. Ridgway to JCS, 27 October 1951, *FR 1951*, Vol. 7, Pt 1, pp. 1068–71.
35. Ruffner, Memo for Acting Seccy, Undated November 1951, RG 330, SecDef CD092 Korea, Box 233, MMR; JCS to Lovett, 15 November 1951, *FR 1951*, Vol. 7, Pt 1, pp. 1168–71.
36. William H. Vatcher, *Panmunjom. The Story of the Korean Military Armistice Negotiations* (New York, 1958) pp. 241–6.
37. JCS to Ridgway, 15 January 1952, CCS383.21 Korea (3–19–45) Sec 79, RG 218 Box 36, MMR.
38. Johnson to Acheson, 2 February 1952, 695A.0024/2–252, DS; Johnson to Matthews, 4 February 1952, 611.959 241/2–452, DS; JCS/State Mtg, 11 February 1952, RG 330, SecDef CD 383.6 1952 TS, Box 363, MMR.
39. Allan E. Goodman (ed.), *Negotiating While Fighting. The Diary of Admiral C. Turner Joy at the Korean Armistice Conference* (Stanford, 1978) pp. 258–9, 251–2.
40. Ibid., pp. 251–2.
41. Ibid., pp. 258–9.
42. Ibid.
43. Memo of Conversation, 27 February 1952, 795.00/2–2752, DS.
44. Goodman, pp. 346–7; Bernstein, p. 283.
45. Tomlinson to Scott, 2 April 1952, FK1071/171, FO371/99570, PRO.
46. Ibid.
47. Ibid.
48. Ministry of External Affairs to Canadian High Commissioner (London), 14 March 1952, FK1071/174, FO371/99570, PRO.
49. Muccio to Acheson, 12 November 1951, 695A.0024/11–1251, DS.
50. Jebb to Johnston, 5 March 1952, FK1551/14, FO371/99631, PRO.
51. Rees, pp. 314–15.
52. Ibid.; Franks to FO, 5 March 1952, FK1071/117, FO371/99567, PRO.

53. Muccio to Armstrong, 12 May 1952, 695A.0024/5–1252, DS.
54. Muccio to Johnson, 19 March 1952, 795.00/3–1952, DS; Johnson to Muccio, 7 April 1952, bid.
55. Goodman, pp. 355–6.
56. Hermes, pp. 170–4.
57. Bernstein, pp. 282–3.
58. Ibid.
59. FO Minute, 29 January 1952, FK1071/52, FO371/99561, PRO.
60. Minute by Lord Reading, 8 May 1952, FK1071/228, FO371/99572, PRO.
61. Minute by Churchill, 25 March 1952, FK1551/33, FO371/99631, PRO.
62. Minute by Eden, FK1071/151, FO371/99568, PRO.
63. FO to Franks, 15 May 1952, FK1071/220, FO371/99572, PRO.
64. O'Neill, p. 288.
65. Ibid, p. 289.
66. Leckie, p. 283.
67. Phillip Deane, *Captive in Korea* (London, 1953) pp. 34–5; William L. White, *The Captives of Korea: An Unofficial White Paper. Our Treatment of Theirs; Their Treatment of Ours* (New York, 1957).
68. Deane, p. 79.
69. William F. Dean, *General Dean's Story* (New York, 1954) pp. 107–8.
70. Deane, p. 85.
71. Ibid., p. 105.
72. Leckie, pp. 152–3.
73. Deane, p. 85.
74. 'The Chinese Communists and UN–US POWs in Korea', 6 February 1953, FW611.959 241/2–1853, DS.
75. Ibid.
76. *Treatment of British POWs in Korea* (London, HMSO, 1955) p. 1.
77. Ibid.
78. Albert D. Biderman, *March to Calumny* (New York, 1979) p. 119.
79. Interview, British Soldier, 3 April 1981.
80. Deane, p. 112; First Cavalry, War Diary, December 1950, RG 319, FRC.
81. René Cutforth, *Korean Reporter* (London, 1952), p. 53.
82. Colonel Percy Thompson to General Stephens, 8 October 1957, RG 319, OCMH, Appleman MS External Review, Box 746, MMR.
83. Francis S. Jones, *No Rice for Rebels* (London, 1956) p. 33.
84. Interview, British Soldier.
85. *Treatment of British POWs*, p. 4.
86. Jones, p. 33.
87. *Treatment of British POWs*, pp. 4–10.
88. Biderman, pp. 48–55.
89. Telecon, 25 August 1950, RG 9, Telecons Numbers 62–78, Box 113, MACL; Edward Hunter, *Brainwashing* (New York, 1958) pp. 83–108; Interview, British Soldier.
90. *Treatment of British POWs*; Interview, British Soldier, Henry O'Kane, Honiley, June 1981.
91. *Treatment of British POWs*, pp. 26–7.
92. Jones, p. 35.
93. *Treatment of British POWs*, p. 21.

94. Ibid., pp. 21–5; White, pp. 178–82.
95. *Treatment of British POWs*, pp. 10–19.
96. Ibid., p. 2; Biderman, pp. 46–7.
97. 'Inter-Camp Olympics 1952' (Pyaktong, DPRK, 1953). See also 'Thinking Soldiers' (New World Press, Beijing, 1952).
98. 'Memo on POWs', Mark Clark Papers (hereafter MCP), Box 19, The Citadel, Charleston, SC.
99. Virginia Pasley, *22 Stayed* (London, 1955).
100. Lockhardt to Anderson, 18 February 1953, 611.95a 241/2–1853, DS.
101. Clark, p. 235.
102. 'The Chinese Communists and UN–US POWs in Korea', 6 February 1953, 611.95a 241/2–1853, DS.
103. Albert D. Biderman, *March to Calumny* (New York, 1979).

9 Deadlock at Panmunjom

1. Cabinet, 4 September 1951, CAB128/20 CC(51)58, PRO.
2. 'The Korean War and the Situation in the Far East', 19 February 1952, Lester Pearson Papers, CNA.
3. Robert A. Hart, *The Eccentric Tradition. American Diplomacy in the Far East* (New York, 1976) p. 193.
4. Truman, pp. 488–92.
5. Ibid., pp. 498–9.
6. Robert A. Divine, *Foreign Policy and US Presidential Elections* (New York, 1974) pp. 64–7, 82–3.
7. Ibid., pp. 10–17.
8. Ibid., pp. 36–7, 43–4.
9. Stephen E. Ambrose, *Eisenhower. The Soldier* (New York, 1983) pp. 546.
10. Divine, pp. 36–7.
11. Ambrose, pp. 541–3.
12. Divine, pp. 34–5.
13. Leonard Mosley, *Dulles* (New York, 1978) pp. 261–5, 306–7; Gaddis, pp. 121–2.
14. Divine, pp. 12–13.
15. Ambrose, pp. 541–3; Divine, pp. 35–6.
16. Ambrose, pp. 563–7.
17. Divine, pp. 51–6.
18. Ibid.
19. Ibid.
20. Truman, pp. 501–2.
21. Stephen E. Ambrose, *Eisenhower the President* (London, 1984) p. 14.
22. Truman, pp. 501–2.
23. Ambrose, pp. 13–14, 42–3.
24. Divine, p. 74.
25. Sherman Adams, *First Hand Report* (London, 1962) pp. 51–2.
26. Divine, p. 83.
27. Ibid., pp. 82–5.
28. Bernstein, pp. 292–3, 305–6.

29. T. R. Fehrenbach, *This Kind of a War* (New York, 1964) pp. 447–8.
30. Minute by Eden, 26 August 1952, FK1071/482, FO371/99582, PRO.
31. Scott to Steel, 6 October 1952, FK1071/540, FO371/99586, PRO.
32. Rees, pp. 323–4.
33. Clark, pp. 14, 41–2.
34. Ibid., pp. 66–70; Dening to FO, 30 May 1952, FK1553/32, FO371/99638, PRO.
35. *Handling of POWs*, pp. 26–38.
36. Ibid., pp. 42–4.
37. Ibid.
38. Ibid. p. 27.
39. Franks to FO, 21 May 1952, FK1551/53, FO371/99632, PRO; FO Memo, 4 June 1952, FK1551/90(A), FO371/99634, PRO.
40. Stairs, pp. 249–55.
41. Ibid.
42. Sargeant to Acheson, 20 May 1952, 695a.0024/5–2052, DS.
43. Rees, pp. 352–63, John Clews, *The Communists' New Weapon – Germ Warfare* (London, 1953); Leckie, pp. 298–302.
44. Jaap Van Ginneken, 'Bacteriological Warfare', *Journal of Contemporary Asia*, Vol. 7, No. 2 (1977) pp. 131–51; McCormack, pp. 150–4; *Observer*, 11 August 1985.
45. Meeting on BW/CW, 11 February 1952, RG 330, SecDef CD385 General, 1952, Box 365, MMR; Memo for SecDef, 25 March 1952, ibid.; Memo for Stohl, 4 February 1952, ibid.
46. John Gittings, 'Talks, Bombs and Germs: Another Look at the Korean War', *Journal of Contemporary Asia*, Vol. 5 (1975) No. 2, p. 217.
47. Charles A. Willoughby and John Chamberlain, *MacArthur 1941–1951. Victory in the Pacific* (London, 1956) pp. 387–93; Van Ginneken, p. 135.
48. McCormack, p. 158; Philip Knightley to author, 26 July 1983.
49. Memo for SecDef, 25 April 1952, CD385 (General) 1952, RG 330, Box 365, MMR; R & D Report, 16 July 1952, RG 233, SecDef CD381 (War Plans NSC114) Box 381, MMR.
50. Clark, p. 72–4.
51. Ibid., p. 75; Robert F. Futrell, *The United States Air Force in Korea, 1950–1953* (New York, 1961) pp. 440–71.
52. FO Minute, 4 June 1952, FK1551 90(A), FO371/99634, PRO; Adams to FO, 24 March 1952, FK1553/5, FO371/99638, PRO.
53. Strang to Washington, 2 June 1952, FK11910/15, FO371/99622, PRO.
54. Lloyd to FO, 19 June 1952, FK1551/112, FO371/99634, PRO; Lloyd to FO, 19 June 1952, FK1551/119, FO371/99634, PRO; Alexander to Minister of State, 17 June 1952, FK1553/59, FO371/99639, PRO.
55. Lloyd to Scott, 10 December 1952, FK1553/121, FO371/99641, PRO.
56. Bliss to Acheson, 21 June 1952, 795.00/6–2152, DS; Franks to FO, 22 June 1952, FK1910/55, FO371/49624, PRO.
57. Murphy to Acheson, 12 June 1952, 795.00/6–1252, DS; Cabinet, 27 May 1952, CAB128/25, CC56(52), PRO; Clark, pp. 113–14; Cabinet, 19 June 1952, CAB128/25 CC61(52).
58. Gifford to Acheson, 24 June 1952, 795.00/6–2452, DS.
59. Ladd to Raynor, 25 June 1952, 795.00/6–2552, DS.

60. Discussions with Lloyd, 25 June 1952, 795.00/6–2552, DS.
61. Acheson, pp. 656–7.
62. Lamb to FO, 10 May 1952, FK1071/235, FO371/99572, PRO; Nehru to Eden, 14 May 1952, FK1071/245(A), FO371/99573, PRO; Memo for Acheson, 21 May 1952, 795.00/5–2152, DS.
63. Eden to Nehru, 14 May 1952, FK1071/245(A), FO371/99573, PRO; UK Draft Proposal, 26 May 1952, Selected Records Relating to the Korean War, Armistice Negotiations 2, Box 11, HSTL.
64. FO to Lamb, 26 May 1952, FK1071/262, FO371/99573, PRO; Bruce to Acheson, 27 May 1952, 795.00/5–2752, DS; Memo of Conversation, 2 June 1952, 795.00/6–252, DS.
65. FO to Washington, 17 June 1952, FK1071/304, FO371/99575, PRO; Memo of Conversation, 19 June 1952, 795.00/6–1952, DS; Memo of Conversation, 18 June 1952, 611.95A 241/6–1852, DS.
66. Memo of Conversation, 14 July 1952, 795.00/5–2152, DS.
67. Simmons, p. 212; UKHC to Commonwealth Office, 16 July 1952, FK1071/405, FO371/99581, PRO; Nehru to Eden, 16 July 1952, FK1071/413, FO371/99581, PRO; Bowles to Acheson, 14 July 1952, 795.00/7–1452, DS.
68. Ringwalt to Johnson, 31 July 1952, 795.00/7–3152, DS.
69. Holmes to Acheson, 23 July 1952, 795.00/7–2352, DS.
70. Clark, pp. 145–6.
71. Henderson, pp. 167–8; Clark, pp. 147–8.
72. Lightner to Acheson, 27 May 1952, 795.00/5–2752, DS; Muccio to Acheson, 12 June 1952, 795.00/6–1252, DS.
73. Memo of Conversation, 2 June 1952, 695.0029/6–252, DS; Memo of Conversation, 28 May 1952, FK1553/38, FO371/99638, PRO.
74. O'Neill, pp. 302–3.
75. Muccio to Acheson, 16 June 1952, 795.00/6–1752, DS.
76. Clark to JCS, 5 July 1952, Selected Records Relating to the Korean War, Box 17, DOD Vol. 7, HSTL; O'Neill, pp. 302–3.
77. Clark to JCS, 31 May 1952, Selected Records Relating to the Korean War, Box 17, DOD, Vol. 7, HSTL; Clark to JCS, 2 June 1952, ibid.
78. Statement by Allison, 5 June 1952, US Congress, House of Representatives, Foreign Affairs Committee, Subcommittee on the Far East, *US Policy in the Far East*, Pt 1, pp. 223–34.
79. Clark, p. 148.
80. Ibid., pp.150–1.
81. Kennan to Acheson, 19 August 1952, 795.00/8–1952, DS; Matthews to Kennan, 27 August 1952, 795.00/8–2752, ES; Kennan to Acheson, 28 August 1952, 795.00/8–2852, DS.
82. Matthews to Kennan, ibid.
83. Murphy to Acheson, 27 August 1952, 795.00/8–2752, DS.
84. Fechtler to Dennison, 17 September 1952, PSF Korea, Armistice Negotiations, Box 243, MMR.
85. Ibid.; Bernstein, pp. 297–8.
86. Future Tactics in the Korean Armistice Negotiations, 17 September 1952, Acheson Papers, Box 67a, HSTL; Connelly, 12 September 1952,

Notes on Cabinet Mtgs, Post–Presidential File, Set 1, Jan 1952–Jan 1953, HSTL.

87. Murphy to SecState, 1 September 1952, 795.00/9–152, DS; Clark to JCS, 1 September 1952, Selected Records Relating to the Korean War, Korean War File–DOD Vol. 7, Box 17, HSTL.
88. Clark to Collins, 9 October 1952, RG 319, Chief of Staff 091 Korea, MMR; Clark, pp. 74–83; Collins, pp. 323–4.
89. Clark, pp. 82–3.
90. Ibid., 78–9.
91. Bernstein, pp. 300–1.
92. Goulden, p. 621.
93. Minute by Eden, 26 August 1952, FK1071/482, FO371/99582, PRO; Scott to Steel, 6 October 1952, FK1071/540, FO371/99583, PRO; FO Minute, 22 September 1952, FK1071/507, FO371/99583, PRO.
94. Stairs, pp. 263–4; Roger Bullen, 'Great Britain, the United States and the Indian Armistice Resolution on the Korean War', *International Studies*, 1984/1, International Centre for Economics and Related Disciplines, LSE, pp. 27–29.
95. Report by Pearson, Korean Discussions in the 7th Session of the General Assembly, 5 January 1953, pp. 2–3, Lester Pearson Papers, CNA.
96. Ibid., pp. 4–8.
97. O'Neill, pp. 320–1; Williams to Mason, 3 December 1952, UP2024/351, FO371/101337, PRO.
98. Acheson to Truman, 15 November 1952, Acheson Papers, Box 67a, HSTL.
99. FO Memo, 17 November 1952, FK1071/661, FO371/99590, PRO.
100. Acheson, pp. 700–1.
101. Memo of Conversation, 24 November 1952, Acheson Papers, Box 79a, HSTL.
102. David Carlton, *Anthony Eden* (London, 1981) p. 321; Memo of Conversation, 13 November 1952, Acheson Papers, Box 79a, HSTL.
103. Memo by Eden, 15 December 1952, CAB129/57, CC(52).
104. Acheson, p. 701. FO memo, 17 November 1952, FK1071/661, FO371/99590, PRO.
105. 'Korean Discussions', p. 12; Bullen, pp. 32–3; Memo by Acheson, 15 November 1952, Acheson Papers, Box 67a, HSTL.
106. Acheson, p. 704; Jebb to FO, 9 November 1952, FK1071/627, FO371/99589, PRO.
107. Acheson, p. 702.
108. Memo by Eden, 15 December 1952, CAB129/57 CC(52), PRO; Carlton, pp. 321–2.
109. Jebb to FO, 25 November 1952, FK1071/694, FO371/99591, PRO; Minute by Eden, 18 November 1952, FK1071/706, FO371/99591, PRO; Carlton, p. 322; Bullen, pp. 37–9.
110. 'Korean Discussions', p. 10.
111. Ibid., p. 15.
112. Memo by Eden, 15 December 1952, CAB129/57 CC(52), PRO.
113. Ibid.
114. Stairs, pp. 269–71.

115. 'Korean Discussions', p. 19.
116. Bowles to SecState, 22 December 1952, 795.00/12–2251, DS.
117. Simmons, pp. 223–8.

10 Eisenhower: Peace with Honour

1. Graham to Eden, 1 December 1952, FK11910/113, FO371/99626, PRO.
2. Clark, pp. 74–5.
3. Ibid., pp. 74–9.
4. Clark to Collins, 1 November 1951, RG 319, Chief of Staff, 091 Korea, MMR.
5. Clark to JCS, 29 September 1952, Selected Records Relating to the Korean War, DOD Korean War Files, 7, Box 17, HSTL; Clark to Collins, 9 October 1952, RG 319 Chief of Staff, 091 Korea, MMR; Clark, pp. 74–83; Hermes, pp. 366–7.
6. Clark, p. 84.
7. Ibid.
8. Memo by Operations Division, 5 July 1951, RG 319 Korea 091 Army Ops, Box 38A, MMR.
9. R & D Report, 16 July 1952, RG 233 SecDef CD381 (War Plans–NSC114), Box 362, MMR.
10. *Daily Worker*, 16 July 1952.
11. Bradley, Post Presidential Files, Box 1, Bradley General Omar, Mar 29–30 1955, HSTL.
12. JSPC Report, 20 May 1953, CCS383.21 Korea (3–19–45) Sec 128, RG 218, Box 44, MMR.
13. Clark, pp. 218–26; Goulden, pp. 623–6.
14. Ibid.
15. Ambrose, *Eisenhower. The President*, pp. 32–5; MacArthur, pp. 464–7.
16. Ibid.
17. Cohen, p. 222; FO Minute, 27 February 1953, FC10345/5, FO371/105221, PRO.
18. Memo by MacDonald, 26 November 1953, FC10345/13, FO371/105221, PRO.
19. Jurika, p. 309; Makins to FO, 30 January 1953, FC1018/6, FO371/105196, PRO.
20. Schnabel and Watson, pp. 940–8.
21. JSPC, 23 March 1953, JCS1176/365 CCS 383.21 Korea (3–19–45) Sec 125, RG 218, Box 43, MMR.
22. JCS for SecDef, 20 May 1953, CCS 383.21 Korea (3–19–45) Sec 128, RG 218, Box 44, MMR.
23. Dwight D. Eisenhower, *Mandate For Change* (London, 1963) p. 180.
24. Ambrose, p. 34.
25. Eisenhower, p. 181; Ambrose, p. 98.
26. Eisenhower, p. 180.
27. Emmett John Hughes, *The Ordeal of Power. A Political Memoir of the Eisenhower Years* (New York, 1963) p. 105.
28. O'Neill, pp. 325–8.
29. Ambrose, p. 97.

30. Ibid., p. 51.
31. Hughes, p. 103–5.
32. Eisenhower, p. 180; Gaddis, p. 164.
33. Hughes, p. 72.
34. Robert A. Divine, *Eisenhower and the Cold War* (New York, 1981) pp. 33–9; Gaddis, pp. 127–63.
35. Memo by Eden, 15 December 1952, CAB129/57, CC(52), PRO; Cabinet, 4 December 1952, CAB128/25CC102(52), PRO.
36. Dening to Scott, 18 November 1952, FK1094/22, FO371/99603, PRO; Dening to FO, 1 December 1952, FK1094/26, FO371/99603, PRO; Cabinet, 30 December 1952, CAB128/25 CC108(52), PRO.
37. *The Times*, 12 November 1952. This was shown to Clark – see Dening to FO, 26 November 1952, FK1094/24, FO371/99603, PRO.
38. Memo by Colville, 8 January 1953, FC10345/1, FO371/105221, PRO.
39. O'Neill, p. 324.
40. Memo by Colville, 8 January 1953.
41. O'Neill, p. 324.
42. *Economist*, 21 March 1953, pp. 779–81.
43. O'Neill, p. 327.
44. T. B. Millar (ed.), *Australian Foreign Minister. The Diaries of R. G. Casey 1951–1960* (London, 1972) p. 110.
45. Harold Macmillan, *The Tides of Fortune 1945–1955* (London, 1969) pp. 507–13.
46. Anthony Eden (Lord Avon), *Full Circle* (London, 1960) pp. 24–5.
47. Clark, p. 227.
48. Eden, pp. 25–6.
49. Bowles to SecState, 22 December 1952, 795.00/12–2251, DS; Gopal, 145.
50. Divine, pp. 30–1.
51. Rees, pp. 414–20.
52. Simmons, pp. 223–31.
53. Ibid.; Divine, p. 107.
54. Simmons, pp. 233–4.
55. Eden, p. 26.
56. O'Neill, p. 328.
57. Cabinet, 1 April 1953, CAB128/24 CC(24) 53, PRO; Memo of Conversation, 13 April 1953, 795.00/4–1365, DS.
58. Memo of Conversation, 1 April 1953, 795.00/4–153, DS; Memo by Dulles, 3 April 1953, 795.00/4–353, DS.
59. Ambrose, pp. 91–2; Divine, pp. 106–7.
60. Hughes, pp. 105–12; O'Neill, pp. 328–9.
61. Hughes, pp. 103–4; Ambrose, pp. 92–3.
62. Eisenhower, pp. 145–7; Hughes, p. 113.
63. Clark, pp. 232–3.
64. Ibid., 240.
65. Ibid, p. 233.
66. Ibid., pp. 245–7.
67. Ibid., p. 246.
68. Memo of Conversation, 19 May 1953, 795.00/5–1953, DS.
69. Ibid., Clark, p. 249.

70. Memo of Conversation, 11 March 1953, 795.00/5–11153, DS.
71. Clark, pp. 246–7.
72. Eisenhower, pp. 181–2.
73. Clark, pp. 246–7.
74. Ibid., p. 250.
75. Ibid., p. 249.
76. Ibid., p. 250.
77. Ibid., pp. 250–1; Smith to Dulles, 12 May 1953, 795.00/5–1253, DS.
78. Clark, p. 251; Smith to New Dehli, 11 May 1953, 795.00/5–1153, DS.
79. Clark, p. 251; *Daily Worker*, 20 May 1953; Memo of Conversation, 16 May 1953, 695.0029/5–1653, DS.
80. Allen to Bonbright, 18 May 1953, 795.00/5–1853, DS.
81. Stairs, p. 277.
82. Memo of Conversation, 16 May 1953, 695.0029/5–1653, DS; Aldrich to Dulles, 15 May 1953, 795.00/5–1553, DS.
83. *The Times*, 12 May 1953.
84. Lord Moran, *Winston Churchill: The Struggle for Survival 1940–1965* (London, 1968) p. 423.
85. Ibid. p. 472.
86. Aldrich to Dulles, 19 May 1953, 795.00/5–1953, DS.
87. Smith to Murphy, 19 May 1953, 795.00/5–1953, DS.
88. *Daily Worker*, 20 May 1953.
89. Smith to Dulles, 18 May 1953, 795.00/5–1853, DS; Memo of Conversation, 19 May 1953, 795.00/5–2353, DS; O'Neill, pp. 352–3.
90. Smith to New Dehli, 23 May 1953, 795.00/5–2353, DS.
91. Ambrose, p. 98.
92. Smith to Bohlen, 26 May 1953, 795.00/5–2653, DS.
93. O'Neill, p. 354.
94. Ibid., pp. 354–7.
95. Ibid., 355; Memo of Conversation, 795.00, 26 May 1953, 795.00/5–2463, DS.
96. Smith to Murphy, 15 May 1953, 795.00/5–1453, DS; Clark, p. 253.
97. Dulles to Eisenhower, 4 June, 1953, 795.00/6–453, DS; Clark, p. 260.
98. Robert H. Ferrell, *The Eisenhower Diaries* (New York, 1981), p. 298.
99. Adams, pp. 92–3.
100. Clark, pp. 253–6.
101. Franklin to McClurkin, 15 July 1953, Relations Between the US and the ROK, April 1–June 22 1953, 611.99B/1553, DS.
102. Clark, pp. 269–70.
103. Young to Johnson, 15 May 1953, 795.00/5–1553, DS; Clark, p. 254.
104. Clark, p. 257.
105. Ibid., pp. 251–9; John Barry Kotch, 'The Origins of the American Security Commitment to Korea', in Bruce Cummings (ed.), *Child of Conflict* p. 247; Young to Johnson, 15 May 1953, 795.00/5–1553, DS.
106. Clark, p. 259.
107. Ibid., pp. 258, 263.
108. Briggs to Dulles, 23 June 1953, 795.00/6–2353, DS.
109. *The Handling of POWs*, p. 77.
110. Clark, p. 265.

111. Ibid.
112. Clark to Howard, 8 July 1953, Clark Papers, Box 9, MCP.
113. Eisenhower, pp. 185–6.
114. Clark, p. 265.
115. Ibid., p. 264.
116. Dulles to Rankin, 24 June 1953, 795.00/6–2453, DS; Clark to JCS, 11 July 1953, 795.00/7–1153, DS.
117. Eisenhower, pp. 186–87.
118. Clark to SecDef, 5 July 1953, 795.00/7–553, DS; Maxwell Taylor, *Swords and Ploughshares* (New York, 1972) pp. 144–7.
119. Memo for Smith, 3 June 1953, 795.00/6–353, DS.
120. Scott to Dulles, 30 June 1953, 795.00/6–3053, DS.
121. Kotch, pp. 246–7; Schnabel and Watson, pp. 991–4.
122. Clark, p. 267.
123. US Congress, House of Representatives, Foreign Affairs Committee, Subcommittee on Far East, *US Policy in the Far East*, Pt 1 (Washington, DC, 1980).
124. Memo of Conversation, 4 July 1953, 795.00/7–452, DS.
125. Schnable and Watson, p. 1019.
126. Ibid., pp. 1019–20.
127. Ibid., p. 1021.
128. Robertson to Dulles, 1 July 1953, 795.00/7–153, DS.
129. Summary of Defense Telegrams, 3 July 1953, 795.00/7–353, DS.
130. Dulles to Robertson, 27 June 1953, 795.00/6–2653, DS; Dulles to USUN, 29 June 1953, 795.00/6–2953, DS; Memo of Conversation, 16 July 1953, 795.00/7–1653, DS.
131. Clark, pp. 270–1.
132. Schnabel and Watson, p. 1039.
133. Robertson to Dulles, 1 July 1953, 795.00/7–153, DS.
134. Memo of Conversation, 21 July 1953, 795.00/7–2153, DS.
135. Taylor, p. 151.
136. Clark, p. 211.
137. Ibid., p. 267.
138. Memo of Conversation, 26 June 1953, 795.00/6–2653, DS; Cabinet, 23 July 1953, CAB128/24 CM45 (53), PRO; Dulles to Aldrich, 28 July 1953, 795.00/7–2353, DS; O'Neill, p. 366.
139. Eisenhower, pp. 188–9.
140. Memo of Conversation, 15 July 1953, 795.00/7–1553, DS.
141. Clark, pp. 273–4.
142. Ibid., pp. 275–6.

11   The War on the Ground

1. Bernard Brodie, *War and Politics* (New York, 1973) p. 63.
2. Almond's views in RG 319 OCMH, Policy and Direction. Schnabel Box 714, MMR; Clark, pp. 296–7.
3. Keyes Beech, *Washington Star*, 8 November 1950, in DeptAr to Echols, 10 November 1950, Box 106, MACL.
4. David Detzer, *Thunder of the Captains* (New York, 1977) pp. 30–1;

MacArthur, pp. 380–1; Observer Team Report, 16 August 1950, RG 319 Chief of Staff, 091 Korea, MMR.

5. Detzer, pp. 30–1,
6. Memo by Deployments Section, Ops G-3, 5 July 1950, RG 319, Army Ops, 091 Korea, Box 121, MMR.
7. David Rees (ed.), *The Korean War, History and Tactics* (London, 1984) p. 18.
8. Manchester, pp. 555–6.
9. Marguerite Higgins, *War in Korea* (New York, 1951) p. 33.
10. MacArthur, p. 393.
11. Major-General Gay to Appleman, 24 August 1953, RG 319, OCMH Appleman MS, External Review, Box 746, MMR.
12. Appleman, p. 61.
13. Denis Warner, *Out of the Gun* (London, 1956) p. 98.
14. Detzer, p. 147; Edwin P. Hoyt, *The Pusan Perimeter* (New York, 1984) p. 44.
15. Appleman, pp. 69–76.
16. Warner, p. 102.
17. Ibid.
18. Ibid, pp. 177–9.
19. Frank E. Lowe, Report to the President, PSF Frank E. Lowe, Box 245, HSTL.
20. Drumright to Allison, 30 August 1950, 795.00/8–3050, DS; Leckie, p. 100.
21. Drumright to Allison, 30 August 1950, 795.00/8–3050.
22. Higgins, pp. 157–8; Acheson to Muccio. 8 September 1950, 795.00/9–850, DS.
23. Letter, Colonel of 24th Division, 5 August 1950, RG 319, Army Ops, 091 Korea, Box 126, MMR.
24. Higgins, p. 124.
25. Memo by Lt-Colonel Moorman, 9 August 1950, RG 319, C Of S, 091 Korea, MMR.
26. Dean to Appleman, 4 June 1954, RG 319, OCMH, Korea 1951, Chp 1–9, Box 746, MMR.
27. *Officers' Call*, Vol. 3, No. 1, July/Dec 1950, p. 8.
28. Higgins, pp. 84–5; Dean to Appleman, 4 June 1954, RG 319, OCMH, Korea 1951, Chp 1–9, Box 746, MMR.
29. Higgins, pp. 114–15; Appleman, pp. 203–9.
30. Memo, 9 August 1950, Ridgway Papers, Historical Record, Aug/Oct 1950, Box 16, MRP.
31. Memorandum, 15 August 1950, ibid.
32. Ibid.
33. Vorhees, pp. 55–6.
34. Leckie, pp. 88–104.
35. FEC Military Intelligence Section, 15 October 1950, *Order of Battle Information NKPA*.
36. Leckie, p. 99.
37. Ibid., p. 102.
38. T. R. Fehrenbach, *This Kind of War* (New York, 1964) p. 258.

39. FEC Military Intelligence Section, 15 October 1950, *Order of Battle Information NKPA*.
40. Appleman, pp. 488–90.
41. Ibid., pp. 490–2.
42. Leckie, pp. 110–11.
43. MacArthur, pp. 395–9; Appleman, pp. 492–5.
44. Appleman, pp. 506–7.
45. Fehrenbach, pp. 281–4.
46. Goulden, pp. 225–6.
47. Appleman, p. 527.
48. Goulden, pp. 228–29.
49. Rutherford, M. Poats, *Decision in Korea* (New York, 1954) pp. 67–9.
50. MacArthur, pp. 403–4.
51. Reginald Thompson, *Cry Korea* (London, 1951) pp. 143, 204.
52. Ibid., p. 94.
53. Ibid., pp. 134–5; See also Vorhees, pp. 148–9.
54. Thompson, pp. 163–4.
55. Major Francis L. Sampson to Ridgway, CICFE Correspondence, Box 19, MRP.
56. CINCFE to CG Army 8, 14 October 1950, RG 9 Outgoing, Misc Jan–Oct 50, Box 51, MACL CG Army 8 to CG X Corps, 16 October 1950, RG 9, Army 8 In, 16–31 Oct 50, Box 34, MACL; CINCFE to CG Army 8, 20 October 1950, RG 9, War Out, Misc, 16–31 Oct 50, Box 50, MACL.
57. War Diary, 1st Cavalry Division, October 1950, Rb 319, Box 4413, FRC.
58. Ibid.
59. Fehrenbach, p. 324.
60. Appleman, p. 669.
61. Ibid., pp. 759–65.
62. Ibid., p. 760.
63. S. L. A. Marshall, *The River and The Gauntlet* (New York, 1953) pp. 1–16; Appleman, pp. 768–9.
64. *Handbook on the Chinese Communist Army*, Dept of the Army Pamphlet 30–51, September 1952.
65. Fehrenbach, pp. 318–19.
66. Appleman, pp. 607–21.
67. Notes on Walker/Almond Relationship, RG 319, OCMH Policy and Direction, Schnabel, Morton Study re Schnabel MS, Box 714, MMR.
68. MacArthur, p. 409.
69. Stueck, p. 239.
70. Appleman, pp. 635–7.
71. Ibid., pp. 689–708, 741–5.
72. Acheson, pp. 463–4.
73. Leckie, p. 169.
74. Memo by Muccio, 17 November 1950, *FR 1950*, Vol. 7, pp. 1175–6.
75. Appleman, pp. 768–9.
76. Memo by Muccio, 17 November 1950, *FR 1950*, Vol. 7, pp. 1175–6.
77. Ridgway, *The Korean War*, pp. 51–65.
78. Drumright to Dept, 27 February 1951, 795.00/2–2751, DS.
79. Appleman, p. 765.

80. MacArthur, p. 422.

81. Ibid., p. 423.

82. Leckie, pp. 171–2.

83. Manchester, p. 606.

84. Goulden, pp. 329–37.

85. Fehrenbach, p. 302.

86. Goulden, p. 354.

87. Manchester, pp. 609–11.

88. Appleman, p. 720.

89. Fehrenbach, p. 357.

90. Leckie, pp. 174–5; 1st Cavalry Division, Command Report, December 1950, RG 319, Box 4419, FRC; 24th Infantry Division, ibid., Box 3522; Julian Tunstall, *I Fought in Korea* (London, 1953) pp. 45–9.

91. Collins, Memo for JCS, 8 December 1950, JCS1776/169, RG 218, Box 29, MMR.

92. Church to Regimental Commanders, 10 December 1950, 24th Infanty Division, Command Reports, RG 319, Acting Chief of Staff, G-1 file, Box 3522, FRC.

93. Acheson to US Embassy, 21 December 1950, 7958.00/12–2150, DS; Cutforth, pp. 34–35; Ridgway to Bolling, 7 March 1951, Special File, Dec 1950–March 1951, Box 20, MRP.

94. Lowe to Truman, 21 January 1951, PSF Lowe, Correspondence 1947–52, Folder 2, Box 245, HSTL; Harris to Gay, 6 February 1951, 1st Cavalry Division, War Diary, RG 319, Command Reports, Box 4416, FRC.

95. G-2 Memo, 10 January 1951, 1st Cavalry Division, RG 319, Command Reports, Box 4434, FRC.

96. Ridgway, *The Korean War* pp. 122–3.

97. Corbyn to Ridgway, 30 November 1972, Postwar Correspondence, Box 21, MRP.

98. *The Royal Ulster Rifles in Korea* (Belfast, 1953) p. 19.

99. Acheson to Holmes, 13 December 1950, 795.00/12–1350, DS; Holmes to Acheson, 15 December 1950, 795.00/12–1550, DS.

100. Letter from the front, Gunner Eric Stowe, 9 January 1951.

101. Acheson to Ankara, 2 December 1950, 7958.00/12–250, DS.

102. MacArthur to Stephens, 15 November 1957, RG 319, OCMH, Manuscript Appleman's Volume, Box 15, MMR.

103. *New York Herald Tribune*, 6 December 1950.

104. Memo for JSPC, 28 November 1950, 383.21 Korea (3–19–5), Sec 39, RG 218, Box 29, MMR.

105. Memo, 2 December 1950, Historical Record, Nov/Dec 1950, Box 16, MRP.

106. Memo for JCS, 8 December 1950, JCS1776/169, RG 218, Box 29, MMR; MacArthur, pp. 429–35.

107. Memo for SecDef, 29 January 1951, Bradley 1949–51, RG 218, Box 3, MMR; Haislip to MacArthur, 25 February 1951, RG 9, Incoming, Dept of the Army, DA-WX Jan–Apr 1951, Box 39, MACL.

108. Manchester, pp. 629–47.

109. Ridgway, *Soldier* pp. 195–211.

110. GHQ Conference, 5 January 1951, Special File Dec 1950–March 1951,

Box 20, MRP; Daily Historical Report, 9 January 1951, ibid.; Ridgway to Collins, 11 January 1951, ibid.; 1st Cavalry Division, Command Report, February 1951, Staff Section, RG 319, Box 4437, FRC.

111. Ridgway, Memo for Commanders, 21 January 1951, 1st Cavalry Division, Command Report, RG 319, Box 4434, FRC.
112. Notes of HQ Meeting, 23 January 1951, Special File, Dec 1950–March 1951, Box 20, MRP.
113. Edgar O'Ballance, *Korea: 1950—1953* (Hamlin, Conn., 1969) pp. 85–6.
114. Ibid., pp. 85–114.
115. Ridgway to JCS, 30 May 1950, CCS383.21 Korea (3–19–45), Sec 49 RG 218, Box 32, MMR.
116. JAMAT to DeptAr, 14 December 1950, RG9, War Misc-In, Dec 1950, Box 49, MACL; Ibid., 9 January 1951.
117. Memo for Record, 4 January 1951, Historical Record, Dec 1950–Jan 1951, Box 22, MRP.
118. Memo for Diary, 14 March 1951, Special File, Dec 1950–March 1951, Box 20, MRP.
119. Rees, pp. 248–51.
120. Ridgway to Van Fleet, 7 May 1951, CINCFE Corr, T–Z, Box 19, MRP; Memo for Diary, 9 November 1951, Special File, Apr 1951–Jan 1952, Box 20, MRP.
121. Ridgway, *Soldier* pp. 219–20.
122. Fehrenbach, p. 549.
123. Ibid., pp. 550–1. DPRK account in *Kim Il Sung. Short Biography*, pp. 40–5.
124. Ibid., pp. 558–64.
125. Rees, p. 386; Hermes, pp. 317–18.
126. Taylor, pp. 142–6.
127. Hermes, pp. 62–3.
128. Vorhees, pp. 149–50.
129. Ibid., p. 149.
130. Ibid., pp. 146–7.
131. Ibid., pp. 144–7.
132. Clark to JCS, 17 July 1953, CCS 383.21 Korea (3–19–45) Sec 133, RG 218, Box 45, MMR.
133. Fehrenbach, p. 692.
134. Taylor, pp. 138–40; Rosenberg, Memo for SecDef, 8 December 1952, RG 330, SecDef CD333 (Far East) 1952, Box 348, MMR; Memo by Major-General Edelman, 20 April 1953, RG 319, C of S, 091 Korea, MMR.
135. Lee Nichols, *Breakthrough on the Color Front* (New York, 1954) pp. 109–117; Richard M. Dalfiume, *Desegregation of the US Armed Forces. Fighting on Two Fronts* (Colombia, Mo., 1968) pp. 201–9.
136. Taylor, pp. 151, 159.
137. Comments by Major Felda, RG 319, OCMH, Policy and Direction, Schnabel, Schnabel Review, Box 714, MMR; 2nd Logistical Command, March 1952, RG 319, Command Report, Provost-Marshall Section Box 6180, FRC; ibid., May 1952; *FEAF Report*, Vol. 3, p. 10.

138. 2nd Logistical Command, March 1952, P–M Section, P–M Conference 29/30 March 1952, RG 319, Box 6180, FRC.
139. Cutforth, pp. 30–1.
140. Ibid.
141. Narcotics Addiction, 16 June 1951, FEAF Intelligence Roundup No. 138, Historical Section, Bolling AFB, K720–607A; Finding and Recommendations of the FEAF Board to Investigate Narcotics Addiction, 16 March 1953, K 720.77.
142. Cutforth, p. 31; Findings and Recommendations of the FEAF Board to Investigate Narcotics Addiction, 5 August 1953, K 720.77.
143. Meeting with Japanese Police Officials, Kanto Area, 1 July 1952, K 720.77.
144. See Christopher Robbins, *The Invisible Air Force: The Story of the CIA's Secret Airlines* (London, 1979) pp. 228–45.
145. Clark to Collins, 9 October 1952, RG 319, Chief of Staff, 091 Korea, MMR; Report by Dr Watkins on trip to Japan and Korea, 28 August 1952, RG 330, SecDef, CD092(Korea) Sept–Oct 1952, Box 318, MMR.
146. Clark, pp. 296–7.
147. Ridgway, *Soldier* pp. 275–9.
148. Clark, p. 307.

12 The War in the Air

1. Donovan, pp. 108–9.
2. Gaddis and Etzhold, pp. 324–4.
3. Herken, pp. 296–8; JCS Memo, 10 February 1950, RG 218, CCS373(10–23–48)BP Prt 2D, JCS1952/11 MMR.
4. David A. Anderson, *Strategic Air Command* (New York, 1976) p. 73; Harry R. Borowski, *A Hollow Threat, Strategic Air Power and Containment Before Korea* (Westport, Conn., 1982).
5. LeMay to Deputy Chief of Staff for Operations, 12 September 1950, Korean Documents, MMR; Richard G. Hewlett and Francis Duncan, *Atomic Shield* (London, 1969) pp. 525–8.
6. Boronowski, pp. 44–5, 189–91; Stephen Pelz, 'US Decisions on Korean Policy, 1943–1950', in Bruce Cummings (ed.), *Child of Conflict* pp. 166–17.
7. Memo for Deputy Sec of Defense, 20 March 1952, RG 330, SecDef CD380 (General) 1952, Box 360, MMR; Rees, p. 277.
8. Memo for Twining, 9 July 1952, Nathan B. Twining Papers (hereafter NTP), Reading File, Box 57, Library of Congress, Washington DC.
9. Boronowski, p. 102.
10. Futrell, pp. 55–8; Detzer, p. 164; Herbert Malloy Mason, *The US Air Force. A Turbulent History* (New York, 1976) pp. 220–4; FEAF Wringer Project, 13 July 1953, RG341 Air Force Plans-OPD823 Korea, Box 393, MMR.
11. Detzer, p. 164.
12. Ibid.
13. Wing-Commander P. G. Wykeham Barnes, 'The War in Korea with

Special Reference to the Difficulties of using Air Power', *Journal of the Royal United Services Institution*, No. 586 (May 1952) p. 151.

14. Robert Jackson, *Air War Over Korea* (London, 1973) pp. 24–5.
15. *FEAF. Report on the Korean War* (hereafter *FEAF Report*), pp. 82–6, Microfilm K720.04D, Air Historical Section, Bolling AFB, Washington DC.
16. Colonel Kalberer to McKinlay Cantor, 7 July 1950, Korean War File, McKinlay Cantor Papers (hereafter McKP), Box 70, Library of Congress, Washington DC.
17. Wykeham-Barnes, pp. 155, 161–6.
18. Richard G. Hubler, *SAC. The Strategic Air Command* (Westport, Conn, 1975) pp. 102–3; Cantor, Notes for the Tame Blue Yonder, Misc Manuscripts, Pkg 32, Item 4, Box 70, McKP.
19. John Pimlott, *B-29 Superfortress* (London, 1980) p. 52.
20. Futrell, pp. 357–62, 595–6; Memo for JCS, 26 December 1951, RG 330, SecDef CD092 (Korea) 1951, Box 234, MMR.
21. Stratemeyer to Edwards, 2 May 1951, RG 341 Air Force-Plans OPD381 Korea, Box 392, MMR.
22. Edwards to Stratemeyer, 18 May 1951, ibid.
23. *The Times*, 17 January 1951.
24. *Military Situation*, pp. 1378–9.
25. Futrell, pp. 357–62, 596–7.
26. Ibid., pp. 357–8.
27. Dean Hess, *Battle Hymn* (New York, 1956) pp. 199–200.
28. John H. Scrivener Jnr, *A Quarter Century of Air Power*, Air University, Maxwell AFB, Alabahma, 1973, 46.
29. Futrell, p. 371; Jackson, pp. 142–56.
30. Letter, USAF Veteran, 3 May 1982.
31. *Fortune*, February 1952.
32. Edward Hunter, *Brainwashing* (New York, 1958) pp. 124–5.
33. Policy on Combat Sorties, 2 December 1950, Hoyt S. Vandenberg Papers (hereafter HVP), Box 83, Library of Congress, Washington DC.
34. *FEAF Report*, pp. 99–102.
35. Malcolm W. Cagle and Frank A. Manson, *The Sea War in Korea* (New York, 1980) pp. 254–7.
36. *Military Situation*, p. 382.
37. James M. Gavin, *War and Peace in the Space Age* (New York, 1958) p. 122; Melvin B. Vorhees, *Korean Tales* (London, 1953) p. 170.
38. Air Attaché Report, 5 March 1951, AU1225/1, FO371/90984, PRO.
39. Cagle and Manson, pp. 13–22; Importance of the Army's Mission in the light of the Current Situation, RG 319, Army Ops 091 Korea, Box 122, MMR.
40. Futrell, pp. 446–9.
41. Vandenberg to Collins, 28 March 1951, File 7, Talks with Pace and Collins Re Tacair, Box 83, HVP.
42. Futrell, pp. 35–42.
43. McKinlay Cantor and Curtis LeMay, *Mission with LeMay* (New York, 1965) p. 382.

44. RG 319, OCMH, 'Policy and Direction', Schnable, File Project 1, Box 714, The Korean Conflict.
45. Schnabel and Watson, pp. 450–6.
46. Acheson, p. 463.
47. HQ FEAF to MacArthur, 8 November 1950, RG 6 FECOM Box 1, General Files 10, Correspondence Nov–Dec 1950, MACL; Acheson, p. 464.
48. *The Times*, 10 January 1951; Hess, pp. 130–1, 233–4.
49. Memo, 14 July 1952, RG 330, SecDef CDO92 (Korea), June–Aug 1952, Box 318, MMR.
50. McCormack, p. 132.
51. JCS to Ridgway, 25 July 1951, *FR 1951*, Vol. 7, Pt 1, pp. 730–1.
52. Memo for Chief of Staff, 4 October 1952, Clark Papers, Box 8, MCP.
53. *Incendiary Weapons*, SIPIRI monograph (London and Cambridge, Mass, 1975) pp. 46–7.
54. Dean, p. 278.
55. Rees, pp. 378–81; JCS to Ridgway, 10 August 1951, CCS383.21 Korea (3–19–45), Sec56, RG 218 Box 33, MMR; JSPC, 23 March 1953, JCS1776/365, CCS 383.21 Korea (3–19–45) Sec125, RG 218 Box 43, MMR; JCS for SecDef, 20 May 1953, CCS383.21 Korea (3–19–45), Sec128, RG 218, Box 44, MMR.
56. Cantor and LeMay, p. 382.
57. *Incendiary Weapons*, p. 43.
58. Clark to JCS, 1 September 1952, Selected Records Relating to the Korean War, DOD Vol. 7, Box 17, HSTL; Scalapino and Lee, pp. 413–35.
59. Dean, p. 273.
60. Bohlen to Dulles, 21 April 1953, 611.95A 251/4–2153, DS.
61. Dean, p. 269.
62. Futrell, pp. 46–55, 504–8; Scrivener, pp. 54–5.
63. Albert F. Simpson, 'Tactical Air Doctrine. Tunisia and Korea', *Air University Quarterly Review*, Vol. 4 (1950–1) No. 9 (Summer 1951) pp. 5–20.
64. Almond to Clark, 23 January 1951, Box 8, MCP.
65. Sykes to Vandenberg and Finletter, 10 December 1951, File 6a, Memos from Colonel Sykes, Box 83, HVP.
66. Memo, 10 January 1951, Korean Evaluation Project, Box 119, NTP; Memo of Understanding, 2 October 1951, File 7B, Box 83, HVP.
67. *FEAF Report*, pp. 129–32.
68. Futrell, pp. 400–38.
69. Ibid., pp. 400–38, 656–7.
70. FEAF Intelligence Roundup (hereafter FIR), 11 August 1952, No. 101, K 720.607A, Air Historical Section, Bolling AFB. Futrell, pp. 408–16.
71. FIR, 15 March 1952, No. 81.
72. Futrell, pp. 418–26.
73. Ridgway, *The Korean War* pp. 75–6.
74. *FEAF Report*, pp. 127–8.
75. Futrell, pp. 656–7.
76. Ibid.

77. Richard K. Betts, *Soldiers, Statesmen and Cold War Crises* (London and Cambridge, Mass., 1977), p. 205.
78. Futrell, pp. 440–58.
79. JIG to JIC, 15 February 1951, JIC557/1, RG 218, CCS–383.21 Korea (3–19–45), s43, Box 31, MMR; Schnabel and Watson, 450–6.
80. Clark, pp. 72–5; Weyland to Twining, 23 July 1952, Reading File 1952, Box 57, NTP.
81. Futrell, pp. 449–53; FIR, 4 November 1951, No. 62.
82. Clark to JCS, 1 September 1952, Selected Records Relating to the Korean War, Korean War File, DOD Vol. 7, Box 17, HSTL.
83. Futrell, pp. 623–8; Rees, pp. 381–2; Gittings, 'Talks, Bombs and Germs', pp. 205–17.
84. Rees, p. 383.
85. Simmons, pp. 216–17.
87. Futrell, pp. 230–3; Richard E. Stockwell, *Soviet Air Power* (New York, 1956) p. 49; *The Encyclopedia of Air Warfare*, p. 171.
88. Futrell, pp. 370–1; Clark to JCS, 9 February 1953, CCS383.21 Korea (3–19–45) Sec122, RG 218, Box 42, MMR.
89. Air Operations in Korea against MIG-15, 21 November 1951, Box 83, HVP.
90. Norman Uphoff and Raphael Litauer, *The Air War in Indochina* (Boston, 1972) p. 209.
91. Futrell, pp. 673–5.
92. Air Ops against MIG, 21 November 1951, Box 83, HVP.
93. Stockwell, pp. 47–8; *Military Situation*, p. 1377.
94. Memo for JCS, 26 December 1951, RG 330, SecDef CD02 (Korea) 1951, Box 234, MMR.
95. FIR, F86E v MIG-15 in the Korean Theater, April 1952.
96. JCS to Clark, 6 March 1953, RG 218, CCS383.21 Korea (3–19–45), Sec 134, Box 43, MMR.
97. David Rees (ed.), *The Korean War, History and Tactics* (London, 1984) p. 110.
98. Analysis of F-86 encounters with Mig-15, FIR, 1 August 1951, K720.3101–47, Critique on F-86E v MIG, FIR April 1952.
99. R & D Report, 18 November 1951, RG 330, SecDef CD 451.1 L951, Box 285, MMR.
100. Stockwell, pp. 138–9; *Encyclopedia of Air Warfare*, 171.
101. *FEAF Report*, Vol. 2, p. 39.
102. FIR, 21 April 1952, No. 85.
103. *Guerrilla Warfare & Airpower in Korea*, Concepts Division, Aerospace Studies Institute, Air University, Maxwell AFB (Maxwell, Alabama, 1964) p. 117–36.
104. FIR 12 August 1951, No. 49.
105. Memo, 23 August 1953, Box 9, MCP.
106. Futrell, p. 610.
107. Ambrose, pp. 112–13; Eisenhower to Smith, 21 September 1953, 795A.00/9–2153, DS; Seoul to Dept, 29 September 1953, 195A.00/9–2453, DS; Memo for President, 23 September 1953, 795A.00/9–2353, DS.

108. Clark to JCS, 22 October 1953, RG 218, CCS383.21 Korea (3–19–45) Sec 139, Box 46, MMR.
109. Clark to JCS, 9 February 1953, CCS383.21 Korea (3–19–48) Sec 122, RG 218, Box 42, MMR; FIR, 18 August 1952, No. 102; Memo for SecDef, 8 June 1951, Fil 1 Misc, Box 83, HVP.
110. Rees, p. 110; Memo for SecDef, 30 June 1953, RG 330, CD092 Korea 1953, Box 10, MMR; Report by Strickland, 11 July 1953, RG 319, Chief of Staff, 091 Korea, MMR.
111. FIR, 22 February 1953, No. 129.
112. Combat Pilots Discuss MIG, FIR, 21 April 1952, No. 85.
113. Ibid.
114. FIR, 9 January 1953, No. 125.
115. *FEAF Report*, Vol. 2, p. 19; Robert A. Kilmarx. *A History of Soviet Air Power* (New York, 1962) pp. 236–41.
116. CINCFE to CG Army 8, 9 October 1950, RG 9, Outgoing, Misc, June–Oct 1950, Box 51, MACL; GHQ Check Sheet, 15 August 1950, FECOM General Folder 3, Box 4, MACL; John M. Carroll, *Secrets of Electronic Espionage* (New York, 1966) pp. 127–46.
117. Kilmarx, pp. 236–41.
118. Futrell, pp. 645–6.
119. Jackson, p. 161.
120. *FEAF Report*, pp. 156–60.
121. Eugene M. Emme (ed.), *The Impact of Air Power* (New York, 1959) pp. 673–6.
122. Colonel Paul for General Burns, 25 June 1953, Reading File, Box 119, NTP.

13 Conclusions

1. Martin Russ, *The Last Parallel* (New York, 1957) p. 317.
2. T. B. Millar (ed.), pp. 102–3; Ambrose, p. 106.
3. Ambrose. p. 107.
4. Clark, p. 298.
5. Ambrose, p. 107.
6. Memo by Johnson, Undated June 1953, 611.95a241/6–2953, DS.
7. Summary of Defense Telegrams, 22 July 1953, 795.00/7–2253, DS.
8. Hansen, pp. 118–29, 144–7.
9. Memo of Conversation, 15 October 1953, 695A.0024/10–1553, DS.
10. Hansen, pp. 160–1.
11. Memo of Conversation, 2 October 1953, 695A.0024/10–253; Briggs to Dulles, 15 October 1953, 695.0024/10–1553, DS; Hansen, pp. 173–4.
12. Hansen, p. 197.
13. Ibid, pp. 173–4.
14. Ibid., pp. 184–229.
15. O'Neill, p. 377.
16. Summary of Defense Telegrams, 6 October 1953, 795.00/10–652, DS; Memo of conversation, 6 October 1953, 795.00/10–653, DS.
17. O'Neill, p. 378.

18. Interim Report of the Neutral Nations Repatriation Commission, 22 January 1954, Korean Documents, MMR.
19. Ibid.
20. O'Neill, p. 377.
21. Dulles to New Delhi, 4 January 1954, 695A.0024/1–154, DS.
22. Hansen, pp. 304–6.
23. Kay to Cabot, 19 January 1954, 695.0024/1–1954, DS.
24. Williams to Mason, 3 December 1952, UP2024/35, FO371/101351, PRO.
25. Jebb to FO, 18 December 1952, FK1071/763, FO371/99593, PRO.
26. Biderman, pp. 1–2.
27. Eugene Kinkaid, *Why They Collaborated* (London, 1960) p. 15 (U.S. title, *In Every War But One*).
28. Major W. E. Mayer, Conference of Professors of Air Science, November 1956, *The Baylor Line*, July/Aug 1957.
29. Lockhardt to Anderson, 18 February 1953, 611.95a 291/2–1853, DS.
30. Kinkaid, pp. 153–4.
31. Ibid., p. 156.
32. Ibid., pp. 16–17; Sec Navy for SecDef, RG 341, Air Force Plans, OPD, 383.6 Korea, Box 392, MMR; USAF Staff Study, RG 341 Air Force Plans, OPD 383.6 Korea, Box 392, MMR.
33. Kinkaid, pp. 202–11.
34. Ridgway, *Soldier* p. 302.
35. Biderman, pp. 24–6, 43–8, 66–8, 86–90, 101–13.
36. Ibid.
37. Ibid., pp. 8–9.
38. US Consul (Southampton) to Dept, 18 September 1953, 695A.0024/9–1853, DS.
39. Stairs, pp. 281–2; Cabinet, 28 July 1953, CAB128/26 CC46(53), PRO; Lodge to Dulles, 13 August 1953, 795.00/8–1253, DS.
40. Stairs, pp. 281–2; Dulles to Lodge, 14 August 1953, 795.00/8–1353, DS; Memo by Dulles, 16 August 1953, 611,95/8–1453, DS; Millar, p. 103.
41. Stairs, p. 282.
42. Ibid.
43. Ibid., pp. 283–4.
44. Eden, p. 117.
45. O'Neill, pp. 388–9.
46. Ibid., p. 397.
47. Herbert B. Bix, 'Japan and South Korea in America's Asian Policy', in Frank Baldwin (ed.), *Without Parallel* (New York, 1974) p. 203; O'Neill, p. 400.
48. JCS to Ridgway, 30 July 1952, CCS383.21 Korea (3–19–45), Sec 134, RG 218, Box 45, MMR.
49. Bix, pp. 204–5.
50. Cameron, pp. 126–7.
51. *Military Situation*, p. 82.
52. I. F. Stone *The Hidden History of the Korean War* (New York, 1969), p. 312.
53. Futrell, pp. 644–65.
54. Burchett, p. 163.

55. Jon Halliday, 'The North Korean Enigma', *New Left Review*, No. 127 (May–June 1981) p. 29.
56. Command Report, 24th Infantry Division, December 1950, G-2 Section, Box 3522, RG 319, FRC. See also War Diary, 1st Cavalry Division, Box 4419, ibid. *Incendiary Weapons*, p. 43.
57. Cagle and Manson, p. 355.
58. *Incendiary Weapons*, p. 43.
59. Bix, pp. 194–200; Robert Murphy, *Diplomat Among Warriors* (New York, 1964) pp. 347–8; Yamamoto Mitsuru, 'US–Japan Economic Cooperation', in Nagai and Iriye (eds), *The Origins of the Cold War in Asia*. (Tokyo, 1977) pp. 908–26.
60. NIE, 15 January 1951, PSF CIA Reports, Box 253, HSTL.
61. Leckie, p. 331; Nakajima Mineo, 'Sino-Soviet Confrontation', in Nagai and Iriye, *Origins of the Cold War in Asia*, pp. 216–27.
62. Cohen, pp. 227–9.
63. Wells, 'Sounding the Tocsin', p. 116–58.
64. O'Neill, p. 407.
65. Millar, p. 110.
66. O'Neill, p. 279.
67. Gaddis, pp. 127–63.
68. NSC-166/1, 6 November 1953, NSC Records, MMR.
69. Bix, p. 202.
70. Stairs, p. x.
71. Eden, p. 519.

Bibliography

MANUSCRIPT SOURCES

Canada

Ottawa Public Archives
Lester Pearson Papers, MG 26
Hume Wrong Papers, MG 30

United Kingdom

London School of Economics
Hugh Dalton Papers

Public Record Office, London
CAB 128
CAB 129
DEFE 4
FO 371
FO 800

Bodleian Library, Oxford
Clement Attlee Papers

United States

Army War College, Carlisle, Pa.
General Edward (Ned) Almond, Oral History
General John E. Hull, Oral History
General James H. Polk, Oral History
General Matthew B. Ridgway Papers

The Citadel, Charleston, Sc.
General Mark Clark Papers

Harry S. Truman Library, Independence, Mo.
Dean G. Acheson Papers
Eben A. Ayres Papers
Matthew J. Connelly Papers
Robert L. Dennison Papers
George M. Elsey Papers
Dan A. Kimball Papers

Charles S. Murphy Papers
Frank Pace Jnr. Papers
Harry S. Truman Papers
Harry H. Vaughan Papers
James E. Webb Papers

Lucius Battle, Oral History
Nathan M. Becker, Oral History
Niles W. Bond, Oral History
John H. Chiles, Oral History
O. Edmund Clubb, Oral History
Thomas K. Finletter, Oral History
Lord Oliver Franks, Oral History
W. Averell Harriman, Oral History
Loy W. Henderson, Oral History
John D. Hickerson, Oral History
U. Alexis Johnson, Oral History
Robert Lovett, Oral History
Edwin W. Martin, Oral History
H. Freeman Matthews, Oral History
Livingston Marchant, Oral History
John H. Muccio, Oral History
Frank Pace Jnr., Oral History
Princeton Seminars

Douglas A. MacArthur Memorial Library, Norfolk, Va.
RG 5
RG 6
RG 9

Federal Records Center, Suitland, Md.
RG 319

Bolling AFB, Washington DC
FEAF History of the Korean War
FEAF Intelligence Roundup

Library of Congress, Washington DC
MacKinley Cantor Papers
General Nathan F. Twining Papers
General Hoyt S. Vandenberg Papers

National Archives, Washington DC
RG 59
RG 218
RG 319

National Archives, Washington DC – continued
RG 233
RG 330
RG 341
RG 407

GOVERNMENT PUBLICATIONS

Australia

Australia In The Korean War, Volume 1, *Strategy and Diplomacy*, Robert O'Neill, The Australian War Memorial and the Australian Government Publishing Service, Canberra, 1981.

Democratic People's Republic of Korea

Documents and Materials Exposing the Instigators of the Civil War in Korea, Ministry of Foreign Affairs, Pyongyang, 1950.

United Kingdom

Our Men in Korea, Eric Linklater, HMSO, London, 1952
The Treatment of British POWs in Korea, HMSO, London, 1953.

United States

USAF, *Guerrilla Warfare and Airpower in Korea, 1950–1953*, Concepts Division, Aerospace Studies Institute, Maxwell AFB, Alabahma, January 1964.

US Congress, Senate, Foreign Relations and Armed Services Committees, *Military Situation in the Far East*, 82nd Congress, 1st session, 3–31 May 1951.

US Department of the Army, *Handbook on the Chinese Communist Army*, Department of the Army Pamphlet 30–51, September 1952.

US Department of the Army, *Order of Battle Information, NKPA*, FEC Military Intelligence Section, 15 October 1950.

US Department of the Army, *The United States Army in the Korean War*, Volume 1, *South to the Naktong, North to the Yalu*, Roy E. Appleman, Washington DC, 1961, Volume 3, *Truce Tent and Fighting Front*, Walter G. Hermes, Washington DC, 1962.

US Department of State, *The Foreign Relations of the United States*.

US Joint Chiefs of Staff, *The History of the Joint Chiefs of Staff*, Volume 3, *The Joint Chiefs of Staff and National Policy, The Korean War*, James F. Schnabel and Robert J. Watson, Volume 4, *The Joint Chiefs of Staff and National Policy*, Walter S. Poole.

NEWSPAPERS AND MAGAZINES

United Kingdom

Daily Worker
Economist
New Statesman
The Times

United States

Fortune
New York Times
Washington Post

BOOKS

DEAN G. ACHESON, *Present at the Creation* (London, 1969).

SHERMAN ADAMS, *Firsthand Report: The Story of the Eisenhower Administration* (New York, 1961).

STEPHEN E. AMBROSE, *Eisenhower, The Soldier 1890–1952* (New York, 1983).

STEPHEN E. AMBROSE, *Eisenhower, The President 1952–1969.* (New York, 1984).

FRANK BALDWIN (ed.), *Without Parallel: The American–Korean Relationship since 1945* (New York, 1973).

C. N. BARCLAY, *The First Commonwealth Division* (Aldershot, 1954).

ELISABETH BARKER, *The British Between the Superpowers* (London, 1983).

JOHN BAYLIS, *Anglo-American Defence Relations 1939–1984* (London, 1984).

MAX BELOFF, *Soviet Policy in the Far East 1944–1951* (London, 1953).

CARL BERGER, *The Korean Knot* (Philadelphia, 1957).

RICHARD K. BETTS, *Soldiers, Statesmen & The Cold War* (Cambridge, Mass. & London, 1977).

RICHARD K. BETTS, *Surprise Attack* (Washington DC, 1982).

ALBERT D. BIDERMAN, *March to Calumny* (New York, 1979).

CLAY BLAIR, *Beyond Courage* (London, 1956).

CLAY BLAIR, *MacArthur* (London, 1977).

ROBERT M. BLUM, *Drawing the Line, The Origin of the American Containment Policy in East Asia* (New York, 1982).

ROBERT BOARDMAN, *Britain and the People's Republic of China, 1949–1974* (London, 1976).

CHARLES E. BOHLEN, *Witness to History, 1929–1969* (New York, 1973).
DOROTHY BORG AND WALDO HEINRICHS (eds), *Uncertain Years, Chinese-American Relations 1947—1950* (New York, 1980).
HARRY R. BOROWSKI *The Hollow Threat, Strategic Air Power and Containment Before Korea* (Westport, Conn. 1982).
ANDREW BOYLE, *The Climate of Treason* (London, 1979).
WILLIAM C. BRADBURY, SAMUEL M. MEYERS AND ALBERT D. BIDERMAN (eds) *Mass Behavior in Battle & Captivity. The Communist Soldier in the Korean War* (Chicago, 1968).
BERNARD BRODIE, *War & Politics* (New York, 1973).
RUSSELL D. BUHITE, *Soviet-American Relations in Asia 1945–1954* (Norman, Oklahoma 1981).
ALAN BULLOCK, *Ernest Bevin as Foreign Secretary* (London, 1983).
WILFRED BURCHETT, *At the Barricades* (New York, 1981).
MACKINLAY CANTOR AND CURTIS LEMAY *Mission with LeMay* (New York, 1965).
MALCOLM W. CAGLE AND FRANK A. MANSON, *The Sea War in Korea* (New York, 1980).
JAMES CAMERON, *Point of Departure* (London, 1978).
RONALD J. CARIDI, *The Korean War & American Politics: The Republican Party as a Case Study* (Philadelphia, 1968).
DAVID CARLTON, *Anthony Eden* (London, 1981).
KIM CHUM-KON, *The Korean War* (Seoul, 1973).
MARK W. CLARK, *From the Danube to the Yalu* (London, 1954).
JOHN CLEWS, *The Communists New Weapon, Germ Warfare* (London, 1953).
WARREN I. COHEN, *America's Response to China* (New York, 1971).
J. LAWTON COLLINS, *War in Peacetime* (Boston, 1969).
PHILLIP CROSBY, *Three Winters Cold* (Dublin, 1955)
BRUCE CUMMINGS, *The Origins of the Korean War* (Princeton, NJ 1981).
BRUCE CUMMINGS (ed.), *Child of Conflict: The Korean–American Relationship, 1943–1953* (Seattle, 1983).
RENE CUTFORTH, *Korean Reporter* (London, 1955).
RICHARD M. DALFIUME, *Fighting on Two Fronts, The Desegregation of the US Armed Forces* (Colombia, Missouri, 1968).
WILLIAM F. DEAN, *General Dean's Story* (New York, 1954).
PHILLIP DEANE, *Captive in Korea* (London, 1953).
DAVID DETZER, *Thunder of the Captains* (New York, 1977).
ROBERT A. DIVINE, *Eisenhower & the Cold War* (New York, 1981).
ROBERT A. DIVINE, *Foreign Policy and US Presidential Elections* (New York, 1974).
CHARLES M. DOBBS, *The Unwanted Symbol: American Foreign Policy, the Cold War and Korea* (Kent, Ohio, 1981).
ROBERT J. DONOVAN, *Eisenhower, The Inside Story.* (New York, 1956).
ROBERT J. DONOVAN, *Tumultuous Years* (New York, 1982).
ANTHONY EDEN, *Full Circle* (London, 1960).
DWIGHT D. EISENHOWER, *Mandate for Change* (London, 1963).
THOMAS H. ETZHOLD AND JOHN LEWIS GADDIS, *Containment.*

Documents on American Foreign Policy & Strategy, 1945–1950 (New York, 1978).

ANTHONY FARRAR-HOCKLEY, *The Edge of the Sword* (London, 1954).

T. R. FEHRENBACH, *This Kind of War* (New York, 1964).

ROBERT H. FERRELL (ed.), *Off the Record. The Private Papers of Harry S. Truman* (London, 1982).

ROBERT H. FERRELL (ed.), *The Eisenhower Diaries* (New York, 1981).

MICHAEL FOOT, *Aneurin Bevan, 1945–1960* (London, 1973).

ROBERT F. FUTRELL, *The United States Air Force in Korea 1950–1953* (New York, 1961).

JOHN LEWIS GADDIS, *Strategies of Containment* (New York & Oxford, 1982).

MARK GAYN, *Japan Diary* (Rutland Vt. & Tokyo, 1981).

LORD GLADWYN, *The Memoirs of Lord Gladwyn* (London, 1972).

ALLAN E. GOODMAN (ed.), *Negotiating While Fighting. The Diary of Admiral C. Turner Joy at the Korean Armistice Conference* (Stanford, 1978).

LELAND GOODRICH, *Korea. A Study of US Policy in the United Nations* (New York, 1956).

SARVEPALLI GOPAL, *Jawaharal Nehru, 1947–1956* (London, 1979).

JOSEPH C. GOULDEN, *Korea. The Untold Story of the War* (New York, 1982).

MARGARET GOWING, *Independence & Deterrence, Britain & Atomic Energy 1945–1952* (London, 1974).

JOHN GUNTHER, *The Riddle of MacArthur*

KENNETH HARRIS, *Attlee* (London, 1982).

ROBERT A. HART, *The Eccentric Tradition. American Diplomacy in the Far East,* (New York, 1976).

KENNETH K. HANSEN, *Heroes Behind Barbed Wire* (New York, 1957).

SHIRLEY HAZZARD, *Defeat of an Ideal. The Self-Destruction of the UN.* (London, 1973).

FRANCIS H. HELLER (ed.), *The Korean War. A 25-Year Perspective* (Lawrence, Kansas 1977).

GREGORY HENDERSON, *Korea. The Politics of the Vortex* (Cambridge, Mass., 1968).

GREGG HERKEN, *The Winning Weapon* (New York, 1980).

RICHARD G. HEWLETT AND FRANCIS DUNCAN *Atomic Shield.* (University Park & London, 1969).

DEAN HESS, *Battle Hymn* (London, 1957).

MARGUERITE HIGGINS, *War in Korea* (New York, 1951).

TRUMBULL HIGGINS, *Korea & the Fall of MacArthur* (New York, 1960).

E. J. HUGHES, *The Ordeal of Power* (London, 1963).

EDWARD HUNTER, *Brainwashing. The Story of Men who Defied it* (New York, 1958).

ROBERT JACKSON, *Air War Over Korea* (London, 1973).

IRVING L. JANIS, *Victims of Groupthink* (Boston, 1972).

E. S. JONES, *No Rice for Rebels* London, 1956).

C. TURNER JOY, *How Communists Negotiate* (New York, 1955).

STEPHEN JURIKA (ed.), *From Pearl Harbor to Vietnam. The Memoirs of Admiral Arthur W. Radford* (Stanford, 1980).

J. H. KALICKI, *The Pattern of Sino-American Crises* (London, 1975).

LAWRENCE KAPLAN, *A Community of Interests, NATO & the Military Assistance Program 1948–1951* (Washington DC, 1982).

GEORGE F. KENNAN, *Memoirs, 1925–1963* 2 vols. (Boston, 1967 and 1972)

EUGENE KINKAID, *Why They Collaborated* (London, 1960).

PHILLIP KNIGHTLEY, *The First Casualty* (New York, 1975).

JOYCE AND GABRIEL KOLKO, *The Limits of Power. The World and US Foreign Policy 1945–1954* (New York, 1972).

NIKITA KRUSHCHEV, *Krushchev Remembers* (London, 1971).

WALTER LAFEBER, *America, Russia and the Cold War, 1945–1984* (New York, 1985).

ROBERT LECKIE, *Conflict. The History of the Korean War 1950–1953* (New York, 1962).

TRYGVE LIE, *In the Cause of Peace* (New York, 1954).

ERIC LINKLATER, *A Year of Space* (London, 1954).

EVAN LUARD, *Britain & China* (London, 1962).

DOUGLAS A. MacARTHUR, *Reminiscences* (New York, 1965).

GAVAN McCORMACK, *Cold War, Hot War* (Marrickville, NSW, 1983).

DAVID S. McCLELLAN, *Dean Acheson. The State Department Years* (New York, 1976).

HAROLD MacMILLAN, *The Tides of Fortune* (London, 1969).

WILLIAM MANCHESTER, *American Ceasar. Douglas MacArthur, 1880–1964.* (Boston, 1978).

S. L. A. MARSHALL, *The River and the Gauntlet* (New York, 1953).

ERNEST R. MAY, *Lessons of the Past. The Use and Misuse of History in Ameican Foreign Policy* (New York, 1973).

PAWEL MONAT, *Spy in the US* (London, 1962).

KENNETH OWEN MORGAN, *Labour in Power 1945–1951* (London, 1984).

K. P. S. MENON, *The Flying Troika*, (London, 1963).

RALPH MILIBAND, JOHN SAVILLE and MARCEL LIEBMAN (eds), *The Socialist Register 1984* (London, 1984).

MERLE MILLER, *Plain Speaking. An Oral Biography of Harry S. Truman* (New York, 1973).

T. B. MILLAR (ed.), *Australian Foreign Minister: The Diaries of R. G. Casey 1951–1960* (London, 1972).

LORD MORAN, *Winston Churchill: The Struggle for Survival, 1940–1965* (London, 1968).

LEONARD MOSLEY, *Dulles* (New York, 1978).

JOHN E. MUELLER, *War, Presidents & Public Opinion* (London, 1973).

J. A. MUNRO AND A. I. INGLIS (eds), *Lester Pearson Memoirs 1948–1957. The International Years* (London, 1974).

ROBERT MURPHY, *Diplomat Among Warriors* (London, 1964).

YONOSUKE NAGAI AND AKIRA IRIYE (eds), *The Origins of the Cold War in Asia* (Tokyo, 1977).

RICHARD E. NEUSTADT, *Presidential Power. The Politics of Leadership* (New York, 1960).

LEE NICHOLS, *Breakthrough on the Color Front* (New York, 1954).

HAROLD JOYCE NOBLE, *Embassy at War* (Seattle, 1975).
EDGAR O'BALLANCE, *The Red Army of China* (London, 1962).
ROBERT T. OLIVER, *Syngman Rhee. The Man Behind the Myth* (New York, 1954).
ROBERT OSGOOD, *Limited War* (Chicago, 1957).
GLENN D. PAIGE, *The Korean Decision* (New York, 1968).
K. M. PANNIKKAR, *In Two Chinas* (London, 1955).
VIRGINIA PASLEY, *22 Stayed* (London, 1955).
RUTHERFORD M. POATS, *Decision in Korea* (New York, 1954).
LEWIS McCAROLL PURIFOY, *Harry Truman's China Policy. McCarthyism and the Diplomacy of Hysteria. 1947–1951.* (New York, 1976).
DAVID REES, *Korea: The Limited War* (London, 1964).
DAVID REES (ed.), *The Korean War. History and Tactics.* (London, 1984).
MATTHEW B. RIDGWAY, *Soldier. The Memoirs of Matthew B. Ridgway* (New York, 1956).
MATTHEW B. RIDGWAY, *The Korean War* (New York, 1967).
RICHARD H. ROVERE AND ARTHUR M. SCHLESINGER, *The MacArthur Controversy and American Foreign Policy* (New York, 1965).
MARTIN RUSS, *The Last Parallel* (New York, 1957).
ROBERT A. SCALAPINO AND CHONG SIK LEE, *Communism in Korea*, Vol. 1., *The Movement* (Los Angeles, 1972).
MICHAEL SCHALLER, *The United States and China in the Twentieth Century* (New York & Oxford, 1979).
WILLIAM SEBALD, *With MacArthur in Japan* (New York, 1965).
ROBERT R. SIMMONS, *The Strained Alliance. Peking. Pyongyang, Moscow and the Politics of the Korean War* (New York, 1975).
GADDIS SMITH, *Dean Acheson* (New York, 1972).
ROBERT SMITH, *MacArthur in Korea. The Naked Emperor* (New York, 1982).
JOHN W. SPANIER, *The Truman–MacArthur Controversy and the Korean War.* (New York, 1965).
DENIS STAIRS, *The Diplomacy of Constraint. Canada, the Korean War and the US.* (Toronto, 1974).
I. F. STONE, *The Hidden History of the Korean War* (London, 1952).
WILLIAM W. STUECK, *The Road to Confrontation, American Policy toward China and Korea 1947–1950.* (Chapel Hill, NC, 1981).
MAXWELL D. TAYLOR, *Swords and Ploughshares* (New York, 1972).
REGINALD THOMPSON, *Cry Korea* (London, 1951).
HARRY S. TRUMAN, *Memoirs* Vols 1 & 2, (New York 1955–56).
TANG TSOU, *America's Failure in China, 1941–1950.* (Chicago, 1963).
JULIAN TUNSTALL, *I Fought In Korea* (London, 1953).
WILLIAM H. VATCHER, *Panmunjom. The Story of the Korean Armistice Negotiations.* (New York, 1958).
MELVIN B. VORHEES, *Korean Tales* (New York, 1952).
DENIS WARNER, *Out of the Gun* (London, 1956).
D. CAMERON WATT, *Succeeding John Bull. America in Britain's Place 1900–1975.* (Cambridge, 1984).
W. L. WHITE, *The Captives of Korea*, (New York, 1957).

ALLEN S. WHITING, *China Crosses the Yalu. The Decision to Enter the Korean War.* (New York, 1960).
COURTNEY WHITNEY, *MacArthur. His Rendezvous with Destiny* (New York. 1956).
PHILLIP M. WILLIAMS, *Hugh Gaitskell* (London, 1979).
CHARLES A. WILLOUGHBY AND JOHN CHAMBERLAIN, *MacArthur 1941–1951. Victory in the Pacific* (London, 1956).
ALAN WINNINGTON, *I Saw the Truth in Korea* (London, 1950).
KENNETH T. YOUNG, *Negotiating with the Chinese Communists* (New York, 1968).

ARTICLES

RUSSELL D. BUHITE, 'Major Interests: American Policy Toward China, Taiwan and Korea 1945–1950', *Pacific Historical Review*. Vol. 47. August 1978.
ROGER BULLEN, 'Great Britain, the US and the Indian Armistice Resolution on the Korean War, November 1952', *International Studies*. 1984, No.1.
RENE CUTFORTH, 'A Generation Ago', *The Listener*. 11 September 1969.
ROGER DINGMAN, 'Truman, Attlee and the Korean War Crisis'. *International Studies*. 1982, No. 1.
STEPHEN L. ENDICOTT, 'Germ Warfare and Plausible Denial', *Modern China*. Vol. 5. No.1. January 1979.
PETER N. FARRAR, 'Britain's Proposal for a Buffer Zone South of the Yalu in November 1950. Was it a Neglected Opportunity to End the Fighting in Korea', *Journal of Contemporary History*. Vol. 18. 1983.
JOHN GITTINGS, 'Talks, Bombs and Germs. Another Look at the Korean War', *Journal of Contemporary Asia*. Vol. 5. No. 2. 1975.
KARUNKER GUPTA, 'How did the Korean War Begin?', *China Quarterly*, 8, October–December 1972.
JON HALLIDAY, 'The North Korean Phenomenon', *New Left Review*, No. 127. May–June 1980.
WILBUR HITCHCOCK, 'North Korea Jumps the Gun', *Current History*. Vol. 20. March 1951.
JAMES I. MATTRAY, 'An End to Indifference. America's Korean Policy During World War Two'. *Diplomatic History*, 2. Spring 1978.
JAMES I. MATTRAY, 'Truman's Plan for Victory. National Self-determination and the Thirty-Eighth Parallel Decision in Korea', *Journal of American History*, 66, September 1979.
STEPHEN E. PELZ, 'When the Kitchen Gets Hot, Pass the Buck: Truman & Korea in 1950'. *Reviews in American History*, December 1978.
WILLIAM W. STUECK, 'Cold War Revisionism and the Origins of the Korean Conflict: The Kolko Thesis,' *Pacific Historical Review*, 42, November 1973.
JAAP VAN GINNEKEN, 'Bacteriological Warfare', *Journal of Contemporary Asia*. Vol. 7, No. 2, 1977.

SAMUEL F. WELLS, 'Sounding the Tocsin. NSC-68 and the Soviet Threat',
International Security, Vol. 4, Fall 1979.
SAMUEL F. WELLS, 'The Origins of Massive Retaliation', *Political Science
Quarterly*, Spring 1981.
JOHN EDWARD WILTZ, 'The MacArthur Hearings of 1951: The Secret
Testimony', *Military Affairs*, Vol. 39, December 1975.

Index